6-30   11.75

WITHDRAWN

New Directions in Organizational Behavior

St. Clair Press Titles
In Management and Organizations

ORGANIZATIONAL BEHAVIOR AND MANAGEMENT:
A Contingency Approach
 Henry L. Tosi and W. Clay Hamner, eds.

CONTEMPORARY PROBLEMS IN PERSONNEL, rev. ed.
 W. Clay Hamner and Frank L. Schmidt, eds.

MANAGEMENT: Contingencies, Structure, and Process
 Henry L. Tosi and Stephen J. Carroll

READINGS IN MANAGEMENT: Contingencies, Structure, and Process
 Henry L. Tosi, ed.

EXPERIENCES IN MANAGEMENT
AND ORGANIZATIONAL BEHAVIOR
 Douglas T. Hall, Roy J. Lewicki, Donald D. Bowen, and Francine S. Hall

THEORIES OF ORGANIZATION
 Henry L. Tosi, ed.

ORGANIZATIONAL BEHAVIOR
 Stephen J. Carroll and Henry L. Tosi

NEW DIRECTIONS IN ORGANIZATIONAL BEHAVIOR
 Barry M. Staw and Gerald R. Salancik, eds.

New Directions in Organizational Behavior

Edited by

Barry M. Staw
Northwestern University

Gerald R. Salancik
University of Illinois

St. Clair Press
4 East Huron Street
Chicago, Illinois 60611

New Directions in Organizational Behavior
Copyright © 1977 by St. Clair Press
All rights reserved. Printed in the United States of America

No part of this publication may be reproduced, stored in a retrieval system, or transmitted in any form or by any means, electronic, mechanical, photocopying, recording, or otherwise, without the prior written permission of the publisher.

Library of Congress Catalog Card Number 76-47795

ISBN 0-914292-06-4

Cover design by H. B. Smith

St. Clair Press
4 East Huron Street
Chicago, Illinois 60611

Contributors

Gerald R. Salancik is a social psychologist and an associate professor of organizational behavior at the University of Illinois at Urbana-Champaign. He is the author of a large number of papers in the areas of commitment, attitude change, and organizational power. He is also co-author with Jeffrey Pfeffer of *The External Control of Organizations: A Resource Dependence Perspective* (1977), and, with Eugene Webb, of *The Interview* (1966).

Barry M. Staw is an associate professor of organizational behavior and psychology at Northwestern University. He is the author of papers in the areas of individual motivation, attribution, and escalation processes in organizations. He is also the author of the psychology module, *Intrinsic and Extrinsic Motivation* (General Learning Press, 1976), editor of the forthcoming book, *Psychological Foundations of Organizational Behavior* (Goodyear Press, 1977), and editor of the annual series *Research in Organizational Behavior* (JAI Press).

Paul S. Goodman is an associate professor of industrial administration and psychology at the Graduate School of Industrial Administration, Carnegie-Mellon University. He is on the editorial board of *Organizational Behavior and Human Performance* and the *Academy of Management Journal*. He has published professional articles in the areas of work attitudes, motivation, and organizational performance.

Camille B. Wortman is an assistant professor of psychology at Northwestern University. She serves as associate editor of *Personality and Social Psychology Bulletin* and has contributed a number of papers within the areas of interpersonal attraction, causal attribution, and reactions to uncontrollable life events. She is also the co-author of the psychology module, *Ingratiation: An Attributional Perspective* (General Learning Press, 1973).

Joan A. W. Linsemeier is a graduate student in the department of psychology at Northwestern University. Her research interests are in the areas of interpersonal attraction and information processing.

Bobby J. Calder is an associate professor of behaviorial science in management and of psychology at Northwestern University. He is the author of many papers in the areas of attitude change, attribution processes, social structure, and consumer behavior. He is also the author of the psychology module, *Attitudes and Behavior* (General Learning Press, 1976), and is editor of a forthcoming book in consumer behavior to be published by St. Clair Press.

Terry Connolly is an associate professor of industrial and systems engineering at Georgia Institute of Technology. He is the author of papers in the areas of decision making and individual motivation in organizations.

Jeffrey Pfeffer is an associate professor of business administration at the University of California at Berkeley. He serves on the editorial boards of *Administrative Science Quarterly, American Journal of Sociology, Industrial Relations,* and *Academy of Management Journal*. He is the author of the forthcoming books, *Organizational Design* and, with Gerald R. Salancik, *The External Control of Organizations: A Resource Dependence Perspective* (1977), and has contributed numerous papers in the areas of organizational power and organization-environmental relations.

Karl E. Weick is professor of psychology and organizational behavior at Cornell University. He is the editor of *Administrative Science Quarterly*. He is the author of *The Social Psychology of Organizing* (Addison-Wesley, 1969), co-author of *Managerial Behavior, Performance, and Effectiveness* (McGraw-Hill, 1971), and numerous papers in the areas of individual behavior, organizational design, and research methodology.

Contents

Preface *page* ix

Chapter One
**Commitment and the Control
of Organizational Behavior and Belief**   1
Gerald R. Salancik

Chapter Two
**Motivation in Organizations:
Toward Synthesis and Redirection**   55
Barry M. Staw

Chapter Three
Social Comparison Processes in Organizations   97
Paul S. Goodman

Chapter Four
**Interpersonal Attraction and Techniques
of Ingratiation in Organizational Settings**   133
Camille B. Wortman and Joan A. W. Linsenmeier

Chapter Five
An Attribution Theory of Leadership   179
Bobby J. Calder

Chapter Six
**Information Processing and Decision Making
in Organizations**   205
Terry Connolly

Chapter Seven
Power and Resource Allocation in Organizations   235
Jeffrey Pfeffer

Chapter Eight
Enactment Processes in Organizations   267
Karl E. Weick

Preface

The development of this volume has been very much a joint venture between the two editors and the contributors. However, because of the practical necessity of having an order of editorship, a randomization procedure was developed. The member chosen first by this procedure would thus be the first editor, while the member chosen second would be assigned the task (and pleasure) of writing a preface to this book. The preface which follows is a narrative on the evolution of the project written by and from the perspective of Jerry Salancik. Barry Staw has restrained himself from any editorial role in this material but can corroborate much of its accuracy.

This book began on one of those hot afternoons common to Champaign, Illinois, in August. My air conditioner had died from overexertion as I was attempting to prepare a reading list for my course on the behavioral foundations of organizations and management. As was becoming my practice, I was late with my list and considered cribbing from a friend. His was neatly typed with indented topic headings such as "leadership" and "motivation," and I began to read the materials listed beneath them. The sun was beginning to set when I found that the book had somehow fallen from my lap. I didn't recall how much I had read, but I realized, of course, that I had not found an answer to my problem that was either simple or satisfying. I decided to talk about some studies I thought should have been in a list of readings on motivation but often were not. One of my favorites was a study by some friends who had given children felt-tipped pens and watched them zoom through reams of blank paper. "Now that was motivation!" was my capsule for the lecture.

Unhappily, a student took me up on a routine offer of "Any questions?" and asked, "Why don't you have us read about Theory X and Theory Y, or something relevant to organization?" Realizing the student had not grasped the organizational relevance of children and felt-tipped pens, I dismissed the class and promised an answer for our next meeting. Fortunately the weekend was coming up. I read some 73 articles and wrote careful comments on each. I found seven pieces that I thought students should read, and figured out a reason why I could not recommend the remainder to them. I had my answer and delivered it the next day to my students.

The answer was really quite simple. I was a social psychologist who viewed individual behavior as quite changeable by the experiences and conditions of social reality. In contrast, much of the literature in organizational behavior seemed to me to take the individual as a given, and inviolate sanctuary. The individual was perceived as having needs and the world was conceived as something one designed around those needs. The only difference between Theory X and Theory Y for me was the different needs imputed to individuals; the differences in managerial or organizational styles were merely logical extensions of the imputation of X or Y needs. Yet for me, the more interesting question was "How do people come to need, believe, and act the way they do?" And the answer I thought was that the conditions and experiences of organizational and personal life produce those needs, beliefs, and actions.

Though the answer seemed meaningful to me, it was not until many months later that I began to do something about the disparity between my own beliefs about what should be taught about human behavior and what was commonly encapsulated under the headings "leadership" and "motivation." So I began to write down some ideas about how I would organize the materials I knew about into traditional topical labels of the management literature. When I had finished I realized I had written an outline for a readings book.

The next day, I showed my notes to Barry Staw and reminded him of our previous conversations about the paucity of new materials in the organizational behavior literature. I suggested that we might possibly know of several individuals who could bring some recent materials from social science into the more traditional organizational behavior framework. He was in the middle of xeroxing something and glanced at my outline in between turning pages to the hungry green light of the machine. When he had finished he said, "That would be an interesting book." Armed with this tacit commitment (see chap. 1 for a discussion of commitment processes), I flew off to Seattle for a meeting.

In Seattle, while touring the book stalls with a friend, we met the owner of the publishing house whose imprimatur marks this book. He was hawking copies of his most recent text and my friend interrupted him to discuss some mutual business matters. He was introduced to me as Bob St. Clair, and having nothing else to converse about—Seattle weather being what it always is—I mentioned my idea for a book to him. His eyes displayed a conservative but judicious interest and I recall he murmured something about "it" being "possible," before turning to a customer who had just entered. I was not sure to what the "it" referred, though I took it to be some hitherto uncalculated market potential. As we walked away, my friend confided to me that St. Clair did not seem very interested in my idea. Though my friend clearly had more experience in these matters than I, I felt he lacked the proper enthusiasm. Otherwise he would have been more sensitized to the salient cues of the situation and concluded, as I had, that this book was a sure winner (see chap. 6 for a discussion of information processing models of judgment and decision making).

I returned to Champaign. It was again hot, and I was again without a completed readings list. I saw Barry Staw who had by then finished his xeroxing and was quite free to talk. I recounted the extraordinary enthusiasm displayed at the Seattle meetings for our book. I reminded him of his own expressed interest and suggested that we should rough out an outline and send it around. He concurred, and things stood like that for the duration of the semester.

In December, Staw went to Atlanta for a meeting. There he met Robert St. Clair and, moved by the spirit of science which enlivens such meetings, they discussed the book at length. Barry returned with a proper level of enthusiasm and we renewed our previous goal by writing a detailed outline. In preparing a prospectus we were forced to think back about why such a book was needed and we discovered that it was because much of the literature in organizational behavior was based on ideas from psychology and sociology that were 10 to 20 years old. The purpose of our book was then obvious: to introduce some different and more recent (not necessarily better) ideas into the mainstream literature; that is, ideas that coincided more with our own graduate student days. Staw subsequently confirmed our hunches about the mainstream literature by conducting a survey and documenting a 15-year lag between basic social science research and its introduction into the organizational literature. Assured that we had a good rationale (see chap. 8 for a discussion of retrospective enactment processes), Staw and I sent a note to St. Clair along with the outline. We signed a preliminary contract.

The next problem we faced was deciding on authors to write the chapters. We decided they had to be bright and capable and somewhat discouraged with the organizational literature as it stood. We drew up a list of persons who fit those qualifications and listed their names alongside the chapter outlines. In all we had some 20-plus names with which to work. A number of them happened to be among our acquaintances, and so the evaluations were easy to make (see chap. 7 for a discussion of the social basis for decision making and resource allocation).

To obtain cooperation from the prospective authors we had listed required extremely careful planning and coordination. Letters and phone calls with unimaginable promises were hurled across the country. Subdued conversations were arranged in convivial places (one of the more memorable being a Spanish hotel lounge in LaJolla, California). Everyone we contacted wanted assurances that the book would be published and that some of the suggested authors would in fact participate. This presented an interesting problem: before we could get one author to agree, he wanted to know which others had also agreed. We solved the problem by calling one person up to solicit his comments about the book, and then recounted these comments to others as we called them; the value of the book soon became apparent to all (see chap. 3 for a discussion of social comparison processes). The first to agree was Jeffrey Pfeffer, who made extremely detailed inquiries about the venture, the publisher, and the market potential for the book. I pointed out certain qualities of character he possessed which made him the only person capable of writing the chapter on power (see chap. 4 for a discussion of ingratiation processes).

The last person committed was Karl Weick, an event that required months of careful discussion at subtle levels. In one conversation we had, every time I mentioned the idea of the book he changed the subject. Some would have taken this as a sign of disinterest, but I assumed it indicated he wanted time to reflect before being pressed into a decision. Finally we proposed two suggestions, since it would increase the chance of acceptance from .50 to .67. One idea was to unlock the meaning of interlocking behavior; the other was to enact the enactment notion. He chose the latter for reasons that should be obvious but are not.

When we sat down to write contracts we decided with St. Clair that the contributing authors should share in the profits of this venture. This is an unusual practice in publishing and the authors seemed pleased to learn they were to receive a percentage of some unknown net income for their writing efforts—in other words, a standard royalty divided among the contributors. I assume it kept up their enthusiasm for their work, since it was just enough to remind them they were being paid but not really enough to justify their investments of time and energy (see chap. 2 for a discussion of motivation and incentive).

The next phase was to insure that the contributors contributed. It

PREFACE

xiii

was by now the spring of 1975, and I decided to take a year off in California rather than meet another class without a completed reading list. We set September 1975 as the due date for manuscripts. Two arrived by August 1975, Pfeffer's and Camille Wortman's. That the former was early was to be expected, but the other was a pleasant surprise. Camille Wortman had been given one of the most difficult assignments. She is an experimental social psychologist who was not familiar with the organizational behavior literature but was being asked to discuss ingratiation as it relates to management. She did the intelligent thing and enlisted her co-author, Joan Linsenmeier, to help her barrel through 50 years of organizational literature. The last manuscript to arrive was, predictably, Bobby Calder's, though it came only a few weeks after the editors'. Calder's task was one of the more challenging of the book. He was to ignore virtually all that had been written about leadership and then fill the vacuum with his own ideas about social processes.

With chapters flooding our mailboxes at the rate of one every two months, we faced the unsettling task of commenting on them and suggesting directions for change. This took skills before unknown to us (see chap. 5 for a discussion of leadership processes). The fewest comments were made on Paul Goodman's chapter; the most, on Terry Connolly's chapter. Connolly had had the least experience at writing this kind of chapter, and this fact alone suggested we should heap volumes of comments on him, including those meant for some other authors. He, as did all the authors, took our comments well and wrote another draft, wisely ignoring many of our suggestions. The most interesting reactions to comments came from Karl Weick. In a lengthy letter, I described several difficulties that I thought readers would have with some of his ideas and pointed out some places where a hint of definition to enactment was emerging and could be expanded. When I later went through his revision, I noticed that he had carefully deleted nearly every sentence that I alluded to. From this experience, I concluded, "To define enactment is to miss the point about it."

With the final edited chapters finished in July of 1976, Staw and I faced the task of arranging our names on the title page. When we began a year and a half earlier we agreed to flip a coin; this now seemed impractical since he was in Evanston and I was in California. To permit chance its due, I created a more interesting version of the numbers game I knew as a child. The alphabet was distributed into two equivalent lists, from which Staw selected one as his own, leaving the other to me. The winning list was determined by the first letter of the last name of the first person listed in the July 26th issue of *Time* magazine's

"Milestone" column. As it happened, Ted Mack of television's Amateur Hour died, making Staw the last person to be chosen by this great man.

Though the title may imply other things, we had no grand expectations of moving the field of organizational behavior into "new directions" through this book. The title came because we had to send one to St. Clair when we first began in earnest. One of us suggested, "Why not 'new directions in organizational behavior'?" and, since we couldn't think of a reason fast enough, the title stuck. What is new to a reader, of course, will depend a lot on where the reader's coming from. I personally would be happy if the contents of this book were old hat to most researchers in organizational behavior.

GRS

Editor's Note: For convenience, *he*, *his*, and *him* have been used throughout this text rather than *he/she*, *his/her*, and *him/her*. All statements in the book, however, are intended to apply to both sexes.

Chapter One

Commitment and the Control of Organizational Behavior and Belief

Gerald R. Salancik

Most articles on organizational commitment extol the virtues of commitment. In them, you will find that the committed employee is the happy employee, the success of the organization is a matter of its members sacrificing their time and effort, and commitment to the values of the organization gives meaning to a person's life. In them commitment enhances productivity, assures quality in the final product, and guarantees the flow of adaptive innovation. In them, you will find, in short, a lot of nonsense mixed with a lot of common sense. But from them your understanding of commitment may not be enhanced.

This chapter will not tell you that commitment is necessarily good or necessarily bad. Whether or not it is will depend on what a person is committed to and on whether or not what he is committed to is appropriate for success in the situation. Sometimes commitment to beliefs can be truly devastating. When asked to explain why a comparatively small number of armed SS guards were able to lead millions of men, women and children to death in the gas chambers, one survivor of the Nazi concentration camps said this: "Why? Why did we walk like meek sheep to the slaughterhouse? Why did we not fight back? . . . I know why. Because we had faith in humanity. Because we did not really think that human beings were capable of committing such crimes" (quoted in Des Pres, 1976). A history of living their own moral lives told people that such things did not happen.

Organizational behavior, as a field, historically has confused theories of human behavior with theories of organizational outcome. The trap is easy to understand. At some point it is believed that productivity is a good thing for an organization. At another point it is recognized that certain behaviors contribute to productivity. Then it is discovered that certain conditions affect behavior. Quickly, those concerned are deluded into thinking that programs to change behavior will enhance productivity. A flurry of research is done to demonstrate this. The research comes back equivocal at best. Usually missing is serious consideration for the way organizational outcomes come about and the way human actions relate to outcomes. Without knowledge of how behaviors affect organizational performance, intensification of the behaviors may only exacerbate ineffectiveness. A person who takes the wrong road may be greatly motivated, but will wind up lost nonetheless, and perhaps a little faster than one who is not motivated.

Our emphasis in this chapter will be on commitment as a psychological and social process. What is commitment? How do people become committed? What are the likely effects of commitment on behavior in organizations? How do you manage and manipulate commitments in organizations? These are the questions we address. The precise and particular ways in which commitment will affect a particular organizational situation can only be understood by looking into the particular situation.

Conceptions of Commitment

The most frequently encountered view of commitment in organizations is one having to do with an individual's psychological bond to the organization. Buchanan (1975) provides a recent review, and suggests commitment is an additive function of three things: organizational identification, job involvement, and organizational loyalty. Similarly, Porter and his associates define commitment as an additive function of a person's desire to remain a member of the organization; his willingness to exert high effort for the organization, and his belief in the values and goals of the organization (Porter and Smith, 1970; Porter, Crampon and Smith, 1972; Dubin, Champoux, and Porter, 1975). These psychological views are compatible with most managerial conceptions of organizational loyalty and commitment (Lee, 1968; Sigband, 1974; Jennings, 1973; Spencer, 1972), a view which Stewart (1961) expresses quite nicely: "Organization-centered loyalty can probably be defined as a man's personal commitment to give more than adequately of his time, energy, talent, judgment, ideas, and moral courage in the best interests of the company" (p. 19). Imagine getting all that for the minimum wage.

Sociologists who have examined various issues of commitment

come at it from a slightly different perspective. They look at the conflicting commitments and multiple role orientations of professionals in organizations. They suggest that involvement in one organization is partly a function of involvements in other organizations. Despite this, their views of commitment are quite similar to those of psychologists and concern the person's willingness to leave or stay with the organization (Hrebiniak and Alutto, 1972) or his orientation to the rewards of his various affiliations (Sheldon, 1971).

While there is nothing particularly wrong with the prevailing conceptions, they do create a few problems for anyone interested in manipulating commitments in organizational settings or for anyone interested in studying the determinants and consequences of commitment. The definitions refer to the attitudes and behavior of committed individuals. A committed person is one who says he will stay on the job and work hard for the organization's interests. But how do people come to do such things? And why?

The above definitions can be used only after the fact to classify persons as committed or not committed. They do not give much direction as to how to create commitment. As such they can guide neither action nor research. One studies commitment partly because one is interested in manipulating it in organizational and social contexts. And the research done has been done to address some striking organizational problems. The 1960s brought a spate of work on the differing role orientations of U.S. engineers and scientists. No small impetus was the National Aeronautic and Space Administration's interest in mobilizing scientific talent. A scientist too oriented to his profession might not do much for the organization, whereas one too oriented to his company might turn into a conforming bureaucrat. Neither condition would foster NASA's goals, and hence the research interest in commitment. Recent interest in commitment research is justified by the general decay of employee interest in working, rising dissatisfaction, absenteeism, and turnover. Add to that union militancy, unsponsored wildcat and membership strikes, and labor's growing political and economic power, and you can quickly see the advantage of making employees feel a bit more concerned and dedicated.

Current conceptions of organizational commitment are too restrictive. There are many more ways in which commitment is relevant to organizations than just staying on the job. Managers become committed to what they are doing. Project directors advance their pet projects. Employees become committed to one another and protect each other from hostile bosses. Organizations become committed to pursuing new goals, or to keeping things pretty much as they have always been. Commitment pervades organizations. To restrict the conception to a person at his desk with his nose to the grindstone is unduly limiting and not justified on any theoretical or empirical grounds.

An Alternative Definition. The view of commitment we present in this chapter is one which is grounded in behavior and the implications of behavior in one situation for behavior in another. The view derives primarily from the model of commitment developed by Kiesler (1971), with intellectual roots going back to Festinger (1957; 1964) and Lewin (1947). We borrow considerably from Kiesler's work, and deviate in significant ways. As a working definition, "commitment is the binding of the individual to behavioral acts" (Kiesler and Sakumura, 1966). The important words are "binding" and "acts."

To act is to commit oneself. A person may talk about how important it is to keep the population growth rate down, but to be sterilized is to give eloquent, unshakeable force to the statement. An adulterer may proclaim unrelenting devotion to a lover, but to give up children, home, and joint bank accounts is to put meaning into the proclamation. Thus, at a minimum, a concept of commitment implies that behavior, or action, be a central focus.

Determinants of Commitment

While action is a necessary ingredient in commitment, all behaviors are not equally committing. There are degrees of commitment. A statement of a belief or attitude is a less committing action than the signing of a petition in favor of the belief, which in turn is less committing than actively advocating the belief to a hostile or skeptical audience.

The degree of commitment derives from the extent to which a person's behaviors are binding. Four characteristics of behavioral acts make them binding, and hence determine the extent of commitment: explicitness; revocability; volition; and publicity. The first is the *explicitness* or deniability of the act, and concerns the extent to which an action can be said to have taken place. Two contributors to explicitness are the observability of the act and the unequivocality of the act. Some acts are not observable and we may know them only by inference from assumed consequences. You leave a dollar bill on a check-out counter, turn away for a moment, then find it missing. The consequence is obvious, but do you know if the customer next to you took it or if it was carried away by a draft from the open door? Acts themselves can be equivocal, forgotten, or otherwise intractable. A person who says, "I sometimes think . . ." is behaving more equivocally than one who says, "I think. . . ."

A second characteristic of behavior affecting commitment is the *revocability* or reversibility of the action. Some actions are like trials. We try them out, see how they fit with us, and if they don't suit us we change out minds and do something else. Few actions are really irreversible. Even a vasectomy can be undone. Promises can be made and broken. Jobs can be quit. Marriages can be dissolved; engagements, broken. Contracts can be torn up. On the other hand, some actions are permanent and having occurred, they cannot be undone. They are committing. Slapping someone in the face can be excused, forgiven, forgotten or reciprocated, but it cannot be taken back. Consumption of food or drink may be regretted but not reversed. Pulling the trigger of a loaded gun pointed at a friend commits all to its gross reality.

The explicitness and irrevocability of an act link action to an indelible reality. *Volition*, a third characteristic of committing behaviors, links action to the individual. This is one of the more difficult characteristics of human action to define precisely, and is frequently associated with such concepts as freedom and personal responsibility. What makes definition difficult is that all human action is both free and constrained, being done under one's own volition and in response to contingencies. Even the most seemingly free and personal action can be perceived as constrained. Artists and writers, such as Dostoevski and George Bernard Shaw, describe their acts of creation as the result of compulsions and external forces. And even the most seemingly constrained acts can be considered free. A person with a gun to his head ultimately is free to choose whether to comply or accept the consequences of noncompliance. The perception of volition, moreover, can vary with the consequences that follow acts. A manager who takes a decision which turns out to be a disaster for his firm may make every effort to divest himself of responsibility. And one can observe in the annual reports of most corporations the following simple relationship: When sales increase from the previous year, the annual report points out how management's ingenious investments and development programs are paying off; when, the next year, sales decrease, an astounding downturn in the economy is lugubriously noted.

Despite difficulties in developing a precise concept of volition, volition wields powerful influences on the attitudes and behaviors of people, at least in Western culture. Some major characteristics found to relate to the degree of perceived volition of action are: (1) choice; (2) the presence of external demands for action; (3) the presence of extrinsic bases for action; and (4) the presence of other contributors to action. Thus a person who works hard in order to make a lot of money is not perceived as having as much volition as a person who works hard for nothing. A person who works hard because his superior stands over him constantly is not perceived as having as much volition as one who does as much on his own. With regard to choice, a person who buys a Ford because that is the only car available for sale is not perceived as having as much volition as one who passes over a hundred other models to make the same purchase.

The perception of one's own causal role in an action is in part a function of the role of others. People feel less responsible for actions taken in groups than alone (Mynatt and Sherman, 1975). More subtle responsibility comes when one has sole determination of outcomes. People feel more confidence that they will win a bet when they flip the coin than when their opponent does, and also that the probability of winning is greater before the coin is flipped than after (Storms, 1971). The importance of self-determination was eloquently demonstrated in a study by Wortman (1975). Lake Forest College men were told they could have one of two consumer products, but that which one they got would depend on a lottery. The students felt more choice if they made the draw themselves than if the experimenter did. And if they received an unwanted item through the experiment's draw they derogated it more than when they themselves made the draw. The belief in control of chance is a pervasive phenomenon hinting at the importance we attach to ourselves as actors (see Langer, 1975).

One issue not dealt with by psychologists concerns whether volition is a personal attribution or a social ascription. That is, if I prefer to deny responsibility for an action and claim I did it because of extreme external pressures—but other people hold me accountable, regardless —am I responsible? Is a person who robs for food guilty? Is a soldier who kills civilians under orders a murderer? Is a government employee who commits political sabotage for his President thereby absolved of personal responsibility? To some extent, the fact that courts make judgments on just such issues as these suggests that personal responsibility is bestowed socially. Moreover, most experimental manipulations of volition are socially ascribed.

A fourth characteristic of action affecting commitment is the *publicity* or publicness of the act. This characteristic links the action into a social context. While all action and behavior is by definition observable, publicity refers to the extent to which others know of the action and the kinds of persons who know of it. Some audiences are unimportant to us, as are their observations of our behavior. One of the simplest ways to commit yourself to a course of action is to go around telling all your friends that you are definitely going to do something. You will find yourself bound by your own statements. The same commitment will not develop from proclamations to strangers you meet on trains. The publicity of one's action places the action in a social context which is more or less binding and, as we shall describe, contributes to directing the effect of those behaviors on subsequent behaviors.

The Implications of Behavior

Commitment is important because commitment to one behavior has implications for other behaviors. Kiesler sets forth two assumptions necessary to predict the effects of commitment. The first is that individuals attempt to resolve inconsistencies between the behaviors they do and the attitudes they hold. The second is that the effect of commitment is to make an act less changeable. For our purposes, the most important assumption is the second. With regard to the first, we will extend it and make it more general by stating that people will tend to behave in ways that are consistent with the implications of their past behaviors. To these two necessary assumptions we add a third: The implications of behavior are not given but are invested into a situation by a person's own beliefs or by the beliefs and expectations of others. Making these three assumptions allows us to predict the effects of commitment.

Behavior carries one into the future. When a person chooses to order a ham sandwich for lunch it implies he will eat it and also implies he likes ham sandwiches. If the choice is free and committing, the consistency assumption predicts the person will in fact eat it and will in fact report he likes it. The prior choice commits him to those courses. The same theory would predict that the less committed a person is, the less consumption will follow from choice. Just such an effect has been observed by Reibstein, Youngblood, and Fromkin (1975). They had college students pour themselves soft drinks. When the students selected from four alternative choices (high commitment), they drank more of the chosen drink than when they selected from only two alternative choices.

Social Basis of Implication. One problem with developing a coherent theory of psychological implication is that it is too often assumed at the outset that implications are inherent properties of behavior or attitudes. Thus the argument that behavior follows from attitude (rarely found empirically) is that an attitude implies something about behavior. Such implications, however, are usually in the minds of the investigators and may not be in the minds of the respondents. For our purposes we shall simply assume that the implications of behavior are the expectations which either we ourselves or others have about what should follow from our behavior. How these expectations develop will not concern us except to note that they are part of our cultural heritage, our desires and beliefs about human activity. The important thing is that we and others have such expectations and that those expectations are salient to us as we act. The implications of a given behavior may be contestable and are a product of social reality, lending spice, flexibility, and potential survival to organizational life.

Divorced from behavior per se, implications can flexibly link one behavior with other behaviors. If you commit someone to a specific goal and it turns out at some future time to be no longer appropriate, how do you get him to switch gears and pursue a new path? Do you tell him that all of his past efforts were worthless and ask him to commit himself to some new effort—that future events may also prove worthless? An alternative strategy is to have several goals, or a goal so general that you can adapt it to fit different activities. Most organizations follow just such a strategy. Behaviors without preset implications can be shaped into new directions. Thus, if a canvasser comes to your door and says, "Do you support Frank Stapleton for mayor?" and you answer "Yes," he may use your answer to suggest, "Well, then, perhaps you would like to sign a petition indicating your support?" And you do. Two days later the same voice calls you on the phone and suggests that you might also be interested in helping out in the campaign. And you are.

Commitment and Social Control. It should be obvious from the above example that commitment is a potentially powerful mechanism of social control. By committing a person to one set of behaviors. with salient implications attached to them, you insure his doing other behaviors. Most organizations employ commitment in just such a way. When an individual joins an organization it is often suggested that he enters into a psychological contract with the organization, and agrees to adhere to the legitimate authority of the organization. The language is aptly colorful. The word "contract" suggests the individual is bound to fulfill certain obligations and duties. But unlike a formal contract, the precise content of obligations and duties is left unspecified—to be filled in later as the need arises with time's unpredictable requirements. The value of doing this is obvious. If all the expectations for future behavior were spelled out beforehand, the participant would know exactly what is needed and there is a high probability that things will remain the same. But if the situation is characterized by unanticipated contingencies, a more broadly drawn commitment is needed. For this reason, recently popular contract marriages are superficial instruments for binding individuals to what at one time was called "the thick and thin of it." People cannot forsee their own interests, expectations and demands for others so far in advance. Rather, they alter and align behavior with ensuing expectations and pressing commitments.

Commitment to Organizations

A careless interpretation of the consistency assumption might lead one to infer that having chosen to join an organization or to do a job, individuals will be willing to stay with it and be quite satisfied. After all, one implication of taking a job is that the person likes it. Choice, however, is not enough. The choice itself must be committing. The person must be bound to this choice. Let us consider an attempt to examine the validity of Festinger's (1964) notion of cognitive reevaluation in an actual job situation. Vroom and Deci (1973) studied the commitment and satisfaction of industrial administration graduates with their first jobs. The students in each case made a job choice from the offers they had received. Immediately after the decision, but before going on the job, the students' evaluations of the rejected and accepted jobs were consistent with their choices and more consistent than they had been prior to the decisions. In follow-ups one year later and three and a half years later, the job-takers reported less satisfaction with their jobs and rated the jobs as being less consistent with what they regarded as important. Twelve of the 37 persons had changed jobs and reported being more satisfied with their new jobs than those in the original jobs reported being. On the other hand, that 25 remained on their original jobs is more than would be expected by chance. But, unfortunately, any interpretation is equivocal, for we do not know the conditions under which the various individuals made their decisions. And details are important. Many first jobs are taken with the expectation of changing them or for instrumental expediency, both of which would reduce the binding effects of the decision.

A more explicitly binding situation was studied by Staw (1974). He traced the development of attitudes toward ROTC programs by college cadets. In some programs, students were required to sign a contract for two years; in others, no such binding arrangements were made. During the years studied by Staw, the United States instituted its first draft lottery; students who had joined ROTC to avoid being conscripted to Vietnam suddenly had a reason to reconsider their decisions. Staw compared cadets who received lottery numbers that virtually eliminated them from the pool of draftees with cadets who received numbers with a high probability of being called for service. In the nonbinding ROTC, following the draft lottery, cadets relieved from the draft soon disliked the program, while cadets in the draft category increased their liking. The same pattern was not evident for those who expected to remain in the organization; in fact, they became somewhat more attracted to the ROTC when they learned they were not to be drafted.

It is clear that making a committing decision, in the ROTC case an irreversible one, is different from just making any decision. And it is also clear that individuals make important decisions under differing circumstances. Consider the following comments from two freshmen engineering students, both of whom decided to pursue careers in engineering. They were asked by Perrucci and Gerstl (1969) to describe how they decided on engineering as a major. The first said:

> "I don't know. My dad started telling me about it when I was in the seventh and eighth grades . . . in the ninth grade we had this orientation course [about] . . . all sorts of jobs. We had to make reports on each job . . . just like an application to come here. . . . So I signed up for engineering. . . . I never really cared for math. . . . I just sort of—well, had to have it. . . . When I filled out my application . . . I was never actually positive. . . . So I figured well, it's your freshman year. . . . So I just signed up for engineering" (p. 44).

The second said:

> "In junior high school the counselors tried to help us pick our careers, and we had tests, these punch board tests, and mine came up engineering, and that's what started my goal . . . different years we'd do something like make reports on engineering— broaden our knowledge on it—and . . . take field trips to different universities . . . we made a trip here" (p. 46).

Neither of these individuals display extraordinary insight into their interests. Yet they differed in the way they made and accepted their initial decisions. The first considers the decision as just a trial. His father told him about engineering and he had to write a report anyway, so why not engineering. He had to list some major, so why not engineering. He constructs the choice as one guided from external pressures and needs, just as the taking of math—it was something he had to do. The second individual, also not too sure of what he wanted, learns that a punch board test decides he is suited for engineering. And just like that he accepts it as his fate. When he has to write a report, he interprets it not as just writing a report but as a broadening of his knowledge. Not surprisingly, the second student finished the program, while the first dropped out after a year.

Sacrifice and Initiation Rites. Some organizations prefer not to leave a member's commitment to the happenstance of his own decision process. Corporations frequently publicize the decisions of their new managers. The *Wall Street Journal* is crammed with advertisements by companies announcing that a particular individual has joined their firm, an act giving instant status to the manager's new role. Friends and past associates call in their congratulations and set into motion a climate of expectation that he is part of that firm. In recent years, insurance companies have been taking full spreads in such magazines as *Time* and *Newsweek* to publish the pictures of their sales personnel. Western Electric has done the same with television scans of their employees working on the job. For a few hundred dollars, an individual is identified with the organization. Next-door neighbors rush to ask, "Say, is this you?" One implication of the advertisement to both the employee and his friends is that the company really cares about its employees, and as a consequence it becomes more and more difficult to complain about it to friends. Harvard Business School uses a particularly effective method of maintaining long-term commitment from its graduates. Entering MBAs are immediately assigned to a group of classmates. This class does everything together from then on. They live in the same dormitories, hear the same lectures, and take the same exams. Virtually everything is scheduled for the class as a whole. Within each class, individuals are identified by namecards so that everyone knows the name of everyone else and is referred to by name in classroom discussions. Twenty years later, when the individuals have long departed the ivy-draped halls, the social network created there continues to operate. One of the things it is used for is to drum donations to the "B School," as it is fondly called.

In addition to advertising a person's commitment, some organizations take pains to make sure the individual is aware he has made a decision. Like the experiments with a well-constructed social psychological choice manipulation, the new employer commits the beginner: "Now, we want to be sure you're taking this job because you want to. We know you've given up a lot to come here and we're grateful. You left your home, your old friends. It must have been very difficult for you. And the salary we're offering, while more than you were making, is never enough to compensate for that."

The idea of giving up something to join the organization is one exploited in many ways. A common form is the initiation rites which still persist in college fraternities and sororities, fraternal clubs like the Masons or Elks, prisons, military organizations, revolutionary cadres, communal living experiments, police academies and religious organizations, orders and cults. An important part of the initiation process is the forcing of a sacrifice, in which members are asked to give up something as a price of membership (Karter, 1968). College fraternities require pledges to do hours of push-ups, to take verbal abuse, to have their privileges restricted, to accept subservient roles; in the end, those who endure love it. The effect is obvious. The individual in order to give meaning to his sacrifices is left to conclude they were made because of his devotion to the organization, a conclusion made more likely by his public pledge to enter the organization out of his own choosing. Other organizations have less colorful forms of sacrifice. Exclusive country clubs require their new members to make large initial donations in addition to yearly fees. The donations themselves provide for no services, and members pay for almost all services. But having given up an initial thousand, or a few thousand, dollars, members feel a certain compulsion to spend $3.00 for a martini at the club's bar rather than half that at a public lounge.

Investments and Tenure. Many organizations do not exploit the idea of sacrifice as a price of membership. Instead they emphasize the instrumental or exchange bases for participation. Members are hired rather than invited into the organization. Commitment under such circumstances will obviously be more difficult.

Studies on commitment to organizations that emphasize the instrumental bases for membership—work organizations—have consistently found two factors as most reliably related to commitment. The two factors are position in the organization and tenure with the organization. Study after study on the issue comes down to: People with good jobs are willing to stay in them; and, the longer a person has been with an organization, the more he wants to stay. Unfortunately, most of the studies were done in such ways that it is difficult, and in many cases impossible, to interpret the meaning of the findings.

The relationship of tenure to organizational commitment is predictable from the model of commitment presented in this chapter and has been discussed in a related manner. Howard Becker (1960) suggested that individuals build up commitment over time through certain "side-bets" they make in the organization. One obvious form of accumulation investments in an organization is the build-up of pension benefits and credits over the course of a lifetime. Until recently, such employee benefits, often called the "golden padlock," were not transferable from one organization to another. If an individual terminated in one organization, he lost some of his future wealth or security and had to begin accumulating it again in another organization. The costs of leaving the organization thus increase the longer one's involvement and one becomes more and more likely to continue where one is.

Regardless of financial investments, mobility also declines with tenure in an organization. As time goes by, one becomes less employable. And one's expertise becomes increasingly specific to one's current organization. Some organizations purposely manipulate the costs of leaving for some individuals. Universities will promote some of their assistant professors at rapid rates, making it more costly for other organizations to entice them away. Some business organizations will give young managers attractive positions unusual for their age, knowing it would be difficult for them to obtain equivalent offers elsewhere and also knowing it is cheaper to buy their commitment at an early age than it would be when they become industry hot-shots.

Test of the side-bets notion have been rare. More frequently, researchers have compared workers of different ages or different lengths of service in the organization. Becker and Casper (1956) observed that the more years graduate students remain in the program, the more they identify with their institutions. Miller and Wager (1971) found that the longer research scientists are educated, the more they orient to their professions. Buchanan (1974) found that older managers in major federal agencies and corporations liked their jobs and were committed more to the organization than were newer managers. Sheldon (1971) observed that scientists who had been in a private research laboratory over ten years were more committed to the organization than those who had been in the organization fewer than ten years. Schoenherr and Greeley (1974) observed that the best predictor of commitment to the Catholic priesthood was the age of the priest. Hrebiniak and Alutto (1972) studied nurses and teachers and found the same general relationship; the younger employees were less willing to stay with the organization than the older ones.

While we could go on with case after case (e.g., Grusky, 1966), there is little to be gained by doing so. The studies we cited, and those we haven't, all share one common problem. There is virtually no way of interpreting the meaning of the observation that young employees are less committed than older employees. It can mean a number of things. It can mean that the less-committed individuals in the history of the organization leave the organization, such that when the researcher asks his questions only committed older employees are around to be asked. Alternatively, the observation could mean that the longer one stays with the organization, the more likely one is to move into good jobs with the organization; having found them, one intends to keep them. There is some evidence that individuals are more committed to their organizations when they have higher positions in them (Sheldon, 1971; Stagner, 1975). Even in an Israeli kibbutz, where norms of equality are held to be strong, it is clear that persons occupying roles considered important by the kibbutz society are more ideologically and emotionally committed than their less prestigeous peers (Antonovsky and Antonovsky, 1974).

Another alternative interpretation of the tenure and commitment relationship is that older workers, rather than having more attractive jobs, have developed confidence and competence in doing them and are thus less likely to be dissatisfied. Vivier (1973), for instance, studied several hundred French railroad chiefs over a six-year period and found that their satisfactions with their jobs and organizations increased as their perceptions of their ability to handle the job increased. Organ and Greene (1974) also looked at changes in individual perceptions over time. Using lagged analyses, they found that with increased tenure (in a large electronics firm), senior scientists and engineers felt themselves to be more in control of their work situation and less ambiguous about their roles and how to do them. In turn, they attributed more purpose and meaning to their jobs, leading to more satisfaction. Hrebiniak and Alutto (1972) also found that nurses and teachers who didn't quite know what was expected of them felt a lot less committed to their employers. It would appear that people stick with jobs when they get the hang of them.

Part of the difficulty of interpreting studies on organizational commitment is that their authors share a tradition of not considering alternative interpretations of their own data and as a consequence rarely analyze their data in such ways that the alternatives can be ruled out. Indeed, some of the most interesting findings are those which contradict the authors' interpretations. The very contradiction sheds light on the process of commitment in organizations. We will present three cases.

Hall and Nougain (1968) argue for a model of commitment based on need satisfaction. They postulate what they call a "success syndrome model." A manager's need for success increases over the years he spends with a company. Those who are successful, as evidenced by their promotion and salary, increase in self-esteem. Their greater satisfaction with their personal esteem leads them to a greater commitment to their work. Hall and Nougain observed just such a pattern in the careers of successful managers. Over time, both commitment and perceptions of worth increased. However, less successful managers also became more committed to their work. Following presumed failure, their work and jobs become even more a central focus of their lives. Though the authors don't mention it, a "success syndrome" model seems inappropriate to account for such data. The findings can be made more explicable by recognizing that the mobility of less successful managers is dampened severely by their failure. Their current work situation becomes more and more an irreversible prospect. Not surprisingly, their attitudes adapt to the reality to which they are committed.

In a study of the commitment of nurses and teachers, Hrebiniak and Alutto (1972) found two factors were most important—years of service, and workers' perceptions about what was expected of them. They determined the importance of these factors by a sequential multivariate analysis. The procedure can delude the analyst into thinking that the variables are additive. The interesting aspect of Hrebiniak and Alutto's analysis, however, is that a re-plot of their reported data shows a nonadditive interactive pattern. It shows that younger employees who were uncertain about what was expected of them were least committed to staying with their current employer, while younger employees who knew their obligations and older employees, regardless of their uncertainties, were all highly committed. What is critical in predicting the commitment of younger employees is irrelevant for older employees, suggesting again that mobility may be an important consideration.

The third study we consider also has some perplexing features. Sheldon (1971), in an attempt to gather evidence on the side-bets notion of Becker (1960), studied Ph.D. scientists in a private laboratory. She argued that the scientists' commitment would follow their investments in the organization. Investments were defined as age, position, and length of service. While there is some suggestion that each of these factors was associated with commitment to the laboratory, the interesting aspect of the data is an unexpected interaction between length of service and position. Since the pattern is difficult to describe, we present below the proportion of scientists classified by Sheldon as displaying high commitment to the laboratory:

Length of Service/High Commitment

Position	Under 2 years	2-10 years	Over 10 years
Low	42%	50%	75%
Medium	12%	27%	75%
High	100%	45%	81%

There are two important features of the data. Individuals were highly committed after ten years of service regardless of their position. For younger employees, those occupying middle-level positions were less committed than those in higher or lower positions. Why should lower-level personnel be more committed than those at the middle level? Perhaps because they know they are not that good and not likely to have many alternatives to consider, so they settle into the job they do have. Why should the higher-level scientists be more committed than the middle-level ones? Perhaps because they know they are good, have had many alternatives to choose from and rejected them in favor of the place where they are. And the middle-level employee? They are in the unique and somewhat disquieting position of constantly having to consider alternative job opportunities without rejecting them. By the fact that they have been given moderately high positions, they know they are good. But they don't know how good or if they're good enough to move into a higher position in the laboratory or if they'd be more likely to get a better position elsewhere. In short, they are in a classic position of not knowing where they are going. As they spend more and more time in the same organization in the same position, it becomes clearer and clearer that where they are going is staying where they are. But until that becomes certain, their most intelligent response is to keep their options open and not settle into the organization with which they happen to find themselves at the moment.

Work Environments and Organizational Commitment

Thus far we have discussed commitment to the organization as the result of the constraints on an individual's ability to leave the organization, and the extent to which the individual himself has made a definite and committing choice. In reading this over, one gets the feeling that commitment to an organization is an entrapment: an individual is either cut off from other alternatives because no one else wants him or because his own situation doesn't allow him to change it. Thus, individuals rarely make job changes involving moves when their children are entrenched in a school. In all, it is a rather negative view of commitment. You are committed because the facts of your life have bound you.

What about more positive features? Do people become committed to their jobs because they are attracted to them and find them enjoyable? The research on this issue is unimpressive. Much is based on termination interviews which find that workers who quit say they quit because they didn't like the job or the pay. Having taken so decisive a step, it would be rather amusing to find them saying that they loved the job. Studies attempting to predict employee turnover or absenteeism from prior reports of job satisfaction have been notoriously unsuccessful from a practical point of view; that is, the studies report statistically reliable relationships of so low a magnitude that they predict little about behavior. Even superior measurement techniques do poorly (Newman, 1974).

The typical relationship found between job attitudes and turnover or absenteeism is clouded by other factors. We have already discussed that one of these factors is the tenure of the employee. Job satisfaction increases with age and tenure, as does commitment to the organization (see Grupp and Richards, 1975; Organ and Greene, 1974; Gow, Clark, and Dossett, 1974 for illustrative studies). Where investigators have bothered to make the necessary causal analyses, they have found that the change is a "real" one and not simply a function of changes in position, jobs, or salary (Stagner, 1975). As a person becomes more experienced in what he does he becomes more able to cope with the negative and positive features of his job.

The idea that turnover is the result of dissatisfaction is one which gained much ground during the industrial turmoil of the 1960s. Both popular and professional analyses of the growing alienation and militancy of industrial workers have placed the balance of blame on the meaningless, boring, repetitive and disintegrative tasks of modern life. Attempts to trace the presumed phenomena to such factors, however, have been rare. In one recent attempt, Flanagan, Strauss, and Ulman (1974) did regression analyses of national data on absenteeism, quit rates, and strikes. They found from analyses across industries and across time that the most commonly associated factors were basic shifts in the demographic characteristics of the labor pool. Absenteeism, turnover, and militancy were associated with changes in the proportion of blacks, young persons, and women in the labor pool. Attitudinal surveys have often shown these groups to be among the most dissatisfied toward their jobs. While the empirical observations do not provide their own explanation, they should be taken as important facts that localize the meaning of "growing industrial dissatisfaction." During the historical period examined, these groups were involved in significant struggles for power and status in society. In the middle of a revolution, one does not go around mouthing off about how lovely and satisfactory everything is. With regard to labor discord, Bok and Dunlop (1970) reviewed strike data and argue that recent lengthy strikes tend to occur in situations where unions are attempting to restructure their relationship with management—that is, to improve their bargaining power.

Commitment and Job Features. Despite the rather unpredictable relationship between job attitudes, absenteeism, turmoil, and turnover, the model of commitment presented here does suggest that certain features of a person's job situation will affect his commitment. In general, any characteristic of a person's job situation which reduces his felt responsibility will reduce his commitment. As for the relationship between commitment and satisfaction, our own view (to be discussed below) is that enjoyment is more likely to follow commitment than the reverse.

Many characteristics of job situations can affect a person's perception of responsibility. Some positions simply carry more responsibility, and persons in higher positions tend to be more committed. Similarly, some jobs offer more discretion and self-determination to their occupants, and it has been found that employees in autonomous positions generally have more favorable attitudes than those with little freedom to decide how to do their jobs (Hackman and Lawler, 1971; Hackman and Oldham, 1974).

In addition to the job and the freedom it permits, the manner by which the job is supervised or monitored can affect perceptions of responsibility. The supervisor who stands over a subordinate provides an excuse for the subordinate's behavior. When unpleasant aspects of the job become apparent, rather than coping with them, and finding some joy in the job, the subordinate can attribute his endurance to the supervisor's tenacious pressure. Lepper and Greene (1975) found that surveillance deteriorates interest in a task. Zanna (1970) found that when students are led to believe they worked very hard for a nasty supervisor, they enjoyed the task more than when they worked very hard for a nice supervisor. When they work for a nice person they attribute their effort to their liking for him, not the job. This would be an unrealistic attribution to a nasty boss, so they like the job more.

If a supervisor merely stands by without taking an active part in determining the subordinate's behavior, his presence may serve to reinforce the subordinate's felt responsibility. Maguire and Ouchi (1975) found that close output supervision improves employee satisfaction but that close behavioral supervision does not. Monitoring and providing an individual with feedback about his work performance can increase a person's felt responsibility. The person, knowing his outcomes and knowing his outcomes are known by others, may become more aware that the outcomes are his responsibility. Hackman and Oldham (1974) found workers' perception of responsibility was in part a function of feedback about their performance. While the precise effects of various supervisory conditions on commitment have not been well studied, we would expect that high output monitoring coupled with low behavioral control would lead to the greatest felt responsibility on the part of the worker. Whether or not these conditions will lead to greater satisfaction, would depend on whether or not the worker can handle the task. Maguire and Ouchi (1975) found more satisfaction among monitored workers who could do their jobs without depending on others (i.e., low interdependence), than those who could not.

Commitment also derives from the relation of an employee's job to those of others in the organization. Some jobs are rather isolated and can be done independently of other jobs in the organization. It has been found that jobs which are not integrated with the work activities of others tend to be associated with less favorable attitudes (Sheperd, 1973). Gow, Clark and Dossett (1974), for instance, find that telephone operators who quit tend to be those who are not integrated into the work group. Work integration can affect commitment by the fact that integrated jobs are likely to be associated with salient demands from others in the organization. If a person has a job which affects the work of others in the organization, it is likely that those others will communicate their expectations for performance of that job. Such expectations can be committing in that the other people implicitly or explicitly hold the person accountable for what he does. Earlier we mentioned that when individuals did not know what was expected of them they tended to be less committed to the organization. One reason an individual will not know what is expected is because no one is telling him. In general, we would expect that anything which contributes to creating definite expectations for a person's behavior would enhance his felt responsibility, and hence commitment. Integration may be one such contributor.

Perhaps the most pervasive condition of a job which affects commitment is its instrumentality, the fact that work is a means to some other end. While all jobs in industrial and commercial organizations are done in exchange for salary, there are perhaps great variations in the extent to which the instrumental basis for the work is salient or not. In general, we would expect that when the instrumental basis for work is salient it will reduce a person's felt responsibility. The attribution, "I am doing this job only for the money," should inhibit commitment. A similar point was raised by Ingham (1970), who analyzed absenteeism and turnover in light engineering firms in Bradford, England. Observing that larger organizations had more absenteeism (but lower turnover), he argued that workers were attracted to large firms because of the higher pay offered, but that this instrumental orientation led to little personal involvement with the organization.

One factor which could make the instrumental basis of a job unlikely to serve as an attribution is the level of reward. If payment is very low, it may not serve as a credible explanation for considerable effort at a task. As a consequence, the person may find it necessary to attribute his activity to the task itself. Salancik (1976a), for instance, compared students who had received course grades which were above or below their grade point average. Some had worked relatively hard in their courses and others had not; those who had worked relatively hard and received a below average grade for the course actually liked the course more than did those who did not work hard or who received an above average grade.

Tasks which are done primarily for instrumental reasons have been found to lead to less enjoyment than tasks which are not justified instrumentally. Most of these studies have been done with laboratory tasks which are initially interesting, such as solving the Soma puzzle (Deci, 1972) or assembling cut-up pages from *Playboy* into shapely figures (Calder and Staw, 1975). It was found that if a salient reward (Ross, 1975) is paid for doing these tasks, the individuals express less enjoyment and are less willing to do them again later. The interpretation given to these phenomena (Lepper, Greene, and Nisbett, 1973; Nisbett and Valins, 1971; Deci, 1972; Calder and Staw, 1975) is that the individual justifies doing the task by intrinsic aspects of the task when not given payment. The precise mechanism by which this occurs is not clear. One interpretation of the degrading effects of payment is that the knowledge of the instrumental basis for one's activity interferes with one's finding enjoyment in the task. This idea has philosophical roots in Marx's concept of alienation (1964; original, 1844), which argues that if an individual's orientation to his work is purely instrumental he becomes alienated from it. He absolves himself of responsibility for it and sees it less and less as something which belongs to him. Indeed, the work is nothing more than an obstacle which needs to be overcome to get to the individual's real goals—food, a summer vacation, and so forth.

On a more mundane level, by focusing on the instrumental basis for an activity, an individual's attention is diverted from the activity itself. The behavior is perfectly understandable to him from the outcomes it provides and there is little need for him to explore the task with regard to anything else. Thus, he does not find enjoyment in the task because he is not looking for it. And he is not looking for it because his attention is focused on the personal outcomes of the task. In a recent illustration of this, Salancik (1976b) induced students to attribute their work in a university course solely to their desire for grades and credit. The manipulation involved little more than having the students answer a few questions such as, "Most students work hard in a course because they want to get a good grade in it. Did you?" At the same time, some of the students were reminded of concrete interesting features about their courses. In spite of these reminders, those persons made to attribute their behavior to instrumental outcomes found the course less interesting and enjoyable.

These hypotheses aside, there is far too little empirical work on the nature of commitment to jobs, and how features of the work situation lead to or detract from feelings of personal responsibility for work. Much more detailed accountings of the particulars of job situations need to be made.

Effects of Commitment on Organizational Behavior

This section describes some effects of commitment on the behavior of individuals. The discussion is organized around three topics: (1) cognitive consistencies; (2) commitment to policies, strategies, and behavior; (3) commitment to norms and goals.

Most of the effects of commitment stem from the constraints which behavior places on us. It is for this reason that the most critical assumption of Kiesler's (1971) model of commitment is that the effect of commitment is to make a behavior less changeable. Commitment suggests that certain things will not change—namely, the behavior to which you are committed. Behavior serves as a constraining reality around which our beliefs, interpretations, attitudes, and justifications revolve. The more committing the action, the more constraining its effects. This important point is implicit in most of what follows.

Cognitive Consistencies: Shaping Attitudes and Beliefs

The beliefs, attitudes and values of people are *generally* consistent with their behavior. This is both because a person behaves in a manner consistent with his attitudes, and because he develops attitudes consistent with his behavior. Our emphasis in this section is on the latter, since we are concerned with the effects of commitment and commitment begins with behavior.

The importance of cognitive consistency for organizations can be summed up simply by noting that people like what they do. After a person takes a job, regardless of earlier uncertainties and second thoughts, he tends to like it. Despite the clamor about alienation in modern life, the truth is that most people are quite satisfied with their jobs and are committed to keeping them.

Another simple truth relevant to cognitive consistencies in organizations is that people believe in the value of what they do. People believe in the importance of what they do, its efficacy and effectiveness. When a supervisor instructs a subordinate in a particular way, he believes that his way is good. When a management consultant instructs a supervisor about the best method of supervision, the consultant comes to believe in the wisdom of his advice. In both cases, the beliefs can develop and persist not because of any verifiable evidence but because the mere performance of an action implies it is worthwhile. William Colby, who had just been removed from his post as director of the Central Intelligence Agency at a time when the Agency was under fire from congressional investigations into illegal political spying on U.S. citizens, was asked about his personal attitude toward keeping tabs on Americans. He replied: "Having lived around the world and being accustomed to having my phone tapped, I don't get emotional about it. Of course, if it's illegal, we're not going to do it, but I don't get horrified" (*Time*, 1976). Believing too much in the efficacy of one's action may even on occasion result in tragedy. It is said that one mistake airline pilots make is relying too much on the elaborate instruments of their modern planes. Flying is made so effortless, the pilots are lulled into thinking everything is under control when it is not. Shealy, Geyer, and Hayden (1974) detected a similar delusion in the epidemiology of ski accidents. They found that formal ski instruction resulted in a significant increase in accidents; the neophyte's assumption of improvement after lessons led him to put aside good judgment.

A third simple truth about cognitive consistency is that people become what they do. When people behave in certain ways, they develop conceptions of themselves which are consistent with their behavior. A person who helps another sees himself as a benefactor and a humanitarian. A President who has impressive papers placed in front of him for signing comes in time to see himself as an important person. The same President who shuttles around the world shaking the hands of kings, prime ministers, and chairmen cannot but image himself as a molder of the world. A manager beset with nagging subordinates seeking a word of approval here or an okay there will in time be amazed by his own brilliance.

A fourth simple truth is that people see others in light of the consequences of their own behavior. The manager, while verifying his own wisdom, will recognize the limitations of his underlings. A supervisor who watches to be sure his subordinates finish work correctly will point out their untrustworthy characters (Strickland, 1958). A soldier who kills a pregnant civilian will "realize" the civilian's whoring about was simply a ruse to pass information to the enemy.

In order to be enlightening, the four simple truths must be tempered by certain conditions. First, the extent to which cognitive justifications will follow from behavior is a direct function of commitment to the behaviors involved. Second, the particular justifications depend on the particular implications made salient to the person. Third, justifications take place in an objective and social reality with which they must be consistent. A President convinced of his importance to the national challenge confronts an environment of other persons' opinions. Occasionally, Presidents buffer themselves amazingly well, but most organizational actors cannot as easily escape the social reality.

Festinger argued in 1964 that people develop attitudes consistent with their choices. He recognized that decisions are committing and carry equivocal consequences for those who make them. After a choice is made, the negative aspects of the decision become real. But the choice has been made, and, if committing, cannot be unmade. One is stuck with the facts and follies of the past. When a person is committed and bound to a choice, he will resolve inconsistencies to produce attitudes consistent with the choice. Bailey and Helm (1974) found that only committed couples—those who made public statements of an intention to marry—judge their partners as similar to their ideals. Those who had known each other for an equivalent period of time but had not made a formal commitment were not likely to idealize their partners. Similarly, Winter (1974) found greater product acceptance among consumers who made committing decisions. He permitted customers to purchase one brand of scouring pads either on a trial purchase basis or a final purchase basis. Customers liked the brand they chose more after a definite adoption than after a trial. One of the grossest cases of cognitive reevaluation following commitment is Comer and Laird's (1975) study giving students choice to participate in or leave an experiment, and when they choose to participate telling them that the task involves eating a dead worm. Stuck, the students view themselves as brave but deserving sufferers, and the worm as not so bad. In fact, when given an opportunity to forego the worm in favor of a more neutral task, they choose to eat the worm.

In addition to resolving the incompatible aspects of one's choices, attitudes are consistent with behavior in part because attitudes are implied in behavior and hence inferable from behavior (Bem, 1972; Nisbett and Valins, 1971). When our feelings are not immediately obvious to us because we have not thought about them before, it is reasonable to look back at behavior to gauge them. Thus, a friend says, "Did you think the movie was funny?" and you think about it a moment and say, "Well, I laughed a lot—I guess I did think it was funny." Evidence that attitudes are inferred from behavior is widespread.

Attitudes are more consistent with behavior when people are induced to behave before reporting their attitudes (Fendrich, 1967), when attitudes involve recurring behaviors (Tittle and Hill, 1967), and when people are reminded of their behavior before reporting their attitudes (Salancik and Calder, 1974). Behavior's salient reality contains information about how one feels. As mentioned earlier, Zanna (1970) illustrated this in a task setting. Students working at their own pace for either a nice or nasty supervisor performed either faster or slower than a confederate. Those working very fast for a nasty person liked the task more than other subjects. The reason? With a nice boss, it is easy to assume you are working fast to please him. Not so with a nasty boss; it is not credible to say, "I am working hard because I don't like this guy." The more reasonable conclusion is that the task is pursued with vigor because it is enjoyable. And so it becomes.

Attitudes will not be inferred from behavior unless the implications of the behavior are salient. Kiesler, Nisbett, and Zanna (1969) provide evidence on this point. Yale students, standing on a street corner, were asked to persuade passersby to sign an antipollution petition, an implication of which was that they believed air pollution was bad. Kiesler, Nisbett, and Zanna made this implication explicit by having a confederate intimate that he wouldn't mind convincing others about something he believed in. When the implication was made salient, the subjects who agreed to solicit signatures became more negative about air pollution. Salancik and Conway (1975) extended this reasoning in a study of students' attitudes toward their courses. Students were reminded of their positive and negative behaviors regarding a course, and then asked their attitudes. Salancik and Conway reasoned that the implications of the behaviors would be more salient for majors than nonmajors, and thus their attitudes would be more consistent with their behaviors. Such was the case. For the majors, those reminded of positive behaviors liked the course more than typical students, and those reminded of negative behaviors disliked the course more.

The implications of behavior can be moderated by future conditions, and thus attitudes can be shaped in many alternative directions and still be consistent with both the committed behavior and the salient implications. Himmelfarb and Arzai (1974) induced people to choose to hear a message discrepant from their own views. One implication of such a choice is that you wanted to hear the message, thus suscepting you to its influence. However, another implication is that you wanted to hear a particular speaker. Himmelfarb and Arzai showed that when the discrepant message was delivered by an attractive source no attitude change followed, but an unattractive source produced attitude change. An attractive source provides a reason for listening independent of attitudes; namely, to watch somebody who is good-looking. Similarly, as mentioned earlier, Salancik (1976a) showed that when students who had worked hard in a course and received a low grade were given an acceptable reason for their hard work, their attitudes were unaffected by the low grade. Without an acceptable reason, they assumed they worked hard because they enjoyed the course, and they reported it to be enjoyable.

The attitudes of people can also be shaped by the anticipated implications of behavior. People behaving at one point in time can anticipate future social contexts within which their behavior might be viewed. They will develop attitudes consistent both with their behavior and with its future consequences. Calder, Ross, and Insko (1973) illustrate this. Female students were led to believe they were responsible for causing a classmate (whom they may meet in future classes) to miss a class exam to continue in the psychology experiment the women were in. The women tell the classmate the experiment was enjoyable (which it was not), and the experiments subtly bind them to their action by removing all justifications. The women given high choice and insufficient incentive for telling the classmate the task was enjoyable actually find the task more enjoyable themselves than others with less choice or sufficient incentive. Considering that they might meet the classmate in the future, the only acceptable thing which justifies their statement is if they themselves believed the task was enjoyable. And so it came to be.

The effect of future consequences on attitudes was investigated more thoroughly in a study by Goethals and Cooper (1975). Princeton students were recruited to supply arguments to university officials in favor of compelling freshmen and sophomores to purchase meal contracts from the university. Compulsory participation in the real program was, at the time, a controversial issue on the campus and most students wanted to be released from mandatory contracts. The students in Goethals and Cooper's study who wrote arguments favoring compulsory contracts subsequently believed what they wrote. But they did so only if they also expected their essays would or might be used by the University's Food Service to decide the issue. On the other hand, when the students knew their essays would not be used, or did not expect them to be used, they were less favorable to compulsory meal contracts even though they had written a favorable essay. Again, the important point is that behaviors which commit an actor to a future reality also shape his attitudes toward it. Merton and Kitt (1950) observed long ago that people alter their attitudes to prepare themselves for the futures they know are coming. Boots in training camp during the Second World War took on attitudes very similar to veteran combat troops if they had already been assigned to combat zones; those as yet unassigned made no such changes.

Postaction Justification in Organizations. There are few studies we can draw on to illustrate the cognitive effects of behavior in organizations. The reason is not that this aspect of humanity is irrelevant to organizations, but that organizational researchers are not used to thinking in such terms. The discussion of postaction cognitive consistency bothers many observers of organizations. Our common working assumption is that attitudes, goals, and values precede action and help to determine it. The analyst chooses an investment because he believes it will satisfy his needs. The consumer buys a detergent because he believes it will clean his dishes better. Human action is rational. We do things because of what they do for us. Most of us are neither fools about nor blind to reality. No doubt. But such facts should not now blind us to the possibility that a good deal of what we think and feel follows from our behavior. And a good deal of what we know about the consequences of action cannot be known until after the action has occurred.

Postaction justification occurs in part because actions have consequences, sometimes unanticipated consequences. These need to be explained to afford comprehension in an otherwise incomprehensible world. Understanding, however concocted, helps one continue to plow ahead with more (possibly meaningless) action. Explanations, properly selected, induce feelings of competence. They support beliefs about the stability and manageability of the world. Such beliefs are not to be taken lightly, either in organizational or personal life. They mobilize and satisfy. Hackman and Oldham (1974) have shown that employees who describe their jobs as meaningful also report they are more motivated to do them. These and many other writers have made much of the meaninglessness of modern jobs, the lack of variety, the deadly boredom, and rigid regulation. We would argue, however, that the very senselessness of many jobs requires that people make sense of them. We would also argue that individuals do make sense of their activities, and that they use any convenient characteristics of the job context which will provide sufficient justification for doing them. However, we would not argue that people will necessarily be more satisfied by making sense of their jobs, or any other activity. If you make sense of your job by noting that your bastard of a boss is the reason for your hard work, and that your need for money is the reason for working at all, then you are not likely to develop much endearment toward either. We would also argue that jobs can be made more satisfying by manipulating their contexts, and thus we disagree vigorously with those who argue that jobs must be redesigned to bring happiness.

In addition to the meaningful interpretations provided, postaction justification is also vital for generating legitimacy for one's actions. As we said earlier, behavior takes place in a social context. In organizations, the social context is unavoidable. Others are all around, and are not indifferent to the behaviors they witness. Individuals and organizations depend on the support of others, often making it necessary to justify actions in ways compatible with maintaining support. Regardless of what goals and beliefs went into taking a particular action, once that action is taken both it and its consequences need to be justified within the framework of those from whom one obtains support. Consider a simple illustration. A sales manager goes to a sales convention that is more luxurious than business-like. To himself he justifies the action as a pleasant and much-needed vacation. To his wife (whom he leaves behind) he justifies the trip as an important professional and business obligation. To his boss and company associates he justifies it as a way of keeping up on the latest in sales techniques and finding out what the competition is up to. In each case, the justifications are developed to solicit continued support from the parties involved—to give meaning to his actions consistent with his relationships with them. Though there is little evidence on the point, we suspect that a good deal of organizational goal-writing is aimed at establishing legitimacy for committed behaviors.

Commitment to Goals and Values

One effect of commitment suggested by the model presented here is that an individual who is committed to an organization (or work group) will tend to adhere to its norms. One implication of membership is that you will behave in ways appropriate for a member; that is, you will conform to the implied or explicit values and expectations of those to whom you are committed. Another implication of the model is that a person who is committed to a goal will try harder to achieve it than if he is not. In this section we discuss both of these effects.

Conformity to Norms. A person committed to interact with a group in the future will conform more to its social norms. The waiting job applicant straightens his clothes before the interview as if he were adjusting his life to the occasion. The anticipated future constrains current behavior because one is aware of behavior's implication for the success of future interactions. Ensuing reality thus makes one susceptible to influence in the present. The influence can be either covert or overt. In overt influence, others tell you how they want you to behave. Covert influence is more subtle, and for that reason more powerful. In covert influence, the person being influenced himself recognizes that his behavior carries certain implications into the future which he may wish to avoid. He shapes his behavior to satisfy the anticipated future interactions. Roering, Slusher, and Schooler (1975) found that opponents in a car-trade made more equitable trades when they expected to meet again with their opponent in a nonbargaining situation. Kaufman (1973) observed that bureau chiefs of federal agencies frequently choose to ignore feedback about their subordinates' work because taking action would strain the mutual feelings of trust they wish to maintain.

A number of organizational studies illustrate how the assignment of an individual to a particular group leads him to reflect the values of that group. Miller and Wager (1971), for instance, studied Ph.D. scientists working for a major U.S. aerospace company. They found that scientists assigned to the research laboratory of the company retained their professional orientation to a greater extent than did scientists assigned to the product development group. Lieberman (1956) documents how dramatically attitudes change with organizational roles. He assessed the attitudes of workers toward management and unions at one point in time. A year later, he interviewed the same individuals, some of whom had become foremen and some of whom had become union stewards. Those who had become foremen expressed more pro-management attitudes than previously, while those who had become stewards expressed more pro-union attitudes. Still some time later, the company demoted some foremen when an economic recession forced a cutback in personnel. Those returned to the ranks of workers expressed the same attitudes they had held as workers before.

The importance of socializing organizational members to the values of the organization is obvious when one realizes that the organization cannot always control who comes into the organization. If the organization altered its values to accommodate each new influx of members, it would be in a poor position to develop coherent strategies for organizing any activities. Garnier (1972) recently examined how England's Royal Military Academy at Sandhust maintained a consistent ideology despite major changes in its membership over 20 years. Sandhurst is the training ground for all regular officers of the British Army, and traditionally recruited its cadets from elite public schools such as Eton and Rugby, from which its values derive. Since the end of World War II, however, the school shifted recruitment to other public and private schools. The attitudes of these new entrants are vastly different from those of the elite schools; yet when they leave Sandhurst, they are the same. The socialization does not take place by means of any elaborate propaganda effort. Rather, it results from the movement of individuals through positions in the organization. When the individual accepts the position he behaves in the manner he observed his predecessor behaving; attitude change is a byproduct of this behavior.

When discussing social norms it is important to recognize that individuals are not committed to only one group or one organization. Rather, they invest their behaviors in many social environments at the same time, and the demands from these various groups may conflict. Dubin, Champoux, and Porter (1975) found that blue-collar workers are less committed to their jobs when they are involved in other life interests than when they are not. Pfeffer and Salancik (1975) have found that supervisors conform more or less to the demands of their bosses and workers as a function of how much of their daily routine is invested in each group.

Given that an individual is simultaneously committed to several environments, it would not be surprising that a single commitment to a single group guarantees little control over a person's behavior. It may be helpful to present our hypotheses about conflicting commitments. A person will act on the implications of commitments as a function of the saliency of the implications and commitments and strength of the commitment. If the implications of some behaviors are not salient, their impact will be less than if they are salient. If a certain social group is not salient, the commitments to that group will be less relevant to current behavior than if the group is salient. Kelly (1955), for example, found that when Catholic girls were reminded of their formal ties to their religion they were more resistant to anti-Catholic propaganda than when not reminded. Analyses of "brainwashing" techniques suggest the utility of isolating persons from other significant social connections (Schein, 1958). Similarly, Newcomb (1943) found that when Bennington College women maintained their communications with their families and friends, they were less influenced by the school's liberal tendencies than when they did not. Thomas (1973) found that convicts were less "prisonized" the more friends visited them from the outside. Although most problems of conflicting roles and commitments are probably handled by the relative salience of each, sometimes individuals actually may have to choose between them. We expect the choice would mirror the degree of commitment to the alternative groups. Salancik, Calder, Rowland, Leblebici, and Conway (1976), for instance, found that supervisors were more likely to conform to the wishes of their subordinates the less interdependent they were with other managers in the organization.

Commitment to Goals. An effective use of commitment within an organization is to induce individuals to pursue specific objectives of the organization, such as performance goals. An amazing fact of organizational life is that by merely telling individuals to achieve a certain performance goal they tend to do so. Steers and Porter (1974) review most of the research on goal setting and suggest that assigning a specific high-performance goal to operators leads to higher performance, than merely telling them to "do your best." Locke (1968) amends this simple statement by arguing that a person must accept the specified goal before it will affect his performance. Our coverage of this literature is restricted to the role of commitment.

The goal-setting situation is one in which a specific concrete goal for performance is stated for the performer. The typical situation studied is one in which the goal is set by some person other than the performer but is communicated to the performer, although it can include situations in which the performer sets his own goal and communicates his intention to another person, such as his supervisor. Other variations include the extent to which the performer has a role in setting the concrete goal or a choice in accepting a goal set by another. A common interpretation for the finding that a specific goal results in better performance than a nonspecific "do your best" is that the specified goal provides an objective around which behavior can be organized.

Careful consideration will show that a goal-setting situation involves an extremely subtle form of commitment. There are several features which make it committing. First, it is a public situation. Second, it is a situation in which definite public expectations are communicated for a performer's behavior. If the performer explicitly or implicitly accepts the goal, he will be making a public commitment which has certain implications for his future behavior. There are two primary implications of accepting a specific goal assignment. First, the statement of a specific goal and its acceptance implies that the performer is capable of achieving the goal. Second, the acceptance of a specific goal implies that the person is willing to attempt to achieve it. When a public commitment to achieve a goal is made and these two implications are salient features of that commitment, we would argue that the effects of goal setting should always be to increase a person's persistence on the task. In many cases this should increase performance. But whether or not performance is affected will depend upon the extent to which performance is affected by persistence.

In a goal-setting situation, the performer's behavior is a critical determinant of the commitment that follows. The performer, by sitting quietly by while the goal is set, behaves in such a way that his silence is a tacit acceptance of the goal. While Locke (1968) believes that goal acceptance is necessary for goal achievement, he errs in thinking that one must therefore ask the performer to accept or reject a goal. In his own experiments, Locke gives performers a considerable amount of power by allowing them an opportunity to evaluate a goal. It is no wonder that he finds that when a person rates a goal as impossible the person does not achieve it. The person's public statement commits both the operator and the goal setter to a justification for acceptable failure. That is, the salient implication of rejecting a goal is that the person is not capable or willing to achieve it. Under such conditions a person does not make a commitment to pursue a goal. Dweck and

Gilliard (1975) provide an interesting illustration of this with children. They compared children who are allowed to state a single initial expectation for achieving solution to a puzzle with children who are allowed to revise their statements in the face of failure. When allowed revision, persistence drops off in later trials proportional to the amount of effort made in earlier trials. When not allowed revision, however, persistence in later trials increases proportional to earlier effort. Without an opportunity to revise expectancies, the children are committed to pursue their prior stated objectives.

In a setting when the goal setter does not give explicit power to subordinates (does not invite their objections to a goal), a goal statement can be committing even if the person is not asked to specifically accept it. The mere fact that subordinates listen without objection commits them to the expectations explicitly communicated by the goal setter. By not explicitly objecting, subordinates give implied consent to the expectations that they are able and willing to pursue the stated goal. Later, when faced with the difficulty of the task, and the knowledge that it will take more effort than might have been anticipated, the person is already stuck by his own past commitment. The important aspect of the situation, however, is that acceptance is implied or specified in the communication of the goal itself. And it is this implied consent which is committing. Anything which detracts from the implied acceptance of a stated goal will reduce commitment to the goal, and hence persistence in attempts to achieve it.

A recent illustration of the subtle power of implied consent comes from a 36-month study of a "management-by-objectives" program (Ivancevich, 1974), perhaps the first test of the productive efficacy of MBO since Peter Drucker (1954) established its value by mere suggestion 20 years earlier. Ivancevich compared three plants. One plant was given no MBO program; a second was introduced to an MBO program by top management and left alone; a third plant was introduced to MBO by top management and left alone for two years, at which point a special department was set up to deal with issues of the MBO program. Initially, there was a slight production improvement for the two MBO plants, but this quickly fell off to normal levels comparable to the non-MBO plant. The plant with a special department introduced after two years began to improve again and surpassed previous improvement. One feature of the special department was that a telephone was installed with a number for plant foremen and supervisors to call if they had problems with the program. The telephone held important implications for the foremen's behavior. If they used it, they would be given advice on how to make the program work which they would have to accept, since they had already agreed to try the program. If they didn't use the phone, they would be implying that the program had no problems. In short, the presence of the telephone undercut the supervisor's ability to argue the program was not working, and implied both management's and their own acceptance of the program.

An important feature of the goal-setting situation is that definite expectations are communicated in a public situation. When a person is told "do your best," it leaves open the question of what is his "best." Since "your best" is left unspecified, any actual outcome is acceptable; that is, any outcome fits the expressed expectations of the subordinate and the supervisor. The importance of salient expectations can be seen from a study of workers in the pulpwood industry (Ronan, Latham, and Kinne, 1973). In a field (or, more correctly, a forest) experiment, these authors found that the per-person output was higher for independent pulpwood producers when goals were set *and* a supervisor was present, even though the goals were not tied to any rewards or threats of punishment. The suggestion is that the presence of the supervisor is a potent reminder of the expectations implicit in the previously-set goal. Munson and Kiesler (1974) set up an experiment in which a bystander attributes a particular attitude to a subject, either the subject's previously stated attitude or a discrepant one. When the subject later reads a communication stating the opposite point of view, his final attitudes were related to the public expectations communicated by the bystander.

The above studies all suggest that a person will become committed to pursue a goal when he listens to another person's expectations for his behavior without objection. It would not be surprising that if a person publicly declares his acceptance of a goal, he would be even more bound to pursue it (Locke, 1968). A person's own statement of an expectancy can significantly affect performance by the fact that the public pronouncement itself is committing. Zajonc and Brickman (1969) showed that when college students were asked to state their expectations for performance they performed better than when they were not given an opportunity to make a statement. Dweck and Gilliard (1975) gave fifth-graders insoluble puzzles to work on during a set time period, allowing them to quit whenever they wanted. They found that for males, but not females, the statement of an expectancy led to greater persistence in the face of failure. Pallak and Cummings (1976) found that Iowa City homeowners publically identified with an agreement to reduce energy consumption did in fact reduce it more than privately-committed homeowners.

Commitment to Failure. We have said that commitment to a goal stems from the public expression of the goal and the presence of salient implications that a person is willing and able to achieve the goal. From this it should be obvious that if salient implications are present in the situation which suggest one is not able, then goal persistence will be reduced. In the course of pursuing a goal, feedback from one's own performance can have a modifying effect on the implication that one is able to achieve the goal. If there is an implicit or explicit expectation of failure, particularly when it is public, then we would expect a person not to persist toward a goal. Locke's (1968) studies on the public rejection of goals is clearly consistent with this argument. There is considerable evidence that when individuals expect to fail, they fail quite effectively. Cetlin (1965), for instance, led subjects to expect failure on a complex key-pressing task testing their suitability for a career program. When the expectation was communicated early in the operator's trials, persistence on the task was less than when the expectation was communicated later, after success expectancies had built. Actual failure, in addition to expectations of failure, has frequently been found to cause subsequent failure in both organizational and laboratory tasks. These studies are conducted in such ways that the "actual" failure is manipulated and the subsequent failure is usually due to reductions in effort and persistence rather than a lack of ability.

The salience of expectations for failure are themselves partly a function of personal characteristics. Failure leads to failure most readily for individuals characterized by low self-esteem; that is, individuals who tend to view themselves as being incompetent or unworthy. High self-esteem persons are frequently unaffected by negative feedback, while low-esteem persons typically perform worse (Stotland and Thorley, 1957; Silverman, 1964; Shrauger and Rosenberg, 1970). One explanation for these individual differences and for the general phenomena is that a person who observes his failure comes to believe he will experience future failure, and because of that he perceives the situation as hopeless, with no reason to try harder. Thus the teacher who watches a child slip up on a problem accepts it as due to the child's level of ability, as does the child, and neither try hard to change the child's performance. Low self-esteem persons by definition are those who hold low opinions of their ability, and thus they are particularly prone to make such attributions.

If a failure experience or expectation diminishes effort because a person attributes his failure to lack of ability, then it should be possible to change his attributions and thus his success. A series of recent studies suggest just this. When individuals are given public expectations that their failure is attributable to changeable causes rather than permanent hopeless causes, it is found that they in fact persist longer and perform better. Dweck (1975) took children who normally attribute their failure to a lack of ability (a presumed unchangeable cause) and taught them to place the blame on more changeable factors, such as effort. When the children made such attributions, she found they did in fact persist longer. Miller, Brickman, and Bolen (1975) showed that telling fifth-graders they were able and motivated to do math problems actually resulted in greater persistence than trying to persuade the children that they *should* be able and willing. A similar effect has been demonstrated with adults. In one study students are given a pill and told it will deteriorate their performance. They then experience failure and are given a related task. Those given a pill persisted longer than others not given the pill (Weiner and Sierad, 1975). The pill becomes a temporary excuse for the first failure, so they do not attribute it to their inability.

Participation in Decision Making. From what we have said of commitment, one would expect enhanced persistence when a person is actively involved in making a decision to pursue a goal. The literature on participation and goal setting is generally consistent with this expectation. But, unfortunately, most of the studies are done with such carelessness that it is nearly impossible to isolate the precise factors contributing to the effects of participation. Part of the befuddlement is with the concept of participation itself. Participation can range all the way from an organizational structure in which "managers" and "workers" share power to veto or elect each other, such as the worker's councils in some plants in Yugoslavia and Poland, through a group planning program in which workers and managers develop a procedure together, down to a situation in which a subordinate agrees to accept a supervisor's idea. The resulting confusion can be monumental. Most participatory management studies allow so many alternative interpretations that they are cryptically uninformative. Alutto and Acito (1974) reported that they asked 80 manufacturing workers how much they participated in organizational decision making and found that the answers were positively correlated with attitudes toward the job. And what one learns is that the more a person tells you he took part in something, the more he tells you he liked it.

Still, when individuals take part in setting goals, it is found in both laboratory and organizational settings that the participation enhances the performance achieved (Steers and Porter, 1974). Latham and Yukl (1975), for instance, assigned some woodworker crews production goals and allowed others to participate in setting the goal. The participating crews had higher production. The results did not obtain for a similar manipulation involving logging crews, which Latham and Yukl attribute to the higher education of loggers. Tomekovic (1962) provides a clearer test of the proposition and shows that when individuals participate they perform better. Lawler and Hackman (1969) had some groups of telephone workers set up incentive plans to improve attendance and compared subsequent attendance with groups assigned the same plans or given no plans. The groups designing the plans showed improved attendance.

The committing aspects of participation in decision making derive from a number of factors. The participant not only publicly agrees to pursue a particular goal, but has some hand in designing the implementation of that goal. The effect of this is that the implications are quite salient to all participants in the situation (management and workers); active participation in the design of a plan of action implies both willingness and ability to accomplish it. Were this not the case, the parties would have to confront the question of why they would decide on something that was not feasible to accomplish. Other factors that would contribute to the degree of commitment are the same as those that contribute to the degree of commitment in any decision—the number of alternatives rejected, the publicity of the decision to all participants, the responsibility attributable to the individuals involved. On this last point, it can be the case that participation in a group decision can diminish an individual's felt responsibility. Thus, participation programs which operate by polling opinions and announcing the majority are not very binding, even on those who agree with the majority. Lack of personal identification provides an escape from compliance. The power of participation in directing future behavior comes from the person being held responsible for a decision with salient implications.

The Cooptation of Personal Satisfaction. In many ways, participation is an elaborate form of cooptation, regardless of whether such intentions are present. Miles (1965) has suggested that in many cases managers who use participation do so intentionally as a cooptation; that is, as a means of getting employees to carry out the objectives of management. Although we cannot speak for the intentions of past or future managers, we would add that it doesn't matter for the outcome what the intentions were. The important fact is that committing someone to do something places constraints around him so that he is more likely to do it. By having a person choose to do something, you create a situation that makes it more difficult for him to say that he didn't want to do it. And the ironic thing is that the more freedom you give him to make the decision, the more constraining you make his subsequent situation.

In the literature published about participatory programs, it is generally the case that the goals workers decide on are goals set by management. The boundaries of the decisions are always controlled and defined by management. In the Lawler and Hackman (1969) study, the goal of reducing absenteeism was a goal set by and very much in the interests of the organization. Workers were merely given an opportunity to figure out how to do it. By placing boundaries around another's decision while giving him complete freedom to make the decision, one not only gets what one wants done but gets it without a tremendous uproar. Galbraith (1973) describes how managers of giant corporations control their boards of directors by giving board members the impression that they are the ones who make the decisions, a much safer strategy than doing battle with them. In this sense, the use of participatory management to obtain commitment to goals and change is a cooptation. What is being coopted is a person's ability to complain, an ability made difficult by his own hand in designing the goal or its implementation. One company averted considerable complaint from employees they laid off by allowing participation of all levels of management and workers in the setting up of guidelines for the lay-offs. Those leaving thought they had been treated quite fairly, or so they said in parting interviews. Some unions, aware of the coopting implications of participatory management, refuse to allow their members to become involved.

Resistance to Change: Commitment to Policies and Beliefs

The last section argued that one effect of commitment is to induce a person to persist on a task to achieve its goals. Another way of describing the same thing is to suggest that the committed individual is resistant to change his behavior in the face of failure. This is how we often think of commitment when exemplified in the dedicated struggles of missionaries and doctors battling disease and starvation in the jungles of South America or Africa. It is also how we think of the junior executive doggedly fighting the battle of hours with his peers. Our admiration for commitment in individuals frequently stems from our agreement with the goals to which their efforts are directed. But what if the goal is the wrong goal? What if the truth lies in another direction? What if the world is different and the old ways of doing things just do not work anymore? In these cases we label the committed, "resistors to change." And we call those who resist, "entrenched conservatives," and "obstacles in the path of committed progressives."

Though the names may change, the phenomena are pretty much the same. People committed to certain beliefs or actions tend to resist changing them in the face of attack (Kiesler and Sakumura, 1966). In organizations, such people are frequently fired or forced to quit.

Whole organizations sometimes become committed to pursue objectives that lead to their failure, or if not failure, the incursion of tremendous cost. The United States' investments in Vietnam were considered by many to represent the disastrous consequences of unwise commitments. With each significant military failure, the response was not a cutback but an escalation of resources. When intelligence reports pointed out the massive task involved in a military victory and documented the erroneous underestimates of the opposition's strength, they were summarily dismissed. Undersecretary of State George Ball anticipated the irreversible nature of our commitment as early as 1965 (Ball, 1971) when he wrote a position paper to President Lyndon Johnson, "Once we suffer large casualties . . . our involvement will be so great that we cannot—without national humiliation—stop short of achieving our complete objectives." The escalation phenomena are similar to other phenomena described by Schelling (1960) as "entrapment," in which investments once begun are escalated beyond the bounds justified by the value of the object. Tom Stoppard, the playwright, noted that Rosencrantz and Guildenstern had simply "traveled too far, and . . . momentum has taken over." Shubik (1971) has created an auction in which the momentum builds so nicely that normal individuals can be found bidding more than a dollar for a dollar just to make sure they get the dollar.

One of the first studies of the effects of commitment on resistance to change was done by Hovland, Campbell, and Brock (1957), who had individuals state their opinions either publicly or privately prior to receiving a counter-communication. The public statements led to less influence from the communication. Kiesler and Sakumura (1966) subsequently showed that if public expressions of an attitude are made for salient instrumental reasons (payment of $5.00), individuals were more likely to change their position to one suggested by a counter-communication than were persons given a small inducement to express their initial opinion (payment of $1.00). In another study (Kiesler, Mathog, Pool, and Howenstine, 1971), residents of New Haven were either given an opportunity to sign a petition or not given such an opportunity. A day later, half of each of these groups was delivered with a broadside attacking the position taken in the petition. On the third day, attitudes were measured and the individuals were asked to volunteer to do work for organizations supporting the petitioned position. The attitudes of residents committed by signing a petition were more favorable than those of residents not given an opportunity to sign the petition. Moreover, the petition signers who were sent the attack volunteered three and a half times as often as all other residents (42% vs. 12%). What is so amazing about this study is that with so little effort (an innocuous petition one day, a counter-argument slipped under the door the next) one can turn quiet New Haveners into ready activists.

The importance of the attack is somewhat uncertain. It may be that the attack acts to remind individuals of their previous behavior and the implications of that behavior in light of present circumstances, presenting them with a challenging test of their newly committed position. When the attack comes, the new information is assimilated into the previous position and the person becomes even more bound to the position because he actively rejects some aspect of the alternative. Thus, when presented with a third opportunity to act, he behaves in a manner consistent with his previous behavior. A number of recent studies suggest the critical variable is not attack per se which is involved, but the implications of a committed behavior for future behaviors (Pallak, Mueller, Dollar, and Pallak, 1972; Kiesler, Nisbett and Zanna, 1969; Pallak and Kleinhesselink, 1976).

There is some evidence that people will act in a particular manner merely as a consequence of having acted in the same way before. In the first demonstration of this, Freedman and Fraser (1966) asked women residents of a pleasant community if they would place a small sign in the window of their homes. They readily complied. Some time later, a different person returned to the same houses and asked the same women if it would be all right to place a large and unsightly placard on the front lawn. These women were more likely to allow the large sign than were another group which had not been asked to comply with the first small request. Synder and Cunningham (1975) approached students on a campus street and asked some to answer a small 8-question survey and others to answer a large 50-question survey. Those asked the small request all complied, while those asked the large request refused. Subsequently, a different experimenter asked the same students if they would do a moderate 30-question survey for another organization. Compared to students not asked an initial request, those who had accepted the initial request complied more readily to the second request, while those who had refused the initial request complied less readily. The interpretation of both of these studies is that the person's response to the first request defines him as a helper; when a subsequent test of his helpfulness arises, he acts consistently. A more elaborate study by Uranowitz (1975) lends credence to this interpretation. He went to a shopping center in Palo Alto and gave female shoppers an opportunity to help a male college student with five bulky grocery bags. The young man put the bags down in front of the shopper and asked her if she would watch them while he went to get something he had left in the store. In some cases what he had to get was extremely important; in other cases it was rather trivial. It was assumed that helping for an important reason would lead the shoppers to assume they were helping because the circumstances demanded it, but that a trivial reason was insufficient and would lead the shoppers to assume they were helping because they were gracious persons who offered help to those in need. Such an assumption seems to be correct, for on a subsequent opportunity to help another person, the insufficiently justified were more likely to give further aid.

A study which seems to contradict the self-perception interpretation of helping was done by Ciadini and associates (1975). They asked students on a campus street to comply with an extremely large request (spend several hours working for an action group). After the students refused, the experimenter asked them to do a smaller favor. They agreed to the smaller favor more readily than did the students not asked the first favor. Thus, nonhelping in this case leads not to more nonhelping but to more helping. The most likely interpretation is that the students did not want to be thought of as apathetic to volunteering help for those in need. The same results probably would not obtain if the second request was made by a different person and the first supplicant had already left the subject with his irreversible refusal to help. For then he would be committed to his previous refusal to help. Just such an effect seems to occur. When individuals refuse an enormous initial request and are not approached again for several days they do not accede to a second request, while they do if asked immediately (Cann, Sherman, and Elkes, 1975).

The studies cited about helping describe rather innocuous and discontinuous outcroppings of behavior. The opportunity to help strangers is neither a recurring nor a frequent event. Many other behaviors individuals do, particularly in organizations, are of a recurring nature. It would not be surprising that the more an individual does a particular behavior, the more his commitment to that behavior would build, particularly when the behavior was not justified by some overwhelming and obvious extrinsic pressures. The adherence to rules in organizations is a good illustration of this. Both sociologists and satirists have described the extent to which bureaucrats follow rules with such devotion it borders on a fetish. In following a rule, the mere act invests the rule with unshakeable authority. Even though one might have adhered to the rule at first because it was official policy and fear of sanction (real or imagined) prevented deviation, over time, as a rule is applied on more and more occasions, it is likely that the original reason for following it becomes forgotten and one is left with the fact that things have always been done that way. Having done things one way in the past alone justifies doing them that way again. Rasmussen and Jensen (1974) observed skilled electronics repairmen trouble-shooting defective plant equipment. To learn how the men located problems besetting the complicated equipment, they asked the men to describe what they were doing as they did it. Though highly skilled and capable of building from scratch much of the equipment they maintained, the men invariably applied simple search routines, testing this condensor and then that transistor until the problem was found. When the tests were unsuccessful, the men, rather than abandoning the procedure and generating a new approach by reasoning, simply repeated the original search routine. When it failed again, they tried it again, until, perhaps by chance alone, something turned up which suggested the next routine to apply.

Kiesler and Mathog (1971) have done one of the few experimental studies of commitment to strategies of action. Commitment was manipulated by the number of times the strategy was used. Students played a card game for which there were four basic strategies of play. Through random assignment, with implied freedom of choice, the students played a particular strategy either zero, one, or three times. After playing, another student attacked the strategy rather strongly. The students were then asked which strategy they would choose to use again. Their choice of the critical strategy was proportional to the number of times they had used it previously. Moreover, when the other student attacked the efficacy of their original strategy they actually chose it more when they had played it three times. The attack, however, did decrease use of strategies played only zero or one time. It is as if the choice of a given policy over and over again convinces one of its efficacy, and when that efficacy is put into question, one reaffirms one's belief rather than alter it according to feedback.

People do manage, perhaps too easily, to continue with policies which evidence indicates are unwise. Staw (1976) had commerce students make investment decisions allocating R&D funds to one of two divisions of a large corporation. Some students personally made an initial decision, while others were told how the company's financial officer had decided. The students were then presented with five years of simulated history which indicated the initial decision was either a failure, causing a decline in profit, or a success, leading to improved earnings. The students were then asked to make another investment of R&D funds. Not surprisingly, those who had personally made the first decision and received feedback of negative consequences increased the investment to the same division as formerly. In essence, they escalated their investments following failure.

To understand the propensity of individuals to escalate their investments into failing enterprises, losing military situations, hopeless tasks, one has to appreciate certain features of these situations.

First, there is a degree of uncertainty about what will happen if you take a particular course of action. The failure you observe following your past action does not guarantee that the future action will also fail. Second, the behavior itself is irreversible. Having chosen, you cannot return to the past to erase the decision. If events in the future suggest that the past decision might have been a mistake, it may be unfortunate but knowing that does not allow you to remove the error. So you are stuck, and perhaps a little embarrassed. Third, in the process of making your initial choice, you bring to your mind information and ideas relevant to the choice and organize the information in a manner consistent with the choice (Salancik, 1970; Salancik and Kiesler, 1971). There is some evidence that when individuals anticipate opposition they tend to develop strong justifications for their initial positions and decisions (Salancik, 1972; Salancik and Snell, 1972).

Stuck with an attacked position, the easiest thing to do is to reaffirm your previous wisdom and try it again, since the future outcomes are not known for sure. It is the relative uncertainty of the future and the relative certainty about your own beliefs in your past action which balances the scales in favor of adhering to the past. As President Lyndon Johnson said on so many occasions following setbacks in Vietnam: We should not let this be an excuse to admit defeat. We must redouble our efforts. The importance of uncertainty for the escalation effect can only be surmised from the studies by Staw and Kiesler. In Staw's study, the feedback that students received following their decision showed that sales were going up but that profit was going down. It is quite possible that the decision makers could have thought they were having an effect on sales but that it wouldn't show up in profits for quite some time. In the Kiesler study, another student's opinion about a playing strategy could certainly be interpreted in many ways. There is always uncertainty about the meaning of events, and as long as there is, the past will live into the future.

Rubin and Brockner (1975) have recently simulated the entrapment situation in which you invest a resource in the hopes that it will pay off but are never sure whether subsequent investments are worth it and are faced with mounting, unrecoupable losses. The feeling of entrapment is like waiting for a bus rather than walking. As each minute passes you wonder if the next minute will bring the bus and you hate to miss it after you've waited so long; so you wait some more, hating to leave, hating to stay. Rubin and Brockner find that when individuals have clear indications that further investments will not pay off, they abandon the effort. Unfortunately, life rarely offers clear cues about payoffs, and thus we are trapped by our commitments. Staw and Fox (1976) recently extended the study of investment decision making to allow individuals to make decisions over time. Some of the students were told that the investment of R&D funds was known to be efficacious and would improve the conditions of either one corporate division or the other. Others were told that it was not certain if R&D investments were useful or not. A re-plot of Staw and Fox's (1976) findings show the following relationship: When students were led to believe that investments were known to be efficacious, they decreased their investments in the failing division (and increased them in the alternatives) as they made more and more decisions. However, when they were uncertain about the efficacy of investment in either corporate division, they increased their investments in the failing division with each decision. Although Staw and Fox did not test for this relationship, our own analysis indicates it accounts for most of the variance. And thus it is the uncertainty of the future action and the clarity of the committed past actions which are critical for resistance to change.

Managing Commitment in Organizations

From what we have said about commitment, it should be obvious why we do not consider that commitment leads necessarily either to good or to bad outcomes. It depends on what a person's commitments are and how those commitments lead to outcomes desired. When commitments induce a person to complete a difficult or unpleasant task which benefits him and others, then one might believe commitment is a good thing. When, however, the commitment leads to the fixation on a policy or behavior of diminishing benefit and rising cost, then the situation is less clear.

The Need for Commitment. All organizations do not need commitment from their employees to function effectively. While all organizations do require support from others, including employees, to implement the activities that accomplish their ends, it is not the case that such support need be given because of commitment to the organization. It is possible in many circumstances to develop support through nothing more than instrumentalities and extrinsic pressures. Indeed, it may be to an organization's advantage to do so. Explicit instrumental exchanges set definite boundaries to a relationship. If an organization knows exactly what it needs from another, it is to the organization's advantage to establish a simple instrumental exchange of the form, "You give me what I need, and I give you what you need." The advantages of such bounded relations are that when one is not getting what one wants, it is easier to sever the relation.

Commitment can be a liability to both the organization and the individual. To the extent that commitment derives from establishing a personal responsibility for behavior, there are situations where it is clearly a disadvantage to do so. National armies face such a situation in shaping individuals into killers. To take 19-year-old kids off the street and set them to the task of doing something which is personally abnormal is more effectively and humanely done by divesting their action of all personal responsibility. The disadvantages of making individuals personally responsible for killing in combat are that such policy would lead to less fighting, more guilt, and after the war a large population of potentially violent citizens. Thus, fighting is turned into a very impersonal business. You are not killing people but "gooks" and "jerries." You are not shooting because you are a murderous villain but because you are fighting for your country, your spiteful lieutenant is ordering you to do so, and your "buddies" will call you dumb if you don't.

Too much commitment can also be disadvantageous to an organization's flexibility. We have said that one of the effects of commitment to groups is adherence to normal and public expectations. And another is an inviolate trust in past policies. Over time, these can lead to an homogenous group speaking and acting as a single mind. But their impression can be wrong, and the world may have changed around them, nullifying their utility. Differences of opinion represent not only disagreements but alternative conceptions that may be more appropriate. Without labels proclaiming the "truth" of opinions, people base their judgments on agreement with others. Commitment thus decreases the available diversity, and thus the probability of finding correct solutions when the correct solutions are not known.

Commitments can also be disadvantageous when they merely lead to the reaffirmation of past mistakes—an entrenchment into the security of traditional practices. When the past is something that is known, and the future is uncertain, the balance of preference will tend to lean one backwards. But that may or may not be the right place to lean. Commitment can also be a disadvantage for the organization depending on who is committed to it and why. To the extent that commitment develops from an individual's constraint to leave the organization, the committed may be the least desired among the organization's membership. Those who are incapable of getting jobs elsewhere may be committed to the organization where they are. But if their lack of mobility is due to a lack of capability, the benefits of keeping them may be questionable.

The benefits of commitment also depend upon the situation. There are times when an organization can achieve support for its activities only through commitment. Indeed, some organizations rely completely on commitment to maintain themselves, either because the payoffs which come from activities are insufficient or because they are uncertain. When the relationship between an individual's actions and efforts are not known beforehand, or cannot be traced easily as leading to definite benefits and payoffs for either the individual or the organization, it is not feasible to establish or maintain instrumental relationships. Adolph Hitler understood this. To develop a strong and fervent attachment to the Third Reich, he used the simplest of commitment manipulations—active participation. He wrote, "Followership demands only a passive appreciation of an idea, while membership demands an active presentation and defense" (1941).

Nations often have only vague ideas about the particular kinds of demands required from their citizens. The particular roles required may become apparent only as history unfolds. Most nations, even in the absence of clear threats, thus foster nationalism; eventually a crisis will develop. To wait for the holocaust before shaping attachments may be too late. President John F. Kennedy, sensing the shifting alliances in Europe, South America, and his own country, wrote in his inaugural speech, "Ask not what your country can do for you . . . but what you can do for your country." However, a history of past Presidents preaching a chicken in every pot and a sharply rising post-war affluence consigned Mr. Kennedy's inspirational to a recruitment campaign for the Peace Corps. The nation was little committed to meet the crises that did come.

Like nations, religious organizations rely on commitment mechanisms. Lifelong commitments are developed by carefully taking novitiates through a series of trials and sacrifices. When beliefs are confronted with disconfirmations, they are thought of as "tests of faith," and if the individual emerges from the intellectual battle unscathed, he emerges more committed than before, more able to withstand future tribulations. By the same mechanism, scientists develop unshakeable commitments to their theories, as Mitroff (1974) so tellingly shows in his descriptions of world-famous scientists whose theories about the origins of the moon were left untouched by disconfirming data brought back by the astronauts.

The benefit of commitment is that through it one can get individuals to push headlong on a course of action when the outcomes of the action are themselves not known. For an organization which faces an uncertain environment, the selective use of commitment can allow it to take actions that may have a payoff or not. The only thing that is clear is that if you don't pursue the action, the payoff is guaranteed not to occur.

One of the most obvious benefits of commitment is in the cooptation of a person's satisfaction. By getting an individual to agree with goals, programs, and actions, by inducing personal responsibility for the same, an organization or a manager constrains the individual's ability to find fault with what he is doing. ("How can you complain? You're the one who decided to do that!") Selznick (1949) and Pfeffer (1972, 1973) have both eloquently described how boards of directors are used by organizations to coopt the support of the organization's critical interest groups. Outsiders are invited into the organization, given a sense of participating, and over time find themselves supporting the organization and defending it to other outsiders. The extent to which this can benefit the organization's freedom to operate can be gauged by looking at the congressional oversight committees of the Central Intelligence Agency. Though empowered to watchdog the Agency, committee members became its most powerful defenders. In 20 years they managed to prevent passage of hundreds of bills curtailing the Agency's power. To repeat: The most ironic aspect of participation is that the more the appearance of freedom is given, the more coopted one becomes.

Avoidance of Commitment. Given that commitment is not necessarily beneficial or disadvantageous, the astute manager will recognize that a selective use of commitment is more effective than blanket use. There are times when it is useful to induce commitment, and there are times when it is more useful to avoid it or to remove it.

It is clear that individuals do not enter into commitments easily. There is some evidence that individuals are often aware of the implications of current behaviors for future behaviors, and that this awareness restricts present behaviors. Hoyt and Centers (1972) found that when individuals were given a real choice and allowed to write any essay they wished on a topic, they espoused quite moderate positions when they knew the positions would be publicized. Anonymous writers took more extremely pro or more extremely con positions. The suggestion is that individuals are aware of the future implications of their essays and they avoid expressing positions which may bind them in the future. Kiesler, Roth, and Pallak (1974) had students tape a speech they agreed with and then asked them if they would like to listen to the same speech and describe how others might react. Publicly-committed students preferred to do another, more irrelevant, task and thus avoid thinking about the implications of their behavior.

There are two major strategies for avoiding the binding and constraining effects of behavior. The first is to diminish the obvious implications. One way of doing this is to avoid the committing behaviors. For this reason organizational leaders rarely disagree with one another openly, as a public disagreement carries with it the implication that a disagreement exists and will need to be resolved by either one party or the other backing down. O'Day (1974) observes that one of the ways superiors handle attempts by subordinates to reform the status quo is to nullify and isolate the suggestion. One walks out of the office with the reformer suggesting they examine the new computer to avoid a public commitment that the problem was serious enough to demand future action. Another tactic is to put your behavior into contexts that avoid unwanted implications. Hewitt and Stoker (1975) have described the use of "disclaimers" by individuals to maintain interaction continuity in the face of behavioral discontinuity. If a person behaves in a way that is unusual for his relationship with another, to avoid the impression that their relationship has changed, the person might alternatively discount the behavior. For instance, a student takes a particular course at a time slot when he traditionally met with a friend for coffee. Rather than leaving the friend with the impression that he doesn't value their meetings, he says he had to take it because his advisor says he needed it. Thus, legitimacy is established for the action in a way that maintains the relationship. This strategy has limits, since it depends on the other person's acceptance. Thus, for an organization to claim that its use of a new supplier does not imply lack of faith in its old supplier might be troublesome to accomplish. One seeks disclaimers that are credible; that is, acceptable to others.

A second strategy for avoiding binding implications from one's behavior is to keep the behavior secret. Politicians are reluctant to take a public stand on an issue early in their campaigns because they may find out it will lose other voters in the future. Thus, they hem and haw to keep their real opinions to themselves and a few trusted friends. Administrators guard their secrets for the same reason, regardless of their beliefs about the worth of openness for organizations. An interesting case is that of Warren Bennis (1976), who at one time was a major advocate of open, humanistic organizations (1966, 1969). He subsequently became the President of the University of Cincinnati, and currently defends the right of administrators to privacy, primarily because it makes his job of getting programs approved easier. Most organizations use secrecy as a matter of course to prevent disclosures of implications about their actions that might prematurely lock them into a position. Salaries are kept secret perhaps for no other reason than to maximize flexibility in negotiations with individuals. If they were public, everyone would know where everyone else stood in the eyes of top management and that could be embarrassing, requiring indefensible justifications.

Removal of Commitments. One aspect of managing commitments in organizations is to know when and how to remove them. The *when* is easy. When the commitments of others create resistance in the path of one's own ends, it is time to remove the obstacle. The *how* is more difficult.

If people are resistant to change, if their past actions commit them to a practice, the value of which has been long lost, then organizations may find it necessary to unfreeze the behavior to make way for change. But how? A common assumption is that you try to persuade the person of his errorful past, and make him see the disadvantages of the old ways and the advantages of the new. We obviously would disagree with this assumption. Attack will not reduce resistance. In anything, the evidence indicates that attack will only entrench a person in the position to which he is already committed. If you tell a person that his behavior, his opinion, is unjustifiable, you place the person in a position, a reality, of having to justify his position. You give him a reason to develop arguments that will convince you he is right.

If not attack, however, what then do you do? You try to unbind his behavior by providing the resistor with justifications for his behavior which "explain" the behavior independent of his own volition. Rather than taking away justifications, you overlay the behavior with so much justification that it is no longer necessary for the person to be burdened with sole responsibility for the behavior. You make it appear the behavior is something everyone would do, something the circumstances demanded, something so reasonable, so justifiable by the situation that the person can neither be held accountable nor even thought unique for having done what he did. The author attempted to illustrate this strategy once in a personally-motivated (but professionally justifiable) experiment. The task was to get people who had voted for President Richard M. Nixon to petition to impeach him. In one condition, supporters were given some newspaper articles reporting on the Senate Watergate hearings' disclosures of Nixon's possible misdeeds. At this time in history there was little talk of impeaching Mr. Nixon, and no one in this condition signed the petition. The second group of Nixon supporters were told that their vote seemed to be the most natural and obvious thing for them to do, something anyone would have done in November of 1972. Nixon had wound down the war, had brought peace with honor, and had kept the country from going bankrupt with his difficult but necessary price controls. The supporters were then told, "Yes, it was the reasonable thing to vote for Nixon. But that was 1972, and in 1972 we did not know everything about Nixon. We didn't know about the Watergate thing, and the way he kept what was going on from the voters." Supporters were then given the same newspaper material given to the first group. Sixty-two percent (of 13) of the justification group signed the petition. The implication is that just as the lack of extrinsic justification induces commitment, the abundance of it removes it.

A second strategy for removing commitments and the binding effects of past action is to eliminate the resistors. When an organization is too entrenched in the past, one of the simplest and surest ways to "unfreeze" it is to get rid of everyone who is associated with the past. While this strategy is not discussed frequently in theories of organizational change and development, a careful reading of the cases in which organizations have made profound changes in policy or direction will probably show that it is accompanied with a major change or shift in personnel. Despite vigorous opposition from citizens to the Vietnam involvement, it still took a change in Presidents and personnel to effect a change in response. In this regard, William E. Colby made an insightful comment about his own exit from the Central Intelligence Agency in January 1976. He was asked by a *Time* reporter whether he regretted leaving after embarrassing disclosures about the Agency's involvement in civilian spying and political assassination. He said, "No. I think it's a good idea to have a new face. That may get people thinking more about the future. You see, I have to identify my career with the whole of the agency back through the years. Mr. Bush [Colby's successor] doesn't. When somebody comes up with a horror story about 1948 or 1952, he can say: 'That's all in the past; let's look to the future.'" And that is the statement of a man committed to an organization even after leaving it.

References

Allutto, J. A., and Acito, F. Decisional participation and sources of job satisfaction: A study of manufacturing personnel. *Academy of Management Journal*, 1974, *17*, 160-67.

Antonovsky, H. F., and Antonovsky, A. Commitment in an Israeli kibbutz. *Human Relations*, 1974, *27*, 303-19.

Ball, G. Memo dated July, 1965 to President Lyndon Johnson. As reported in N. Sheelan (ed.), *Pentagon Papers, The New York Times*. New York: Bantam, 1971.

Bailey, R. C., and Helm, B. Matrimonial commitment and date/ideal-date perceptions. *Perceptual and Motor Skills*, 1974, *39*, 1245-46.

Becker, H. S. Notes on the concept of commitment. *American Journal of Sociology*, 1960, *66*, 32-40.

Becker, H. S., and Casper, J. Identification with an occupation. *American Journal of Sociology*, 1956, 289-96.

Bem, D. J. Self-perception theory. In L. Berkowitz, *Advances in Experimental Social Psychology*, vol. 6, New York: Academic Press, 1972.

Bennis, W. G. Have we gone overboard on "the right to know"? *Saturday Review*, March 6, 1976, 18-21.

———. *Changing Organizations*. New York: McGraw-Hill, 1966.

Bok, D., and Dunlop, J. T. *Labor and American Community.* New York: Simon and Schuster, 1970.

Buchanan, B., II. Building organizational commitment: The socialization of managers in work organizations. *Administrative Science Quarterly,* 1974, *19,* 533-46.

Calder, B. J., Ross, M., and Insko, C. A. Attitude change and attitude attribution: Effects of incentive, choice and consequence. *Journal of Personality and Social Psychology,* 1973, *25,* 84-100.

Calder, B. J., and Staw, B. M. Interaction of intrinsic and extrinsic motivation: Some methodological notes. *Journal of Personality and Social Psychology,* 1975, *31,* 76-80.

Cann, A., Sherman, S. J., and Elkes, R. Effects of initial request size and timing of a second request on compliance: The foot in the door and the door in the face. *Journal of Personality and Social Psychology,* 1975, *32,* 774-82.

Cetlin, I. G. Persistence, defensive behavior and self-evaluation as a function of early or late anticipation of failure. *Dissertation Abstracts,* 1965, *25,* 4248.

Cialdini, R. B., Vincent, J. E., Lewis, S. K., Catalan, J., Wheeler, D., and Darby, B. L. A reciprocal concessions procedure for inducing compliance: The door-in-the-face technique. *Journal of Personality and Social Psychology,* 1975, *31,* 205-15.

Comer, R., and Laird, J. D. Choosing to suffer as a consequence of expecting to suffer: Why do people do it? *Journal of Personality and Social Psychology,* 1975, *32,* 92-101.

Deci, E. L. The effects of contingent and noncontingent rewards and controls on intrinsic motivation. *Organizational Behavior and Human Performance,* 1972, *8,* 217-29.

Des Pres, T. *The Survivor.* Oxford: Oxford University Press, 1976.

Drucker, P. F. *The Practice of Management.* New York: Harper, 1954.

Dubin, R., Champoux, J. E. and Porter, L. W. Central life interests and organizational commitment of blue-collar and clerical workers. *Administrative Science Quarterly,* 1975, *20,* 411-21.

Dweck, C. S. The role of expectations and attributions in the alleviation of learned helplessness. *Journal of Personality and Social Psychology,* 1975, *31,* 674-85.

Dweck, C. S. and Gilliard, D. Expectancy statements as determinants of reactions to failure: Sex differences in persistence and expectancy change. *Journal of Personality and Social Psychology,* 1975, *32,* 1077-84.

Fendrich, J. M. A study of association among verbal attitudes, commitment and overt behavior in different experimental situations. *Social Forces,* 1967, *45,* 347-55.

Festinger, L. *A Theory of Cognitive Dissonance.* Stanford, Ca.: Stanford University Press, 1957.

———. *Conflict, Decision, and Dissonance.* Stanford, Ca.: Stanford University Press, 1964.

Flanagan, R. J., Strauss, G., and Ulman, L. Worker discontent and work place behavior. *Industrial Relations,* 1974, *13,* 101-23.

Freedman, J. L., and Fraser, S. C. Compliance without pressure: The foot-in-the-door technique. *Journal of Personality and Social Psychology,* 1975, *4,* 195-202.

Galbraith, K. J. *Economics and the Public Purpose.* Boston: Houghton Mifflin, 1973.

Garnier, M. A. Changing recruitment patterns and organizational ideology: The case of a British military academy. *Administrative Science Quarterly,* 1972, 17, 499-507.

Goethals, G. R., and Cooper, J. When dissonance is reduced: The timing of self-justificatory attitude change. *Journal of Personality and Social Psychology,* 1975, *32,* 361-67.

Gow, J. S., Clark, A. W. and Dossett, G. S. A path analysis of variables influencing labour turnover. *Human Relations,* 1974, *27,* 703-19.

Grusky, O. Career mobility and organizational commitment. *Administrative Science Quarterly,* 1966, *10,* 488-503.

Hackman, J. R., and Lawler, E. E. Employee reactions to job characteristics. *Journal of Applied Psychology,* 1971, *55,* 259-86.

Hackman, J. R., and Oldham, G. R. Motivation through the design of work: Test of a theory. Technical Report no. 6, Administrative Sciences, Yale University, 1974.

Hall, D. T., and Nougaim, K. E. An examination of Maslow's need hierarchy in an organizational setting. *Organizational Behavior and Human Performance,* 1968, *3,* 271-81.

Hewitt, J. P., and Stoker, R. Disclaimers. *American Sociological Review,* 1975, *40,* 1-11.

Himmelfarb, S., and Arzai, D. Choice and source attractiveness in exposure to discrepant messages. *Journal of Experimental Social Psychology,* 1974, *10,* 516-27.

Hitler, A. *Mein Kampf.* New York: Reynal & Hitchcock, 1941.

Hovland, C. I., Campbell, E. H., and Brock, R. C. The effects of "commitment" on opinion change following communication. In C. I. Hovland et al. (eds.), *The Order of Presentation in Persuasion.* New Haven: Yale University Press, 1957, pp. 23-32.

Hoyt, M. F., and Centers, R. Temporal situs of the effects of anticipated publicity upon commitment and resistance to counter-communication. *Journal of Personality and Social Psychology,* 1972 *22,* 1-7.

Hrebiniak, L. G., and Alutto, J. A. Personal and role-related factors in the development of organizational commitment. *Administrative Science Quarterly,* 1972, *17,* 555-73.

Ingham, G. K. *Size of Industrial Organizations and Worker Behavior.* Cambridge: Cambridge University Press, 1970.

Ivancevich, J. M. Changes in performance in a management by objectives program. *Administrative Science Quarterly,* 1974, *19,* 563-73.

Jennings, K. Employee loyalty: Relationship between theory and practice. *Personnel Journal,* October, 1973, 864-71.

Karter, R. M. Commitment and social organizations. *American Sociological Review,* 1968.

Kaufman, H. Administrative feedback: Monitoring subordinates behavior. Washington, D. C.: Brookings Institute, 1973.

Kelley, H. H. Salience of membership and resistance to change of group anchored attitudes. *Human Relations,* 1955, *8,* 275-90.

Kiesler, C. A. *The Psychology of Commitment: Experiments Linking Behavior to Belief.* New York: Academic Press, 1971.

Kiesler, C. A., and Mathog, R. Resistance to influence as a function of number of prior consonant acts. In C. A. Kiesler (ed.) *The Psychology of Commitment,* 66-73.

Kiesler, C. A., Mathog, R., Pool, P., and Howenstine, R. Commitment and the boomerang effect: A field study. In C. A. Kiesler (ed.) *The Psychology of Commitment,* pp. 74-84.

Kiesler, C. A., Nisbett, R. E., and Zanna, M. P. on inferring one's belief from one's behavior. *Journal of Personality and Social Psychology,* 1969, *11,* 321-38.

Kiesler, C. A., Roth, T. S., and Pallak, M. S. The avoidance and reinterpretation of commitment and its implications. *Journal of Personality and Social Psychology,* 1974, *30,* 705-15.

Kiesler, C. A., and Sakumura, J. A test of a model for commitment. *Journal of Personality and Social Psychology,* 1966, *3,* 349-53.

Langer, E. J. The illusion of control. *Journal of Personality and Social Psychology,* 1975, *32,* 311-28.

Latham, G. P., and Yukl, G. A. Assigned versus participative goal setting with educated and uneducated woods workers. *Journal of Applied Psychology,* 1975, *60,* 299-302.

Lawler, E. E., and Hackman, J. R. The impact of employee participation in the development of pay incentive plans: A field experiment. *Journal of Applied Psychology,* 1969, *53,* 467-71.

Lee, J. W. Organizational loyalty: A second look. *Personnel Journal,* July, 1968, 464-66.

Lepper, M. R., and Greene, D. Turning play into work: Effects of adult surveillance and extrinsic rewards on children's intrinsic motivation. *Journal of Personality and Social Psychology,* 1975, *31,* 479-86.

Lepper, M. R., Greene, D., and Nisbett, R. E. Undermining children's intrinsic interest with extrinsic rewards: A test of the "over-justification" hypothesis. *Journal of Personality and Social Psychology,* 1973, *28,* 129-37.

Lewin, K. Group decision and social change. In T. M. Newcomb and E. L. Hartley (eds.), *Readings in Social Psychology,* New York: Holt, 1947. p. 330-44.

Lieberman, S. The effects of changes in roles on the attitudes of role occupants. *Human Relations,* 1956, *9,* 385-402.

Locke, E. A. Toward a theory of task motivation and incentives. *Organizational Behavior and Human Performance,* 1968, *3,* 157-89.

Maguire, M. A., and Ouchi, W. Organizational Control and work satisfaction. Research Paper no. 278, Graduate School of Business, Stanford University, 1975.

Marx, K. *The Economic and Philosophical Manuscripts of 1844.* New York: International Publishers, translated, 1964.

Merton, R. and Kitt, A. Contributions to the theory of reference group behavior. In R. E. Merton and P. F. Lazarsfeld (eds.), *Studies on the Scope and Method of "The American Soldier".* Glencoe, Il.: The Free Press, 1950.

Miles, R. E. Human relations on human resources. *Harvard Business Review,* July/August, 1965.

Miller, R. L. Brickman, P., and Bolen, D. Attribution versus persuasion as a means for modifying behavior. *Journal of Personality and Social Psychology,* 1975, *31,* 430-41.

Miller, G. A., and Wager, L. W. Adult socialization, organizational structure and role orientation. *Administrative Science Quarterly,* 1971, *16,* 151-63.

Mitroff, I. *The Subjective Side of Science.* Amsterdam: Elsevier Scientific Publishing, 1974.

Munson, P., and Kiesler, C. A. The role of attribution by others in the acceptance of persuasive communications. *Journal of Personality,* 1974, *42,* 453-66.

Mynatt, C., and Sherman S. J. Responsibility attribution in groups and individuals: A direct test of the diffusion of responsibility hypothesis. *Journal of Personality and Social Psychology,* 1975, *32,* 1111-18.

Newcomb, T. M. *Personality and Social Change.* New York: Dryden Press, 1943.

Newman, J. E. Predicting absenteeism and turnover: A field comparison of Fishbein's model and traditional job attitude measures. *Journal of Applied Psychology,* 1974, *59,* 610-15.

Nisbett, R. E. and Valins, S. Perceiving the causes of one's own behavior. In Jones, E. E. et al. (eds.), *Attribution: Perceiving the Causes of Behavior,* Morristown, N. J.: General Learning Press, 1971. pp. 63-79.

O'Day, R. Intimidation rituals: Reactions to reform. *Journal of Applied Behavioral Science,* 1974, *10,* 373-86.

Organ, D. W., and Greene, N. The perceived purposefulness of job behavior: Antecedents and consequences. *Academy of Management Journal,* 1974, *17,* 69-78.

Pallak, M. S., and Cummings, W. Commitment and voluntary energy conservation. *Personality and Social Psychology Bulletin,* 1976, *2,* 27-30.

Pallak, M. S., and Kleinhesselink, R. R. Polarization of attitudes: Belief inference for consonant behavior. *Personality and Social Psychology Bulletin,* 1976, *2,* 55-58.

Pallak, M. S., Mueller, M., Dollar, K., and Pallak, J. Effect of commitment on responsiveness to an extreme consonant communication. *Journal of Personality and Social Psychology,* 1972, *23,* 429-36.

Perrucci, R., and Gerstl, J. E. *Profession without Community: Engineers in American Society.* New York: Random House, 1969.

Pfeffer, J. Size, composition and function of hospital boards of directors:·a study of organization-environment linkage. *Administrative Science Quarterly,* 1973, *18,* 349-64.

―――. Organizational ecology: A system resource approach. Ph. D. dissertation, Stanford University, 1972.

Pfeffer, J., and Salancik, G. R. Determinants of supervisory behavior: A role set analysis. *Human Relations,* 1975, *28,* 139-54.

Porter, L. W., Crampon, W. J., and Smith, F. J. Organizational commitment and managerial turnover: A longitudinal study. Technical report no. 13. Irvine, Ca.: University of California, 1972.

Porter, L. W., and Smith, F. J. The etiology of organizational commitment: A longitudinal study of the initial stages of employee-organization reactions. Unpublished paper, Graduate School of Administration, University of California at Irvine, 1970.

Rasmussen, J., and Jensen, A. Mental procedures in real-life tasks: A case study of electronic trouble shooting. *Ergonomics,* 1974, *17,* 293-307.

Reibstein, O. J., Youngblood, S. A., and Fromkin, H. L. Number of choices and perceived decision freedom as determinants of satisfaction and consumer behavior. *Journal of Applied Psychology,* 1975, *60,* 434-37.

Roering, K. J., Slusher, E. A. and Schooler, R. O. Commitment to future interaction in marketing transactions. *Journal of Applied Psychology,* 1975, *60,* 386-88.

Ronan, W. W., Latham, G. P., and Kinne, S. B., III. Effects of goal setting and supervision on worker behavior in industrial situations. *Journal of Applied Psychology,* 1973, *58,* 302-7.

Ross, M. Salience of reward and intrinsic motivation. *Journal of Personality and Social Psychology,* 1975, *32,* 245-54.

Rubin, J. Z., and Brockner, J. Factors affecting entrapment in waiting situations: The Rosencrantz and Guildenstern effect. *Journal of Personality and Social Psychology,* 1975, *31,* 1054-63.

Salancik, G. R. When hard work and failure lead to happiness: A quasi-experiment of attitude inference from behavior. Unpublished manuscript, University of Illinois, Urbana, 1976a.

———. Extrinsic attribution and the inference of attitude from behavior. *Journal of Personality and Social Psychology,* December, 1987b.

———. Two faces of commitment: The need to justify one's position and the need to be consistent. Unpublished manuscript, University of Illinois, Urbana, 1972.

———. The role of decision and organization in cognitive resistance to change. Ph. D. Dissertation, Yale University, 1970.

Salancik, G. R., and Calder, B. J. A non-predispositional information analysis of attitude judgments. Unpublished manuscript, University of Illinois, Urbana, 1974.

Salancik, G. R., Calder, B. J., Rowland, K. M., Leblebici, H., and Conway, M. Leadership as an outcome of social structure and process: A multidimensional analysis. In J. G. Hunt and L. L. Larson (eds.), *Leadership Frontiers,* Kent, Oh.: Kent State University Press, 1975, pp. 81-102.

Salancik, G. R., and Conway, M. Attitude inferences from salient and relevant cognitive content about behavior. *Journal of Personality and Social Psychology,* 1975, *32,* 829-40.

Salancik, G. R., and Kiesler, C. A. Behavioral commitment and retention of consistent and inconsistent attitude word-pairs. In C. A. Kiesler (ed.), *The Psychology of Commitment,* New York: Academic Press, 1971. pp. 109-21.

Salancik, G. R., and Snell, M. Commitment and prior support and the resistance of beliefs to attack. Unpublished manuscript, University of Illinois, Urbana, 1972.

Selznick, P. *T V A and the Grass Roots.* Berkeley, Ca.: University of California Press, 1949.

Schein, E. H. The Chinese indoctrination program for prisoners of war: A study of attempted brainwashing. In E. E. Maccoby, T. M. Newcomb, and E. L. Hartley (eds.), *Readings in Social Psychology,* New York: Holt, 1958, p. 311-34.

Schelling, T. C. *The Strategy of Conflict.* Cambridge, Ma.: Harvard University Press, 1960.

Schoenherr, R. A., and Greeley, A. M. Role commitment process and the American Catholic priesthood. *American Sociological Review*, 1974, *39*, 407-26.

Shealy, J. E., Geyer, L. H., and Hayden, R. Epidemiology of ski injuries: Effect of method of skill acquisition and release binding on accident rates. *Human Factors*, 1974, *16*, 459-73.

Sheldon, M. E. Investments and involvements as mechanisms producing commitment to the organization. *Administrative Science Quarterly*, 1971, *16*, 143-50.

Shrauger, J. and Rosenberg, S. Self-esteem and the effects of success and failure feedback on performance. *Journal of Personality*, 1970, *38*, 404-17.

Shubik, M. The dollar auction game: A paradox in noncooperative behavior and escalation. *Journal of Conflict Resolution*, 1971, *15*, 113-20.

Sigband, N. B. What's happened to employee commitment? *Personnel Journal*, February, 1974, 131-35.

Silverman, I. Self-esteem and differential responsiveness to success and failure. *Journal of Abnormal and Social Psychology*, 1964, *69*, 115-19.

Spencer, H. Designing commitment into the organization. *Personnel Journal*, December, 1972, 892-97.

Stagner, R. Boredom on the assembly line: Age and personality variables. *Industrial Gerontology*, 1975, *21*, 23-44.

Staw, B. M. Knee-deep in the big muddy: A study of escalating commitment to a chosen course of action. *Organizational Behavior and Human Performance*, 1976, *16*, 27-44.

———. Attitudinal and behavioral consequences of changing a major organizational reward: A natural field experiment. *Journal of Personality and Social Psychology*, 1974, *6*, 742-51.

Staw, B. M., and Fox, F. V. Escalation: The determinants of commitment to a previously chosen course of action. *Human Relations*, in press.

Steers, R. M. and Porter, L. W. The role of task-goal attributes in employee performance. *Psychological Bulletin*, 1974, *81*, 434-52.

Stewart, N. A realistic look at organizational loyalty. *Management Review*, January, 1961, 19.

Storms, M. Personal communication. Yale University, 1971.

Stotland, E. and Thorley, S. The effects of group expectation and self-esteem upon self-evaluation. *Journal of Abnormal and Social Psychology*, 1957, *54*, 55-63.

Strickland, L. H. Surveillance and trust. *Journal of Personality*, 1958, *26*, 200-15.

Snyder, M., and Cunningham, M. R. To comply or not to comply: Testing the self-perception explanation of the "foot-in-the-door" phenomenon. *Journal of Personality and Social Psychology*, 1975, *31*, 64-67.

Thomas, C. W. Prisonization or resocialization? *Journal of Research in Crime and Delinquency*, 1973.

Time, January 19, 1976, p. 17.

Tittle, C. R., and Hill, R. J. The accuracy of self-reported data and prediction of political activity. *Public Opinion Quarterly*, 1967, *31*, 103-6.

Tomekovic, T. Level of knowledge of requirement as a motivational factor in the work situation. *Human Relations*, 1962, *15*, 197-216.

Uranowitz, S. W. Helping and self-attributions: A field experiment. *Journal of Personality and Social Psychology*, 1975, *31*, 852-54.

Vivier, J. F. Personal and organizational factors in career development. *Psychologie Francaise*, 1973, *18*, 111-125.

Vroom, V., and Deci, E. L. The stability of postdecision dissonance: A follow-up study of the job attitudes of business school graduates. *Organizational Behavior and Human Performance*, 1971, *6*, 136-49.

Weiner, B., and Sierad, J. Misattribution for failure and enhancement of achievement strivings. *Journal of Personality and Social Psychology,* 1975, *31,* 415-22.

Winter, F. The effect of purchase characteristics on post-decision product reevaluation. *Journal of Marketing Research,* 1974, *11,* 164-71.

Wortman, C. B. Some determinants of perceived control. *Journal of Personality and Social Psychology,* 1975, *31,* 282-94.

Zanna, M. P. Attitude inference in a low choice setting. Ph. D. dissertation, Yale University, 1970.

Chapter Two

Motivation in Organizations: Toward Synthesis and Redirection

Barry M. Staw

Organizational researchers and practitioners have long sought methods to increase the likelihood that individuals will join a particular organization and work hard once within its confines. Historically, both of these problems have been characterized as issues of individual motivation. As a result, motivational research has been one of the most prevalent forms of organizational inquiry. This chapter will present an overall model of motivation which reflects current theorizing and will then examine several new directions for research. Because of the tremendous body of previous work in the area and the availability of highly competent reviews (e.g., Campbell, Dunnett, Lawler, and Weick, 1970; Korman, 1974; Lawler, 1971; Weiner, 1973), the principal goal of this chapter will be to reexamine and then revise our conception of motivation. This chapter's introductory statements on motivation are presented primarily to provide background for an integrated perspective on the area.

An Overview of Task Participation and Performance

Figure 1 presents a rudimentary model of an individual's interaction with an organization. The individual is shown to engage first in a search activity for possible organizations in which to participate. After some alternatives are isolated, the individual engages in a cognitive process to evaluate the relative merits of various organizational memberships, with motivation to participate resulting from such cognition.

After entering an organization, the individual is shown to engage in another search process to determine which behaviors to perform on the job. By evaluating the relative merits of possible behavior-outcome sequences, the individual becomes motivated for high or low task performance. After behavior is emitted and outcomes (both positive and negative) are received, the individual may be more or less satisfied with his outcomes. If dissatisfaction results, the individual may search his environment (this time the intraorganizational environment) for a potentially more satisfying course of action; he may work harder if less work did not previously lead to positive outcomes or he may perform less work if hard work did not pay off as expected. If dissatisfaction persists or remains at a high level, the individual is predicted to search for new organizational memberships. The decision to join a new organization is obviously predicated upon the availability of salient alternatives and their expected value as compared to the present situation (cf. March and Simon, 1958).

FIGURE 1   Flow Model of Task Participation and Performance

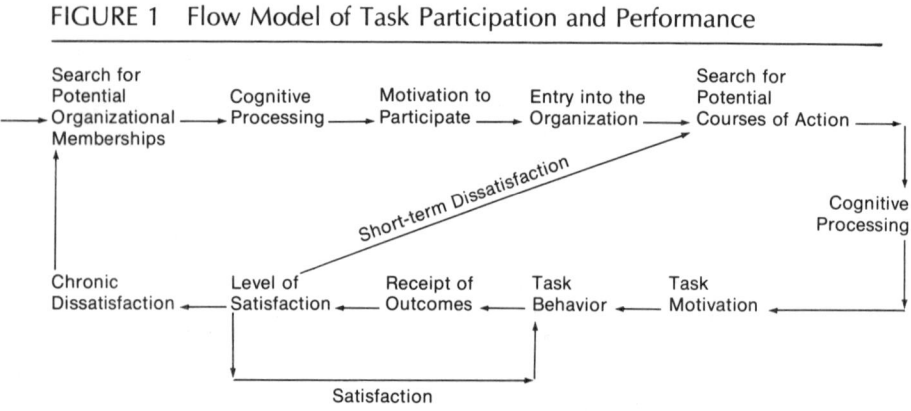

Presentation of this rudimentary model is useful in several respects. First, even in its elemental form, it does not depart too greatly from prevailing theory on task participation and performance. Second, it highlights the psychological emphasis of theory in this area. Both task participation and task performance are generally researched in terms of individual motivation rather than other constructs such as reference-group behavior, conformity, or social structure. Moreover, the motivational theories used to explain task participation and performance have tended to be cognitive in nature. Following the development of *value x instrumentality* theories of motivation in general (e.g., Lewin, 1938; Tolman, 1955; Peak, 1955; Rosenberg,

1956), and expectancy theories of work motivation in particular (e.g., Vroom, 1964; Porter and Lawler, 1968; Lawler, 1971), cognitive models of task participation and task performance have been predominant in the field of organizational behavior. The exact form of the cognitive representation of motivation has varied among theorists, but the primary characteristics of the process are the same. For instance, it is widely posited that the individual possesses certain values or desired goals and that he will embark upon that course of action which is most likely to lead to goal attainment. Of course, due to shortages of information, limited capacity for processing information, and sheer fatigue, the individual may not be perfectly rational in his choices (Simon, 1957). Also, as Locke (1975) points out, there may be important individual differences in ability to assess long- as well as short-term consequences of actions, and in the use of deliberate choice versus impulse in decision making. Each of these factors complicates behavioral predictions. However they do not refute the basic subjective expected-utility model (Edwards, 1954) of motivation in which individuals are posited to *strive for rationality* in their decisions to join and work in organizations.

The Content of the Cognitive Process

The cognitive model of motivation—be it motivation to participate or motivation to perform—is predicated upon two key elements. First, the individual is assumed to possess expectancies that certain behaviors will lead to either positive or negative outcomes, and second, the individual is assumed to be able to assess the valence or perceived value of such outcomes. Within organizational settings, there may be many different kinds of outcomes for which an individual will work, and these outcomes may be differentially tied to behavior or task accomplishment. The expectancy model of motivation posits that individuals attempt to predict both the valence of ensuing outcomes and also the likely contingencies between behavior and future rewards or punishments.

Figure 2 shows the various behavior-outcome sequences that can occur within an organizational setting. In filling an organizational role, the individual must generally perform a certain set of behaviors (e.g., visiting customers and talking about a product), and this set of behaviors may or may not lead to a high level of task accomplishment (e.g., high volume of sales). Some extrinsic rewards such as pay, promotion, and special bonuses may be contingent upon task accomplishment, but other extrinsic rewards are often tied only to specific task behaviors, regardless of accomplishment. That is, salary, fringe benefits, and other rewards can be based upon mere role occupancy or the execution of a set of requisite task behaviors rather than being tied directly to accomplishment. Although such systems rewards can serve to bind individuals to their roles (Katz and Kahn, 1966), their link to task behavior rather than accomplishment is often due to the difficulty of evaluating high as opposed to low task performance (Lawler, 1971).

As shown in figure 2, there are also other outcomes received by individuals in addition to those administered by organizations following task behavior and accomplishment. Individuals may enjoy the activities which comprise an organizational role merely for their own sake. That is, the physical and cognitive stimulation provided by a task may be rewarding to many people (Scott, 1966; Staw, 1975) and these rewards are internally mediated by the individual. In addition, the accomplishment may provide value to the individual even if it does not lead to specific extrinsic rewards (cf. McClelland, 1961). Thus, figure 2 shows three types of value which an individual can derive from his organizational role: intrinsic valence associated with task behavior (IV_{beh}), intrinsic valence associated with task accomplishment

FIGURE 2   The Behavior-Outcome Sequence

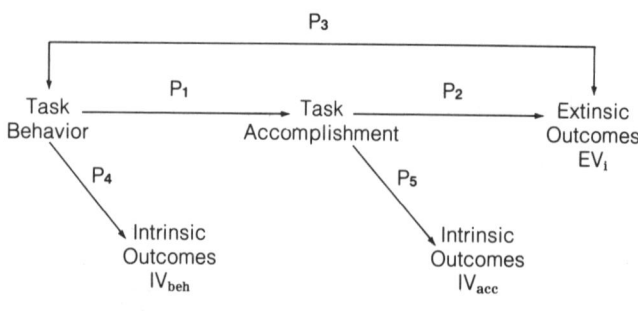

(IV_{Acc}), and extrinsic valences associated with extrinsic rewards (EV_i). Also shown in figure 2 are five separate contingencies or paths between behavior and outcomes. The expectancy theory of motivation assumes that individuals attempt to assess both the valence of various outcomes and the contingencies between these outcomes and behavior.

Determination of Expectancies

The individual anticipates behavior-outcome contingencies by utilizing several sources of information. A chief source of data is obviously first-hand experience in the focal organization or in settings of a similar nature. Once an individual has worked in an organizational setting and experienced both intrinsic and extrinsic outcomes, his motivation to continue or discontinue his participation will be affected primarily by such experiential learning. However, in initially deciding whether to join a particular organization, the individual must make use of both linguistic instruction and observational learning. Linguistic instruction may be in the form of advertising, promotional booklets describing career opportunities in the organization, or information provided by recruiters. Observational learning comes from those situations in which the individual learns behavior-outcome contingencies by watching others encounter them. This type of learning may affect the individual's expectancies both in the recruiting stage (e.g., if an acquaintance is also a member of the organization) and once the individual occupies a given organizational role

Determination of Valences

What determines whether an outcome provides positive or negative value to an individual? One determinant of valence is the set of individual needs that the person possesses. If the individual has a high need for achievement, for example, the opportunity to work on a difficult and challenging task will have a positive valence. If, on the other hand, the individual places a low value on success or achievement, challenging work may provide little motivation. The terms "individual need" and "valence" have been used correspondingly here, even though in certain cases there may be a disparity between the two. As noted by Locke (1975), one may not always value what he needs (e.g., an overweight man may not wish to walk to work). However, when dealing with socially-based rather than physiological needs, this problem diminishes. For example, the higher one's need for social interaction, self-esteem, autonomy, and achievement, the more likely are job outcomes involving these factors to be valued.

A second factor which may affect the cognition of valence is the set of values (and needs) of referent others. As shown in the conformity literature, people may value outcomes if they are valued by salient others (see, e.g., Campbell, 1961; Kiesler, 1969). Obviously, the values of one's reference group help to form one's *own* values, but others' needs and values may also directly affect our cognitions of what outcomes are positively and negatively worth.

A Model of Task Participation and Performance

Now that we have briefly examined the main features of a cognitive model of motivation, it is possible to reexamine more thoroughly the task participation and performance processes. As shown in figure

3, the initial search for organizational alternatives leads to the cognition of both valences and expectancies, and the motivation to participate is a product of this cognitive process. What comprises the expectancies the individual holds are his perceptions of the most likely behavior-outcome sequences for a given organizational membership. As mentioned, the individual's perception of behavior-outcome sequences is determined by his previous reinforcement history as well as linguistic instruction and observational learning. The individual's cog-

FIGURE 3   Flow Model of Task Participation

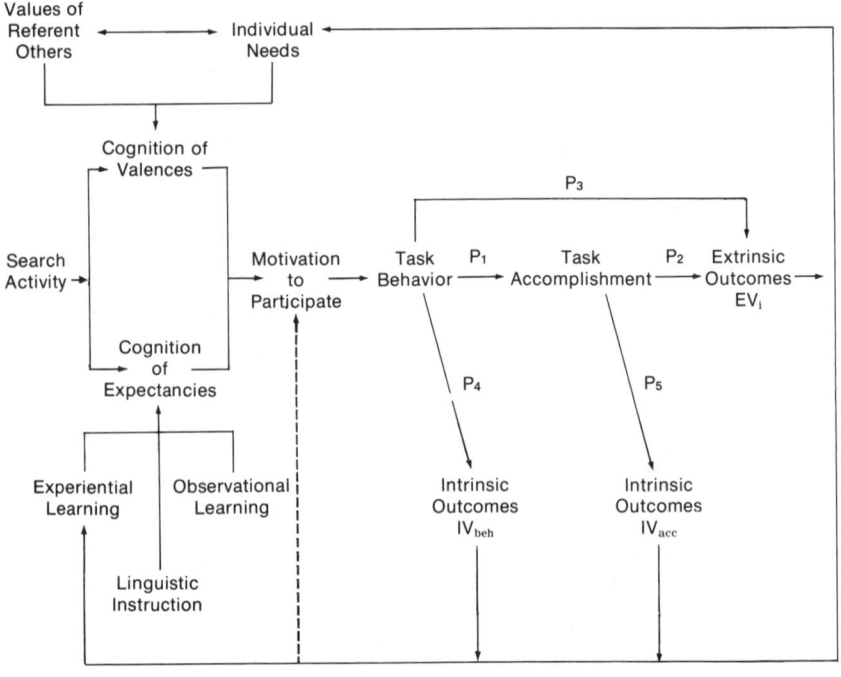

nition of valences will be the value of those outcomes highly desired (e.g., monetary rewards, achievement, social interaction) and those outcomes which it may be important to avoid (e.g., physical labor, nervous tension, shortened lifespan). Motivation to join a particular organization has been generally conceptualized as the multiplicative product of expectancy and valence summed across a series of the most salient outcomes or weighted by the relative importance of those outcomes. There is substantial empirical support for this general theoretical formulation (e.g., Vroom, 1966; Vroom & Deci, 1971; Sheard, 1970; Wanous, 1972; Mitchell and Knudsen, 1973; Sheridan, Richards, and Slocum, 1975; Lawler, Kuleck, and Rhode, 1975).

Figure 4 shows a theoretical model of the task performance process. With one important exception, the model resembles that of task participation. It is hypothesized that the individual, in deciding how hard to work, can perceive at least two behavior-outcome sequences—one associated with high effort, another with low effort. As a concrete example, let us imagine a door-to-door salesman who must decide how much effort to put into his job. One behavior-outcome sequence would consist of long hours of knocking on doors and walking from neighborhood to neighborhood, while a second behavior-outcome sequence would have a more leisurely pace. Clearly, each of these sequences will involve differing intrinsic valences associated with task behavior and, most likely, differing levels of task accomplishment. Whether or not there exist different intrinsic and extrinsic valences associated with task accomplishment will depend on both the individual's need for achievement and his company's compensation scheme. Thus, if the individual is not particularly achievement-oriented but has a great desire for money, he will choose the high performance path when the intrinsic outcomes of the behavior do not decline faster than his increase in extrinsic rewards.

The research on task performance has been generally supportive of the *expectancy x valence* formulation, but has not explicitly tested the model presented in figure 4. Most empirical studies have measured the perceived link between working hard (effort) and accomplishment, and, the link between accomplishment and extrinsic rewards. However, few studies have assessed the intrinsic outcomes of working at different paces or the link between minimal work behavior and extrinsic outcomes (e.g., systems rewards). Generally, empirical tests of expectancy theory inquire about the likelihood that "high effort" leads to "good performance" and the probability that "good performance" leads to extrinsic outcomes. Measuring motivation in this way may not lead to a highly accurate prediction of behavior because the individual may perceive the high effort path to be reasonably rewarding, but still not substantially more rewarding than another, less effortful alternative. In addition, by not considering the impact of systems rewards, one may be led to overestimate the effect of contingent rewards upon task motivation. Even if some rewards are highly contingent on accomplishment, their impact upon resultant motivation may be negligible when large systems rewards are already provided. Thus, we would argue that variance in task performance can

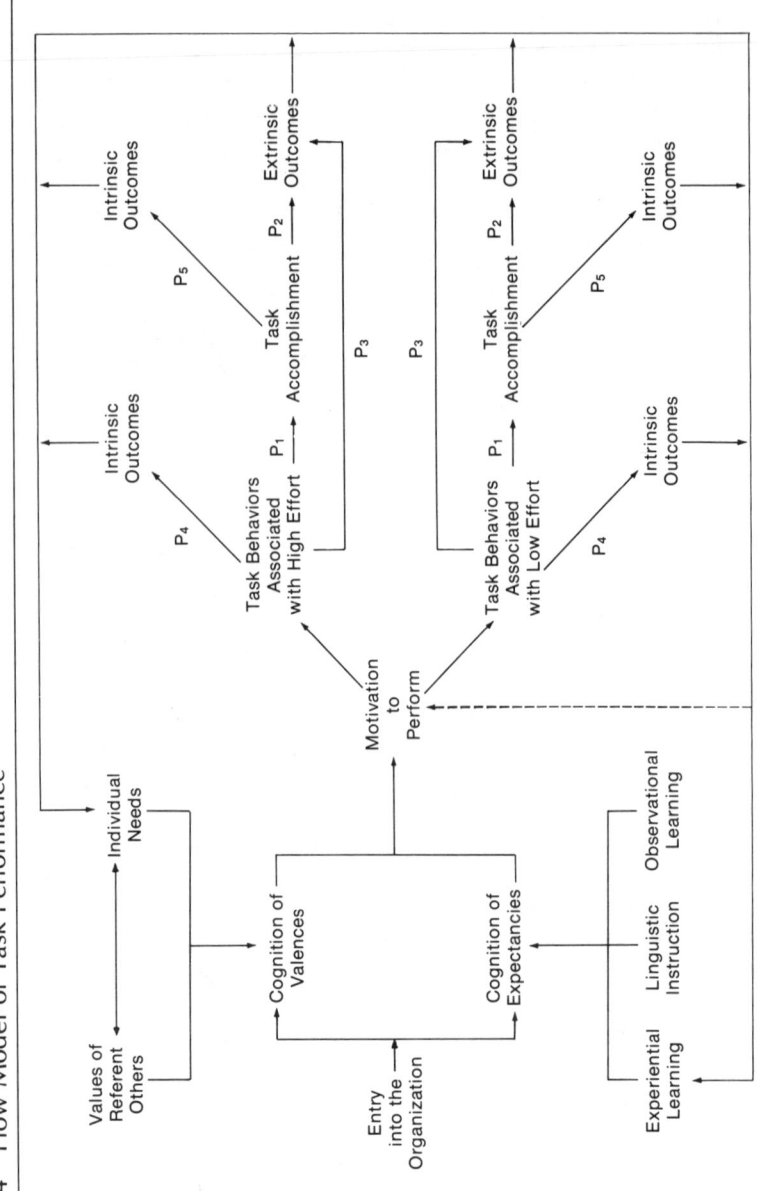

FIGURE 4 Flow Model of Task Performance

be best accounted for by measuring the *difference* between the expected values of two behavior-outcome sequences, one associated with working hard and another with working at a more leisurely pace.

The model of task performance in figure 4 could be operationalized by asking individuals to think of the consequences of working at two or more levels of effort. Items could then be designed to assess the likelihood that each type of task behavior would lead to various intrinsic and extrinsic outcomes. The importance or relative valence of each of these outcomes could be assessed and aweighted average of expected value could then be computed for working hard and for not working so hard. Using only two behavior-outcome sequences would simplify the data collection process and the calculation of a motivational index.[1] Also, given individual limits to cognitive information processing (cf. Simon, 1957; Miller, 1956; Slovic, 1972), this simplification may not depart too radically from empirical reality. An operationalization of this formulation of "motivation to produce" is presented below:

$$\text{Motivation to Produce} = \begin{bmatrix} \text{Expected} \\ \text{Value of} \\ \text{Working} \\ \text{Hard} \end{bmatrix} - \begin{bmatrix} \text{Expected} \\ \text{Value of} \\ \text{Working at} \\ \text{Leisurely} \\ \text{Pace} \end{bmatrix}$$

where:
Expected Value = $IV_{beh} + P_1(IV_{acc}) + \sum_{i=1}^{n} P_1 P_2(EV_i) + \sum_{i=1}^{n} P_3 EV_i$
and:

IV_{beh} = intrinsic valence associated with task behavior (e.g., working 5 hours vs. 12 hours).

IV_{acc} = intrinsic valence associated with task accomplishment
EV_i = extrinsic valences associated with extrinsic rewards
P_1 = probability that task behavior will lead to accomplishment
P_2 = probability that task accomplishment will lead to extrinsic rewards
P_3 = probability that task behavior will lead directly to extrinsic rewards

Note: P_4 and P_5 have not been included, since they should approximate a probability of 1.00.

Cognition versus Reinforcement

In discussing the models of task participation and performance we have emphasized the cognitive determinants of motivation. The individual has been treated as an incessant information processor and, as a result, it may have been assumed that conscious decision making precedes all human actions. This assumption is obviously questionable with respect to individual actions based directly upon physiological reflexes or tied to them via classical conditioning. However, the assumption of conscious decision making also may not hold when a behavior-outcome sequence has become extremely well learned. The automobile driver does not consciously plan his actions once the behavior-outcome sequences of driving are routinized and, likewise, the worker who has always done his job a certain way with satisfactory results may engage in none of the motivational arithmetic outlined above. Thus, on both figures 3 and 4 a dotted arrow-head line is inserted between the behavior-outcome sequence and the motivational construct. It is intended that these models show that reinforcing cycles can occur in which both motivation to participate and motivation to perform can remain high even without preceding cognitions of valence and expectancy.

Although a high level of task behavior can be maintained without cognitive awareness, this does not mean that cognitions of expectancies and valences are not of importance. On the contrary, cognitive information processing is especially important when the individual is making an initial decision to participate in an organization and when the individual has recently entered the organization and is beginning to learn a new role. However, once a person has routinized a behavior-outcome sequence, it may take one of two major events to cause a search of alternative courses of action and recalculation of expected value. First, if the behavior-outcome sequence becomes highly dissatisfying, the individual is likely to begin searching for other, more profitable courses of action. Such dissatisfaction could be caused by an initial failure to accurately anticipate the consequences of the behavior-outcome sequence or by changes in the environment after an initial decision. Second, if courses of action are saliently presented to the individual which yield markedly greater rewards than the present course of behavior, the cognitive process of assessing expectancies and valences is then likely to be reevoked.

In sum, the picture of the individual portrayed here is one of a limited information processor. Once the individual has discovered a reasonably satisfying behavior-outcome sequence, he is not likely to continue his search for better sequences or to consciously assess future returns (Simon, 1957). The reinforcement analysis of behavior with its emphasis on noncognitive learning may thus closely parallel much of the individual's behavior in work settings. But, when the individual is dissatisfied with his present state or is confronted with another promising alternative, the cognitive approach to motivation may provide a closer fit to human action.

Contingent versus Noncontingent Rewards

The models of both task performance and participation emphasize that it is the contingency between behavior and outcomes that largely controls behavior. The individual's perception of causal relationships, whether accurate or not, is a primary determinant of his choice of action. Therefore, it comes as no surprise that a great deal of practitioner-oriented research has gone into techniques of tying rewards to behavior.

One technique currently enjoying wide popularity within organizations is that of "positive reinforcement." Basically an application of B. F. Skinner's work on operant conditioning, positive reinforcement programs endeavor to tie verbal praise, pay, time off work, or special incentives to specific task behaviors desired by management. Examined in terms of figure 4, there are two ways by which behavioral change can be instituted via reinforcement. First, as in the early studies emphasizing the noncognitive elements of behavior control, an individual's behavior can be observed and reinforcements can then be applied when a desired response is achieved. The "shaping" of behavior would involve the gradual application of stricter and stricter criteria for rewarded responses so that only the most "desired" behavior would remain over the longer term. Other behavior which is less desirable would presumably be extinguished. Reexamination of figure 4 shows, however, that a second, and preferable, way to change an individual's behavior is through clear and distinct changes in expected contingencies. Rather than relying merely on learning to occur out of awareness or upon the individual to guess the allocator's scheduling of reinforcement (Spielberger and DeNike, 1966), it would seem more efficient to announce the contingencies between reward and behavior and to deliver as expected. Some of the newer applied motivational techniques such as goal setting and management by objectives (MBO) are embodiments of this latter motivational strategy. Research in this area has generally shown that setting clear goals and tying rewards to the accomplishment of such goals can produce significant changes in task performance (for reviews, see Lawler, 1971; Locke, Cartledge, and Koeppel, 1968; Latham and Yukl, 1975).

The power of contingent rewards to change behavior has been greeted by both controversy and accolades throughout the behavioral sciences. Few have challenged the ability of contingent rewards to change behavior, but debate has centered on the potential use of this power. Reinforcement theory applied on a societal level raises crucial political questions of both the right to control and who potentially would be setting the priority of desired behaviors. Applied within organizational settings, reinforcement techniques do not, however, face such ethical dilemmas. In deciding to work for an organization, the individual exchanges some of his control over his behavior for financial and other inducements. The labor contract is formal recognition of such a trade and it is supported by both social and legal standards. Of course, this does not mean that the organization can alter and shape an individual's behavior at will. As Barnard (1938) noted, there is a zone of indifference within which individuals will comply with organizational directives and outside of which the individual will resist influence attempts. To date, there has been little research on the nature of this zone of indifference for participants at different levels in the organization or for different types of organizations. One would expect, however, that individuals are susceptible to a broader scope of influence in higher- rather than lower-level jobs and in normative rather than utilitarian organizations (Etzioni, 1961). The critical variable determining the acceptance of influence may be the extent of partial versus full inclusion of the individual in his work role (Allport, 1962; Katz and Kahn, 1966) or the extent to which work comprises a "central life interest" for the person (Dubin, Champoux, and Porter, 1975).

Although contingent reward schemes may not involve the same ethical issues for work organizations as they do for the society at large, this is not to say that there are not some vital, unresolved problems here. The primary issue for organizational behavior is whether or not the use of contingent reward schemes actually contributes to effectiveness. While some glowing testimonials (Hamner and Hamner, 1976) and quantitative reports of planned interventions (see Lawler, 1971, and Nash and Carroll, 1975) seem to lead one to answer with an unqualified "Yes," it is necessary to delve into the theoretical nature of contingent reward schemes to really answer this question.

Returning to figure 4, it can be seen that the individual's choice of a specific behavior is largely determined by its reward contingency. Thus, manipulating contingencies and setting goals (which is the same as specifying the contingency between behavior and reward) can be viewed as devices to channel behavior in a particular direction. The key question which remains, however, is whether the direction in which behavior is channeled will facilitate or inhibit organizational effectiveness. Is it possible, for example, to specify exactly which behaviors will lead to improved performance and how this performance will be measured? The answer may be positive for most lower-level positions in an organization, but not for many middle- and top-level positions. The problem is simply that a number of organizational roles cannot be preprogrammed; they involve the resolution of uncertainty and responses to events which cannot be specified in advance. In addition, the higher one goes in an organizational hierarchy, the longer it takes to know if a particular action is useful or not. These problems make contingent reward schemes especially difficult to implement except at the lower levels of an organization.

It is interesting to note that most successful applications of positive reinforcement schemes have been confined to relatively routine jobs for which desired behaviors can be easily specified (Latham and Yukl, 1975). However, even here care must be taken to encompass *all* of the desired behaviors within a reinforcement scheme. When goals are specified in objective terms (e.g., number of units produced, sales per week, etc.), the individual may become so motivated to accomplish the concrete goal that he neglects other unspecified aspects of his role. Thus, although goal clarity and specificity of the behavior-reward linkage does lead to increased motivation, this motivation channels behavior in the direction of reinforcements and away from unrewarded activities. In short, you get what you pay for.

An Ecological Approach to Reward Systems

The very act of designing and implementing a reward scheme implies some knowledge of the cause-effect relationships within an organizational system. However, as Willems (1974) has perceptively noted, sometimes our knowledge is incomplete at best. Just as within the biological sciences where one seemingly positive intervention (e.g., fertilizer or insecticides) can create ecological disturbances of severe magnitude, so can social interventions create dysfunctional consequences which are unanticipated by its change agents. Weick (1974) has observed, for example, that suboptimal performance by a single organizational subgroup may be preventing a more serious problem of bottlenecks throughout the larger organizational system. In many ways the organization and the units within it may have evolved to a point in which they are imperfect, yet positive, adaptations to their environment.

On a more micro level, one should look critically at outwardly successful applications of positive reinforcement and ask about possible side effects. In examining the use of verbal praise in a positive reinforcement scheme (e.g., the Emery Freight example discussed in Tosi and Hamner, 1974), one must ask, for example, whether there have been any long-term changes in how participants react to verbal feedback. As discussed in depth by Wortman and Linsenmeier (1976; see chap. 4), there is often a thin line between praise and ingratiation, and the receiver's perception of both the supervisor and the task situation may determine whether praise yields positive or negative effects. From an ecological point of view one must also ask if conscious manipulation of verbal praise may substantially alter the fabric of one's social interactions. If praise is presumed to be consciously manipulated, the individual may no longer confidently attribute personal attributes to the supervisor such as generosity or liking for subordinates (cf. Jones and Davis, 1965). Research on the effects of leader consideration might therefore find possible negative effects of manipulated verbal praise. My own prediction would be that reinforcement schemes using verbal praise will only be successful when there is initial trust and positive affect between superior and subordinate. In other cases, manipulated verbal praise will likely be interpreted as an ingratiation attempt and lead to a decline in both attitudinal and performance variables.

A second example of an ecological approach to reward systems can be brought out by examining a well-known experiment by Lawler and Hackman (1969). In this study, absenteeism was reduced by applying a contingent reward (bonus pay) for showing up for work. Although the results seem straightforward enough, they point to an interesting issue never addressed by organizational researchers. It is quite possible that absenteeism should *not* be reduced to zero, and that efforts to sharply lower absenteeism may bring on more serious side effects.[2] In understanding this prediction it is useful to think of absenteeism in the same manner as economists view unemployment. Below 2 percent to 3 percent unemployment, there will be too little mobility in the labor force and there will be serious economic consequences. Similarly, below a given level of absenteeism, the individual may not be able to cope effectively with his job. High absenteeism may be a functional adjustment of individuals to extremely boring or dissatisfying tasks, and external efforts to reduce absenteeism may only cause a reduction in work quality (e.g., it is often better to have fatigued or uninterested workers absent from the job on Monday mornings rather than physically present to perform shoddy work). It may also be true that the routinized 40-hour week does not fit adequately with certain individual or subgroup values and that high absenteeism has provided a functional equilibrium or safety valve. Unfortunately, the Lawler and Hackman (1969) experiment did not provide data on behavioral consequences of the monetary bonus other than absenteeism. Future research should be specifically directed toward this problem and endeavor to find the "optimal floor" for certain long-accepted criterion variables such as absenteeism and turnover. Eventually, an inventory of optimal levels of absenteeism and turnover could be compiled by type of job and personal characteristics of the role occupant.

To date, the only side effect of contingent reward schemes which has generated substantial research has been the effect of extrinsic rewards (e.g., monetary incentives, prizes, etc.) upon individuals' intrinsic interest in performing a task. The nature of the data generated to answer this question will be discussed in the sections which follow. Suffice it to say at this point that more research effort should go into such "nonobvious" or unanticipated consequences of traditional motivation schemes. We need to develop a more cautious, ecological perspective toward our most powerful behavioral tools such as contingent reward schemes.

Intrinsic versus Extrinsic Rewards

When discussing reward schemes and the contingency between behavior and outcomes, what comes immediately to mind is the manipulation of financial incentives such as pay raises, bonuses, and fringe benefits. However, as mentioned earlier, individuals are motivated by intrinsic as well as extrinsic inducements. Thus, one important method by which task motivation can be increased is by alteration of the physical or cognitive dimensions of the tasks an individual performs (IV_{beh}) or the sense of personal accomplishment he derives from them (IV_{acc}).

Several factors can be expected to account for the intrinsic valences associated with both behavior and accomplishment, but not all of them are easily alterable. For example, it would be most difficult to change individual needs for activity, manipulation, or exploration, except on a temporary basis. McClelland and his associates have had some success in increasing individuals' achievement needs and motivating entrepreneurial behavior through intensive training sessions (see McClelland and Winter, 1967). However, it is doubtful that achievement training can, by itself, affect the performance of persons on routine organizational tasks or other activities which are not highly achievement-oriented (McClelland, 1973a, 1973b).

Perhaps the most practical method of increasing a person's intrinsic motivation to perform a task is to purposely alter the characteristics of the work activities he faces. Assuming that individuals possess at least a moderate need for activity and achievement, many tasks can be changed so that individuals derive greater satisfaction from either their task behavior or accomplishment. Many industrial firms have, in effect, followed these principles in programs of job enlargement and job enrichment. For example, the intrinsic rewards associated with task behavior are often improved by increasing the variety of skills necessary to perform a task or by rotating workers among several different tasks. Similarly, the intrinsic rewards associated with task accomplishment can be improved by increasing the responsibility of workers or the importance of the tasks they perform.

Increasing intrinsic motivation has several advantages as a motivational strategy. When individuals can derive satisfaction from task behaviors or accomplishment, there may, for example, be a reduced need for extrinsic rewards to motivate behavior. This may be especially important in cases where organizations (e.g., voluntary organizations) have a limited supply of extrinsic inducements or where individuals do not value those that are readily available. A second advantage of intrinsic motivation is that the need to monitor another's task behavior is reduced. With intrinsic motivation, it may not be necessary to rely totally upon financial incentive systems or periodic performance appraisals to induce a high level of task performance. Instead, a task can be designed so that the quantity and/or quality of performance fulfills the individual's need for achievement. When this is done, the worker who values achievement can monitor his own task accomplishment and reward himself on a completely contingent basis.

In discussing job design it is important to note that changes in some factors should, theoretically, affect IV_{beh} while other factors should more directly affect IV_{acc}. For example, increases in job variety, utilization of cognitive skills, and social interaction should directly affect the intrinsic valence associated with performing the activities of a task. Therefore, increases in these factors should be related to increases in job satisfaction and role participation (i.e., lower absenteeism and turnover). However, other job characteristics such as Hackman and Oldham's (1976) dimensions of task identity, task significance, autonomy and feedback might be expected to more directly affect work quality as well as satisfaction. Task identity, significance, and autonomy should, theoretically, increase the valence associated with task accomplishment, while feedback should increase the link (P_1) between behavior and accomplishment. Of course, there are important individual differences (e.g., need for achievement, cognitive complexity, adherence to middle-class work ethics) which may moderate these effects. Still, existing data show that for most individuals there is a positive relationship between these factors and attitudinal and behavioral criteria.

The model which we have sketched here is slightly different from that of Hackman and Oldham (1976) and Hackman and Lawler (1971), but not inconsistent with their reported data. For example, in Hackman and Lawler (1971) interpersonal relations are positively related to job satisfaction but not to work effectiveness. In Hackman and Oldham (1976), skill variety is similarly related to attitudes but not performance, while identity, significance, autonomy, and feedback correlate positively with both satisfaction and performance.

Although the Hackman and Oldham and Hackman and Lawler studies provide evidence that job characteristics are related to task attitudes and behavior, it should also be noted that current support for any particular theory of job design is at best only suggestive. Because these data are correlational, it is quite possible that individuals who regularly produce high-quality work and who enjoy their task activities are exactly those persons who are *assigned* the most interesting and challenging tasks. Furthermore, it is possible that this reversed effect would be most pronounced in persons with salient higher-order needs, since these individuals are most likely to actively seek out or bargain for the responsible jobs. Thus, it must be emphasized that correlational results showing positive relationships should be viewed with a measure of skepticism. Such skepticism is warranted until more data are available from controlled field experiments and interpretable quasi-experiments in which jobs are purposely altered and the effects documented.

Combining Intrinsic and Extrinsic Motivation

Even though it has not been fully tested empirically, it should be apparent from our discussion that intrinsic as well as extrinsic rewards are likely to be effective methods of energizing behavior. Either of these motivational factors may be manipulated to get an individual to perform a task, and both intrinsic and extrinsic factors probably can bring satisfaction to the individual. The question remains, however, whether or not these two sources of motivation can be combined effectively to yield overall positive effects on the individual's task attitudes and behavior.

In *expectancy x value* models of motivation, intrinsic and extrinsic factors are generally added to form an overall measure of motivation. Expectancy formulations like those of Galbraith and Cummings (1967), House (1971), Porter and Lawler (1967), and Lawler (1971, 1973) *assume* that the cognition of intrinsic rewards and the cognition of extrinsic rewards are additive in their effect on anticipated work satisfaction. They assume that intrinsic motivation $[(IV_{beh}) + (P_1)(IV_{acc})]$ and extrinsic motivation $[P_1P_2(EV_i) + P_3\,EV_i]$ summate to produce overall task motivation, and that intrinsic and extrinsic motivation are separate, independent factors.

Whether or not intrinsic and extrinsic sources of motivation are independent or do in fact have an effect upon each other is a question of considerable practical as well as theoretical significance. For example, if they are positively interrelated, then we might expect that extrinsic rewards will increase a person's intrinsic interest in a task, whereas, if they are negatively interrelated, the administration of an extrinsic reward could drive out intrinsic motivation. Because this issue is of importance to any setting (e.g., industrial organizations, schools, or voluntary work situations) in which extrinsic rewards are administered, we will go into it in some detail.

The Interrelationship of Intrinsic and Extrinsic Motivation

Historically, the relationship of intrinsic and extrinsic motivation has been the subject of considerable controversy. Long ago, Woodworth (1918) suggested that in the process of acquiring a set of skills toward some end, the skills themselves could develop their own motivating force which might endure even after the end is no longer sought. He stated this point in reference to mastering a business:

> ... while a man may enter a certain line of business from a purely external economic motive, he develops an interest in the business for its own sake ... and the motive force that drives him in the daily task, provided of course this does not degenerate into mere automatic routine, is precisely an interest by which he is able to deal with those problems. The end furnishes the motive force for the search for means but once the means are found, they are apt to become interesting on their own account (p. 104).

Allport (1937) has argued in a similar vein that certain behaviors develop their own motive power or "functional autonomy." He noted that while many activities such as making money, solving problems, and so forth, may have originally served some other motive, their persistence in many people, despite an absence of external forces, necessitates their having developed value on their own.

The notion that an activity or task behavior can become valued by an individual through its continued association with an external reward can be explained by the process of secondary reinforcement. Secondary reinforcement refers to a process by which an originally neutral stimulus acquires reinforcing properties through its pairing with a primary reinforcer (see Keller, 1969; Ferster and Skinner, 1969; Uhl and Young, 1967). In these terms, it is possible to assert that an intrinsically motivating activity is simply one in which the reinforcement value of an extrinsic goal has associatively rubbed off on the behavior. Thus, no matter what one's original reaction to a task is, secondary reinforcement implies that it may improve over time if it leads to valued extrinsic rewards.

An Attribution Approach to the Problem

Recently, there has begun an investigation into the relationship between intrinsic and extrinsic motivation from a more cognitive perspective. Instead of asking how intrinsic motivation might be derived from extrinsic reward contingencies, several researchers have concluded that both intrinsic and extrinsic motivation may be more usefully studied as perceptions on the part of individuals. From a perceptual approach, it is not necessary to know how specific behaviors originally acquired reinforcing properties, but only that an individual at a given point in time may perceive a task to be rewarding in and of itself. That is, if individuals think they are intrinsically or extrinsically motivated, these self-perceptions alone may be enough to influence future behavior and attitudes.

The self-perception approach to intrinsic and extrinsic motivation leads one to the prediction that there may be a negative interrelationship between these two motivational factors. The basis for this prediction stems from the assumption that individuals may work backward from their own actions in inferring sources of causation (Bem, 1967, 1962; Kelly, 1971, 1974). For example, if external pressures on an individual are so high that they would ordinarily cause him to perform a given task regardless of the internal characteristics of the activity, then the individual might logically infer that he is extrinsically motivated. In contrast, if external reward contingencies are extremely low or nonsalient, the individual might then infer that his behavior is intrinsically motivated.

There are two particular situations which provide good tests of the self-perception prediction. One is a situation in which there is insufficient justification for a person's actions, a situation in which the intrinsic rewards for an activity are very low (e.g., a dull task) and there are no compensating extrinsic rewards (e.g., no monetary payment, verbal praise, etc.). Self-perception theory (Bem, 1967) predicts that in situations of insufficient justification the individual may cognitively reevaluate the intrinsic characteristics of an activity in order to justify or explain his own behavior. For example, if the individual performs a dull task for no external reward he may "explain" his behavior by thinking that the task was not really so bad after all.

Sometimes a person may also be fortunate enough to be in a situation in which his behavior is oversufficiently justified. For example, a person may be asked to perform an interesting task and at the same time be lavishly paid for his efforts. In such situations, the self-perception theory predicts that the individual may actually reevaluate the activity in a downward direction. Since the external reward would be sufficient to motivate behavior by itself, the individual may mistakenly infer that he is extrinsically motivated to perform the activity. He may conclude that since he is forced to perform the task by an external reward, the task probably is not highly satisfying in and of itself.

Empirical Evidence: Insufficient Justification

A large number of studies have shown that when an individual is induced to commit an unpleasant act for little or no external justification he may subsequently conclude that the act was not so unpleasant after all. Generally, there have been two types of experiments designed to assess the consequences of insufficient justification. One type of design has involved the performance of a dull task under varied levels of reward (e.g., Brehm and Cohen, 1959; Weick, 1964; Freedman, 1963; Weick and Penner, 1965). A second, more popular design has involved some form of counter-attitudinal advocacy, either in terms of lying to a fellow subject about the nature of an experiment or writing an essay against one's own position on an important issue (e.g., Festinger and Carlsmith, 1959; Carlsmith, Collins, and Helmreich, 1966; Linder, Cooper, and Jones, 1967). Fundamentally, the two types of designs are not vastly different. They uniformly have required subjects to perform an intrinsically dissatisfying act under varied levels of external inducement, and they uniformly have predicted that in the low-payment condition the subject will change his attitude toward the activity (i.e., think more favorably of the task or begin to believe the position advocated).

Recently, a strong test of the insufficient justification paradigm has been conducted outside the laboratory by Staw (1974). A natural field experiment was made possible by the fact that many young men had joined an organization (the Army ROTC program) in order to avoid being drafted, *and* these same young men subsequently received information (a draft lottery number) which changed the value of this organizational reward. Of particular relevance was the fact that persons who joined ROTC, did so not because of their intrinsic interest in the activities involved (drills, classes, summer camp), but because they anticipated a substantial extrinsic reward (draft avoidance). As a result, persons who received draft numbers which exempted them from military service subsequently faced a situation of low extrinsic as well as intrinsic rewards—a situation of insufficient justification. In contrast, persons who received draft numbers which made them vulnerable to military call-up, found their participation in ROTC perfectly justified—they were still successfully avoiding the draft by remaining in the Reserve Officer Training Corps. To test the insufficient justification effect, both the attitudes and performance of ROTC cadets were analyzed by draft number before and after the national draft lottery. The results showed that persons in the insufficient justification condition enhanced their perception of ROTC and even performed somewhat better in ROTC courses after the lottery. It should be recognized, however, that this task enhancement occurred only under very similar circumstances to those found in previous laboratory research to be necessary for the insufficient justification effect: high commitment or irrevocability of behavior (Brehm and Cohen, 1962), free choice (Linder, Cooper, and Jones, 1966), and substantial adverse consequences (Calder, Ross, and Insko, 1973; Collins and Hoyt, 1972).

Empirical Evidence: Oversufficient Justification

There have been several empirical studies designed to test the self-perception prediction within the context of overly sufficient justification. A study by Deci (1971) is probably most well known. In an experiment specifically designed to test the effect of contingent monetary rewards on intrinsic motivation, Deci (1971) enlisted a number of college students to participate in a problem-solving task. All of the students were asked to work on a series of intrinsically interesting puzzles for three experimental sessions. After the first session, however, one-half of the students (the experimental group) were told that they would also be given an extrinsic reward (money) for correctly solving the second set of puzzles, while the other half of the students (the control group) were not told anything about the reward. In the third session, neither the experimental nor the control subjects were rewarded.

Deci had hypothesized that the payment of money in the second experimental session might decrease subjects' intrinsic motivation to perform the task. That is, the introduction of an external force (money) might cause participants to alter their self-perception about why they were working on the puzzles. Instead of being intrinsically motivated to solve the interesting puzzles, they might find themselves working primarily to get the money provided by the experimenter. Observations of the amount of time subjects spent on the task during a free-time period was the indicator of intrinsic motivation.

The Deci experiment possessed some serious flaws in design (see Calder and Staw, 1975) and its results were only marginally significant. However, it provided the first empirical data with human subjects (Harlow's monkey studies were much earlier) which demonstrated a possible decrement in intrinsic motivation following the administration of extrinsic rewards. A number of recent studies have replicated the "overjustification effect" (e.g., Lepper, Green, and Nisbett, in press; Lepper and Green; Kruglanski, Friedman, and Zeevi, 1971; Kruglanski, Alon and Lewis, 1971) using designs which are more interpretable and yielding results which are more statistically reliable. Still, it must be noted that there appear to be several necessary conditions for this overjustification effect. The task for which external rewards are administered must be interesting (Calder and Staw, 1975b; Hamner and Foster, 1975); the rewards themselves must be salient (Ross, 1975); and there should be no pre-existing norms for payment (Staw, Calder, and Hess, 1976). Without these necessary conditions, one is more likely to find a reinforcement effect.

The necessary conditions for the overjustification effect reduce its applicability to industrial work organizations. First, within industrial organizations, a large number of jobs are not inherently satisfying enough to foster high intrinsic interest. Persons would not ordinarily perform many of the tasks of the industrial world without extrinsic inducements, and this initial lack of intrinsic interest may preclude an overjustification effect (see Calder and Staw, 1975b). Second, even when an industrial job is inherently interesting, there exists a powerful norm for extrinsic payment. Not only do workers specifically join and contribute their labor in exchange for particular inducements, but the instrumental relationship between task behavior and extrinsic rewards is supported by both social and legal standards.

The recent work of Staw, Calder, and Hess (1976) suggests that overjustification effects would more likely be found within voluntary organizations or with the application of external rewards to tasks which are usually voluntarily performed within a work organization. With voluntary tasks, individuals are often motivated to perform without extrinsic inducements and a norm for no payment may exist. Therefore, in these situations one is likely to find that external rewards inhibit intrinsic interest or behavior which extends to settings free of external reinforcers. When there are strong norms against the use of money to motivate behavior, or if its use is quite unexpected, individuals may view money as a salient external force, thereby weakening the self-perception of intrinsic motivation. However, when payment is administered in an "appropriate" manner (i.e., in line with normative expectations), the value of the extrinsic reward has been found to generalize to the task itself, producing increased task satisfaction and persistence.

Toward Some New Ideas on Motivation

It can be said that there is nothing so central to an organization's functioning as the motivation of its members. It can also be said that there has been more research on individual motivation than on any other topic within organizational behavior. Yet, somehow, most of the research in this area has either added little to what we already know from early experimental psychology (see, e.g., Thorndike, 1911; Tolman, 1932; Lewin, 1938), or has provided us with few insights which go beyond prevailing common sense. Recent work on the interaction of intrinsic and extrinsic motivation has helped to broaden the perspective of traditional motivation theory and that is why we have considered it in such depth. However, we must actively seek out other promising research questions if our understanding of motivation is to increase.

In the past decade, a great deal of research has, for example, gone into the question of whether a multiplicative model (*expectancy x valence*) is appropriate to specify motivational force (see Heneman and Schwab, 1972; Behling and Starke, 1973; House, Shapiro, and Wahba, 1974; and Mitchell, 1974, for reviews). This issue has been fraught with methodological and empirical difficulties (Schmidt, 1973; Connolly, in press) and shows little prospect of being resolved. One might contend, therefore, that research on expectancy theory would be more fruitful if some of its basis questions were rephrased. Instead of testing the statistical significance of an expectancy model or comparing multiplicative versus additive models of motivation, one should ask under what conditions would individual motivation be expected to approximate a subjective expected utility (SEU) model, and when would it be less rational?

It may be true, for example, that many individuals and subgroups do not engage in detailed cognitive arithmetic to decide which organization to join and at what level to perform. Unlike the processes outlined in figures 2 and 3, many individuals may merely model the behavior of salient others or follow the path that appears appropriate for a person from a particular family background or socioeconomic group. Individuals may join an organization or perform at a certain level because it "seems the right thing to do," rather than its being the product of subjective expected utility. As Salancik has shown in a series of original studies (Salancik, 1974; Salancik and Conway, 1975), individuals may analyze their behavior in rationalistic terms only when faced with such a task presented to them by an outside researcher.

Although many studies testing expectancy models are subject to the bias that rationality has been retrospectively recalled (cf. Staw,

1975) rather than concurrently tapped by the researcher, these studies are still unimpressive in their support for the theory. The magnitude of unexplained variance should lead us to look for moderating variables. One such variable might be the fit between occupational status of the job and socioeconomic background of the role occupant. When the individual is upwardly mobile in status, his behavior may be better predicted by an expectancy-value model than when he is satisfied with his social station. Alternatively, if the individual's job occupies a small aspect of his "central life interest" (Dubin, Champoux, and Porter, 1975), the individual should be expected to do little cognitive work in deciding to join a particular organization or perform within it. Expectancy-value formulations may be appropriate only for the most important decisions an individual must make. For those un-involved in work, day-to-day performance questions or the choice of one of many perceived-to-be similar organizations (e.g., an auto worker's choice of Ford, GM, or Chrysler) may closely resemble impulse purchase decisions of consumers. Many workers may reserve their cognitive prowess for decisions about the allocation of leisure time and durable goods.

Finally, as discussed earlier, we should not expect individuals to engage *continually* in a cognitive motivational process. As noted in figure 3, individuals are most attentive to behavior-outcome contingencies in learning a new task or when confronted with a large discrepancy between present reward levels and a salient alternative (e.g., when a new pay plan is introduced). In other situations, the individual's behavior has probably become routinized and this patterning could be represented either in terms of an operant conditioning model (Skinner, 1953, 1974) or as a decision subroutine (March and Simon, 1958).

A Divergent Approach

Mapping the cognitive antecedents of behavior is important and research should no doubt continue on it. But at the same time we should begin to examine alternative formulations of individual behavior. One strategy which is helpful in developing new theoretical propositions is to alter the point of view or perspective from which current theorizing addresses behavior.

Many existing theories of individual behavior can be viewed as formulations of individual adaptation to the environment. Certainly Skinner's theory of reinforcement and operant conditioning represents the view that man is extensively shaped by the reward/punishment contingencies around him. However, other motivational models can also be viewed, as White (1959) pointed out, as manifestations of an individual's motivation to be "competent" or positively adapted to his particular social and physical surroundings. For example, Festinger's (1957) theory of cognitive dissonance as well as the attribution models of Kelly (1969), Bem (1967, 1972), and Jones and Davis (1965) are theories about how individuals make sense of their physical and social worlds. Even the maximizing notions of expectancy theory and Simon's (1957) alternative of satisficing can be viewed in this way.

At the organizational level of analysis there has been a concomitant degree of theory development on how organizations can best be adapted to their environments. Work on centralization-decentralization (e.g., Blau and Schoenherr, 1971; Hage and Aiken, 1969; Mackenzie, 1975), integration and differentiation (e.g., Lawrence and Lorsch, 1967; Child, 1974, 1975; Khandwalla, 1974), and matrix organizational designs (Shull, 1965; Galbraith, 1973), are examples of this perspective. The central research question in this line of research has been how the particular structure of an organization interacts with characteristics of the organization's environment (such as uncertainty and technological change) to produce a given level of effectiveness.

Figure 5 represents the above two theoretical perspectives as the directed lines A and B. In figure 5, the organization is fitted within its environment, while top levels of the organization are shown to constitute the environment of lower participants. From a top-management perspective, societal institutions (including other organizations and the market economy) comprise the external context in which behavior must be enacted. This environment determines many of the behavior-outcome contingencies which will shape and alter the organization's behavior. From the perspective of lower levels within the organization, the environment primarily consists of the actions and policies set by higher-level management. These policies frequently describe the behavior-outcome contingencies the lower-level participant faces on his job.

As illustrated in figure 5, each level in the organizational system tends to determine the behavior-outcome contingencies under which the lower level must operate. This is obviously an oversimplification, but it tends to fit a large body of theory and empirical research in organizational behavior. At the micro level, for example, organizational research is often concerned with the individual's response to incentive schemes, leadership practices, and control mechanisms exerted from higher levels in the organization. Individual behavior is studied largely to show why individuals respond positively to some actions and policies of management but negatively to others. In essence, much of the micro-level research has implicitly taken the perspective of higher management who attempt to control behavior-outcome contingencies and endeavor to increase worker response to them. From this perspective, the individual is viewed as an adaptive organism who responds to the reward contingencies facing him. Thus, if there is little positive response from the individual to a new program (e.g., job enlargement), the problem is conceptualized as due to the

FIGURE 5 Flow of Influence in Intra- and Extraorganizational Environments

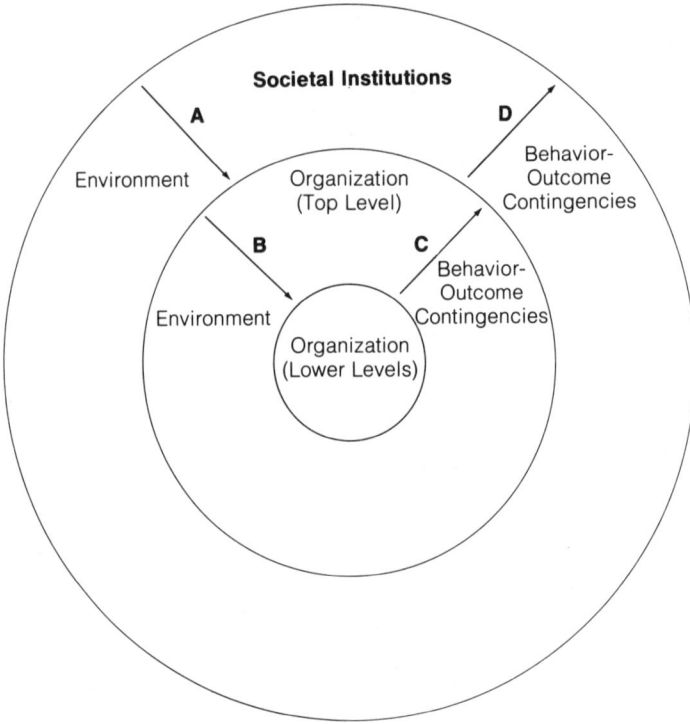

fact that the proper valences were not tapped (e.g., individuals may have low growth needs) or the contingencies between behavior and accomplishment or between accomplishment and reward were not clearly specified (e.g., task goals were not clearly set).

I would advocate that we enlarge our perspective of individuals in organizations, and that we attempt to creatively reverse our point of view. As shown in figure 5, there is an influence process that flows upward in the organization (cf. Mechanic, 1962) and also from the organization to its environment (cf. Thompson, 1967). By reversing our perspective, we not only recognize this upward influence but can build specific hypotheses which are not evident without it. This practice has already occurred to a large extent in the macro literature on organizations. Following Thompson's (1967) seminal work, the organization is viewed as an entity which attempts to shape its environment, reduce potential sources of uncertainty, and enlarge its bases of resources. The organization does not merely adapt to behavior-outcome contingencies facing it from the environment, but it alters these contingencies by *acting on* the environment. A number of empirical studies have tested this basic hypothesis (see, e.g., Selznick, 1949; Zald, 1967; Pfeffer, 1972, 1973).

Micro-level theory could profit by testing the same kinds of hypotheses that are now centered in the sociological literature. The individual should not be viewed as a passive acceptor of behavior-outcome contingencies or merely as an adapter to them, but also as an entity which strives to alter its environment. The individual, like the organization, strives to reduce sources of uncertainty in his day-to-day relations with superiors. One particular source of uncertainty the individual strives to reduce is uncertainty over the allocation of resources. From the individual's perspective, improvement may come in the form of increased control over reinforcement contingencies so that the individual is assured of a given level of reward for a specific behavior. In this regard it should be noted that unionization of the workplace brings increased power to workers and that this power is usually manifested in control over behavior-outcome contingencies. Union demands for weekly wages, rather than piece-rate incentives, and for the implementation of strict work rules can be interpreted as evidence for a demand for control over reinforcement contingencies.

A second method by which the individual may actively improve his situation in the organization is by ingratiation (Wortman and Linsenmeier, 1976). If the individual can manipulate his supervisor's attitudes and opinions of him, he can improve his share of resources allocated by the supervisor. Through ingratiation, the individual may receive more than he deserves for a given level of work or at least assure himself of a positive evaluation of his task output. (See chap. 4 for a complete discussion of the antecedents and consequences of ingratiating behavior.)

In developing a theory of individual action within the organizational environment, one caveat should be kept in mind: Individuals may indeed strive to reduce sources of uncertainty but they do not strive for high probabilities of receiving low rewards. This oversight in the macro-organizational literature has led to an overemphasis on environmental conditions leading to uncertainty and a virtual neglect of the scarcity-munificence of environments. As noted by Staw and

Szwajkowski (1975), organizations strive to improve their quantities of resources in addition to reducing uncertainty in resource procurement. Thus, at the individual level of analysis, we must develop hypotheses which include both the magnitude of reinforcement received and the contingency between behavior and outcomes. A sample set of general hypotheses from which specific testable propositions can be derived is stated below:

Hypothesis 1: Individuals strive to increase the probability of receiving positive outcomes and to reduce the probability of receiving negative outcomes within the organization.

Hypothesis 2: Individuals attempt to control the reinforcement contingencies leading to both desirable and undesirable outcomes.

Hypothesis 3: If direct control of the reinforcement contingencies is impossible, individuals attempt to personally influence the allocator of resources so as to improve personal outcomes.

Hypothesis 4: If direct control of the reinforcement contingencies or indirect control through personal influence is impossible, individuals attempt to make the contingencies more predictable.

Hypothesis 5: Individuals strive to reduce the possibility of negative outcomes before attempting to control or make predictable positive outcomes from the organization.

From these hypotheses and others similar to them, it is possible to build a testable theory of upward influence in the organization. The individual, like the organization, may attempt to carve a niche for himself which is both highly munificent and low in uncertainty. The individual can attempt to do this in a one-to-one role relationship with his supervisor, and relations with subordinates and peers. Graen (1976), for example, has suggested that roles are negotiated between the superior and subordinate, and that the role-making process is determined by both interpersonal attraction and bargaining. We would contend that individuals generally follow a strategy of improving interpersonal attraction or ingratiation in one-to-one relationships with supervisors. Outright bargaining with supervisors runs the risk of future sanctions or negative outcomes, except when the individual's expertise is especially high or the individual is nearly irreplaceable. High-skill personnel, and especially those with ready opportunities in alternative organizations are, however, more likely to utilize either overt or implied bargaining in shaping their organizational roles. Low-skill personnel and those with fewer outside opportunities are more likely to use bargaining agents such as unions to help control behavior-outcome contingencies on the job.

A relevant question which follows from the above analysis is, "What are the consequences of behavior-outcome contingencies which are unpredictable or uncontrollable by the individual?" As implied by the above hypotheses, lack of individual control or predictive ability may be aversive to organizational participants. Several separate areas of research provide data which bear on this question.

Prediction of Behavior-Outcome Contingencies

The most familiar body of research data which is relevant to this issue is that of role conflict and ambiguity (Kahn et al., 1964). When the individual's task is inadequately defined or there is substantial disparity in demands placed upon the individual from his supervisor, peers, or subordinates, the individual may find the situation to be aversive. Under these conditions, the individual has been found to possess low job satisfaction, low trust in supervisors, and poor mental health (Kahn et al., 1964).

In a theoretical sense, both role conflict and ambiguity can be interpreted as factors which reduce the individual's ability to predict behavior-outcome contingencies. When an individual does not know what is expected of him due to the absence of information (i.e., role ambiguity) or conflicting information (i.e., role conflict), his predictive power is reduced. House and his associates' recent work on leadership (House, 1971; House and Dessler, 1974; Szilagyi and Sims, 1974) suggests that increased clarification and supervision (i.e., initiating structure) will improve individual attitudes and behavior on ambiguous tasks. However, when a task is already highly structured and routine, initiating structure has been found to be negatively related to task satisfaction. Presumably, once behavior-outcome contingencies are relatively clear, increased supervision and work directives add little of positive value and may be viewed by many workers as threatening.

If individuals do indeed strive to make the behavior-outcome contingencies they face more predictable, how can this fact be reconciled with the research and theory on achievement motivation that shows high achievers tend to seek out risk-taking situations (Atkinson and Raynor, 1974)? Fortunately, this paradox is more apparent than real. Individuals high in achievement motivation should not be viewed as deriving pleasure from uncertainty itself but from the *process of reducing it*. Behavior-outcome sequences which are either hopelessly impossible or trivially easy do not appeal to high achievers. They view 50-50 situations (termed "calculated risks" by McClelland) as most motivating because of the negative relationship between valence and expectancy (i.e., the most difficult tasks being the most rewarding) and the positive relationship between expectancy and goal attainment. Therefore, the primary contribution of achievement theory is to revise our expectancy-valence models so that the two factors of valence and expectancy are not independent. Achievement theory does not refute the notion that individuals strive to reduce uncertainty.

Control of Behavior-Outcome Contingencies

In recent years there have been a number of experimental studies designed to compare individuals' reactions to controllable and uncontrollable aversive outcomes (see Averill, 1973 and Glass and Singer, 1972, for reviews). Subjects in these studies, are typically subjected to aversive stimuli and then either provided or not provided with information on how to terminate the stimulation (e.g., Corah and Boffa, 1970; Glass et al., 1971; Sherrod and Downs, 1974). In most of the studies in this area, subjects who can control aversive outcomes experience less stress than subjects without such control (see Wortman and Brehm, 1976).

Desire to control aversive outcomes makes sense intuitively and can be explained by any number of psychological theories. What is more compelling, in terms of testing an individual need or desire for control per se, is to examine the consequences of receiving positive outcomes under high and low choice. Tests of Brehm's (1966, 1972) theory of psychological reactance provide the most relevant data on individuals' striving for control.

Reactance

Brehm posited that when behavioral freedom is threatened, the individual will become motivationally aroused or experience reactance. The predicted consequences of psychological reactance are efforts to restore freedom and an increased desire for any lost options. Among empirical studies designed to test reactance theory, it has been shown, for example, that subjects will devalue positive outcomes if they are "forced" to receive them. If the individual expects to choose his outcomes, he will react negatively if they are selected for him—even if they are the very outcomes he had previously preferred (see Hammock and Brehm, 1966). The implications of psychological reactance for applications of reinforcement theory in organizations are quite profound. Will the individual react negatively to the allocation of positive and negative outcomes by supervisors or will he react more positively if he can reduce his dependence on higher authorities?

An answer to this question is likely to be found by examining the parameters posited by Brehm as underlying psychological reactance. According to Brehm (1966, 1972), reactance should only result when there is an initial expectation of freedom, when this freedom is of importance to the individual, and when there is a significant threat of elimination of the freedom. In the experiment described above (Hammock and Brehm, 1966), for example, simply giving the preferred alternative to subjects with no expectation of control led to an increase in its evaluation. Thus, it would seem reasonable to conclude that in organizations with a tradition of hierarchical relations there should be no reactance aroused in employees who have come to expect a top-down approach. Reactance would be more of a problem in organizations with a history of participative management that attempt to institute hierarchical controls. Participation and freedom, following Brehm, are thus easier to expand than to contract.

Learned Helplessness

Recently, a large number of studies have been conducted on a related phenomenon labeled, "learned helplessness" (see Wortman and Brehm, 1976, for a review). In a series of studies using laboratory animals, Seligman (1975) and his associates have found that exposure to uncontrollable, inescapable electric shock leads to a reduction in subsequent avoidance learning. The learning that one's behavior and outcomes are independent apparently leads to a reduction in the ability to respond adaptively to future learning situations. This general finding has also been replicated in a number of task settings using human subjects (Hiroto and Seligman, 1975).

The practical implications of "learned helplessness" seem to conflict directly with those of reactance theory. One model posits that individuals react negatively to reductions in freedom and actively attempt to restore control, while the other posits that exposure to uncontrollable outcomes results in passive acceptance of any negative consequences. However, as noted by Wortman and Brehm (1976), it is possible to integrate learned helplessness and reactance into a single theoretical statement. Their model is presented in figure 6. If a person expects to be able to control or influence outcomes that are of importance to him (i.e., at point a in the figure), exposure to uncontrollable events should arouse psychological reactance and the individual should be motivated to re-exert control. But, if the individual comes to learn through extended helplessness training that he cannot control his environment, he will stop trying. When a person has no expectation of control (i.e., at point b in the figure) then reactance will *not* precede helplessness and the individual is predicted to quickly become a passive receiver of future outcomes. Wortman and Brehm report some tentative support for this model from animal research (e.g., Seligman and Maier, 1967; Sidman, Heinstein, and Conrad, 1957) and research using human subjects (e.g., Shaban and Welling, 1972; Glass and Singer, 1972; Krantz, Glass, and Snyder, 1974; Roth and Kuban, in press; Roth and Bootzin, 1974).

FIGURE 6   The Integrative Model

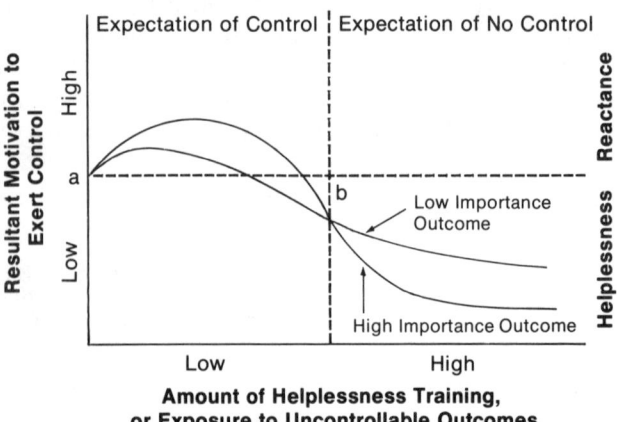

From Wortman and Brehm, 1976

The Wortman and Brehm model of individuals' reaction to uncontrollable outcomes has some direct implications for everyday behavior, but these implications appear to turn on the critical variable of "expectation of control." Unfortunately, it is this same variable which is the most difficult to extrapolate across situations and individuals. Thus, following from the model, we must have some knowledge of both the history of upward and downward influence in the organization and the individual's personal reinforcement history in order to make accurate predictions. This is not a shortcoming of Wortman and Brehm's theory, but an empirical reality with which we must deal in applied research.

One factor which *is* a shortcoming of the Wortman and Brehm model is its lack of specificity of the notion of control. Much of the empirical work on reactance theory has dealt with the reduction of control over the distribution of outcomes, while the work on learned helplessness has been concerned with exposure to outcomes (primarily aversive) which are not contingent on the individual's actions. Thus, we can see that the crucial dimension of "exposure to uncontrollable outcomes" in figure 6 can be interpreted as either inability to influence the allocation of resources or merely as inability to predict the linkage between one's behavior and subsequent allocations by others. The reason that this vagary is so important is that the Wortman and Brehm model, as it stands, can be used to support either increased *or* decreased control by lower-order participants in an organizational setting. If one uses the argument that predictive ability is the most important factor (citing the learned helplessness research as evidence), it is possible to conclude that the organization needs tighter top-down controls and increased power of supervisors to reward and punish contingently.[3] If, however, one uses the argument that control over resource allocation is the crucial factor (as per reactance theory), then one would be hesitant to institute any top-down controls which inhibit freedom and tend to avoid behavior modification schemes (Luthans and Krietner, 1975). Recall that reactance theory predicts that even positive outcomes may be devalued if they are not freely chosen by the individual.

It is my opinion that individuals do strive for control over their social environments and that one important source of control is that over behavior-outcome sequences. If no control is possible, then the ability to predict will be preferred by individuals over random or noncontingent outcomes. Thus, it is possible that individuals *will* prefer top-down controls and contingent reinforcement schemes over situations in which there is no apparent link between behavior and reward. However, this is not to deny that *control over the allocation of outcomes* is probably more preferred than a highly predictable supervisor who controls the rewards.

An alternative model to that of Wortman and Brehm is presented in figure 7. It shows that individuals follow a decision-making sequence in which they seek first to control and then, if control is not possible, to at least predict behavior-outcome sequences. If neither control nor prediction is perceived to be possible, the individual will either leave the field or become a passive acceptor of externally-imposed outcomes. In figure 7, expectations of control are shown as a moderating variable which determines where individuals begin this decision-making process. With no prior expectations of control, individuals are shown to strive primarily for prediction or clarity in behavior-outcome sequences. Clarity would be sought both in the specification of tasks to be completed and also in the rewards which would result from various levels of task performance. Individual differences in need for autonomy are also shown to affect the entry point in this decision process. With a low need for autonomy the individual may not be as interested in actual control over the allocation of resources as in predicting their distribution by supervisors. In addition, individual differences are relevant for one's personal history of control. Some individuals have had very little exposure to situations in which they were able to influence the allocation of external rewards, while others (e.g., children raised on a communal farm) may have had little experience with highly authoritarian relationships. Finally, as touched upon earlier, the organization's own history of participative versus autocratic style of management will influence initial expectations of control.

FIGURE 7   Flow Diagram of Upward Control

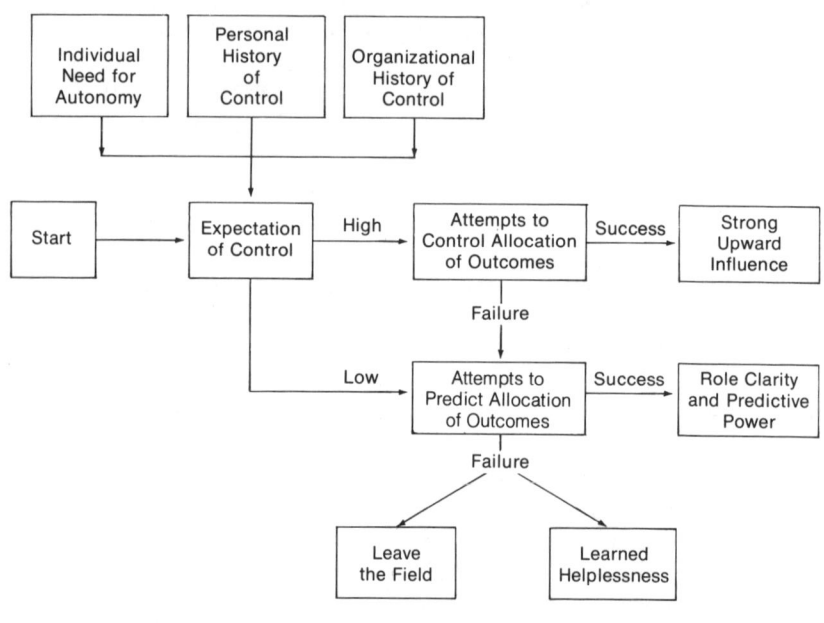

As shown in the revised model of figure 7, if attempts at both control and prediction fail, the individual becomes resigned to his fate or decides to leave the field. This latter option is added to make the model applicable to real-world settings in which turnover is a definite option to the individual faced with uncontrollable outcomes. In laboratory research on learned helplessness, the subject either has no option to leave the field (especially in the studies using animal subjects) or this option is extremely restricted. In organizations, factors such as external labor market conditions, the educational or skill level of the individual, and his visibility to other organizations may determine ease of turnover.

Summary and Conclusions

The synthesis of motivation presented here is one in which the individual is an active constructor of his social reality. The individual is viewed not merely as an information processor confronting a number of possible behavioral paths—each with their attendant rewards and costs—but as an actor who can attempt to change the parameters or "givens" of traditional motivation models. The individual can bargain, cajole, and ingratiate in order to change the contingencies between behavior and outcomes. In addition, the individual may be able to change the valences attached to the particular outcomes he faces. (For example, an individual may consciously give up security and achievement to concentrate on social gratification.[4]) What we are facing therefore in describing a theory of individual motivation in organizations is a highly complex system in which individuals have constructed a social and physical niche for themselves within the larger environment. This niche is built upon relationships developed over time with supervisors, subordinates, and peers in the organization and rests, in part, upon a role negotiation process (Graen, 1976). This niche is also built upon the individual's idiosyncratic construction of his social reality (Berger and Luckman, 1967; Weick, 1969). The processes of self-perception, dissonance arousal and reduction, and psychological reactance are but a few of the ways by which individuals come to grips with their social world. We need to know more about how individuals psychologically cope with the demands placed upon them by an organization and how these demands are in turn changed, redefined, or met by subordinates.

To date, the investigation of individual motivation in organizations has been extremely narrow in both direction and scope. Nearly all efforts have been expended upon explaining the determinants of job choice, productivity, absenteeism, and turnover. While these are important criterion variables, they are not the only behaviors of interest in organizational systems and not the only behaviors related to organizational effectiveness. Similarly, nearly all efforts to explain motivation in organizations have focused upon either expectancy or reinforcement models of behavior. While these theories are certainly relevant, other psychological processes have been unduly neglected. Thus, there has been an unfortunate restriction in theory building at both the independent and dependent variable ends of our models. It is hoped that this chapter will serve as an impetus toward a broadening of our conceptualization of motivation and a reconsideration of established theory in the area.

Notes

1. An experiment by Graen (1969) tested an expectancy model very similar to the one presented here. The present formulation also does not depart too greatly from the "within individuals" formulation of expectancy theory originally posited by Vroom (1946), and later advocated by Mitchell (1974) and Campbell and Pritchard (1976).
2. This point was also raised by Jerry Ross in a graduate seminar in organizational behavior at Northwestern University, 1976.
3. William E. Scott, for example, has previously used the learned helplessness literature as evidence for greater use of contingent reward systems.
4. This point was also raised by William Simons in a graduate organization behavior seminar at Northwestern University, 1976.

References

Allport, F. H. A structuronomic conception of behavior: Individual and collective. *Journal of Abnormal and Social Psychology,* 1962, *64*, 3-30.

Allport, G. W. *Personality: A Psychological Interpretation.* New York: Holt, 1937.

Atkinson, J. W., and Raynor, J. O. *Motivation and Achievement.* New York: Wiley, 1974.

Averill, J. Personal control over aversive stimuli and its relationship to stress. *Psychological Bulletin,* 1973, *80*, 286-303.

Barnard, C. I. *The Functions of the Executive.* Cambridge, Mass: Harvard University Press, 1938.

Behling, O., and Starke, F. The postulates of expectancy theory. *Academy of Management Journal,* 1973, *16,* 373-88.

Bem, D. J. Self-perception: The dependent variable of human performance. *Organizational Behavior and Human Performance,* 1967, *2*, 105-21.

———. Self-perception theory. In L. Berkowitz (ed.), *Advances in Experimental Social Psychology* (vol. 6), Academic Press, 1972.

Berger P. L., and Luckman, T. *The Social Construction of Reality.* New York: Anchor, 1967.

Blau, P. M., and Schoenherr, R. A. *The Structure of Organizations.* New York: Basic Books, 1971.

Brehm, J. W. *A Theory of Psychological Reactance.* New York: Academic Press, 1966.

———. *Responses to Loss of Freedom: A Theory of Psychological Reactance.* Morristown, N. J.: General Learning Press, 1972.

Brehm, J. W., and Cohen, A. R. *Explorations in Cognitive Dissonance.* New York: Wiley, 1962.

Calder, B. J., Ross, M. and Insko, C. A. Attitude change and attitude attribution: Effects of incentive, choice, and consequences. *Journal of Personality and Social Psychology,* 1973, *25*, 84-100.

Calder, B. J., and Staw, B. M. The interaction of intrinsic and extrinsic motivation: Some methodological notes. *Journal of Personality and Social Psychology,* 1975, *31*, 76-80.

———. The self-perception of intrinsic and extrinsic motivation. *Journal of Personality and Social Psychology,* 1975, *31*, 599-605.

Campbell, D. T. Conformity in psychology's theories of acquired behavioral dispositions. In I. A. Berg and B. M. Bass (eds.) *Conformity and Deviation*, Harper and Brothers, 1961.

Campbell, J. P., Dunnette, M. D., Lawler, E. E., and Weick, K. E. *Managerial Behavior, Performance, and Effectiveness.* New York: McGraw-Hill, 1970.

Carlsmith, J. M., Collins, B. E., and Helmreich, R. L. Studies in forced compliance: The effect of pressure for compliance on attitude change produced by face-to-face role playing and anonymous essay writing. *Journal of Personality and Social Psychology,* 1966, *4,* 1-13.

Child, J. Managerial and organizational factors associated with company performance, Part I: A contingency analysis. *The Journal of Management Studies,* 1974, *11,* 175-89.

———. Managerial and organizational factors associated with company performance, Part II: A contingency analysis. *The Journal of Management Studies,* 1975, *12,* 12-27.

Collins, B. E., and Hoyt, M. F. Personal responsibility-for-consequences: An integration and extension of the forced compliance literature. *Journal of Experimental Social Psychology,* 1972, *8,* 558-94.

Connolly, T. Some conceptual and methodological issues in expectancy-type models of work motivation. *Academic Management Review,* in press.

Corah, N. L., and Boffa, J. Perceived control, self-observation, and response to aversive stimulation. *Journal of Personality and Social Psychology,* 1970.

Deci, E. L. The effects of externally mediated rewards on intrinsic motivation. *Journal of Personality and Social Psychology,* 1971, *18,* 105-15.

———. The effects of contingent and noncontingent rewards and controls on intrinsic motivation. *Organizational Behavior and Human Performance,* 1972, *8,* 217-29.

Dubin, R., Champoux, J. E., and Porter, L. W. Central life interests and organizational commitment of blue-collar and clerical workers. *Administrative Science Quarterly,* 1975, *20,* 411-21.

Edwards, W. The prediction of decision among bets. *Journal of Experimental Psychology,* 1955, *50,* 201-14.

Etzioni, A. *Complex Organizations.* New York: The Free Press, 1961.

Ferster, C. B., and Skinner, B. F. *Schedules of Reinforcement.* Appleton-Century-Crofts, 1957.

Festinger, L. *A Theory of Cognitive Dissonance.* Stanford University Press, 1957.

Festinger, L., and Carlsmith, J. M. Cognitive consequences of forced compliance. *Journal of Abnormal and Social Psychology,* 1959, *58,* 203-10.

Freedman, J. L. Attitudinal effects of inadequate justification. *Journal of Personality,* 1963, *31,* 371-85.

Galbraith, J. R. *Designing Complex Organizations.* Reading, Mass.: Addison-Wesley, 1973.

Galbraith, J. R. and Cummings L. L. An empirical investigation of the motivational determinants of task performance: Interactive effects between instrumentality-valence and motivation-ability. *Organizational Behavior and Human Performance,* 1967, *2,* 237-57.

Glass, D. C., Reim, B., and Singer, J. E. Behavioral consequences of adaptation to controllable and uncontrollable noise. *Journal of Experimental Social Psychology,* 1971, *7,* 244-57.

Glass, D. C. and Singer, J. E. *Urban Stress.* New York: Academic Press, 1972.

Graen, G. Instrumentality theory of work motivation: Some experimental results and suggested modifications. *Journal of Applied Psychology Monograph* , 1969, *53,* 1-25.

———. Role making processes within complex organizations. In M. Dunnett (ed.) *Handbook of Industrial and Organizational Psychology.* Chicago: Rand McNally, 1976.

Hackman, J. R., and Lawler, E. E. Employee reactions to job characteristics. *Journal of Applied Psychology Monograph,* 1971, *55,* 259-86.

Hackman, J. R., and Oldham, G. R. Motivation through the design of work. *Organizational Behavior and Human Performance,* 1976, *16,* 250-79.

Hage, J., and Aiken, M. Routine technology, social structure and organization goals. *Administrative Science Quarterly,* 1969, *14,* 366-76.

Hammock, T., and Brehm, J. W. The attractiveness of choice alternatives when freedom is eliminated by a social agent. *Journal of Personality,* 1966, *34,* 546-54.

Hamner, W. C. Reinforcement theory and contingency management in organizational settings. In H. L. Tosi and W. C. Hamner (eds.) *Organizational Behavior and Management: A Contingency Approach.* Chicago: St. Clair Press, 1974.

Hamner, W. C., and Foster, L. W. Are intrinsic and extrinsic rewards additive? A test of Deci's cognitive evaluation theory of task motivation. *Organizational Behavior and Human Performance,* 1975, *14,* 398-415.

Hamner, W. C., and Hamner, E. P. Using positive reinforcement principles to increase worker productivity. *Organizational Dynamics,* April, 1976.

Heneman, H. G., and Schwab, D. P. Evaluation of research on expectancy theory predictions of employee performance. *Psychological Bulletin,* 1972, *78,* 1-9.

Hiroto, D. S., and Seligmen, M. E. P. Generality of learned helplessness in man. *Journal of Personality and Social Psychology,* 1975, *31,* 311-27.

House, R. J. A path-goal theory of leader effectiveness. *Administrative Science Quarterly,* 1971, *16,* 321-35.

House, R. J., and Dessler, G. The path-goal theory of leadership: Some post hoc and a priori tests. In J. G. Hunt (ed.), *Contingency Approaches to Leadership.* Carbondale, Illinois: Southern Illinois University Press, 1974.

House, R. J., Shapiro, H. J., and Wahba, M. A. Expectancy theory as a predictor of work behavior and attitude: A reevaluation of empirical evidence. *Decision Sciences.* 1974, *5,* 481-506.

Jones, E. E. and Davis, K. E. From acts to dispositions: The attribution process in person perception. In L. Berkowitz (ed.) *Advances in Experimental Social Psychology,* New York: Academic Press, 1965.

Kahn, R. L., Wolfe, D. M., Quinn, R. R., Snoek, J. D., and Rosenthal, R. N. *Organizational Stress: Studies in Role Conflict and Ambiguity.* New York: Wiley, 1964.

Katz, D., and Kahn, R. L. *The Social Psychology of Organizations.* New York: John Wiley, 1966.

Keller, F. S. *Learning: Reinforcement Theory* (2nd ed.). Random House, 1969.

Kelley, H. H. Attribution theory in social psychology. In D. Levine (ed.) *Nebraska Symposium on Motivation* (vol. 15), University of Nebraska Press, 1967.

———. The process of causal attribution. *American Psychologist,* 1974, *28,* 107-28.

Khandwalla, P. N. Mass output orientation of operations technology and organization structure. *Administrative Science Quarterly,* 1974, *19,* 74-97.

Kiesler, C. A., and Kiesler, S. B. *Conformity.* Reading, Massachusetts: Addison-Wesley, 1966.

Korman, A. K. *The Psychology of Motivation.* Englewood Cliffs, N. J.: Prentice-Hall, 1974.

Krantz, D. S., Glass, D. C., and Snyder, M. L. Helplessness, stress level, and the coronary-prone behavior pattern. *Journal of Experimental Social Psychology,* 1974, *10,* 284-300.

Kruglanski, A. W., Friedman, I., and Zeevi, G. The effects of extrinsic incentive on some qualitative aspects of task performance. *Journal of Personality,* 1971, *39,* 606-17.

Kruglanski, A. W., Alon, S., and Lewis, T. Retroactive misattribution and task enjoyment. *Journal of Experimental Social Psychology,* 1972, *8,* 493-501.

Latham, G. P., and Yukb, G. A. A review of research on the application of goal setting in organizations. *Academy of Management Journal,* 1975, *18,* 824-45.

Lawler, E. E. *Pay and Organizational Effectiveness: A Psychological View.* New York: McGraw-Hill, 1971.

———. *Motivation in Work Organizations.* Monterey, Calif.: Brooks/Cole, 1973.

Lawler, E. E. and Hackman, J. R. Impact of employee participation in the development of pay incentive plans: A field experiment. *Journal of Applied Psychology,* 1969, *53,* 467-71.

Lawler, E. E., Kuleck, W. J., and Rhode, J. G. Job choice and post decision dissonance. *Organizational Behavior and Human Performance,* 1975, *13,* 133-45.

Lawrence, P. R., and Lorsch, J. W. *Organization and Environment.* Boston: Harvard University, Graduate School of Business Administration, Division of Research.

Lepper, M. R., and Greene, D. Turning play into work: Effects of adult surveillance and extrinsic rewards on children's intrinsic motivation. *Journal of Personality and Social Psychology,* in press.

Lepper, M. R., Greene, D., and Nisbett, R. E. Undermining children's intrinsic interest with extrinsic rewards: A test of the "over-justification" hypothesis. *Journal of Personality and Social Psychology,* 1973, *28,* 129-37.

Lewin, K. *The Conceptual Representation and the Measurement of Psychological Forces.* Durham: Duke University Press, 1938.

Linder, D. E., Cooper, J., and Jones, E. E. Decision freedom as a determinant of the role of incentive magnitude in attitude change. *Journal of Personality and Social Psychology,* 1967, *6,* 245-54.

Locke, E. A. Personnel attitudes and motivation. *Annual Review of Psychology* (vol. 26), 1975.

Locke, E. A., Cartledge, N., and Koeppel, J. Motivational effects of knowledge of results: A goal-setting phenomenon? *Psychological Bulletin,* 1968, *70,* 474-85.

Luthans, F., and Kreitner, R. *Organizational Behavior Modification.* Glenview, Ill.: Scott, Foresman and Co., 1975.

Mackenzie, K. D. *A Theory of Group Structures.* Monograph, Lawrence, Kansas: University of Kansas, 1975.

March, J. G., and Simon, H. A. *Organizations.* New York: John Wiley, 1958.

McClelland, D. *The Achieving Society.* Princeton, N. J.: Van Nostrand, 1961.

———. The role of educational technology in developing achievement motivation. In D. C. McClelland and R. W. Steele (eds.) *Human Motivation: A Book of Readings.* General Learning Press, 1973a.

———. What is the effect of achievement motivation training in the schools? In D. C. McClelland and R. S. Steele (eds.) *Human Motivation: A Book of Readings.* General Learning Press, 1973b.

McClelland, D. C., and Winter, D. G. *Motivating Economic Achievement.* New York: Free Press, 1969.

Mechanic, D. Sources of power of lower participants in complex organizations. *Administrative Science Quarterly,* 1962, 7, 249-364.

Miller, G. A. The magical number seven, plus or minus two: Some limits on our capacity for processing information. *Psychological* Review, 1956, *63,* 81-97.

Mitchell, T. R. Expectancy models of job satisfaction, occupational preference and effort: A theoretical, methodological, and empirical appraisal. *Psychological Bulletin,* 1974, *81,* 1053-77.

Mitchell, T. R., and Knudsen, B. W. Instrumentality theory predictions of students' attitudes towards business and their choice of business as an occupation. *Academy of Management Journal,* 1973, *16,* 41-52.

Nash, A. N., and Carroll, S. J. *The Management of Compensation.* Monterey, Calif: Brooks/Cole, 1975.

Peak, H. Attitude and motivation. In M. R. Jones (ed.) *Nebraska Symposium on Motivation.* Lincoln: University of Nebraska Press, 1955, 149-88.

Pfeffer, J. Merger as a response to organizational interdependence. *Administrative Science Quarterly,* 1972, *17,* 382-94.

———. Size, composition, and function of hospital boards of directors: A study of organization-environment linkage. *Administrative Science Quarterly,* 1973, *18,* 349-64.

Porter, L. W. and Lawler, E. E. *Managerial Attitudes and Performance.* Homewood, Ill.: Irwin, 1968.

Rosenberg, M. J. Cognitive structure and attitudinal affect. *Journal of Abnormal and Social Psychology,* 1956, *53,* 367-72.

Ross, M. Salience of reward and intrinsic motivation. *Journal of Personality and Social Psychology,* 1975, *32,* 245-54.

Roth, S., and Bootzin, R. The effects of experimentally induced expectancies of external control: An investigation of learned helplessness. *Journal of Personality of Social Psychology,* 1974, *29,* 253-64.

Roth, S., and Kubal, L. The effects of non-contingent reinforcement of tasks of differing importance: Facilitation and learned helplessness. *Journal of Personality and Social Psychology,* in press.

Salancik, G. R. Inference of one's attitude from behavior recalled under linguistically manipulated cognitive sets. *Journal of Experimental Social Psychology,* 1974, *10,* 415-27.

Salancik, G. R. and Conway, M. Attitude inferences from salient and relevant cognitive content about behavior. *Journal of Personality and Social Psychology,* 1975, *32,* 829-40.

Schmidt, F. L. Implications of a measurement problem for expectancy theory research. *Organizational Behavior and Human Performance,* 1973, *10,* 243-51.

Scott, W. E. Activation theory and task design. *Organizational Behavior and Human Performance,* 1966, *1,* 3-30.

Seligman, M. E. P. *Helplessness.* San Francisco: W. H. Freeman, 1975.

Seligman, M. E. P., and Maier, S. F. Failure to escape traumatic shock. *Journal of Experimental Psychology,* 1967, *74,* 1-9.

Selznick, P. *TVA and the Grass Roots.* Berkeley: University of California Press, 1949.

Shaban, J., and Welling, G. The effects of two kinds of bureaucratic harassment. In D. C. Glass and J. Singer (eds.) *Urban Stress.* New York: Academic Press, 1972.

Sheard, J. L. Intrasubject prediction of preferences for organizational types. *Journal of Applied Psychology.* 1970, *54,* 248-52.

Sheridan, J. E., Richards, M. D., and Slocum, J. W. Comparative analysis of expectancy and heuristic models of decision behavior. *Journal of Applied Psychology,* 1975, *60,* 361-68.

Sherrod, D. R., and Downs, R. Environmental determinants of altruism: The effects of stimulus overload and perceived control on helping. *Journal of Experimental Social Psychology,* 1974, *10,* 468-79.

Shull, F. A. Matrix structure and project authority for optimizing organizational capacity. *Business Monograph* no. 1, Business Research Bureau, Southern Illinois University, 1965.

Sidman, M., Herrnstein, R. J., and Conrad, D. G. Maintenance of avoidance behavior by unavoidable shocks. *Journal of Comparative and Physiological Psychology,* 1957, *50,* 553-57.

Simon, H. A. *Administrative Behavior.* New York: Macmillan, 1957.

Skinner, B. F. *Science and Human Behavior.* New York: Macmillan, 1953.

―――. *About Behaviorism,* New York: Alfred A. Knopf, 1974.

Slovic, P. From Shakespeare to Simon: Speculations—and some evidence about man's ability to process information. *Oregon Research Institute Monograph,* 1972, *12,* no. 2.

Spielberger, C. D., and DeNike, L. D. Descriptive behaviorism versus cognitive theory in verbal operant conditioning. *Psychological Review,* 1966, *73,* 306-25.

Staw, B. M. Attitudinal and behavioral consequences of changing a major organizational reward: A natural field experiment. *Journal of Personality and Social Psychology,* 1974, *6,* 742-51.

―――. Attribution of the causes of performance: A new alternative interpretation of cross-sectional research on organizations. *Organizational Behavior and Human Performance,* 1975, *13,* 414-32.

―――. *Intrinsic and Extrinsic Motivation.* Morristown, N. J.: General Learning Press, 1976.

Staw, B. M., Calder, B. J., and Hess, R. Situational norms and the effect of extrinsic rewards on intrinsic motivation. Working Paper, Northwestern University, 1976.

Staw, B. M., and Szwajkowski, E. The scarcity-munificence component of organizational environments and the commission of illegal acts. *Administrative Science Quarterly,* 1975, *20,* 345-54.

Szilagyi, S., and Sims, H. An exploration of the path-goal theory of leadership in a health care environment. *Academy of Management Journal,* 1974, *17,* 622-34.

Thompson, J. D. *Organizations in Action.* New York: McGraw-Hill, 1967.

Thorndike, E. L. *Animal Intelligence,* New York: Macmillan, 1911.

Tolman, E. C. *Purposive Behavior in Animals and Men.* New York: Appleton-Century Crofts, 1932.

———. Principles of performance. *Psychological Review,* 1955, *62,* 315-26.

Tosi, H. L., and Hamner, W. C. *Organizational Behavior and Management: A Contingency Approach.* Chicago: St. Clair Press, 1974.

Uhl, C. N., and Young, A. G. Resistance to extinction as a function of incentive, percentage of reinforcement, and number of nonreinforced trials. *Journal of Experimental Psychology,* 1967, *73,* 556-64.

Vroom, V. H. *Work and Motivation.* New York: John Wiley, 1964.

———. Organizational choice: A study of pre- and post-decision processes. *Organizational Behaviors and Human Performance,* 1966, *1,* 212-25.

Vroom, V. H., and Deci, E. L. The stability of post-decision dissonance: A follow-up study of the job attitudes of business school graduates. *Organizational Behavior and Human Performance,* 1971, *6,* 36-49.

Wanous, J. P. Occupational preferences: Preferences of valence and instrumentality and objective data. *Journal of Applied Psychology,* 1972, *56,* 152-55.

Weick, K. E. Reduction of cognitive dissonance through task enhancement and effort expenditure. *Journal of Abnormal and Social Psychology,* 1964, *68,* 533-39.

———. *The Social Psychology of Organizing.* Reading, Mass.: Addison-Wesley, 1969.

———. Reward concepts: Dice or marbles, unpublished paper, Cornell University, 1974.

Weick, K. E., and Penner, D. D. Justification and productivity. unpublished manuscript, University of Minnesota, 1965.

Weiner, B. *Theories of Motivation: From Mechanism to Cognition.* Chicago: Rand McNally, 1972.

White, R. W. Motivation reconsidered: The concept of competence. *Psychological Review,* 1959, *66,* 297-333.

Willems, E. P. Go ye into all the world and modify behavior: An ecologist's view. *Representative Research in Social Psychology,* 1973, *4,* 93-105.

Woodworth, R. S. *Dynamic Psychology.* New York: Columbia University Press, 1918.

Wortman, C. B. and Brehm, J. W. Responses to uncontrollable outcomes: An integration of reactance theory and the learned helplessness model. In L. Berkowitz (ed.) *Advances in Experimental Social Psychology,* New York: Academic Press, 1976.

Wortman, C. B., and Linsenmeier, J. A. W. Interpersonal attraction and techniques of ingratiation in organizational settings. In B. Staw and G. Salancik (eds.) *New Directions in Organizational Behavior.* Chicago: St. Clair Press, 1977.

Zald, M. N. Urban differentiation, characteristics of boards of directors and organizational affectiveness. *American Journal of Sociology,* 1967, *73,* 261-72

Chapter Three

Social Comparison Processes in Organizations

Paul S. Goodman

Social comparison processes (SCP) are one of the most pervasive phenomena in our organizational and nonorganizational lives. In such a process the individual compares some characteristic to a reference point in order to evaluate the characteristic in question. The most common example of SCP in organizations is the evaluation of pay. Let us assume an individual gets a 10 percent raise. Is that a good or bad raise? There is nothing inherent in the percentage to answer this question. To evaluate the raise, the individual adopts a variety of comparison procedures. The simplest may be to compare the raise with other raises offered to people with similar backgrounds. If the person's raise relative to his contributions (e.g., how hard he works) is comparable to a comparison person's raise and contribution, he can infer that the level of his raise is fair.

Many other rewards, or outcomes, that are allocated in an organization are subject to the same type of analysis. For example, how does one evaluate a promotion or sequence of career moves? There is nothing inherent in a promotion to identify it as good or bad. Somehow, one must identify an appropriate comparison point to evaluate the meaning of the promotion. Although the evaluation of pay and promotion are the most obvious examples of SCP in organizations, many others can be identified, such as evaluations of working conditions, supervision, or performance.

Social comparison processes are not restricted to evaluating outcomes or rewards. A supervisor uses SCP in evaluating subordinates' performance, especially where no objective standard is present. In evaluating the effectiveness of an organization, the SCP is also a critical factor (see Pennings and Goodman, 1976). In this context, performance of the organization may be compared with past performance, performance of other organizations, or other referents. The point is that SCP is a pervasive process in organizations.

People are as involved in SCP in their nonorganizational lives as they are in their organizational lives. Is my marriage successful? How good is my tennis game? Have I done a good job raising my children? Am I a good driver? All of these questions concern some characteristic the individual possesses. In each case, the individual wants to evaluate this characteristic. Since there is nothing in the characteristic to provide the evaluative information, some other reference point must be selected to provide a comparison.

These organizational and nonorganizational examples are presented to illustrate the meaning and generality of SCP. The major objective in this chapter is to develop a framework that can be used to explain and to predict SCP in organizations, with the focus on conceptualizing the process by which people evaluate themselves in organizational settings.

Some of the questions to be explored are: What types of referents do individuals select? Why are certain referents selected over others? What factors affect the selection of referents? What is the process by which referents are selected? To what extent are the types of referents, or process of selecting referents, generalizable over evaluations of different objects (e.g., extrinsic vs. intrinsic rewards)?

To investigate these questions some alternative theoretical approaches to SCP are presented. Then a framework for explaining SCP in organizations is delineated, followed by an examination of the generalizability of that framework for different classes of evaluations that might occur in an organizational setting.

Theoretical Approaches to Social Comparison Processes

This section outlines different theoretical perspectives dealing with SCP. The goal is not to provide an extensive examination of these theories and supporting research but to identify some critical issues that need to be solved.

Social Comparison Theory

Leon Festinger's 1954 article, "A Theory of Social Comparison," is probably the most influential single piece on SCP. His major theme is that people have a drive to evaluate their abilities or opinions and that they select others similar in ability or opinions to accomplish this evaluation. Festinger postulated that the greater the similarity, the greater the stability in the evaluations. He also discussed the effects of discrepancies in abilities or opinions between the evaluating person and the reference person and the drive to reduce the discrepancy. As one would expect, most of the controversy and research has centered on the similarity argument. The basic criticism is that the concept is not well specified and that there are alternative information-seeking strategies that an individual might select when evaluating some object (e.g., looking at the extremes of the distribution).

In one major experimental paradigm used to examine the similarity issue, subjects take a "personality" test measuring traits valued both positively and negatively. After receiving false feedback placing their score in the middle of the distribution for their group, the subjects may select one or two scores of members in their groups. Some of the studies support the similarity argument (cf. Darley and Aronson, 1966; Wheeler, 1966), while other experiments indicate that the subjects select the most able person *or* the least able for comparison to their own score (cf. Arrowood and Friend, 1969; Wheeler, Shaver, Jones, Goethals, Cooper, Robinson, Gruder, and Butzine, 1969).

We will not examine the merits of the competing studies concerning the similarity issue, because it is not clear that such a review would be valuable, since the experimental paradigm in these studies seems very constrained. While it is relatively simple to run, the paradigm really does not reflect the social complexities and major issues of SCP. Also, few of the studies have tried to conceptualize the similarity concept. Nevertheless, some useful observations can be derived. First, the comparison process is more complex than Festinger suggests; subjects can use a wide range of different referents to evaluate their abilities or opinions. Second, similarity can be an important referent when it involves a positive attribute, when objective referents are unavailable, and when the range of the attribute's distribution is known (Pettigrew 1967, p. 248). Third, the drive to evaluate oneself is only one of the motivating forces; feelings of self-esteem and self-enhancement are probably also important.

Reference Groups and Relative Deprivation

Two other concepts, reference groups and relative deprivation, were formulated at the time Festinger's theory was published. Reflecting a sociological rather than psychological viewpoint, they paralleled in some ways the SCP and they also afford new perspectives.

Reference Groups. Reference groups are those groups which individuals belong to or aspire to belong to (Kelley, 1952; Merton, 1957). They provide two general functions—a normative function that establishes and enforces standards or norms, and a comparative function that enables people to evaluate their attitudes and opinions against those of the group. It is the comparative function that parallels the SCP of Festinger. The classic research study on this, titled *The American Soldier* (see Merton, 1957), has been an important source for the early theorizing about reference groups, and it provides a good example of their comparative function (Merton, 1957). The data source for this project was a series of studies about various phases of the life of the U.S. soldier during World War II. Some of the questions examined concerned the relative satisfaction of different groups, and the satisfactions were explained in terms of reference groups.

For example, the answer to the question, "Would black enlistees stationed in the North be more satisfied with their lot than black enlistees in the South?" depended on the reference group selected. If the black soldier stationed in the North compared himself to the black soldier stationed in the South, he would probably be more satisfied. This conclusion assumes that the position of the black soldier was better in the North (i.e., there was more tolerance and freedom) than in the South. On the other hand, if the black soldier in the North compared himself to the black civilian in the North he would be less satisfied, while the black Southern soldier would feel better off than his civilian counterpart. The findings showed that the black soldier stationed in the North was less satisfied than the black soldier in the South. The example shows that there are alternative comparison or reference groups and that predicting the level of satisfaction is not an easy task. Although Merton and others have pointed to the need for elaborating a framework for predicting comparison groups, little has been done in that area.

Relative Deprivation. The concept of relative deprivation also grew out of *The American Soldier* studies. The most-cited example of this phenomenon concerned the degree of satisfaction with promotion exhibited by two groups in the military. Promotions were rapid in the air corps and slow in the military police, yet air corps men were more frustrated over promotion. The concept of relative deprivation points out that it is not the absolute level of promotions that is significant in producing satisfaction but the relative discrepancy between what one attains and what one expects to receive. Air corps expectations for promotion were increased by the rapid promotion rate.

The utility of the relative deprivation concept is that it focuses attention on the nature of the discrepancy between the individual and the comparison group. In this way it complements the reference group concept by giving more understanding to how the discrepancy alters attitudes.

Equity Theory

Equity theory is a more recent attempt to conceptualize the process by which people evaluate outcomes or rewards. The critical aspect of equity theory for our discussion is that it uses an independent reference point to evaluate outcomes. Although there have been a variety of theoretical variations of equity and the use of SCP in evaluating outcomes (Adams, 1965; Jacques, 1965; Smith, Kendall, and Hulin, 1969), Adams' work has been most influential.

Adams (1965) defines the inequity as follows: Inequity exists for a person whenever he perceives the ratio of his outcomes to inputs are unequal to the ratio of another's outcomes to inputs. This may occur when the two individuals are in a direct exchange relationship or when both are in an exchange with a third party, such as a superior. Outcomes are defined as the rewards which the individual receives from his job; inputs represent the contributions (e.g., age, effort) that the individual brings to the job. Adams postulates that inequity leads to tension. The greater the tension, the greater the drive to reduce it. Tension reduction strategies can take many forms, such as increasing outcomes, decreasing inputs, changing the comparison or compared person, and so forth. Other postulates of the model are that inequity results from outcome-input discrepancies relative to another's outcome-input ratio versus absolute discrepancies in outcomes. That is, if A earned more than B, but A had an M.B.A. and B only a B.A., then the relationship between ratios would be in balance. If A and B had the same education, then discrepancies in outcome-input would exist and inequity would result. Adams also states that the tension threshold for underpayment inequity is lower than for overpayment.

The equity model has a number of attractive features relative to other theories. First, it is stated in more theoretical detail than the others we have discussed thus far. Second, it has instigated more research, not just in terms of number of studies but also in terms of the substantive issues tested, and there is general support for many of the model's postulates. (See Goodman and Friedman, 1971, and Pritchard, 1969 for examinations of this research.) Third, much of the recent research has been done to expand the concept of equity to a variety of social relationships (Walster, Bersheid, and Walster, 1973). This attempt to generalize the theory's application may lead to a redefinition and improvement of the theory's application in organizational settings.

It is probably useful to note that another concept—the concept of distributive justice—emerged around the same general time as Adams' theoretical pieces. The concept functions in the same manner as equity—to explain how people evaluate outcomes. According to

Homans (1961), a person in exchange with another will expect profits —representing the difference between rewards and costs and paralleling the equity concept of outcomes—to be directly proportional to his investments; investments are what the individual contributes to work. Negative affect appears when the rule of distributive justice is violated.

Distributive justice is cited because it represents the sociological counterpart of equity theory and because there have been some recent attempts to extend the concept theoretically. Compared to equity theory, there has been much less theorizing and empirical work on distributive justice, but a theoretical piece by Berger, Zelditch, Anderson and Cohen, (1972) and a recent experiment by Cook (1975) focus on an important issue not discussed in any of the theories considered thus far. Their concept—the "distribution rule"—deals with how rewards should be allocated. The rule is a set of cognitive and normative expectations of how outcomes and inputs are related. Mostly equity research had taken distribution rules as a given; that is, people believe more effort or performance deserves more pay. This assumption is obviously critical when one evaluates outcome-input ratios. How the distribution rules are formed, the degree to which they are perceived as legitimate, and their role in evaluations, are important questions raised by this recent work on distributive justice.

Other Theories

Adaptation level theory (Helson, 1964) attempts to explain relativity in perceptual judgment. Whether an object is light or heavy is judged in terms of a neutral reference point—the adaptation level. Helson formally defines adaptation level as the weighted log mean of three types of stimuli: (1) stimulus being judged, (2) background stimuli, and (3) residual stimuli. The level is dynamic in the sense that it constantly changes as a function of variables such as frequency and intensity, size, and nearness of new stimuli.

Although adaptation level theory has primarily been applied to various psychophysical judgment experiments, there have been some attempts to tie it to social psychological processes (Appley, 1971). Also, with some modifications it bears on our interest in SCP processes in organization. For example, the adaptation level is a dynamic entity constantly being modified by current stimuli. In the context of evaluating organizational rewards, we need to deal with the fact that what might be considered an attractive outcome-input ratio at one time may be considered less attractive over time. That is, what is considered an excellent pay-performance ratio at one period may be considered only average at another period; assuming that an upward shift in the adaptation level changes the attractiveness of the pay-performance ration.

Thibaut and Kelley's work (1959) on small groups is also relevant to the social comparison process. They introduce the concept of comparison level, which is a standard against which members evaluate the attractiveness of a relationship and by which rewards and costs are evaluated in terms of their just allocations. The comparison level is influenced by all past relevant outcomes and thus is dynamic in character. The parallel between comparison level and adaptation level seems relatively clear. The major difference seems to be on the focus of the theories. The comparison level concept and a related concept called "comparison level for alternatives" concern the evaluations of outcomes from interpersonal relationships, whereas adaptation level concerns problems in psychophysical judgment. The contribution of Thibaut and Kelley's concept is that it suggests a new area for social comparison processes. That is, individuals in organizations can evaluate not only the attractiveness of an object such as pay, but also the attractiveness of the relationship with others (e.g., supervisor) through social comparison processes.

A number of common elements are evident from this review of SCP-related theories. One is the assumption that an individual is motivated to learn about himself by comparison to outside referents. These other referents are not necessarily other people. A related issue is that there may be competing motivational forces—that is, some comparisons are made to gain accurate information about oneself, while others are made to enhance feelings of self-esteem. In addition to a complex motivational context, the comparison itself is a complex process of evaluating individual dimensions against independent referent points that are also multiple in nature. The consequences to the individual from this comparison process are new data about himself and associated positive and negative affect.

Despite these common elements, the theories are neither well integrated with each other nor conceptually well developed (Pettigrew, 1967). Nor are they supported by a large body of empirical research. The Festinger paper was published in 1954, and the first flurry of significant papers began in 1966; but while equity research was popular in the late 1960s, today one finds fewer such studies in the major journals.

A more profitable way to view the literature is by identifying unsolved problems. The chief problem is that we know very little about factors that affect the selection of referents and little about the process by which referents are selected. A second problem is that there is little specification about the kinds of referents people select. The traditional focus has been on another person, but varying types of referents (e.g., the individual at a different point in time) might be considered. Third, given a particular referent, we know little about how the individual weights the relevance of the different input or outcome terms. In addition, there is the issue of the distribution rule—for example, how does one learn to accept as legitimate the rule that length of service, rather than performance level, should be related to pay level? The nature of distribution rules and the degree to which they are accepted is critical to the social comparison process. Another problem is how to combine information from multiple referents providing conflicting information. A sixth issue concerns the dynamic characteristics of the referents. Adaptation level suggests that referents will have constantly shifting significance as a function of past and current stimuli. The final point is that we know little about the generalizability of the SCP model. Initially it was applied to understanding how people evaluate attitudes, but more recent research concerns the evaluation of outcomes such as pay. An important issue is whether there is a general framework cutting across a variety of objects subject to social evaluation.

General Framework

After first identifying a set of terms, we will describe basic assumptions or characteristics of our framework of SCP. Then we will focus attention on the types of referents people use in evaluations. Our position is that the classes of referents we identify are sufficiently generalizable to cover a wide range of SCP in organizations. The next step will be to identify the factors which affect the selection of a specific class of referents. That is, why are some referents selected and others not? Lastly, we will develop a simple process model describing how SCP operates.

Inputs. Inputs represent the contributions an individual brings to the job. Some inputs are ascriptive, including such variables as age and sex. Other inputs are achievement-oriented, including variables such as effort. The nature of each individual input may be positive or negative. That is, the dimension (input) which the individual brings to the exchange relationship may be considered an asset (e.g., intelligence) or a liability (e.g., poor interpersonal skills). In this analysis the definition of "input" will be expanded to include characteristics of the individual's job, the job environment, and the organization.

Outcomes. Outcomes refer to the rewards or punishments received by the individual in exchange for his other contributions. The outcomes may be extrinsic (e.g., pay) or intrinsic (e.g., feeling of accomplishment).

Outputs. Outputs refer to performance; that is, the products or end results of some work or exchange relationship. Outputs are produced in order to receive outcomes. Meeting a sales quota, producing X number of units, fulfilling a contract, are all outputs. The concept of output is introduced for two reasons. First, we assume that people are interested in evaluating their own performance—that is, knowing how well they are doing in a particular job. Second, outputs are sometimes used as a surrogate for inputs. Because it is often difficult to accurately assess inputs (such as effort or ability), output or performance is used as a measure of input. In this case outputs are used as substitutes for inputs in the evaluation of outcomes.

Distribution Rule. The distribution rule is a statement with a cognitive component defining the expected relationship between inputs and outcomes (e.g., pay related to seniority), and a normative component legitimating that relationship. Distribution rules are used to determine whether a particular referent is appropriate for evaluating a particular outcome-input ratio. For example, a distribution rule might be that pay should be related to seniority. In evaluating an outcome such as pay, we would expect the individual to select referents which provide information about pay and seniority and to reject referents which do not provide this information.

Performance Rule. The performance rule is a statement about the expected relationship between inputs and outputs (e.g., educational level related to job performance). It is similar to a distribution rule in that it determines the appropriateness of a referent when evaluating a particular output-input ratio, but it differs in that it does not have a normative component or evoke feelings of equity or injustice.

Input, Output, or Outcome Comparisons. In input, output, or outcome comparisons, only one dimension is examined—by definition, either an input, output, or outcome. This type of comparison is very descriptive in nature. That is, a particular dimension of an individual is examined in the context of some distribution of that dimension. For example, a salesman might compare his output (performance) to that of other salesmen to determine whether he is in the upper quartile in terms of units sold. In this type of comparison, there is no positive or negative label attached to the dimension under evaluation. The salesman simply learns where his score fits in a particular distribution of scores.

Input and Output Comparisons. With an input-output comparison, the issue is not simply whether one performs better, but how performance relates to inputs. Let us consider two tennis players, A and B. Both are the same age and sex and have the same playing experience (inputs). A consistently beats B by scores of 6-3 (output). In this example, B might evaluate his performance as poor relative to A. However, let us assume that A and B are the same except that A has 10 years more tennis experience and national ranking as a tennis player. In this case, although A might consistently beat B by 6-3 scores, B's rating of his tennis performance is likely to be high, since it is relative to A. The performance rule in this comparison specifies that tennis experience is related to tennis performance and that a referent containing information about tennis experience is appropriate to use in evaluating tennis performance.

Input and Outcome Comparisons. In an input-outcome comparison, the individual compares the ratio of his outcome and input to another outcome-input ration. If the ratios are in balance, the outcome is perceived as fair. This is the traditional equity or distributive justice model and what is being evaluated is the question of fairness or equity.

There has been some controversy about mathematical representations of outcome-input ratios. (The interested reader can consult Walster, Bersheid, and Walster, 1973; and Zuckerman, 1975.) It is to be hoped that this particular controversy will not get out of hand. Since we know very little about how people judge the proportionality between input and output or input and outcome, and since the estimates or rules are, at best, crude approximations (cf. Dawes, in press), to ask for mathematical precision at this point would seem premature.

Assumptions and Characteristics of the Comparison Process

There are a number of characteristics and assumptions which describe the three types of comparison processes delineated above. Our primary focus is on the outcome-input comparison.

1. The comparison process can be initiated by a set of external or internal events. These events evoke a set of motivational forces which provide energy for the social comparison processes.

2. Following Festinger, we assume that people have a general need to evaluate their performance, abilities, attitudes, and outcomes. For any particular evaluation, other needs (e.g., self-esteem) may also

be evoked. Given that there are individual differences in need strength, we would expect differences in the motivation directed toward the evaluation process and, hence, individual differences in the results of the process.

3. The evaluation is subjective in nature. Two persons may evaluate the same inputs-outputs or outcomes differently.

4. The evaluations of output-input or outcome-input ratios are on the relative versus absolute characteristics of stimuli. That is, it is not that A earns more than B, but whether A's earnings relative to inputs is greater, less, or the same as B's ratio.

5. Individuals can use multiple comparison points, and the character of these comparison points will vary between individuals and over time.

6. Comparison points are not limited to other individuals. (See the discussion below on "Types of Referents Used in Evaluation.")

7. An evaluation of output-inputs or outcome-inputs requires, respectively, knowledge of a performance or distribution rule. Such a rule is formed from social consensus and exists outside of any particular evaluation.

8. Balance between inputs and outputs or inputs and outcomes can be achieved in a variety of forms. Using equity terminology, Person and Other can be described as in balance if their inputs and outcomes (or outputs) are both high (H/H, H/H), where the first item refers to Person's high inputs and outcomes and the second refers to Other's. There are, of course, other balance combinations (L/L, H/H), (H/L, H/L), and so forth.

9. There are two general conditions of imbalance. Outcomes (or outputs) can be in greater proportion to inputs relative to a comparison point. Where the individual has an excess of outcomes relative to another outcome-input ratio, there is profitable inequity. When outcomes relative to inputs are less than in a comparison ratio, the reverse holds true and there is unprofitable inequity.

10. Imbalance leads to tension in output-input or input-outcome evaluations. Tension occurs in the outcome-input model because social norms of equity and justice have been violated. In the output-input comparison, tension can occur if central traits or values of the individual are being judged. For example, the nationally ranked tennis player who only marginally beats the inexperienced player may experience threats to feelings of self-esteem.

11. The greater the tension, the more likely it is that the individual will try to reduce it through behavioral strategies (e.g., increasing outcomes or inputs) or by cognitive strategies (e.g., distorting information about the referent).

Types of Referents Used in Evaluation

One problem in the literature on SCP is that little attention has been given to the types of referents people select. In this section we will delineate three classes of referents which we assume can describe comparisons of any organizational outcome or output. (In the section on "Application of Framework," we will explore the generalizability of these referent classes.)

Other. The most common class of referents discussed in the social comparison literature is other individuals. To evaluate oneself on a particular dimension one compares outcomes-inputs or outputs-inputs to another's ratio. Most often this comparison is with similar Others, but as we suggested earlier, the concept *similarity* has never been clearly defined and therefore our knowledge of the range of possible referents is limited.

As an alternative to similarity, Goodman (1974) has suggested categorizing others in terms of their role relationships with the focal individual. In an organizational context, others can be described as either inside or outside the organization. Inside Others can be further defined on dimensions such as level, type of job, department, and Outside Others can be subdivided into those who are work-related, socially-related, or who fall into a residual category.

Work-related Outside Others are those the focal person directly interacts with as a part of his job (e.g., customers, or members of a professional organization). Socially-related Outside Others are persons the focal person interacts with but not on a work basis (e.g., neighbors, or relatives). The residual category primarily includes Outside Others whose inputs, outputs, and outcomes the focal individual has some knowledge of. A newspaper story about a strike settlement, for example, could provide this type of information.

Another way to categorize Others is in terms of time. Others selected could represent output-input or outcome-input ratios in the past, present, or future. For example, one could compare one's current pay-input ratio with the expected pay-input ratio of another or with the pay-input ratio of someone who previously worked on a similar job.

There are many possible comparison Others. Others in similar jobs represent only one type. Also, many of the referents exist outside the focal organization. This is important, since the performance or distribution rules inside the organization may not be generalizable outside the organization. Therefore, the more the individual uses nonorganization members to evaluate outputs or outcomes, the more likely it is that situations of imbalance will arise.

Self. Self-referents are those output, output-input, or outcome-input ratios unique to the individual but different from his current ratios. Self-referents can be distinguished on a time basis. That is, past output-input ratios can be compared to current output-input ratios, or an expected outcome-input ratio can be compared with a current outcome-input ratio.

Another type of Self-referent is derived from internal concepts of self-worth. This assumes that individuals develop ideal ratios which they compare with current ratios. For example, people develop ideal outcome-input ratios related to what they consider to be an acceptable standard of living. This can be compared to their actual ratio. Others develop internal views of their self-worth which can be applied to outcomes such as pay. For example, an individual may expect to earn X thousand dollars a year by age 30. This expectation is then compared to his actual pay at 30. The distinguishing characteristic of the Self-referent is that the comparison is specific to the individual, with no comparison to an Other. While it is clear that conceptions of self-worth are derived from interactions with others, the use of a self-referent at any point in time requires only a cognition of one's current outcome-input ratio and the Self outcome-input ratio. Theoretical work by Helson (1964) and Jacques (1965) argues for the existence of Self-referents. Also, research by Pritchard, Jorgenson, and Dunnette (1972) and Goodman (1974) has demonstrated that Self-referents can be used independently of Other referents.

System. System referents are formed in the exchange between the employee and the organization. When an individual joins the organization there is an explicit or implicit contract about inputs and outputs rendered by the individual and inducement (outcomes) provided by the organization. The contract contains potential referents for evaluation. For example, a company might say its salesmen must meet their quota to get an X percent raise. This ratio (raise performance) can be compared to the focal person's eventual performance and raise. In this example it is important to note that whether or not the individual's cohorts receive a raise on meeting their quota is irrelevant. What is important is that the organization has promised an outcome-input ratio that can be used for comparison purposes.

The initial contract provides the first source of System referents. Over time the normative expectations between the employer and employee can change. We do not expect that organizational promises in terms of inducements for contributions are invariant. However, the critical feature of the System referent does remain the same—it concerns the comparison between Focal's output-input or outcome-input ratio and that ratio expected from the employer. In terms of time, the System comparison examines what was promised in the past to what is experienced in the present; Other referents concern comparison between ratios for the person and Others. Self-referents concern the comparison of a current ratio and some other ratio unique to the individual.

This categorizing of Other, Self-, and System referents was first presented in a paper about how people evaluate pay referents (Goodman, 1974). The conclusions were that (1) people use all three types of referents; (2) people tend to use multiple referents both within and between the Other, Self-, and System categories; (3) Other as a referent class is selected but primarily in conjunction with a second referent and its relative frequency does not seem greater than the Self- and System referent categories; (4) all three types of referents are significantly related to a pay satisfaction criterion which is an indicator of their validity (i.e., imbalance between current outcome-input ratios as compared to the Other, Self-, or System ratios leads to dissatisfaction, while balance leads to feelings of satisfaction); and (5) that the different referent categories are relatively independent, each contributing to the pay satisfaction criterion index. In addition, there were some data indicating the findings were stable across two very different firms.

Despite this support for the validity of Other, Self-, System categorization, there is no evidence yet to suggest that these categories will fit outcome-input or output-input ratios other than the pay-input ratio. The "Application of Framework" section of this paper, however, argues that these categories are generalizable. Although, their relative importance might change with varying kinds of outcomes or outputs, the categories should be a viable way for identifying the potential referents an individual uses when making social evaluation in an organization.

Selection of Referents

The selection of referents is a function of the availability of information and the relevance or attractiveness of a given referent.

Availability of Information. An important factor in selecting a referent is the availability of information; that is, the amount of information pertaining to inputs, outputs, and outcomes an individual possesses about any single referent, as well as the number of referents for which this information is known. The information may be very detailed about distributions of potential referents, or it may be only a gross description of a particular referent. Availability of information about an outcome-input ratio is a necessary condition in the process of referent selection. At this point no assumptions are being made about the quality of the information, defined in terms of its perceived reliability and validity, or the relationship between quantity and quality of information.

Predictors of availability of information can be classified as either structural or individual in character. The structural factors can be defined primarily in terms of the individual's role characteristics and role set (work and nonwork), which can provide important sources of information about referents. A job in the company's payroll department, for example, can provide an opportunity to learn about others' salaries. Other roles strategically placed in the organization's communication network provide information about input, output, and outcome information which can be used by the role occupant for comparison purposes. Similarly, level in the organization is related to the amount of information available. For example, higher-level individuals will probably have a broader range of information about certain outcomes than lower-level participants. Also, occupancy in outside or boundary roles should provide greater information about potential outside comparisons than would occupancy in primarily inside roles.

The availability of information can also be affected by individual factors such as an individual's propensity to search in the environment for information about referents. In one study on antecedents of organizational maps, differences in level of aspiration were positively related to the degree of knowledge the individual had about the organization (Goodman, 1968). The assumption is that people who want to move up in an organization engage in search activities to acquire information relevant to their upward movement. An individual may also "dream up" information on inputs, output, and outcome. If the individual is in a high frustration-conflict situation, one consequence of various cognitive defense mechanisms could be the generation of potential referents. The validity and/or frequency of this particular phenomenon has not been documented, but it does seem a possible source of referents for individuals under extreme stress.

In evaluating the relative importance of structural versus individual phenomena on the availability of information, our hypothesis is that structural factors are probably more important. First, roles (a structural source of information) are composed of normative expectations that are considered legitimate by relevant others. It is legitimate for the clerk in payroll to know other people's salaries, for example. It is generally not legitimate, however, given the secrecy surrounding most pay systems, for an individual to inquire about his peers' salaries. Second, it is the nature of certain roles to have certain information about inputs, outputs, and outcomes. In the course of performing the role, this information is available without any additional cost. For the individual outside this type of role, search activities are costly simply in terms of time and may be perceived as not legitimate.

Relevance or Attractiveness of the Referent. The relevance or attractiveness of a particular referent is a function of the instrumentality of the referent in satisfying needs. In our daily life we encounter many possible referents. Why is it that some are selected and others not? To explore this issue we will examine the functional relationship between needs, instrumentality, and relevance.

Needs affect the relevance of referents in the following ways. First, needs vary in strength. Individuals may or may not want to evaluate their pay, performance, or the relative merits of their working conditions. Holding instrumentality constant, we expect that people with low need to learn about outcomes such as pay will find referents about pay as not particularly relevant. That is, there will be no force to select these referents.

Second, as we have said, research indicates that referent selection in SCP can be related to multiple needs. In addition to the general need to know about oneself in relation to such dimensions as outputs and outcomes, other needs such as recognition, esteem, and affiliation may be activated during the social comparison process.

Third, the relationship between the need and referent may be positive, negative, or neutral. If a referent satisfies the need, the relationship is positive. If it blocks need satisfaction, the relationship is negative. For example, a strong need to know how one is doing at work initiates the SCP, and appropriate referents which afford accurate information about the relative level of one's performance and outcomes are identified. So far, the referents are positively instrumental for the need to know. However, if the comparison process indicates that the individual's performance and outcomes are low relative to others, then feelings of self-esteem may be threatened. In this case the referents are negatively instrumental in relation to the need for self-esteem. The task is to identify the multiple needs and to determine whether the characteristics of the referent or information from the evaluation process facilitates or hinders the satisfaction of the needs under consideration.

The degree to which a referent satisfies a person's needs (degree of instrumentality) is based on the characteristics of the information about the referent and the characteristics of distribution or performance rules relevant to the particular SCP at work. The most important characteristic of the information about the referent is the computational ease it affords the comparer. Earlier we stated that a certain *quantity* of information must be available for the SCP to occur. Here we are talking about the *quality* of the information. The more reliable and valid the information about a referent is perceived, the higher the quality, and the easier it is for the focal person to compute the relationship between his ratio and the ratio afforded by the other referent. The easier the computations, the more likely the referent will be selected. Reliability in this context refers to the stability of information about outcomes, outputs, and inputs. That is, if the individual searches again, would the same outcomes, outputs, or inputs be identified for a particular referent? Validity refers to the accuracy of information. That is, does the outcome-input information we have about an individual describe the actual outcomes and inputs of that individual? The basic hypothesis is that the greater the perceived reliability and validity of a referent, the greater its instrumentality and the more likely its selection.

The performance and distribution rules are the second major factor affecting the degree of instrumentality. (In this section we concentrate on distribution rules, although the reasoning should apply equally to performance rules.) Distribution rules are norms which can reside in society in general and/or be found in educational, work, professional, or social organizations to which the individual has belonged. They are statements about the relationship between outcomes and inputs with both cognitive and normative components. The latter component legitimates the appropriate outcome-input comparison.

The distribution rule determines whether a particular referent is appropriate. If a referent falls within the range defined as appropriate or acceptable by the distribution rule, it is accepted. Regarding the selection of referents in the Other category, a general norm in our society is that people performing similar work should receive similar outcomes. If one belongs to a particular profession (e.g., engineering), then the distribution rule is likely to be that engineers with similar training, service, and jobs should get similar pay. This rule is derived from the more general rule of equal pay for the same work and specifically introduced in educational and professional experiences (e.g., professional association). In the context of evaluation of pay, it means that professional engineers, for example, are likely to consider others in engineering as more appropriate referents than those in— say—medicine, the trades, or other occupations.

Distribution rules also apply to the selection of Self-referents. Consider someone working as an engineer who has worked both as an engineer and as a salesman. Given the general rule of equal pay for someone with similar professional experience, we would expect the Self-referent from the past engineering job would be accepted. The issue in this example is that besides being computationally easier to compare against similar jobs (i.e., engineering), it is also more appropriate to compare within the same profession.

The function of the distribution rule for System comparison is the same, but the form of the rule is somewhat different from that in Other and Self-comparisons. System referents are those generated in the contract between the individual and the employee. They entail the comparison of what the employer promised as outcomes with what he delivered. The issue in the case of distribution rules is whether it is appropriate to use what the employer promised as a referent. In societies with strong personal relationships between employer and employee and low labor mobility, we would expect norms supporting the appropriateness of System referents. On the other hand, when the original employer is changed because of political succession or economic merger, it is less likely that the old "contract" will appear as an appropriate referent.

Since the concept of the distribution rule is fairly new, it might be useful to review some additional issues related to it. First, there is not much information on how distribution rules are formed. Second, distribution rules can vary in terms of their formalization, legitimacy, and visibility. In cases where the rules are formalized and visible, the application of the rule to the outcome-input evaluation seems quite straightforward. In the case where the rule is diffuse and not visible, the process by which evaluation takes place is more complicated. Cook (1975) argues that when the rule is not visible, an individual forms expectations of what the rule should be from the actual outcomes-inputs ratios. That is, the ratios between Focal and Other referents are accepted as equitable and a distribution rule is inferred. This leads to a state of balance between the focal person and the referents, and assumes that people attempt to maintain the status quo. An alternative position is that, faced with no visible distribution rule, the individual tries to construct a rule from available stimuli in a way that will maximize his own outcomes. This point of view contrasts with the status quo features of the earlier argument.

A third issue is that there may be more than one type of distribution rule and these rules may be in conflict. Yuchtman (1972) in an analysis of work behavior in a kibbutz states that both equality and equity are possible rules. Equalitarianism in the economic sphere has been central to the development of most kibbutzim. However, as these organizations become more complicated, and as role differentiation increases (input), there is a competing claim for equity. Greater inputs should lead to greater outcomes. In the case of competing rules, we would expect the greater the visibility and perceived legitimacy of a rule, the more it would be used. In the case where rules were competing on an equal basis, we would expect to find frequent reports of inequity with the outcome-input ratio.

To review, the selection of referents is a function of the availability of information and the relevance or attractiveness of the referents. Availability of information is primarily affected by structural characteristics of the comparer's role and role set. Relevance or attractiveness is a function of the number and strength of needs related to a referent and the degree of instrumentality of that referent for satisfying the needs. Instrumentality, in turn, is a function of the computational ease in evaluating a referent and the appropriateness of the referent as determined by distribution and performance rules. We do not know enough about the instrumentality-need relationship to identify its functional form.

The Selection of Referents in a Process Model

A stimulus event evokes some search process, resulting in a set of outcome-input ratios. These are subject to an evaluation or testing process—the result of which is a set of relevant outcome-input ratios. The selected ratios are then compared with the focal person's outcome-input ratio. Portraying the selection of referents as a process model provides a useful way to examine the interrelationships among the concepts identified and defined separately above. The process model, thus, takes us one step further by examining the interrelationship among these concepts. In addition, the process model itself can assist in generating hypotheses. By focusing on the processes individuals go through in making comparisons, a large set of assumptions and alternative hypotheses are generated.

This model makes certain assumptions about the individual as an information processor which are derived directly from the work of Simon and his associates (cf. Newell and Simon, 1972). It is assumed, first, that the individual is a limited information processor. He cannot entertain all possible outcome-input ratios simultaneously. Therefore, in a comparison he would consider only his own outcome-input ratio and one other ratio at a time, although an individual uses multiple referents. Second, outcome-input ratios are generated by search processes which operate in a serial fashion. Third, the criteria for search and for the other evaluation processes use satisficing versus optimizing rules. Referents which meet the necessary constraints are considered acceptable and are used. There is no effort made to identify the most relevant or best comparison referent; rather, the first acceptable referent is selected. This occurs because the search process follows certain heuristics; it is not a random process. Workable referents from past experience are likely to be identified early in the search process. Fourth, the time required for evaluating a particular outcome-input ratio depends on the unit of analysis. We view the SCP as being composed of a set of cycles, each of which includes the basic processes of search, testing, and comparison that are applied to a particular referent. We assume that one evaluation cycle—the basic building block of the total SCP—will occur in a very small time period (e.g., few seconds). The total SCP for a given outcome-input ratio, however, may demand many cycles, and these may occur over a period of time.

The elements or components of the process model include certain constraints (limiting conditions), programs, and data. Constraints represent conditions that must be satisfied—in a sense, these are tests to determine whether information will be included in the comparison process. A constraint in the selection of referents for the evaluation of pay could be that both input and outcome about pay must be specified. Information about outcome by itself, or information about some other reward, would be rejected.

Each evaluation cycle is comprised of programs which select and evaluate referents. A search program generates the outcome-input ratios. Constraints, such as the ones specified above, would be imbedded in the search programs. Another program—the testing program—would serve to evaluate against certain criteria the set of outcome-input ratios generated by the search program. Then a comparison program would evaluate the individual's ratio in light of the selected outcome-input ratio. In addition, there are switching programs which store information and initiate the other programs. These programs have the executive function of organizing the different subprocesses.

The third component in the model is the data. In the case of evaluating pay, for example, the outcome-input ratio would be the major data.

Let us examine now how the process model might work. Only the simplest model describing the evaluation cycle is presented first. Again, we will use pay as the example, though any outcome or output could have been used.

1. An external event about a recent wage settlement activates an individual's need to know about his pay. Also, since pay is a multiple reinforcer, other needs such as self-esteem are activated. The needs evoke the search program for outcome-input referents.

2. The search process scans long-term memory for potential

information on referents. Individual memories will differ in terms of the information available for comparison as a function of membership in different roles. The search process proceeds serially, guided by a set of constraints. The constraints represent conditions that must be satisfied in the search process. For example, a constraint might be to identify any information about pay, or any information about outcome-input ratios concerning pay. Once the constraints have been satisfied, the search process would terminate and a switching program (i.e., a program to initiate other programs) would be activated. We assume that information units identified in the search process are treated one at a time. That is, each referent will go through the following steps before a new referent is identified in the search process.

3. The switching program initiated two different programs. First, the information identified in the search process is stored for immediate evaluation. Second, a testing program whose function is to evaluate the relevance of the information is evoked.

4. The testing program is broken into a set of linked subprograms. One is designed to test the computational ease of the potential referent identified in the search process. The other subprogram is designed to test the degree to which the potential referent fits the distribution rule for the class of outcomes being examined. Both represent rather complex processes. Our expectation is that evaluation of computational ease or closeness of fit to distribution rules (appropriateness of referent) operates at a fairly crude level. That is, there are not very precise cutoff points for accepting or rejecting a potential referent. Once these subtests have been made, the testing programs are terminated and new switching programs evoked.

5. The switching programs store the newly screened information and initiate the comparison program.

6. The function of the comparison program is to evaluate the individual's outcome-input ratio with the selected referent ratio. One result of this process is a new belief about the degree of equity in the relationship of the ratios. Another result would be feelings of affect. The third consequence of this process would be to terminate the selection and evaluation process or the evoking of a new stimulus event.

This conceptualization presents a very simplified view of the process of social comparison (see fig. 1). We have only identified one cycle of the model: stimulus event → search program → testing program → comparison program → psychological reaction → stimulus event. We assume that the social comparison process is made up of linked sets of these cycles that may be defined by a particular time period or over a series of time periods. The model becomes complex when multiple cycles are linked together.

Another source of complexity in the model is found in the various feedback loops and in the fact that the constraints and programs are not fixed, and they can be modified during the process.

One obvious feedback point occurs in the search process. If the search process cannot find ratios that satisfy the constraints, we would expect two possible options. First, the search can switch from long-term memory to actively collecting information in the individual's

FIGURE 1   Simplified Social Comparison Process Model

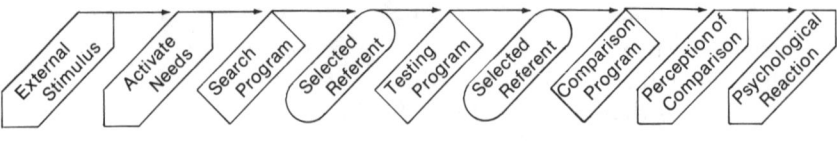

environment (e.g., ask peers). The second option is to modify or relax the constraints. We expect these two options would be tried until a satisfactory outcome-input ratio is identified. If neither option produces a satisfactory ratio, the process will terminate.

A second feedback point would occur in the testing program. Here, if the outcome-input ratio fails to satisfy all the subtests, the search process would be evoked.

Feedback also occurs in the comparison program. Two options are likely. First, if a person identifies outcome-input ratios which provide accurate information (positive instrumentality for need to know), and the information is equitable, the need to know is satisfied and the cycle is terminated. Second, the selected outcome-input ratio might provide accurate information, but the comparison might reveal an inequitable relationship which induces tension, and which might lead to feelings of threatened self-esteem (negative instrumentality for self-esteem). If the need for accurate feedback outweighs the tension derived from the inequitable comparison and from the threats to self-esteem, the comparison point will be accepted and the evaluation process may terminate. Another option is that the search process will be reinitiated to locate other inequitable comparison points. There is some evidence (Patchen, 1961) that people seek inequitable relationships as a bargaining strategy to gain more of the desired outcome at a future time.

If the threats to self-esteem outweigh the need for accurate information, we expect the resulting feelings of tension and conflict will initiate the search for another referent or initiate the testing programs to reevaluate the relevance of the selected referent. In the latter case, characteristics of the comparison referent may be distorted so the referent will fail to meet the criteria in the testing program, or the criteria from the testing program might be modified so that this class of referents is defined as unacceptable (i.e., not relevant).

Application of Framework

The framework just outlined is essentially divided into 4 parts—a set of definitions and a set of 11 assumptions, a delineation of 3 classes of referents used in SCP, and a model which postulates a process by which particular referents are considered relevant and selected. Our basic thesis is that this framework can be generalized to any evaluation processes that occur in the organization. We will focus on some of the major assumptions and certain aspects of the process model as they apply to the evaluation of extrinsic and intrinsic rewards (i.e., outcomes) and to outputs (i.e., performance). It would be too cumbersome in this chapter to examine how each of the 11 assumptions or the complete process model applies to each of the different outcomes and outputs.

To demonstrate the generalizability of the framework, the following questions will be analyzed: To what extent can the object of evaluation be represented in output-input or outcome-input terms? To what extent are referents used in the evaluation, and do they fit into the Other, Self-, System classification? To what extent does the process model describe the evaluation of the different outcomes and outputs?

Organizational Outcomes: Extrinsic
Pay. Much of our discussion thus far has used pay as an example of how evaluation processes occur in organizations. Research on pay indicates that it is evaluated in outcome-input terms (Goodman and Friedman, 1971). Also, there is evidence that individuals use multiple referents that fall into the Other-Self-System category scheme (Goodman, 1974). Although there is no test of the process model, there is some indirect support for the effects of information availability and relevance on referent selection (Goodman, 1974).

Promotion. Since pay and promotion levels are highly correlated (Heneman, 1973), and promotions generally lead to pay increases, promotion or promotion opportunity evaluations must be quite similar to pay evaluations. Like pay, promotion is one of the few well-defined rewards that organizations provide as inducements to their employees. Nevertheless, there has been no research on how promotion opportunities are evaluated.

Translating the evaluation of promotion into outcome-input terms seems straightforward. The individual could compare the level of his promotion or time-to-promotion over input factors such as age, education, and effort. The comparison referent for evaluation could be a person, or the individual could compare his present promotion level over inputs to past promotion level over inputs (Self-referent). He could also compare the time-to-first-promotion to the expected time-to-first-promotion established in the "contract" with his employer (System referent). In terms of the process model, the evaluation of promotion would parallel that for pay. There would be a search process to identify referents. Testing programs would be needed to assess the quality of the information (computational ease), as well as the appropriateness (distribution rules) of the referents. Thus, the evaluation of promotions seems congruent with the process model.

Working Conditions. Although quite different from pay or promotion outcomes, working conditions are another extrinsic reward that can be evaluated with this framework. How do people evaluate or decide whether they are satisfied with their working conditions?

The writer is currently conducting a study of the quality of working life in a coal mine. It might be useful to examine how working conditions are evaluated in this setting. The conditions of the coal mine in terms of dust, cold, water, and ability to stand up seem objectively poorer than those found in most work settings. However, when asked for their evaluation of working conditions, the majority of miners questioned expressed satisfaction. Why did they make this judgment? Although data were not systematically collected on this question, there are some qualitative observations that seem congruent with the process model.

When the miners discussed working conditions, it was in the context of some other variable. Conditions such as the amount of dust or water were evaluated in terms of the type of mine or type of job (input). For example, dust conditions at the face are different from those in the back area of a mine. In other words, working conditions were viewed in the context of other variables, which we would classify as job and environmental inputs. Personal inputs such as age and health were also used in evaluating working conditions. A miner with "black lung" would view dust levels differently from a person without black lung. Therefore, working conditions can be viewed in outcome-input terms.

Do the miners use referents in the evaluation of working conditions? Again, the answer is yes. A common referent was some other mine. "Other," then, in this context, is not a person but perceptions of working conditions in another mine. System referents could also be used in this type of evaluation. That is, it would appear that in the employment contract the employer promises, at least implicitly, certain levels of working conditions for worker participation. This promise is reinforced through federal and state mining-industry safety regulations. The miner could then compare the current working conditions with those expected from the "contract." Self-referents could also be used in the evaluation of working conditions. A miner could compare working conditions in past jobs to the present job. Miners with black lung are likely to evaluate high dust levels negatively, regardless of the type of job or type of mine (inputs). That is, they would have some expected ratio of working conditions to inputs and compare this to their current outcome-input ratio. Of the three classes of referents, Self-referents (e.g., past perceptions of working conditions in other jobs) and Other referents (e.g., perceptions of conditions in other mines) would be the most dominant comparison points for evaluating working conditions. System referents, although possible comparison points, are less likely to be used, since working conditions as outcomes are not likely to be explicit in the contract between employer and employee.

The postulated process model should also describe evaluations of working conditions. Some external event such as a sudden change in conditions could initiate the SCP. The search processes would be the same, although there are probably fewer potential referents relevant for evaluations of working conditions as compared to evaluations of pay. This was especially true with the miners studied. They have lived in isolated rural areas for most of their lives. Most have worked only in mining. This limited opportunity to experience different roles (a structural source of information about referents) greatly constrained the information they had and, hence, the kinds of judgments they could make.

The concepts of computational ease and distribution rules in the testing phase of the model also seem applicable. Our observation is that miners have some general idea about how working conditions should be, given certain characteristics of work (inputs). These rules, or norms, have their origin in the mining community, the union, government regulations, and work experiences. The nature of the distribution rule (determining the appropriateness of the information), however, would be less formalized and less visible as contrasted with pay. Nevertheless, in evaluating working conditions, some crude programs testing computational ease and the distribution rules are probably used. Imbalance between the ratios should lead to tension and dissatisfaction with working conditions. The point is that, although there are differences between evaluating pay, promotion, and working conditions, the general process of evaluation is the same.

Supervisory Outcomes. The supervisor is an important source of outcomes at work. In this context, we are looking at outcomes tied specifically to supervisory behavior such as degree of recognition or supportiveness, rather than rewards such as pay that the supervisor provides in behalf of the company. We know from job attitude literature that workers express satisfaction or dissatisfaction with supervisory behaviors. In other words, supervisory behavior is evaluated by workers. How does this evaluation take place?

Our basic hypothesis is that supervisory behavior evaluations can be represented in outcome-input terms. Outcomes represent the rewards (e.g., recognition) or punishments the supervisor provides to his subordinates. Inputs represent those things the workers contribute to the job.

When the evaluation processes occur we expect a wide range of possible referents. One could compare the present supervisory behavior-input ratio to past supervisory behavior-input ratios (Self-referent). Also, one could observe how one's supervisor treats employees, given the level of the employees' inputs. This ratio (Other referent) could then be compared to one's own supervisory behavior-input ratio. System referents—primarily concerning an expected outcome-input ratio derived from the "contract" between the employer and employee—may also be used, but their frequency of occurrence is probably lower than the other two referent classes. It is possible, but rather unlikely, that an employer would state in the "contract" what the supervisor's behavior should be.

The process model, including the stimulus event, search, testing, and comparison programs, seems applicable to the evaluation of supervisory behaviors. A stimulus even such as a new superior might initiate the evaluation process. The search process, following the rules identified in the original process model description, proceeds in a serial manner, with one object considered at a time, and constraints (e.g., only consider supervisors in this company) applied to determine which referents are selected. During the testing phase, distribution rules specifying how supervisory behaviors should be related to subordinate inputs are applied. One form of a distribution rule, for example, may be that a boss should not "chew out" a subordinate in front of the subordinate's peers. During the evaluation process, this and other rules would be applied to the referents generated during the search process. If the referents fit the classes of behavior specified by the distribution rules, they are passed on to the comparison program. If the referents do not fit, the search process would be reinitiated.

Imbalance in the supervisory behavior-input model can be expected to lead to tension and dissatisfaction. Imbalance could be in the form of profitable (i.e., I get more than I should from my boss) or unprofitable inequity. In the case of unprofitable inequity, we would expect the subordinate either to lower his inputs or to increase his outcomes. Withdrawing physically or psychologically would represent other reactions to tension.

Work Group and Organization Rewards. As a supervisor can be a source of rewards, so can one's work group or the organization itself. When people evaluate their well-being in a group or in the organization, they consider outcomes received from their participation in the group or organization relative to their contributions or inputs. Group or organization functioning is partly based on this exchange between outcomes and inputs. In analyzing supervisory behavior outcomes, we argued that the assumptions and structure of the process model are congruent with the way people evaluate supervisory behavior outcomes. There is no reason to believe these assumptions or the model would not apply to the evaluation of work group outcomes or general outcomes from the organization. The evaluation of supervisory behavior, work group, and organizational outcomes all follow the pattern of examining the exchange of outcomes and inputs relevant to some other outcome-input ratio.

Organizational Outcomes: Intrinsic

One of the major interests in motivational research on organizations is intrinsic motivation and its relationship to extrinsic motivation (Staw, 1974; Lepper, M., and Greene, D., 1975). An interesting test of our framework is to see how it applies to evaluating intrinsic outcomes.

Intrinsic outcomes are positive or negative rewards derived from performing a particular activity. The outcomes are not mediated by an outside source but inherent in the activity itself. Activities which provide opportunities for accomplishment, freedom, variety, responsibility, and exploration enhance intrinsic motivation.

Assuming that people evaluate the intrinsic rewards offered at work, how does the process differ from evaluating pay? Our hypothesis is that intrinsic rewards are evaluated according to the same process as extrinsic rewards, although some of the specific substantive dimensions in the model receive different weights. The major difference between these two rewards is the mediating source (internal or external). However, there is no reason to believe that this difference would affect the general parameters of the comparison model we have presented.

The following example highlights the similarities between evaluating extrinsic and intrinsic rewards. Mr. A's job has been successfully enriched. Mr. A reports he has greater feelings of accomplishment in his job and more satisfaction with the level of accomplishment. How does Mr. A make these judgments? First, evaluation of accomplishment must be made in the context of a particular job and the inputs contributed by Mr. A. Second, any judgment about levels of accomplishment must be made relative to some other referent. There are no objective ways to measure increasing levels of accomplishment. Although all three categories—Other, Self-, and System—could be selected as referents, we hypothesize that Self-referents would more likely be selected because intrinsic rewards, such as accomplishment, are not visible. Rather, they are experienced, and it is difficult to evaluate the degree of intrinsic rewards experienced by others. Therefore, outcomes such as accomplishment are more likely to be compared to Self-referents such as levels of accomplishment in past jobs or internal standards of how much accomplishment one should experience. Nevertheless, Other or System referents could also be used. A co-worker might express feelings of accomplishment which could be used as a comparison point (Other referent), or the organization could promise the worker the opportunity to work on achievement-oriented jobs (System referent).

In the process model, the search process should be the same for intrinsic outcomes, although the population of potential referents is much more limited than, for example, in the case of pay. This is again because intrinsic outcomes are internal, and it is difficult to learn about those experienced by others. As hypothesized, most potential referents would be Self-referents about feelings of accomplishment in past jobs.

In the test subprogram, assessing computational ease should be generalizable across all comparisons. If the information is unreliable or invalid, it will be rejected whether it concerns intrinsic or extrinsic rewards. Also, the testing of distribution rules can be applied to intrinsic rewards. For example, if an individual moves to a higher-level job, the general expectation (distribution rule) is that the job, with its greater stress and responsibility, will provide greater opportunities for accomplishment. If an individual promoted to a higher-level job experiences greater responsibilities (inputs), but no stronger feelings of accomplishment, we would say that comparison is in imbalance—

current outcome-input ratio is less than the previous outcome-input ratio. In this example, imbalance should lead to feelings of dissatisfaction and tension, as is the case with extrinsic rewards. Similarly, the level of tension should lead to different conflict-resolution strategies.

At the present time, there is no data to substantiate the above assumptions about evaluation of intrinsic rewards. We have argued that the processes of evaluating objects are quite general and that the mediating source, which is the major difference between intrinsic and extrinsic rewards, does not warrant a separate process model even though there are differences in dimensions used in the model and their characteristics. For example, availability of information and computational ease probably explain why it is easier to use Self-referents rather than Other or System referents in evaluating intrinsic rewards. It is often difficult to know what intrinsic rewards another individual received or how to translate these into some common scale. In addition, distribution rules for intrinsic rewards may be less visible than for extrinsic rewards. Extrinsic rewards such as pay are often tied to formal structures in the organization (i.e., pay system), and expectations about appropriate behavior would probably develop around these structures. Since intrinsic rewards are specific to a particular individual experience, it probably is more difficult for visible and widely held norms to develop about appropriate relationships between intrinsic rewards and inputs. Therefore, we would expect greater variability among individuals in the SCP of intrinsic rewards.

Organizational Outputs. Performance is another object that is subject to evaluation in an organizational context. Am I a good manager? Did I have a good year in sales? Am I a good teacher? All these questions concern the evaluation of performance from the viewpoint of the individual performer. In this context (as opposed to performance evaluation by a superior), it is quite similar to a person's evaluation of his outcomes.

To evaluate one's performance, an output-input ratio is used. Adding information on inputs provides a better context in which to evaluate outputs. For example, information that salesman A made his quota (output) is different from the information that he made his quota and had a difficult territory (input). Similarly, knowing that salesman A with the difficult territory made his quota and all other salesmen made their quotas provides a basis for evaluation that would be different from knowing only that Mr. A made his quota. The point is that both the individual's output-input ratio and another ratio are necessary to evaluate a person's output.

It is possible in evaluating performance to use Other, Self-, and

System referents. Another salesman's performance can be used as a referent in evaluating salesman A's performance, or past performance-input ratios also can be compared (Self-referent). Similarly, ratios can be derived from a System class. For example, an accounting firm might tell its new hires that they should bring in X amount of billings after five years. This is an output-input ratio that can be used for evaluating individual performance.

In the process model, search processes would generate a referent, while testing programs would examine issues such as computational ease and performance rules, which specify the expected relationships between inputs and outputs. If the particular referent contains information which falls into the behavior delineated by the testing program, the referent is switched to the comparison program. Imbalance between output-input ratios determined by the comparison program has two consequences. As in the case of underpayment, where negative feelings derived from violations of equity were experienced, "underperformance" imbalance produces tension from threats to self-esteem. Second, in the case of "overperformance," the imbalance does not lead to tension as is characteristic of overpayment. One simply has performed better than expected and positive feelings should result.

This discussion deals with performance only in its most general sense. Performance can vary in terms of its specificity and operationality (e.g., selling X units vs. the quality of a manager's decisions). Similarly, there are other outputs—such as creativity, effort, and leadership—which can be evaluated. Again our basic thesis is that the evaluation would be the same process. The more specific and operational the outputs, the quicker the SCP and the more stable the results of the process over time.

Organizational Beliefs

Organizations present individuals with complex sets of cues. To operate within the organization, the individual reduces these cues into a simplified representation of the organization, one part of which comprises beliefs about the organization. Two types of beliefs—one about objects and one about the relationship between objects—are pertinent to this discussion. The statement that people trust each other in an organization is an example of a belief about objects. The statement that the organization rewards people on the basis of seniority is a belief about the relationship between objects. How are these beliefs developed or modified? Although there are many processes that contribute to the development of these beliefs, SCP as discussed here, represents one important process.

An individual can develop beliefs about the organization itself (as an "object") through SCP-type evaluations. For example, an individual who believes that there is a high degree of trust and cooperation within his organization has possibly derived this belief from comparing the present degree of trust in the organization to his perceptions of trust levels in other organizations he has worked in (Other referent). This comparison using Other referents can be made on two levels. First, the individual can simply compare the level of trust in one organization versus another. Second, the individual can compare levels of trust in the context of the organizational setting. For example, the perceived level of trust in company A may be greater than in B, but the organizational context of A indicates that the trust level should be higher. Company A in this example, might be a small family business, while B might be a large, impersonally run organization. In this case, beliefs are evaluated in the context of organizational characteristics (inputs), and thus parallel our earlier discussion of evaluations of outcomes-inputs or outputs-inputs.

In the process model many of the same routines should apply to evaluating the organization in terms of degrees of trust. It would be necessary to search for other referent points (i.e., organizational situations where trust levels are known). The testing program would determine the computational ease of the comparison. Distribution rules "per se" would probably not be evoked in such a comparison. There is no issue of equity or fair exchange in evaluation of beliefs about the organization. However, there are probably some general beliefs linking organizational factors (e.g., size of firm) with expected levels of trust. The comparison process of our model would seem applicable to evaluating levels of trust between two organizations.

Beliefs about the relationship between objects (e.g., promotion and educational training) are affected by many processes. Various forms of communication, persuasion, and reinforcement contribute to the development of these beliefs (cf. Goodman and Moore, 1976). Another means of acquiring these beliefs is by observing others' behaviors and forming inferences about the relationships between objects in question. For example, in one company in which this author conducted research, managers reported that getting an M.B.A. from a certain university was the only path for promotion. Respondents reported that they arrived at this belief by observing who had been promoted and making an inference about the relevant instrumental behaviors for promotion. At first this seems an example of social learning and modeling research such as conducted by Bandura (1969) and others (Berger, 1975). An important aspect in this learning process, however, is determining appropriate models or referents to select. In this particular context, it would seem that the process by which models or, in our terminology, referents are selected is critical to the more general process of learning from observing others' behaviors. It is our assumption that the social comparison model presented in this chapter could be used to identify the types of models that are selected during social learning processes. The process of selecting appropriate models in the social learning paradigm is the same process that we have suggested operates in the evaluation of outputs or outcomes.

Nonorganizational Objects

Although the objective of this chapter has been to examine social comparison processes in an organizational context, the general framework postulated here to describe evaluations of outcomes or outputs should apply to either organizational or nonorganizational contexts.

In our analysis of extrinsic outcomes, the primary setting was an exchange relationship. An individual contributed certain inputs and received certain outcomes. The individual's evaluation of outcomes from his superior should follow the same process as the evaluation of outcomes from his spouse or friends. Inputs such as skills, effort, and status are exchanged for outcomes such as recognition or supportiveness. A person's evaluation of outcomes from his work group should also have the same properties as his evaluation of outcomes from social or community type groups. The basic point, then, is that extrinsic rewards in either organizational or nonorganizational settings have the same general properties. This generalization should also apply to intrinsic rewards; evaluating intrinsic rewards at work versus those outside of work (e.g., a hobby) is not an inherently different process.

In analyzing outputs, an individual compares a current output-input ratio with referent ratios. In nonorganizational life there are many tasks to be performed and, accordingly, many potential outputs. For example, how does a person evaluate his driving ability? First, there has to be some stimulus to evoke consideration of this issue and sufficient motivational force to sustain the comparison. The output of driving must be examined in terms of inputs (e.g., number of miles driven, or driving experience). To make the evaluation, it is necessary to identify a referent. Therefore, a search process following the description outlined in the process model would be initiated. The identified referent would be tested using programs assessing computational ease and congruence with the performance rules. An example of a performance rule might be the number of miles driven related to the number of accidents. Referents containing this information would more likely be accepted and passed on to the comparison program which would, in turn, provide information on one's driving ability relative to the selected referent ratio and would result in feelings of satisfaction or dissatisfaction.

There are many other objects outside of the organizational context in which social comparisons are important. One pervasive activity is evaluating the purchase of goods and services. This evaluation can be expected to follow the same processes outlined in this chapter. A purchase can be described as providing certain inputs (e.g., money) for certain outcomes (e.g., the utility of the product). To evaluate a purchase, one can compare this outcome-input ratio with another outcome-input ratio. For example, in the context of a car, one can evaluate present car purchases to past car purchases (Self-referent) or to other individuals' purchases (Other referent). The same processes of search, testing, and comparing would seem relevant to evaluating purchases.

Conclusion

The objective of this chapter is to develop a framework for explaining and predicting the nature of social comparison processes in organizations. A related objective is to develop a framework that will be generalizable over a broad class of organizational outcomes and outputs. Our basic contention is that evaluations of objects such as rewards and performance are a pervasive form of behavior in organizations, yet there is little conceptual or empirical research dealing with these processes.

Our approach has been addressed to a number of issues. First, to identify the types of referents people use in evaluations. The Other, Self-, and System typology was presented as a generalizable set of categories which people use in evaluating outcomes and outputs. It was also noted in our discussion that the relative importance of these categories would differ across different objects (e.g., extrinsic vs. intrinsic outcomes). A second focus was to identify major variables (e.g., availability of information, instrumentality of referents) which affect the selection of referents. Failure to develop a framework to predict the selection of referents has been an important problem in the SCP literature. Third, we summarized the major variables in our framework into a process model. The functions of the process model are to interrelate the concepts in the model and to describe how people make comparisons between their own outcomes and inputs and others' outcomes and inputs. Finally, we applied the framework to a wide range of objects that could be evaluated in an organizational context, noting that some substantive dimensions in the model receive different weights for different objects.

The proposed framework is theoretical in nature and identifies a wide range of potential research projects. An immediate and significant task is to test these aspects of the framework.

One line of research could test the generalizability of the Other, Self-, and System concepts. To what extent can these concepts be applied to such diverse outcomes as working conditions and promotion? To what extent can we predict the relative importance of these categories over different types of outcomes (e.g., intrinsic vs. extrinsic)?

Another avenue of research concerns the process model itself. One approach might be to develop an actual simulation model from the proposed process model. Another level of research would focus on the micro assumptions of this process model. For example, we know very little about the length of an evaluation episode; the characteristics of the constraints in the search process are largely unknown; we know little about the relationship between testing programs for computational ease and distribution rules—which program goes first? How do they interact? The comparison program is based on individuals making estimates of outcomes to inputs. How do people consider proportions or ratios? In what sense can people combine dissimilar inputs? The attractive feature of the process model is that it forces us to think of the social comparison process in fairly specific terms and, thus, it generates a lot of testable assumptions and hypotheses.

Empirical testing of the proposed framework can have significant consequences for our knowledge of social comparison processes in organizations and related attitudes and beliefs. Although there have been thousands of studies on job attitudes and beliefs, we really know very little about these concepts. Much of the research has focused on measurement and on the relationship between job attitudes and other behaviors (e.g., absenteeism). Very little attention has been given to the process by which these attitudes or beliefs develop, or to their structure. It is our hypothesis that the more we can understand the process by which attitudes and beliefs about organizational objects are formed, the better can managers make decisions about these objects. For example, as our framework becomes more refined through empirical testing, we can better predict the consequences of managerial decisions about modifying extrinsic or intrinsic rewards. This should substantially contribute to our knowledge about designing organizational systems.

Empirical testing of the framework can also have significant consequences for our knowledge about social comparison processes in nonorganizational settings. Indeed, one of the objectives of this analysis has been to state a generalizable model which would deal with social comparison processes in organizational and nonorganizational settings. Although we have primarily applied the model in an organizational context, the framework is designed to deal with some of the unresolved issues of social comparison theory and to deal with social evaluation processes in nonorganizational settings.

References

Adams, S. J. Inequity in social exchange. In L. Berkowitz (ed.), *Advances in Experimental Social Psychology,* New York: Academic Press, 1965.

Appley, M. *Adaption Level Theory.* New York: Academic Press, 1971.

Arrowood, A., and Friend, R. Other factors determining the choice of comparison other. *Journal of Experimental Social Psychology,* 1969, *5,* 233-39.

Bandura, A. *Principles of Behavior Modification.* New York: Holt Rinehart and Winston, 1969.

Berger, J., Zelditch, M., Anderson, B., and Cohen B. Structural aspects of distributive justice: A status value formulation, in J. Berger, M. Zelditch, and B. Anderson (eds.), *Sociological Theories in Progress,* vol. 2, Boston: Houghton Mifflin, 1972.

Berger, S. Social comparison, modeling and perseverance, unpublished manuscript. University of Massachusetts, Amherst, Massachusetts, 1975.

Blau, P. *Exchange and Power in Social Life.* New York: Wiley, 1964.

Cook, K. Expectations, evaluations and equity. *American Sociological Review,* 1975, *40,* 372-88.

Darley, J., and Aronson, E. Self-evaluation vs. direct anxiety reduction as determinants of fear affiliation relationship. *Journal of Experimental Social Psychology,* supp. 1, 1966, 55-65.

Dawes, R. M. Shallow Psychology, in J. S. Carroll and J. W. Payne (eds.), *Cognition and Social Behavior,* Hillsdale, N. J.: Lawrence Erlbaum Associates, (in press).

Festinger, L. A theory of social comparison. *Human Relations,* 1954, *7,* 117-40.

Goodman, P. Measurement of an individual's organizational map. *Administrative Science Quarterly,* 1968, *13,* 246-65.

―――. "An Examination of Referents Used in the Evaluation of Pay," *Organizational Behavior and Human Performance,* 1974, *12,* 170-95.

Goodman, P., and Friedman, A. An examination of Adam's theory of inequity. *Administrative Science Quarterly,* 1971, *16,* 271-88.

Goodman, P., and Moore, B. Factors affecting the acquisition of beliefs about a new reward system. *Human Relations,* 1976, *29,* 571-88.

Helson, H. *Adaptation-Level Theory.* New York: Harper and Row, 1964.

Heneman, H. Impact of performance on managerial pay levels and pay changes. *Journal of Applied Psychology,* 1973, *58,* 128-30.

Homans, G. C. *Social Behavior.* New York: Harcourt Brace, 1961.

Jaques, E. *Measurement of Responsibility.* London: Tavistock, 1965.

Kelley, H. Two functions of reference groups, in G. E. Swanson, T. M. Newcomb, and E. L. Hartley (eds.), *Readings in Social Psychology,* New York: Holt, 1952.

Lepper, M., and Greene, D. Turning play into work: Effects of adult surveillance and extrinsic rewards on children's intrinsic motivation. *Journal of Personality and Social Psychology,* 1975, *31*, 479-86.

Merton, R. *Social Theory and Social Structure.* Glencoe, Illinois: Free Press. 1957.

Newell, A., and Simon, H. *Human Problem Solving.* New York: Prentice-Hall, 1972.

Patchen, M. *The Choice of Wage Comparisons.* Englewood Cliffs, N. J.: Prentice-Hall, 1961.

Pennings, J., and Goodman, P., Toward a framework of organizational effectiveness. Paper for a workshop on Organizational Effectiveness, Graduate School of Industrial Administration, Carnegie-Mellon University, Pittsburgh, Pa. 15213, June 28-29, 1976.

Pettigrew, T. Social evaluation theory: Contingencies and applications, in M. R. Jones (ed.), *Nebraska Symposium on Motivation,* Lincoln, Neb.: University of Nebraska Press, 1967, *15*, 241-311.

Pritchard, R. Equity theory: A review and critique, *Organizational Behavior and Human Performance,* 1969, *4*, 176-211.

Pritchard, R., Jorgenson, D., and Dunnette, M. The effects of perception of equity and inequity on worker performance and satisfaction, *Journal of Applied Psychology,* 1972, *56*, 75-94.

Smith, P., Kendall, L., and Hulin, C. *The Measurement of Satisfaction in Work and Retirement.* Chicago: Rand McNally, 1969.

Staw, B., *Intrinsic and Extrinsic Motivation.* General Learning Press, 1974.

Thibaut, J., and Kelley, H. *The Social Psychology of Groups.* New York: Wiley, 1959.

Thornton, D., and Arrowood, A. Self-evaluation, self-enhancement and the locus of social comparison. *Journal of Experimental Social Psychology,* supp. 1, 1966, 40-48.

Walster, E., Bersheid, E., and Walster, G. New directions in equity research. *Journal of Personality and Social Psychology,* 1973, *25*, 151-76.

Wheeler, L., Motivation as a determinant of upward comparison. *Journal of Experimental Social Psychology,* supp. 1, 1966, 27-31.

Wheeler, L., Shaver, K., Jones, R., Goethals, G., Cooper, J., Robinson, J., Gruder, C., and Butzine, K. Factors determining choices of a comparison other. *Journal of Experimental Social Psychology,* 1969, *5*, 219-32.

Yuchtman, E., Reward distribution and work-role attractiveness in the kibbutz—Reflections on equity theory, *American Sociological Review,* 1972, *37*, 581-95.

Zuckerman, M. A comment on the equity formula by Walster, Berscheid, and Walster (1973). *Representative Research in Social Psychology,* 1975, *6*, 63-67.

Chapter Four

Interpersonal Attraction and Techniques of Ingratiation in Organizational Settings

Camille B. Wortman

Joan A. W. Linsenmeier

This chapter is about ingratiation strategies—strategies designed to enhance one's interpersonal attractiveness—and how they affect organizational behavior. The importance of enhancing one's attractiveness in organizational settings is implicit in the writings of many past theorists. For example, Schein (1970) has suggested that it is clearly to a supervisor's advantage to consider the impression he is creating among his workers:

> If workers feel that their boss does not act too officious, does not interfere too much with social relationships built up on the job, and does not demand production in an impersonal and callous way, they will not only feel better but will *work more effectively* (p. 42).

Sofer (1970) and Downs (1967) have implied that subordinates should make every effort to impress their supervisors. Both writers have pointed out that the subordinate's chances for advancement are heavily dependent on how his immediate supervisor evaluates him. Since

---

Work on this chapter was supported by a grant from the National Science Foundation (SOC75-14669) to the first author.

objective evidence of a subordinate's effectiveness is often lacking, the senior management making promotion decisions "will often have to rely mainly on the subjective, personal judgments of the man's present and recently past immediate work supervisors" (Sofer, 1970, p. 323). As we will show later, a supervisor's evaluation of a subordinate's work can be strongly influenced by whether he likes or dislikes the subordinate. There is also evidence that liking can be managed through the use of ingratiation tactics.

Formally, we can define ingratiation as a class of strategic behaviors employed by a person to make himself more attractive to another. Ingratiating actions are usually directed toward an objective that is not made explicit by the parties involved. The ingratiator tries to behave as though the issue at hand were his only concern, when in fact he is also interested in enhancing himself in the target person's eyes. An ingratiator may seek attraction because he is personally gratified by liking and approval from others, or he may value attraction or positive evaluation not as an end in itself, but because it is instrumental in achieving other goals.

Understanding how people attempt to make themselves more attractive to others provides insight into such areas as organizational advancement and survival, influence processes within the organization, alteration of power relationships, and organizational change. Some authors have recommended that individuals make conscious efforts to impress their co-workers. For example, Whyte (1955) has said, "An executive cannot have it said about him that he is an authoritarian; he must, above all, be permissive. Or, as is more customary, make a good show of it" (p. 172). On the basis of interviews with contemporary executives, Martin and Sims (1956) have suggested that executives keep the following in mind: "Concessions . . . should be more apparent than real" (p. 30). . . . The man who constantly gives the impression of knowing what he is doing—even if he does not—is using his power and increasing it at the same time" (p. 34). Other investigators (see, e.g., Mills, 1962; Sofer, 1970) have implied that ingratiation tactics are used quite frequently. According to Sofer, "It is said that the would-be successful executive learns when to simulate enthusiasm, compassion, interest, concern, modesty, confidence and mastery, when to smile, with whom to laugh, and how intimate or friendly he can be with others. If the operation succeeds he will have fabricated a personality in harmony with his environment" (p. 61).

Though interpersonal attraction and ingratiation are topics that have received much attention from social psychologists (see Jones and Wortman, 1973, for a review of the literature), systematic study of ingratiation tactics within organizational settings has been rare. Perhaps it is felt that there is something shady or illicit about ingratiation, and that it therefore does not deserve the attention of organizational theorists. However, we would agree with Martin and Sims (1956) that

> . . . it is neither immoral nor cynical to recognize and describe the actual daily practices of power. After all, sweeping them under the rug—making believe that they are not actually part of the executive's activity—does not cause them to vanish. . . . They exist; therefore we had better take a look at them and see what they are really like (p. 36).

Regardless of the setting in which he is operating, the ingratiator's task is primarily one of manipulating the attributions made by the target person he is trying to impress. For example, suppose a manager compliments a peer on the efficiency of his office. The co-worker might make a number of attributions about this comment. First, he may decide that the compliment was offered not because his colleague really meant it, but because he had an ulterior motive (e.g., "He's just trying to be nice to me so I'll help him with those production reports this weekend."). In our opinion, attribution of ulterior motivation or manipulative intentions is likely to result in a decrease in liking rather than an increase. A second attribution that the recipient of a compliment may make is that his co-worker complimented him because he is the kind of person who is almost always positive toward others. We feel that if a person has a reputation for making positive comments in almost all circumstances, he is unlikely to gain in interpersonal attractiveness when such a comment is made.

A third attribution that the target person might make is that his colleague's response was triggered by situational demands or pressures. In many situations, it is probably normative to offer a compliment. When a colleague has just been promoted, for example, it may be normative to offer congratualtions. If an associate has gone to considerable lengths to redecorate his office, it may be normative to comment on how nice it looks. If a person fails to deliver a compliment in such a setting, he will probably suffer a decrease in interpersonal attractiveness. At the very least, his behavior will signify that he is lacking in the social graces; at most, his silence will be understood to imply a negative evaluation of the target person. But complimenting a person in such a setting is probably regarded as a simple social courtesy, and therefore may not increase one's attractiveness very much.

A fourth attribution that the recipient of the compliment might make is that his co-worker may not have been completely honest when he delivered the compliment, but that his motivation was benign (e.g., "He can see that I'm worried about how I'm doing on this job, and he's just trying to be nice"). Most people appreciate the attempts of others to consider their feelings and make them feel more comfortable. Thus, an attribution to this cause will probably result in some increased attractiveness.

Finally, a person who is complimented on the job might conclude that his co-worker really meant what he said. We feel that people who offer their compliment in such a way that others believe they are sincere, and thereby convey their "genuine high regard" for the target person, will be very successful in eliciting interpersonal attraction.

Of course, we believe that the target person's attributions will strongly influence his reaction to the would-be ingratiator, regardless of the particular tactic selected by the ingratiator. In addition to compliments, such tactics as positive self-presentation, opinion conformity, and even rendering favors can easily elicit a wide variety of attributions. Unfortunately for the potential ingratiator, attributions of manipulative intentions are especially likely in those settings in which he has the most to gain by making a good impression on the target person.

In this chapter we will first discuss the tactics that might be employed to enhance one's interpersonal attractiveness in organizational settings. The only determinant of attractiveness that has generated much research by investigators in the field of organizational behavior has been level of performance or competence. Numerous studies have suggested that a person can make himself more attractive to his co-workers by performing well on a job, and these studies will be discussed briefly. Some possible exceptions to this statement, as well as some suggestions for broadening future research on the relationship between performance and attraction, will also be considered. We will then go on to discuss the tactics of a more social nature that might be employed to increase one's interpersonal attraction: other-enhancement, opinion conformity, rendering favors, and self-presentation.

In discussing these tactics, two kinds of information are examined. First, we describe the results of experiments in which subjects have been exposed to a stimulus person engaged in various attraction-seeking tactics, and have been asked to indicate their feelings toward him. These studies provide information about the effectiveness of various tactics in eliciting interpersonal attraction. Second, we describe studies in which subjects have been placed in a setting where it was to their advantage to make themselves as attractive as possible, and where their behavior was compared with that of subjects who had nothing to gain by impressing a target person. These studies provide information about the naïve psychology of ingratiation—what people think will make them attractive to others, and what tactics they employ in various settings. Throughout our discussion, we keep in mind that the effectiveness of the various tactics, as well as the inclination to use them, may depend on such factors as the stage in one's career, or the relative status of the parties involved.

The chapter concludes with a discussion of some possible effects of ingratiating overtures. We argue that these tactics have pervasive effects on both the target person who receives them, and on the ingratiator himself. The use of these tactics is characterized by a number of dilemmas for all parties involved, and may be expected to have some rather serious implications for the quality of interpersonal relationships in organizational settings.

Tactics of Ingratiation

Good Performance

A number of studies suggest that one way that a person can impress others in his organization is by maintaining a high level of performance at his job. These studies indicate that a person who performs well will not only be viewed as more competent, but will also be better liked than a person who performs less well.

Evaluations of Co-workers. In a laboratory study conducted by Staw (1975), groups of undergraduate business students worked on a task which involved estimating the values of certain parameters of a company's performance. Some groups were randomly told that their estimates were quite accurate, while others were told that their answers were far from correct. After learning of their group's performance, subjects were questioned about their perceptions of and attitudes toward the group. Individuals randomly assigned to high-performance groups rated their groups as more cohesive and enjoyed working with their teammates to a greater extent than did those assigned to low-performance groups. Subjects in the high-performance groups also tended to indicate greater liking for their teammates than did low-performance subjects, although this difference fell short of statistical significance. Prior to Staw's experiment, many correlational studies were interpreted as evidence that group cohesion and liking cause high performance. Staw's results may occur as a consequence of group performance a well.

In Staw's (1975) experiment, however, it is quite difficult to tell whether subjects responded more positively to their co-workers in the high-performance condition because their co-workers had done well, or because they themselves had done well. Perhaps subjects' good feelings about their own performance generalized to their feelings about the others on their team. Another possibility is that people respond favorably to good performers if they have performed well, but are threatened by indications of competence in others if their own performance level has been poor. Although the research on this point is not entirely consistent (see, e.g., Mettee and Riskind, 1974; Senn, 1971) most of the experiments to date have suggested that people prefer competent or well-performing others regardless of their own level of performance. In a laboratory study by Fromkin, Klimoski, and Flanagan (1972), for example, subjects worked in three-person groups and were led to perform either well or poorly. A newcomer was then added to the group; the newcomer was described as either highly competent or relatively incompetent to do the task the group was working on. The subjects continued performance for a while with the newcomer. In order to avoid confounding newcomer competence with group performance, however, they received no information about their performance after the newcomer joined their group. Ultimately, subjects were asked to rate the newcomer on a number of scales. Interestingly, high-competent newcomers were not only judged to be more competent than low-competent newcomers, but were judged to be more intelligent, more persuasive, more likeable, and tended to be viewed as more interesting, more pleasant, and more similar in attitudes. These findings emerged both for subjects who had been performing well when the newcomer joined, and for subjects who had been performing poorly.

Evaluations of Subordinates. An individual may be dependent not only on those at his own level in the hierarchy, but also on those individuals who report to him. Evaluations of a department manager by higher management are linked to the performance of those who work in his department. If their performance level is high, the department manager is more likely to receive promotions and raises, to be thought highly of by his colleagues, and to view himself as successful. Thus it is to be expected that a manager will prefer subordinates who do their job well. Several studies have demonstrated that this is indeed the case. For example, Wall and Adams (1974) found that subjects playing the part of sales director evaluated their salesman more favorably if they believed that the salesman had performed effectively. The manipulation of effectiveness affected not only subjects' evaluations of the salesman's performance, but also their evaluations of the salesman as a person, the amount of autonomy they granted him, and the degree to which they trusted him. Additional evidence that people will react more favorably to subordinates who perform their jobs well comes from studies by Lowin and Craig (1968) and Farris and Lim (1969).

Evaluations of Superiors. Bachman (1968) found that faculty members reported greater satisfaction with faculty deans who had more influence on the policies and actions of their schools than with those who had less. This research implies that subordinates will prefer superiors who can exert influence on the higher levels of management. Such superiors are probably better liked because they are generally more successful in securing benefits for their subordinates.

Unfortunately, few experiments have explored how subordinates evaluate their superiors as a function of various performance characteristics. There is some indication from social psychological experiments, however, that superiors should attempt to convey to workers that they are approachable as well as highly competent. These studies will be discussed in more detail in the section on self-presentation.

Conclusions. While it is not surprising that competent workers are liked better than less competent ones, it is interesting that a worker's performance affects others' impressions of him on a wide variety of dimensions. A person who is very motivated to have others like him or think well of him may think that the best way of assuring this outcome is to act friendly to those around him. He may not realize that attributions of friendliness and pleasantness may be free byproducts if he is judged as highly competent or a good performer by others.

Since it is obviously very important for a worker to have his colleagues evaluate his performance favorably, the following question comes to mind: In a complex organizational setting, how do people decide when a subordinate is performing well and when he is performing poorly? We have already mentioned that the criteria applied are often likely to be subjective. Could the clever subordinate use some of the ingratiation tactics to be discussed later, such as flattering the supervisor or conforming to his opinions, to enhance the supervisor's evaluation of his performance? Suppose a subordinate was able to elicit attraction from a superior. Would a superior who liked a worker evaluate his performance differently than one who did not?

A laboratory experiment by Regan, Straus, and Fazio (1974) has addressed this question, and provides good evidence that attractiveness does affect the evaluation of one's performance on a skill task. Subjects were induced to interact with a confederate of the experimenter. This interaction was prearranged so that half of the subjects would like the confederate, and half would dislike her. In the "like" condition, the subject observed the confederate behave in a very pleasant manner, and received information that the confederate held attitudes that were very similar to her own. In the "dislike" condition, subjects observed the confederate behave rather rudely, and received information that the confederate's attitudes were quite different from hers. Subjects then watched the confederate play a game requiring skill. For half of the subjects, the confederate performed objectively well; for the remaining subjects, her performance was relatively poor. Subjects in the like condition evaluated the confederate as more skillful than did subjects in the dislike condition, regardless of the confederate's objective level of skill. Thus, it seems that if a person can get his co-workers to like him, they may judge his performance to be better than it really is. A study by Kipnis and Vanderveer (1971) has suggested that flattering one's supervisor can tend to increase one's attractiveness, and also one's performance ratings.

Some Possibilities for Future Research. Are there exceptions to the general rule that a person can make himself attractive to others by performing at a high level? Are there conditions under which people react negatively to those who perform well? Are there circumstances when poor performance does not elicit negative reactions?

One factor that has received little investigation, but that may affect reactions to different performance levels, is the attribution of causality that the evaluator makes for a person's performance. A coworker or subordinate who performs well because of high ability may be judged differently than one who performs well because of high motivation. Of course, these parameters of performance can combine in different ways to create dilemmas for those evaluating performance. How should a superior evaluate a subordinate who is able to perform his job well but clearly isn't trying? Or an employee who is working very hard, but who may have less than average ability?

In addition to assessments about a worker's ability and motivation, judgments concerning one's *reasons* for good performance may affect others' evaluations of that performance. The performance of a superior who works hard and drives himself because of his own need for power may be judged differently by his subordinates than that of a superior who works hard because he is dedicated to the company.

Another factor that may influence a superior's judgments of a subordinate's performance is whether the subordinate has followed the superior's advice, directives, and recommendations. In the laboratory experiment by Wall and Adams (1974) mentioned earlier, subjects were led to believe they were supervising a salesman, and were told to make a recommendation about how the salesman should proceed with his job. Subjects then received false feedback that the salesman either had or had not followed their recommendation, and either had increased the resources of the organization or had decreased them. Subjects were then asked to evaluate the performance of the salesman. When the salesman was successful in increasing the resources of the firm, his performance tended to be rated better if he had followed the supervisor's recommendations than if he had not. Salesmen who decreased the resources of the firm were rated quite negatively regardless of whether they had followed the supervisor's directive. These results suggest that a subordinate will be rated more highly if he can perform well while using the supervisor's recommendations. Perhaps more important, they imply that if a subordinate follows a supervisor's recommendations and fails, it is the subordinate who will get most of the blame for the failure.

In past research studies, the range of performance that subjects were exposed to has been rather limited. It would be interesting to know whether judgments of the quality of one's performance are affected as the quantity of work increases to a very high level. In some settings, turning out an extraordinary amount of work may elicit negative reactions. In academic settings, for example, people who publish 20 articles per year may inspire comments by their colleagues that their work must be of low quality, or that they must manipulate and exploit others to accomplish so much. Perhaps the worker who produces a great quantity of excellent work either through sheer brilliance, incredibly hard work, or a combination of the two, is actually doing himself a disservice.

The tendency of less productive individuals to draw negative inferences about their more productive colleagues may occur because they find their colleagues' superior performance threatening. It would be worthwhile to delineate the conditions under which we are especially likely to be threatened by others' high performance and, hence, react negatively (cf. Mettee and Riskind, 1974). Attention to these factors should help us determine the conditions under which the relationship between high performance and attraction does not hold.

Other-Enhancement

One tactic that an ingratiator may use to make himself more attractive to a target person is to express a favorable evaluation of the target person. He may emphasize the target person's positive qualities, while calling little attention to his more negative attributes, or he may go so far as to distort reality by exaggerating the target person's strengths and virtues. The intent of these communications is to lead the target person to believe that the ingratiator admires and likes him. The effectiveness of such communications as ingratiation tactics seems to stem from the fact that when a person perceives that another is favorably disposed towards him, he tends to like that other individual in return.

The premise that liking tends to be reciprocated was put forth by Heider (1958, p. 205), who maintained that people have a preference for balanced states and that a dyad will be unbalanced if one person likes the other, but is disliked by him. Hence, if a person perceives that another likes him, he will feel uncomfortable unless he likes the other person as well. To reduce this discomfort, he will come to like the other person. Consistent with this reasoning, a number of studies (e.g., Jones, Gergen, and Davis, 1962; Lowe and Goldstein, 1970) have demonstrated that subjects increase their liking for a stimulus person who expresses approval of them.

Effects of Low Self-Esteem. A strict interpretation of Heider's balance theory suggests that perceived liking will lead to reciprocal liking only when a person likes himself. Consistent with this interpretation, many investigators (e.g. Bachman and Secord, 1959; Deutsch and Solomon, 1959) have hypothesized that while people with high self-esteem will respond favorably to those who express positive evaluations of them, those with low self-esteem will prefer negative evaluators to positive ones. Others, however, have disagreed with this stand (e.g., Dittes, 1959; Harvey and Clapp, 1965; Walster, 1965). They have argued that since individuals with low self-esteem are generally dissatisfied with themselves, they will be especially grateful for compliments.

Unfortunately, the research that has focused on this problem has not produced consistent results. One attempt to explain the contradictory findings has been made by Jones (1973). Jones agrees that under most circumstances people with low self-esteem will appreciate compliments and respond favorably to those who approve of them. He has suggested that their low feelings of self-worth will lead them to react negatively to compliments in two settings, however. First, low self-esteem people will not appreciate compliments if they expect their true level of competence to be exposed. Since low self-esteem people are insecure about their abilities, they feel uncomfortable with praise which they fear they will be unable to live up to. Second, Jones suggests that a low self-esteem person may not respond favorably to a compliment that is ambiguous. According to Jones, low self-esteem people often interpret ambiguous remarks as negative, and therefore react negatively to the person who has complimented them. There is some research evidence consistent with this reasoning (see, e.g.,

Jacobs, Berscheid, and Walster, 1971), although these hypotheses have not yet been put to a strict empirical test.

Other investigators have suggested that the credibility of feedback received from another person determines the reaction to it. A person with low self-esteem may be suspicious of a compliment that contradicts his beliefs about himself and may react negatively to it for this reason. This argument received support in a study by Jones and Schneider (1968). After taking a written test of social sensitivity, some students were led to believe that they were definitely insensitive, while others were made to feel uncertain about their sensitivity. Subjects then answered some test items orally and received evaluations of their sensitivity from two peers. Subjects made to feel uncertain about their social sensitivity responded more favorably to a peer who told them that they were sensitive than to a peer who told them that they were insensitive. However, those who were made to feel certain of their insensitivity subsequently sent slightly more positive evaluations to the peer who had evaluated them negatively. These results imply that people do not appreciate positive feedback that they believe to be inaccurate.

Further evidence of the importance of the credibility of feedback comes from a study by Potter (1973). In this study, too, students first took a written test and received false feedback about their social sensitivity. They then received a message from a partner indicating both how socially sensitive he thought the subject was and how much he liked the subject. Potter expected that a partner whose judgment of a subject's sensitivity agreed with the test feedback he had received would be judged as highly credible. He predicted that subjects would be most inclined to like a person who liked them, and to dislike a person who disliked them, if the person was regarded as especially credible. The results supported his predictions. According to Potter, "It is pleasant to be liked, and painful to be disliked; but when this liking or disliking is seen as being based on an inaccurate appraisal of our own characteristics, it at once moves us less . . . than when someone likes or dislikes us because of what we really are" (p. 196).

Taken as a whole, these studies suggest that using compliments to ingratiate yourself with a person low in self-esteem is not easy. Ambiguous comments may strike him as negative and give offense, while overly positive comments may not be believed. Similarly, a compliment that is not viewed as genuine may undermine the credibility of later compliments and impair their potential for eliciting attraction. The ingratiator should, then, avoid positive assessments that contradict the target person's own assessments of himself. He should also avoid compliments that challenge or threaten a low self-esteem person, and should avoid compliments in settings where the target fears his true level of competence will subsequently be exposed. Thus, for example, an ingratiator should probably not compliment a low self-esteem target on his apparent physical fitness and then invite him to play a game of handball. The compliment alone would probably be more effective.

Perceived Intent and Credibility. Another situation in which a compliment may lack credibility is when the complimenter is seen as having ulterior motivation. Dickoff (1961) conducted an experiment in which female subjects received compliments from an individual who did or did not have something to gain by making a favorable impression. The compliments came from a graduate student who was actually a confederate of the experimenter. Subjects in the accuracy condition were told that the graduate student would try to be as accurate as possible in evaluating them. Those in the ulterior motive condition were told that, after the experiment, the graduate student would try to get them to participate in an experiment of her own. The graduate student observed while the subject answered some questions about herself, and then gave an evaluation of the subject. For some of the subjects the evaluation was uniformly positive; for some it was identical to the way in which the subject had evaluated herself in an earlier situation; and for the remaining subjects the evaluation was uniformly neutral. After receiving the evaluation, subjects evaluated the confederate both on a number of questionnaire items and in their own words.

Subjects were least attracted to the graduate student when her evaluation of them was neutral. Evaluations which matched the subject's view of herself generally resulted in an intermediate amount of liking. As predicted, the effect of a consistently positive evaluation depended upon whether or not the subject believed that the complimentor had an ulterior motive. A positive evaluation led to greater liking when the subject thought the complimentor was trying to be accurate, but not when she knew the complimentor had something to gain by obtaining her good will. In addition, subjects' free descriptions of the complimentor differed sharply among conditions. The neutral complimentor was disliked, but was given credit for honesty and candor. Among the subjects who were told that the complimentor was trying to be accurate, those who received opinions of themselves that matched their self-opinions rated her as brighter and more perceptive than those who had received uniformly positive evaluations. Those who received positive evaluations stated that they liked the complimentor more, however. In the accuracy-positive condition, the graduate student was described as naïve, optimistic, and kindhearted.

In the ulterior-motive-positive condition, however, she was described as behaving out of weakness, insecurity, and fear of rejection.

Lowe and Goldstein (1970) have also found that subjects respond favorably to a positive evaluation from another only if they believe that the other is trying to be accurate. These studies suggest that the would-be ingratiator should keep in mind that if he is obviously dependent on another, the other may attribute his compliments to ulterior motivation and react negatively.

How can the attribution of ulterior motivation be avoided? First, the subject might time his compliments so that the benefit desired from the target person is not salient. That is, a would-be ingratiator may be less than completely successful if he says to his boss, "I really like the way you handled the staff meeting last week. By the way, I've been meaning to ask you for a raise."

Another way that the ingratiator may avoid the attribution of manipulative intentions is by arranging to have his compliment delivered by a third person. If a manager is told by one of his colleagues that another colleague made favorable remarks about him, he is unlikely to conclude that the remarks were made to obtain his affection. Lord Chesterfield once suggested to his son the value of "flattering people behind their backs, in the presence of whom, to make their own court, much more than for your sake, will not fail to repeat and even amplify the praise to the very party concerned. This is, of all flattery, the most pleasing and consequently the most effectual" (1901, I, p. 179). Its effectiveness is probably due to the fact that the recipient has no evidence that the person who originated the compliment hoped that it would be repeated to him.

Combining Positive and Negative Evaluations. We have suggested that an ingratiator should try to convey the impression that his compliments are a sincere reflection of the target person's positive attributes. As discussed above, he should try to prevent attributions of ulterior motivation. He should also try to avoid the attribution that he is the type of person who always makes positive comments to others. If the target person draws this inference when complimented, he is unlikely to accept the remark as evidence of his true self-worth. One way that the potential ingratiator can avoid this attribution is to refrain from complimenting others in the target person's presence. He may also locate the target person with reference to others, implying that he thinks the target person is better than those other persons.

Another tactic that may enhance the apparent sincerity of a compliment, while avoiding the attribution that the ingratiator is uniformly positive in his evaluation of others, is that of making both negative and positive comments about the target person. For example, an ingratiator might compliment the target person on attributes that are important to him, while pointing out a few trivial weaknesses. This strategy should be especially effective if the ingratiator can identify areas in which the target person is both certain of his weaknesses and willing to acknowledge them. As the studies cited earlier have suggested, a person can enhance his credibility as a communicator by evaluating a target person negatively but accurately. As a result, later compliments should be especially effective in eliciting attraction.

Mettee (1971) conducted a study that bears on this issue. Subjects were asked to work on a real-life decision problem. Some subjects first received a positive evaluation about a major aspect of their work and then received a negative evaluation about a minor aspect. They were asked how much they liked the evaluator after each evaluation. As expected, subjects responded very favorably after receiving the major positive evaluation. Surprisingly, they did not change their opinion of the evaluator after they received the minor negative evaluation. Mettee's experiment also included a condition in which subjects first received the minor negative evaluation, and then received the major positive one. Interestingly, these subjects rated the evaluator much less highly than subjects who had first received the major positive evaluation followed by the minor negative one. This information could be useful to supervisors who wish to bring minor shortcomings to the attention of their subordinates. Mettee's results imply that the subordinate will react more positively to the supervisor if he begins with a supportive statement before mentioning the weakness.

Aronson and Linder (1965) were interested in a related question: How do individuals react to evaluations of their personality that change over time? They had subjects engage in a series of short interactions with a confederate and comment about her to the experimenter following each interaction. Interestingly, the confederate was liked better when her comments were initially negative, but became more favorable by the end of the session than when she was uniformly positive. Not surprisingly, uniformly positive evaluators were preferred to uniformly negative ones. The confederate was liked least when her evaluation changed from positive to negative during the sessions.

A number of explanations have been proposed for Aronson and Linder's findings. First, a negative-positive evaluator may be preferred to a uniformly positive one because the former is judged to be more discerning—not the type of person who reacts positively to everyone. Another explanation for this result may be that if we are evaluated negatively by someone, we may consciously try to get him to change his mind. Subjects in the negative-positive condition may have felt especially good because they judged themselves to be successful in accomplishing this goal. A third explanation concerns anxiety reduction. A negative evaluation may make a person feel hurt and anxious, and he may especially welcome a subsequent positive evaluation since it will reduce the anxiety.

A number of investigators have been unable to replicate Aronson and Linder's (1965) results, however (see, e.g., Hewitt, 1972; Taylor, Altman, and Sorrentino, 1969; Tognoli and Keiser, 1972), suggesting that reactions to negative feedback may be strongly affected by situational variables that have differed from study to study. For example, in the experiments by Taylor et al. (1969) and Hewitt (1972), the confederate's evaluations were communicated directly to the subject, while in the Aronson and Linder (1965) study the subject "accidentally" overheard them. An individual who expresses his negative feelings about a person directly to that person may be regarded as rude and tactless. This judgment of him may remain even if his subsequent positive comments remove the subject's anxiety about his own personal attributes.

In summary, it seems clear (Mettee, 1971) that a negative remark may be more palatable if a person has just praised us in an important area. But if a person praises us and then changes his mind (cf. Aronson and Linder, 1965), the value of the prior positive comment is vitiated. We will react as negatively to such a person as we will to a person who is continually negative—perhaps even more so. The really interesting question, of course, is whether mentioning a combination of positive and negative characteristics will be more effective in eliciting attraction than mentioning only positive characteristics. Unfortunately, this question has not yet been addressed.

Subtle Strategies for Enhancing Another. One way that an ingratiator can flatter the target person without giving the impression that he is trying to curry favor is to employ other-enhancing tactics that are more subtle than direct verbal compliments. Nonverbal behaviors, such as smiling and maintaining eye contact, fall into this category. To quote Dale Carnegie, "Actions speak louder than words, and a smile says 'I like you. You make me happy. I am glad to see you' " (1940, p. 72). An interesting experiment by Holstein, Goldstein, and Bem (1971) has demonstrated that these tactics can be quite effective in eliciting interpersonal attraction. Subjects were asked to interview a male confederate for 15 minutes. For half the subjects, the confederate employed positive expressive gestures: He maintained steady eye contact as he replied to questions, gave frequent smiles, and avoided the use of distracting hand gesticulations. For the remaining subjects, he avoided eye contact during his replies, did not smile, and used distracting gestures such as drumming his fingers on the chair or table top. Subjects rated the confederate more highly (i.e., thought him to be more sincere, intelligent, etc.) when he made positive expressive gestures than when he did not, and also indicated greater preference to participate with him in future experiments. While this study suggests that positive nonverbal gestures are effective in eliciting interpersonal attraction, some experiments (see, e.g., Scherwitz and Helmreich, 1973) have implied that the relationship between nonverbal gestures and attraction may be complex. For example, if the conversation is already positive or highly personal, high eye contact may bring the encounter to a level of intimacy that is uncomfortable, and thereby reduce interpersonal attraction. In everyday business encounters, however, we would expect these gestures to be effective.

We would surmise that positive nonverbal gestures are effective in eliciting attraction because they convey to the other that we have a high opinion of him. Related tactics, such as listening closely to the other person, discussing the topics that he brings up, and asking him to expand on his comments, should also be effective in this regard (cf. Geller, Goodstein, Silver, and Sternberg, 1974). There is some evidence from a study by Rosenfeld (1966) that subjects engage in such tactics when they are trying to make themselves more attractive to others. In this experiment, each subject was told that he or she would be interacting with another subject. Half of the subjects were told to try to get the other to like them; the remaining subjects were told to convey to the other that they did not like him and were not interested in becoming friends. Subjects in the approval-seeking condition emitted a significantly greater percentage of smiles, positive head nods, and recognitions (brief utterances that indicate attentiveness to the preceding statement, e.g., "Really," "Um-humm") than subjects who were trying to avoid the other's approval.

Among the other more subtle tactics that an ingratiator can use to indicate that he thinks his relationship with another person is a good one is to ask that person for a favor or for advice. An ingratiator may also tease the target person with friendly insults and sarcasm, implying that he does not really think the person has the weaknesses of which he is being accused. At worst, such insults suggest that the fault is much too minor to interfere with the ingratiator's warm feelings towards the other person.

Another way of letting a person know that you like him and are interested in him is to encourage him to tell you about himself. A related tactic—one that has received far more research attention—is to talk intimately about yourself to the other person. Such self-disclosure should imply that you trust the other person and consider him to be both discreet and understanding. A review of the research on self-disclosure is obviously beyond the scope of this chapter (see Chaiken and Derlega, 1975, and Cozby, 1973). We might mention, however, that disclosures seem to be most effective in eliciting interpersonal attraction if they are not extreme in nature (Cozby, 1972), and if the discloser takes care to avoid the impression that he is the kind of person who would be intimate with anyone. Wortman, Adesman, Herman, and Greenberg (1976) found, for example, that if a person is intimate with a stranger at the very beginning of their interaction, the stranger will react negatively. If a person waits until the two have been talking for awhile before making a highly personal remark, the target person seems to take the disclosure as more of a compliment, and reacts much more favorably.

Concrete Rewards for Flattery. Most of the studies that have examined subjects' responses to compliments or flattery have used liking as the major dependent variable. Obviously, people in business settings are often interested in enhancing more than their interpersonal attraction. Is other-enhancement an effective strategy for eliciting additional rewards from the system, such as higher pay raises? This question was pursued in a laboratory study by Kipnis and Vanderveer (1971). Subjects were led to believe that they were supervising technical high school students located in another room. They were told that they could send messages to their workers by microphone and could receive written notes from them. There were actually no workers present. Notes from the "workers" were actually prepared by the experimenter.

The output of one of the workers indicated that his performance was far superior to that of the others. Two workers performed at an average level, and one of them sent ingratiating messages to the subject. This ingratiating worker mentioned that he thought the boss was a "nice guy" and that the boss could count on him for assistance. In evaluating the performances of their subordinates, subjects gave equally high ratings to the superior worker and the ingratiating worker. Performance scores assigned to the non-ingratiating average workers were significantly lower than these. Thus, the ingratiator's comments actually influenced the subject's evaluation of his performance. In general, he received more promises of pay raises than the average worker, and tended to receive more actual pay raises than the average worker as well.

Opinion Conformity

Another set of tactics available to an ingratiator involves the expression of opinions that agree with those of the target person. Much research by Byrne and his colleagues (e.g., Byrne, 1961; Byrne and Griffit, 1966; Byrne and Rhamey, 1965) has supported the assertion that people prefer those whose attitudes and values are similar to their own. In Byrne's experiments a stimulus person's opinions are usually explicitly communicated to the subject, and the subject knows little about the stimulus person aside from his opinions on a few topics. In an experiment by Griffit and Veitch (1974), however, the same result occurred in a much less structured situation. Thirteen previously unacquainted male students lived together for 10 days under simulated fall-out shelter conditions. Their attitudes on several issues were assessed the day before their confinement. At the end of the first, fifth, and ninth days subjects filled out a sociometric choice questionnaire on which they indicated which other subjects they would most and least like to have remain in the shelter with them. Attraction to group members, as indicated by the sociometric choices, was positively and significantly related to attitude similarity on each of the three assessment days.

Why It Works. Several explanations for the relationship between attitude similarity and attractiveness have been proposed. Byrne (1969) suggested that agreement leads to attraction because it increases a person's confidence that his beliefs are correct. Consistent with this view, Byrne, Nelson, and Reeves (1966) found that opinion conformity was especially effective in producing liking when the opinions involved could not be objectively verified. This is precisely when social validation should be most valuable. Another reason why people may like those who agree with them is that they expect that the agreement will facilitate their attainment of goals and thereby result in more rewarding interactions. Johnson and Johnson (1972) showed that subjects expected similar others to be more cooperative in a situation in which they were interdependent, and a cooperative partner is more likely to enable a person to obtain desired rewards.

In the section on "Other-Enhancement," we discussed Heider's balance theory and his premise that people will like others who appear to like them. This premise provides another explanation for the similarity-attraction relationship if we assume that people believe that similar others will probably like them. In a complicated series of experiments designed to shed light on this issue, Insko, Thompson, Stroebe, Shaud, Pinner, and Layton (1973) found that the most likely explanation of the similarity-attraction relationship is that similarity causes liking, that liking another makes us think that the other probably likes us, and that the belief that the other probably likes us causes us to like him even more.

Avoiding Negative Trait Attributions. Because creativity and independence are important traits in organizational settings, a person who slavishly conforms to the opinions of his superiors, or to the norms and values of the company, may run the risk of eliciting negative reactions. Schein (1968) has stated, for example, that individuals who accept all the values and norms of an organization should be regarded as socialization failures. According to Schein, "The conforming individual curbs his creativity and thereby moves the organization toward a sterile form of bureaucracy."

Experiments by Jones, Jones, and Gergen (1963) and Jones, Stires, Shaver, and Harris (1968) have suggested that people can even get "extra credit" for resisting the urge to be conforming when it is obvious that they have something to gain by impressing the target person. In the experiment by Jones, Stires, Shaver, and Harris, female subjects were asked to discuss their opinions with another subject, who happened to be an experimental confederate. The confederate had been instructed to either come to agree with the subject or to remain autonomous and stick to her own opinion. Following the discussion, half of the subjects were told that the confederate had been trying to get them to like her. The remaining subjects were told that the confederate had been instructed to be spontaneous during the discussion. The major dependent measure was subjects' ratings of how much they liked the confederate. As we would expect, the agreeing confederate was liked better in the condition where she had nothing to gain from the subjects than in the condition where she had been trying to elicit their approval. In contrast, the autonomous confederate created an especially favorable impression by retaining her own views in the face of incentives to elicit the subject's attraction.

Mixing Disagreement and Agreement. These results imply that opinion conformity may not be wise when one's dependence is obvious. In such cases, the attribution of manipulative intent, and perhaps even the attribution that one lacks independence and creativity, may be forthcoming. The potential ingratiator could avoid this problem by trying to anticipate a target person's opinions and expressing them himself before the target person has had a chance to make them explicit. He might also consider the strategy of agreeing with the target person on some views and disagreeing on others. For example, the ingratiator might express agreement with his superiors on pivotal organizational values, but retain autonomy on more peripheral issues (Schein, 1968). In fact, Schein has referred to this response pattern as "creative individualism," and has suggested that it should be encouraged by the organization.

One strategy that may be regarded as mixing disagreement and agreement is yielding: In yielding, the ingratiator makes it clear initially that he disagrees with the target person, and then comes to agree over time. In some ways, this tactic is similar to one that we mentioned in our discussion of other-enhancement: beginning with a negative evaluation of a person and gradually becoming more positive. Such a strategy may indicate that the ingratiator is not the kind of person who is always in agreement with others. Initial disagreement might also make a target person experience anxiety concerning the validity of his opinion, and he may be very gratified when this anxiety is later reduced through yielding. Furthermore, the knowledge that one has effectively influenced another person to move toward his own opinions can be very gratifying because it indicates that one has been persuasive (see, e.g., Sigall, 1970).

Although the research evidence is somewhat mixed (see, e.g., Gerard and Greenbaum, 1962), there is evidence that at least under certain circumstances, yielding is a more effective strategy than mere agreement with another. In a laboratory experiment, Lombardo, Weiss, and Buchanan (1972) led subjects to believe that they would be exchanging opinions with another subject, actually a confederate of the experimenter, on ten different issues. Confederates who yielded to the subject on half of the issues (i.e., expressed initial disagreement, listened to the subject's view, and then changed their mind) and disagreed on half of the items were liked better than confederates who merely agreed with the subject on half of the issues (i.e., listened to the subject's view and then expressed a similar view) and disagreed on half. The authors argue that these results occurred because yielding is reinforcing since it removes the anxiety created by the initial disagreement. We believe that yielding would be much less effective when not coupled with disagreement, as it was in this study. A person who yields every time may be viewed as weak, spineless, or possessing ulterior motivation. Furthermore, we would not recommend yielding as an ingratiation tactic if one's dependence on another is obvious. The evidence (cf. Jones, Stires, Shaver and Harris (1968) suggests that a person who is autonomous will be preferred to a yielder under such conditions.

While some studies have focused on the effects of disagreement and agreement from a single person, others have exposed subjects to different individuals who agree with them to varying degrees. In a study by Stapert and Clore (1969), subjects saw five attitude surveys supposedly filled out by other students. The results revealed that subjects were more attracted to another who agreed with them if they had previously been exposed to disagreement. This study supports the notion that agreement will be especially valued when it can reduce the anxiety aroused by prior disagreements. The results suggest that the ingratiator should try to plan his remarks so that they come at a time when the target person is experiencing anxiety over his views. A manager who has just been criticized by his superior, for example, may be an especially vulnerable target for opinion conformity from his subordinates.

Using Opinion Conformity to Gain Rewards in an Organizational Setting. A study by Baskett (1973) has suggested that a co-worker who expresses attitudes that are similar to his superior's may be rated as more competent, and be given a higher salary, than a worker who does not. In this study, subjects were asked to pretend that they worked for a large company and had been instructed to evaluate a potential vice president of the company. They received dossiers containing background information about the stimulus person, including his responses to an attitude questionnaire containing questions which the subjects had responded to earlier. The responses of the job candidate indicated that he agreed with the subject on either 20 percent or 80 percent of the items. In addition, the background information indicated the candidate's level of competence was either low, average, or high. Not surprisingly, subjects recommended high-competence persons more strongly for the job, and higher salaries were suggested for them than for low-competence persons. Applicants whose opinions agreed with those of the subjects 80 percent of the time were seen as more competent than those whose opinions were in agreement only 20 percent of the time. Subjects showed a tendency to recommend similar candidates more strongly for the job and also suggested higher salaries for them. We should be cautious in generalizing from these results, however, since they involve a role-playing methodology. Nonetheless, the findings suggest that opinion conformity may be instrumental in attaining rewards in an organizational setting.

Rendering Favors
People usually react positively when someone does something nice for them. Thus the giving of favors can also be an effective strategy for an ingratiator. Favors resemble other-enhancement in that they convey to the recipient that the favor-doer likes him and cares about his well-being. They are also related to the self-presentational

strategies to be discussed later, since they may indicate that the favor-doer is a thoughtful person. If these are the messages conveyed by the giving of a favor, then the recipient's liking for the favor-doer is likely to increase.

Perceived Intent. As with other ingratiation tactics, the effectiveness of favor-giving depends upon the attributions which the recipient makes about the ingratiator's motives. Both Greenberg and Frisch (1972) and Nemeth (1970) have shown that helping another will not increase his liking for you unless it is clear to him that you intended to help him. Greenberg and Frisch had a confederate give help to subjects. In both experimental conditions the confederate provided information which the subject needed to solve a problem. In the deliberate-help condition the confederate indicated that he thought the subject might find the information useful, while in the accidental-help condition the information was contained in a question which the confederate asked the subjects. In the deliberate-help condition, more help was reciprocated, and liking increased to a greater degree. Thus, the attribution of intent to help seems to be important.

An experiment by Morse (1972), however, suggests that good intentions alone are not enough. Half of the subjects in Morse's experiment were led to expect help on a difficult task from an experimental assistant; the remaining subjects were not. Half of the subjects actually received the proffered help, while half did not. Subjects who had been led to expect help, but did not receive it, rated the assistant as less helpful and less attractive than subjects who were never promised or given help. These results suggest that we should remain silent about our intentions to help others unless we intend to carry them through.

Should the potential ingratiator offer help spontaneously, or wait until it is asked for? This issue is complicated, and the answer probably depends on situational factors yet to be explored. An experiment by Broll, Gross, and Piliavin (1974) suggests that we like helpers more when help is offered than when we must ask for it. These investigators have suggested that there are negative features associated with asking for help, since such a request may imply that one is inadequate and unable to take care of his own needs. Furthermore, we gain less information about others' intent to help us if we must ask for it.

These studies suggest that an ingratiator should try to insure that the recipient knows both that he intended to be helpful and that being helpful was his own idea. However, it seems to us that he should also avoid making the recipient feel that he holds an especially low evaluation of the recipient's abilities. Help which carries with it the implication that the donor considers the recipient to be incompetent and incapable of succeeding without assistance is unlikely to be received warmly. Individuals in the supervisor role must often spend considerable time giving orders and making suggestions; the foregoing discussion suggests that they should be very careful how they proceed.

Favors that Reduce Freedom. Brehm and Cole (1966) have suggested another situation in which a favor is unlikely to be an effective ingratiation technique. They propose that when an individual receives a favor which reduces his freedom, he will experience "psychological reactance" and will be motivated to assert his freedom by failing to reciprocate the favor. In their study each subject expected to fill out a first-impression rating of the other subject present, who was actually a confederate. Half of the subjects were told that it was important for the ratings to be accurate, while the others were told that accuracy was unimportant. In addition, half of the subjects received a favor from the confederate. During a delay announced by the experimenter at the beginning of the session, the confederate left the room. In the favor condition only, he returned to the lab with a soft drink which he handed to the subject.

This study contained two dependent measures: subjects' first impression ratings of the confederate and how quickly, if at all, they began to help the confederate when an opportunity arose. Of primary interest to us is the finding that when it was important that the subject's judgments be accurate, he was much less likely to return a favor than when accuracy was less important. As a matter of fact, subjects in the high-importance-favor condition were less likely to help the confederate than were those subjects who didn't receive a favor. The ratings of liking for the confederate, however, did not differ among the experimental conditions.

Brehm and Cole's findings suggest that when an ingratiator wants something from a person who wishes to be free to evaluate him in an accurate and unbiased manner, the ingratiator should avoid performing a favor for that person. This would be the case if the target person were an employer and the ingratiator wanted a job. Since an employer generally wants to hire the best workers he can, it will be important to him to be able to judge the job applicant's qualifications without bias. Hence, if the applicant performs a favor for the target person, he may actually hurt his chances of getting the job.

While performing favors for another person can increase that person's liking for you and his willingness to benefit you, the successful ingratiator will be very careful in his use of this strategy. He should do all he can to insure that his action will not appear to signify manipulative intentions, and he should try to convey the impression that he intended to benefit the target person. Finally, he should avoid performing favors which reduce the target person's freedom to judge him objectively when it is important to the target person that his judgments be unbiased.

Self-Presentation

If an ingratiator knows what type of individual the target person will consider attractive, he can attempt to behave as though he were that type of person. The tactic of self-presentation encompasses both verbal statements and behaviors intended to convey the impression that one possesses certain characteristics. Two different sources of information can suggest to the ingratiator what characteristics he should appear to possess. First, he can try to figure out the target person's idiosyncratic likes and dislikes. An ingratiator who uses this strategy will present himself differently to different individuals. Alternatively, he may present himself as having characteristics which are positively valued in his culture and avoid the impression that he possesses negative attributes.

What type of self-presentational strategy is likely to be effective for a new recruit who has just begun his job in an industrial organization? A recruit may feel that it is to his advantage to present himself as highly educated and motivated to work hard. Schein (1964) has implied, however, that such a strategy could well be disastrous. In an article on managerial attitudes toward the college graduate, Schein has suggested that managers hold negative stereotypes toward this group. In general, they feel that college graduates are overambitious and unrealistic about how much responsibility they should be given, that they are too theoretical, idealistic, and naïve, and that they lack understanding of practical problems. From the manager's perspective, the average recruit "tends to think that his education has given him some kind of special privilege to move up fast in the organization" (p. 69). Apparently, the recruit should try to impress his manager with his practical expertise rather than with his formal education. Furthermore, Schein's article implies that a recruit should not "push" for challenging job assignments until the manager feels that he has been "broken in" and is ready for them.

In most organizational settings, the superiors and the new recruits may have quite different perspectives on a number of issues. In their study of the priesthood, for example, Hall and Schneider (1973) found this to be the case. Apparently, new priests are quite enthusiastic and unrealistic about the possibility of changing the church in particular, and the world in general. Older priests are more aware that any kind of change is difficult. A recruit with an understanding of these different perspectives could exploit this knowledge for tactical purposes. Thus, a new priest may be able to impress his superiors with his maturity and sophistication by indicating his awareness of the obstacles to change.

The Special Case of Modesty. One attribute which is considered undesirable in our society is boastfulness, while the quality of modesty is usually admired. This causes some problems for an ingratiator. If he mentions that he is extraordinarily considerate of others, very productive, and extremely intelligent, his strategy may backfire and he may be disliked because of his apparent conceit. But modesty is a risky strategy as well. Suppose a person applying for a job is asked how well qualified he is, and modestly points out that his qualifications are "fair." The interviewer may admire the candidate's modesty. But if he believes the applicant's claim, he probably will not hire him.

The above reasoning suggests that one situation in which modesty may be an effective tactic is when the ingratiator's admirable qualities are already known. If the interviewer has before him a person's college transcript which shows that he has nearly a straight-A average, commenting that he has had some trouble with a few of his courses is unlikely to do much harm. If the admitted difficulties are irrelevant to the skills required by the present job, this approach may be quite effective. An engineer who confesses that he had a hard time with medieval history can gain credit for being modest without appearing to be less qualified for an engineering job.

Modesty may also be a useful strategy when a person expects that someone else is likely to mention his weaknesses.

> Say about yourself all the derogatory things you know the other person intends to say, and say them before he has a chance to say them—and you take the wind out of his sails. The chances are a hundred to one that he will then take a generous, forgiving attitude [toward you] and minimize your mistakes (Carnegie, 1940, p. 130).

The same applies when a person expects his drawbacks to become apparent in some other manner (e.g., when he will be performing a task at which he knows he is not very good). Self-deprecation is also likely to be more effective than self-enhancement when a more positive self-presentation would cause the target person to feel threatened. As we implied earlier, superiors with a limited amount of formal education may feel quite threatened by recruits who are highly educated. A recruit who modestly mentions that his formal education at Yale is "no big deal" may gain considerably in attractiveness. Finally, even in situations where self-enhancement seems more appropriate, the ingratiator would do well to avoid seeming conceited. While the content of positive statements about oneself may enhance one's appearance, giving an impression of conceit and boastfulness will detract from it.

For this reason, it would probably be wise for the ingratiator to look for subtle, indirect ways of communicating his positive attributes to others. One way that he can avoid appearing conceited is to manipulate the conversation so that his positive qualities are mentioned as responses to direct questions. He also might consider having his virtues conveyed to the target person by a third party. Or he may try to demonstrate his positive attributes by having the target person observe his performance on some dimension. A subordinate who is seen in the office on weekends may be more effective in convincing his boss that he is industrious than one who tells his boss how hard he works. It is to be hoped that future research will corroborate these speculations.

Preference for Particular Personality Style. Just as people generally like others who share their opinions, it also appears (see Byrne, Griffit, and Stefaniak, 1967; Secord and Backman, 1964) that people like others whose personalities resemble their own. DiMarco (1975) developed a questionnaire designed to assess people's "life-style orientations." People's responses on the questionnaire reflect the extent to which they believe their actions should be guided by formal authority, social norms, and/or personal feelings. Engineers from two large manufacturing organizations completed this questionnaire and one measuring satisfaction with co-workers and superiors. Satisfaction with co-workers was positively related to the similarity between an individual's scores on the life-style questionnaire and those of the engineers with whom he worked. These results imply that an ingratiator should be able to enhance his attractiveness by emphasizing those aspects of his personality and life style that are similar to those of the target person.

There is, however, a qualification to the general finding that people like similar others. In applying this finding to organizations, Hansson and Fiedler (1973) have pointed out:

> An extension of the similarity-attraction research from individuals to organizations requires one important consideration. We must recognize that individuals join an organization for a wide variety of reasons, and that they will elect to remain because the organization continues to satisfy their needs. An employee's perceived

similarity to members of the organization would be expected to be important to him only if friendships on the job and a feeling of belonging to the organization were also of importance to him. If the person has joined primarily because of such other benefits as high wages, opportunity for advancement, or technical challenge, perceived similarity to members of the organization is unlikely to affect his attraction to the organization (p. 259).

Consistent with this reasoning, Hansson and Fiedler (1973) found that perceived similarity to members of an organization was related to attraction to the organization only for relationship-motivated persons, and not for task-motivated persons.

Contrast Effects. Research on the evaluation of job applicants suggests that the impression that an individual creates is influenced by the characteristics of the applicants who preceded him. In particular, being preceded by a poor candidate improves the impression one makes, while being preceded by an exceptionally qualified candidate can make one look worse (cf. Hakel, Ohnesorge, and Dunnette, 1970; Wexley, Yukl, Kovaks, and Sanders, 1972). Wexley et al. showed that this contrast effect was particularly strong in the case of job applicants with average qualifications.

A number of studies dealing with the evaluation of job applicants have considered the effects of various patterns of negative and positive attributes within a single individual. The results of a study by Carlson (1971) suggest that negative information about job applicants has more impact than positive information. In fact, Webster (1964) has argued that the interview is basically a search for negative evidence. According to Webster, the interviewer will be criticized or punished if a poorly qualified person is hired. In contrast, praise for hiring good employees is rarely given. For this reason, interviewers are usually very sensitive to negative evidence. This suggests that the potential recruit should try to present himself as favorably as possible on his application blank, and try to structure the interview so that no negative information is elicited from him. It also suggests that he should adopt a rather conventional, normative style in his interaction. That is, rather than trying to convince the interviewer that he is outstanding, he should concentrate on avoiding the attribution that he is unimpressive.

Blakeley and McNaughton (1971) found that information presented earlier has a greater effect on evaluations of applicants than that presented later. Apparently, an interviewer decides fairly early whether or not he likes the interviewee, and then interprets later evidence in such a way that it is consistent with his first impression

(Mayfield, 1964; Webster, 1964). This suggests that if a person must make known certain deficits in his personality or background, he should probably do so only after he has first communicated the fact that he possesses a number of strengths as well. However, an experiment by Jones and Gordon (1972) suggests that it may be disadvantageous to appear to be hiding certain types of negative information. Hence it might be best if an ingratiator revealing past misdeeds avoided giving the impression that he was reluctant to do so.

Physical Attractiveness. In a review of the research on selection interviews, Mayfield (1964) noted that irrelevant factors such as facial expression and personal appearance play an important role in the decision. A number of social psychological experiments have also revealed that subjects express greater liking for physically attractive individuals than for unattractive ones (see, e.g., Layton and Insko, 1972). Walster, Aronson, Abrahams, and Rottman (1966) found that a person's physical attractiveness was important in determining how much a partner liked him after their first date. Research by Dion, Berscheid, and Walster (1972) suggests that college students of both sexes rate physically attractive men and women as possessing more socially desirable traits than unattractive men and women. Further, Dion et al.'s study revealed that subjects expected attractive people to have better things in store for them in the future (e.g., more prestigious occupations and happier marriages).

Do people evaluate the actual performance of attractive individuals more positively than that of unattractive people? A study by Landy and Sigall (1974) suggests that they do. Subjects were asked to judge an essay that had supposedly been written by another student. Before reading the essay, they were asked to examine some nondescript background information about the writer. This background material was either accompanied by a photograph of the writer as extremely attractive, by a photo of the writer as unattractive, or unaccompanied by a photograph. The objective quality of the essay itself was also experimentally varied to be either high or low. Both the writer and the essay were evaluated most favorably when the writer was attractive, intermediately when no photograph was provided, and least favorably when the writer was unattractive. There was also some indication from the results that physical attractiveness exerted the strongest influence on subjects' evaluation of the work when it was objectively poor. "Thus, if you are ugly you are not discriminated against a great deal as long as your performance is impressive. However, . . . you may be able to get away with inferior work if you are beautiful" (p. 302).

The attractive and unattractive girls in the Layton and Insko study were actually the same person made up in two different ways. This demonstrates that an individual can do much to alter how attractive he appears. The results cited above suggest that making oneself as attractive as possible is a wise strategy.

Differences in Status

Giving the appearance of successful performance seems to be an effective ingratiation tactic whether the target person is a subordinate, a superior, or someone at one's own level. The effectiveness of other ingratiation strategies, however, may depend upon one's position in the status hierarchy. A person depends upon his superiors for raises, promotions, letters of reference, and even for the definition of his job. We have mentioned several times that if a person's dependence on another is obvious, his ingratiation attempts may elicit suspicions of ulterior motivation. This suggests that when trying to win the approval of superiors, the ingratiator should proceed with subtlety and finesse.

A superior who is interested in gaining the support of his subordinates is in an entirely different position. His motives are less likely to be suspected, since his dependence on his subordinates is less salient than their dependence on him. Furthermore, subordinates may attribute a superior's ingratiation attempts to a desire to improve productivity or morale for the sake of the organization as a whole, rather than to a desire to benefit himself alone. However, the superior is faced with one problem: In obtaining subordinates' support, he must avoid losing his power or lessening their respect for him.

Thus, the strategies that are likely to be effective in gaining approval may differ considerably, depending on whether one is trying to impress his superiors or his subordinates. From our past discussion of the ingratiation tactics, what strategies can be recommended in each case?

Impressing One's Superiors. An ingratiator trying to impress a more powerful other should probably avoid the more obvious tactics. Most types of other-enhancement fall into this category. Directly praising the target person should be avoided, both because it is such an obvious tactic and because it may seem presumptuous. The tactic implies that the subordinate has the capacity to evaluate his superior, that he knows how his superior should behave and how his job can best be done. Other-enhancement of a superior may be effective, however, if the subordinate compliments the superior on job areas in which the subordinate is recognized to be knowledgeable, or on personal qualities that are unrelated to job performance (see, e.g., Kipnis and Vanderveer, 1971). More subtle other-enhancing strategies, such as positive nonverbal gestures, may also be quite effective, as may other-enhancement if the compliment is conveyed by a third party.

Rendering favors may not be an especially good tactic, since it so often gives rise to the feeling that something is expected in return. Opinion conformity is also risky. Jones, Stires, Shaver, and Harris (1968) and Jones, Jones, and Gergen (1963) have found that when a person's dependence on another is obvious, he is liked better when he avoids slavish agreement with that person. Strategies such as anticipating the target person's views and expressing them before he has had a chance to do so, or mixing agreement on major issues with disagreement on minor ones would seem to be more prudent.

What type of self-presentational style should be adopted by a subordinate? One question that may arise is how self-enhancing he should be. Since boasting is not admired, and since extolling one's virtues is such an obvious tactic, self-enhancing statements are unlikely to help his cause. He should probably try to convey his strengths by his actions rather than by explicit comments.

A more basic question about self-presentation style that may occur to a new recruit, especially if he has aspirations to become a manager, is the following: Should he behave in an aggressive and forthright manner, express his ideas with confidence, and indicate his decisiveness and forcefulness when interacting with his superiors? Or should he be more cautious, conform to others' wishes, and not "rock the boat" while he is new? As Porter and Lawler (1968) have indicated, several "classic" books written in the early 1950s suggested that the second approach is preferable. In *The Organization Man*, Whyte (1955) argued that noncontroversial, conforming behavior is demanded by the organization.

Some recent studies, however, have brought the validity of this view into question. In a correlational study Fleishman and Peters (1962) examined managers' responses on a "Survey of Interpersonal Values." Subjects were shown triads of items that had been equated for social desirability and asked to state the item of most and least importance to them. The survey included a conformity scale designed to assess to what degree the worker valued doing what is accepted and proper, following rules and regulations closely, following social standards of conduct, and doing things in the approved manner. A significant negative correlation between conformity scores and evaluation of the subjects' job performance was discovered. Individuals who scored lower on conformity were rated higher on job performance by their superiors. Similar results were obtained by Porter and Lawler (1968), who found that managers who endorsed "inner-directed" traits (forceful, imaginative, independent, self-confident, decisive) were rated higher by their superiors than those who endorsed "other-directed" traits (cooperative, adaptable, cautious, agreeable, tactful).

Roadman (1964) also tried to determine which personal qualities are related to success as a manager. Managers enrolled in a training program in a large corporation were asked to rate their peers on 13 characteristics. The author also obtained data concerning the promotion rates of these managers over the next two years. Those with high promotion rates were significantly more likely to be rated by their peers as being high on a variety of traits, including originality, independence of thought, aggressiveness, self-expression, and leadership qualities, and relatively low in cooperation with others and in tact.

Conforming individuals may not, then, be as successful in organizational settings as people who exhibit more independence. It should be noted, however, that since these studies were correlational, the direction of causality is difficult to specify. As Fleishman and Peters (1962) state,

> Any causal relationship is uncertain here; on one hand, it may be that managers who value conformity highly display a restricted range of behavior and this hinders effectiveness; on the other hand, it may be that the managers who feel themselves to be ineffective will value the protection that explicit rule conformity affords (p. 137).

It may also be that people who are forthright and independent succeed despite these qualities, not because of them. Perhaps these qualities are positively correlated with more important traits such as energy level or intelligence, and it is the latter traits that are responsible for differences in functioning. Alternatively, the relative value of conformity versus originality may vary with economic conditions. The books stressing conformity were written in the 50s, when conditions were tight; the correlational studies suggesting that independence is preferable were written in the 60s, when conditions had improved and originality may have been more affordable.

The correlational studies described above dealt with people in managerial positions. Even if independence and originality are correlated with one's performance as a manager, it may nonetheless be unwise to present oneself in this manner to one's superiors before one has management status. As we indicated earlier, superiors may resent displays of independence and leadership until it is clear that a new recruit has been "broken in" and has been around long enough to know what he is doing. Most people who aspire to managerial status start out lower down in the organizational hierarchy. While a person who hopes eventually to be a manager may help his cause by displaying some leadership ability and some ability to think on his own, it is probably most important for him to concentrate on those characteristics which will make him effective in his present position.

Unfortunately, the self-presentational strategy that a new recruit employs may be influenced not by the qualities that are actually correlated with success in the organization, but the qualities that he thinks are important. Especially since it has been popularized for so long that organizations want docile, conforming men, recruits may try hard to mold themselves to this. Furthermore, unless recruiters are sophisticated about these matters, they themselves may believe that new recruits should be docile and conforming, and may select and hire the very type of individual who is unlikely to succeed in the organization.

It is to be hoped that future research will clarify the conditions under which a decisive and independent manner is an asset in the business world. We might note, however, that such a style may be considerably more effective for men than for women. Johnson (1976) has argued that if a woman attempts to use a forceful, direct approach in her interpersonal relations, she runs the risk of "becoming known as pushy, overbearing, unfeminine, and/or castrating" (p. 101). At least one experiment (Johnson and Goodchilds, 1976) has suggested that women who adopt a direct, expert stance in trying to influence others are rated as more aggressive than men who adopt exactly the same stance. The results of this study also indicated that women are more likely to employ a helpless, dependent interpersonal style when interacting with others than men are. Although this tactic may be effective in increasing a woman's rewards in the short run (see e.g., Gruder and Cook, 1971), Johnson (1976) has stressed that there are real disadvantages to the use of dependence as a strategy: "Certainly the use of this type of power by females (or any group) does not establish them as strong influencers; it may be a contributing factor both to their low power status and to their low self-esteem" (p. 103). In our opinion, more research is needed to determine whether certain ingratiation strategies are more effective for one sex than another. It would also be interesting to learn whether the success of a given tactic depends on the sex of the target person.

Ingratiating One's Subordinates. The task facing most managers or superiors is a complex one. They must be successful in motivating their employees to be highly productive. They may also wish to maintain the support and respect of those who work for them, although this latter factor will be more important to some managers than others (see, e.g., McClelland, 1975). What tactics are likely to facilitate these aims?

Opinion conformity would seem to be a very poor choice for a high-status person, for it is inconsistent with the behavior of one who has the capacity to make independent judgments. Besides, unless all of a leader's subordinates have the same opinions, the leader who tries to agree with all of them will be forced to contradict himself. A person whose opinions appear to vacillate will be viewed as weak rather than powerful. Rendering favors may be a good choice. Doing favors is consistent with the role of possessing more skills than subordinates. However, research (McClelland and Burnham, 1975) has suggested that the executive should avoid doing special favors for employees who request them. "When a manager bends the rules for particular individuals, he often alienates other workers. His failure to treat people equally destroys the worker's faith in the corporate reward system" (p. 69). This suggests that, above all, the manager must strive to maintain fairness in their treatment of employees.

Is other-enhancement a wise choice for the superior? It would seem to be, since the ability to pass judgment is consistent with the role. Furthermore, we have stated earlier that compliments are especially likely to be effective when they reduce a person's anxiety about poor performance. As a number of investigators have noted (see, e.g., Gomersall and Meyers, 1966), subordinates often feel extremely anxious about their performance, particularly if they are new on the job. A superior who compliments new recruits on what they have done well and indicates that he has faith that they will succeed at their job will not only elicit interpersonal attraction, but may enhance workers' morale and performance and minimize problems with absenteeism and high turnover.

Just because a superior's dependence on his workers is less obvious than their dependence on him does not mean that the superior can use compliments without regard to their credibility. If initial trust is low, or if the compliments are blatantly inaccurate, the worker may infer manipulative intentions and react negatively. Results of an interesting role-playing experiment by Organ (1974) suggest that while an expression of confidence in a subordinate's ability may lead to increased compliance under conditions of low surveillance, it may actually lead to less compliance if the degree of surveillance is high.

Organ has theorized that under high surveillance conditions, the supervisor's expression of confidence will be viewed as manipulative. If the subordinate feels that the compliment was intentionally given in order to increase compliance with his superior's decisions, he may feel that his freedom to make decisions of his own is being threatened. Under these circumstances, he may be motivated to demonstrate that he is free to do as he pleases by failing to comply with his superior.

What type of self-presentation should a manager or superior employ? Blau (1960) has noted that a high-status person may want to impress others without losing their affection. A very impressive person can seem unapproachable, while affection implies a feeling of closeness. High-status persons may be able to obtain affection while retaining respect by employing modest self-presentations. As Given (1964) has advised in his book on how to be a successful manager, if you are a high-status person, "it is a good idea now and then to 'let your hair down' and confess the mistakes you've made. . . . You don't have to pretend to bat 1.000. In fact, you might even boast about your mistakes now and then!" (p. 42). However, a high-status person may wish to avoid self-deprecation with respect to attributes which are central to his position. Such statements may well undermine his power and authority.

A question that is relevant to ingratiation, but that has not yet been mentioned explicitly in this chapter, is the following: What type of leadership should a superior employ if he wishes to insure high productivity and morale from his workers? Specifically, the following questions present themselves:

1. How much consideration should he show toward his employees? To what degree should his relationships with them be characterized by mutual trust, warmth, willingness to listen, etc.?

2. How much structure should he initiate in interacting with his subordinates? To what degree should he play an active role in organizing and directing their behavior?

3. To what degree should he allow his subordinates to participate in the decision-making process? Should he be authoritarian or democratic in his approach to supervisory relations?

Literally hundreds of studies have addressed these questions, and a comprehensive review is obviously beyond the scope of this chapter (see Fleishmen and Hunt, 1973; Kerr and Schriesheim, 1974; Korman, 1966; Vroom and Yetton, 1973, for detailed considerations of these issues). Nonetheless, it is possible to make a few general comments about these concepts and their relevance to ingratiation.

As other investigators have noted (e.g., Kerr and Schriesheim, 1974; Korman, 1966), most of the research in these areas is correlational in nature. Attempts have been made to correlate the above leader behaviors with such dependent variables as worker satisfaction, morale, and productivity. When correlations have been attained, it has generally been assumed that the productivity or morale were caused by the leadership behavior in question. However, this is not necessarily the case. In an interesting laboratory experiment, Lowin and Craig (1968) found that the reverse might also be true.

These investigators recruited male students for what was supposedly a part-time job supervising Job Corps employees. After a brief interview, each subject was told that he could have the job and was asked to keep an eye on one of the Job Corpsmen (actually a confederate of the researchers). Sometimes the confederate appeared to be highly competent at his job, while for other subjects his competence appeared to be quite low. At specific times during the session the confederate delivered verbal probes designed to assess the subject's level on each of the three dimensions of managerial style. The results indicated that low-competence confederates elicited closer supervision, more initiation of structure, and less consideration from the subjects. This study is provocative, but unfortunately has one serious flaw. The confederate was always aware of the experimental condition. This awareness may have caused him to behave differently with different subjects. He may even have delivered his probes differently, and he may have been biased in his recording of subjects' responses.

There are a few experimental studies that have explored the effects of these various leadership patterns, but unfortunately, the results from these experiments are far from consistent (see Kerr and Schriesheim, 1974, for a review). It is not clear how these concepts affect productivity and morale or how they relate to one another.

Recently, a great deal of research has focused on the possibility that the effectiveness of a particular leadership style may interact with situational or personality variables (see, e.g., Hunt and Larson, 1974). Some early research by Pelz (1952) has suggested that consideration will be effective only if the supervisor is influential with the higher levels of management. "The supervisory behaviors of 'siding with employees' and 'social closeness to employees' will tend to raise employee satisfaction only if the supervisor has enough influence to make these behaviors pay off in terms of actual benefits for employees" (p. 216). According to Pelz, noninfluential supervisors will only raise false hopes by employing these behaviors. "Employee expectations will be frustrated, and consequently their satisfactions will not rise and may even fall" (p. 216). In a provocative theory, too complex to be given justice here, House (1971) made a number of predictions concerning the interaction between situational variables and leadership behaviors. For example, he suggested that if the job in question is a higher-level one in which the behaviors expected of employees are ambiguously defined, initiating structure will reduce role ambiguity. Theoretically, structure will increase the employee's expectation that his behavior will result in goal attainment, and consequently result in increased worker satisfaction. Since lower-level jobs are more routine, a leader's initiation of structure may be viewed by subordinates as imposition of external control designed to keep them at work on unsatisfactory activities. Under these circumstances, initiation of structure should reduce worker satisfaction.

Although some laboratory studies have suggested that workers will prefer a participatory style of leadership (see, e.g., Scrontrino, 1972), research by Vroom and Mann (1960) has suggested that such preferences may depend on personal and situational variables. These investigators found, for example, that men who are dependent and authoritarian in nature will prefer authoritarian supervision, while those who are more independent fare better when allowed to participate in the decision-making process. Schein (1970) has reviewed several lines of research which provide examples of workers who are not alienated by authoritarian work situations, either because they have a genuine respect for authority and status, or because they have no desire for autonomy.

In summary, at present little practical advice can be given to the manager who is interested in the relationship between various leadership styles and the attitudes and productivity of his workers. We have discussed some of the difficulties in interpreting past research in this area. We might also point out that in most of the studies on leadership style, the dependent variables have been gross measures of productivity and worker satisfaction. Specifically how these leadership behaviors affect attitudes toward the leader, and how these attitudes might mediate morale and performance, have not yet been explored.

However, the research on the interactions between situational and personal variables and leadership behavior provides one recommendation for the potential ingratiator. As Schein (1970) has said,

> ... the successful manager must be a good diagnostician and must value a spirit of inquiry. If the abilities and motives of the people under him are so variable, he must have the sensitivity and diagnostic ability to be able to sense and appreciate these differences. . . . If the needs and motives of his subordinates are different, they must be treated differently (pp. 70-71).

The successful ingratiator is one who tailors his other-enhancement, opinion conformity, rendering of favors, and self-presentation to the particular characteristics of the individual whose affection and respect he is trying to win at the moment.

Effects of Ingratiating Overtures

Thus far in this chapter, we have discussed a variety of ingratiation tactics and their probable effectiveness, as well as status differences in tactical use. We would like to conclude the chapter with a discussion of some of the effects of engaging in ingratiating behaviors.

Reactions of Subordinates. We have already mentioned that the ingratiation tactic most likely to be successfully employed by superiors in trying to win the favor of their subordinates is other-enhancement. Many investigators have suggested that superiors should encourage and frequently praise their subordinates. For example, Tracey (1973) has advised managers that "people tend to become what we expect them to be. Have faith in your subordinates; both you and they will be rewarded" (p. 38).

Experimental evidence that positive expectations enhance a subordinate's productivity comes from an experiment by Bavelas (1965). Female applicants in a large industrial complex underwent an evaluation procedure, and the foreman who was to supervise each employee received information about her supposed scores. The foremen were led to believe that some of the women had scored quite high on the tests, while others had scored quite low. Some time later, the objective production record was examined. It was found that those women from whom the foremen had expected superior performance did better than women for whom the foremen held low expectations.

Unfortunately for organization theorists, most of the subsequent research on the effects of positive expectations has been conducted in classroom rather than organizational settings. Perhaps the most publicized of this work is that of Rosenthal and Jacobson (1968), who purported to show that children in a classroom would demonstrate greater intellectual growth if their teacher expected such growth. This work has received much criticism on methodological grounds (see Jones, in press, for a review). However, the finding has been replicated in later studies, and even most of the original critics now agree that expectations can alter one's performance.

Surprisingly, little research has been designed to explore exactly how positive expectancies operate. Perhaps a supervisor who holds such expectations for a recruit is more likely to provide a challenging initial assignment for him. There is certainly ample evidence that those who receive challenging first assignments are likely to develop greater competence and become more successful in their field (e.g., Berlew and Hall, 1966; Bray, Campbell, and Grant, 1974; Kaufman, 1974). Perhaps providing subordinates with such an opportunity facilitates the development of mutual trust, and creates an atmosphere in which the subordinate's good performance is especially reinforcing to the supervisor. As Gomersall and Myers (1966) have noted, "A supervisor who, in his first experience as a manager, learns to expect and seek information from his subordinates, and discovers that they are creative and responsible, is conditioned or permanently 'programmed' to look to, and rely on, subordinates for assistance in solving problems" (p. 71).

Another possibility is that perhaps supervisors who have positive expectations for their subordinates tend to praise their work more than supervisors who do not. Since praise is one of the most common of ingratiation tactics, it is surprising that more research has not focused on how praise affects performance. Again, most of the studies dealing with this problem have been conducted in the classroom, rather than an organizational setting (see Kennedy and Willcut, 1964, for a review). Criticism as well as praise has been shown to improve performance in certain situations. However, one of the most methodologically sound of these experiments (Hurlock, 1925) has shown that improvements in performance that are brought about by criticism tend to dissipate quickly over time, while those stemming from praise persist longer.

Of course, there are potential dangers in the use of positive expectations and praise. If a supervisor's expectations are unrealistically high, the subordinate may merely become frustrated in his efforts to meet them. And if a supervisor's positive expectations or praise are presented in such a way that attributions of ulterior motivation are made, we would expect them to backfire. The subordinate who feels that such statements are made to enhance his performance is likely to respond with considerable ill will (see, e.g., Organ, 1974). Perhaps the greatest threat to the subordinate, however, comes from praise that is insincere but believed. A worker's attempt to accurately assess his skills and make a rational decision about the kind of work he should pursue will be seriously hampered by inaccurate positive feedback from a supervisor. A person may be seduced into sticking with a career for which he is ill-suited and not particularly talented on the basis of such information.

Effects on Superiors. We have mentioned several times that those who wish to ingratiate people in high positions of power are in somewhat of a dilemma. Although the ingratiator has a great deal to gain by impressing a powerful target person, the tactics are likely to be less effective when the target person is aware of his position of power. We should now mention the other side of this coin—the fact that powerful target persons have an especially hard time assessing the reliability of the information they receive from others. The more powerful a person is, the more difficult it is for him to tell whether dependent others genuinely admire him and/or share his beliefs. There is an alternative explanation for virtually every compliment he receives—that the person who offers it is doing so for his own gain.

There is a second reason why the feedback received by a powerful person is likely to be ambiguous. Since supervisors have the power to enforce compliance and obedience, it is difficult for them to tell whether others' compliance is spontaneous or done in fear of recrimination. Strickland (1958) designed an ingenious laboratory experiment to highlight this dilemma. Subjects were led to take the role of supervisors, and were told that they would be in charge of two workers. They were told that for the purposes of the experiment, they would be permitted to monitor one worker fairly frequently; the other worker could only be monitored once or twice throughout the study. "Supervisors" were led to believe that both workers performed well. They were asked to answer some questions about how much they trusted each worker, and how dependable they felt each worker was. Then, during a second phase of the experiment, they were permitted to monitor each worker as frequently as they liked. Subjects attributed greater trust and dependability to worker B, the nonmonitored worker, and elected to monitor him less during the second phase of the experiment. According to Strickland:

> ... a supervisor cannot know first-hand the nature of the loyalty of his subordinates until he perceives that they have had an opportunity to be disloyal. In this experiment, S could perceive that subordinate B had this opportunity; B had been under low surveillance, yet he had apparently worked diligently. Subordinate A, on the other hand, had been under high surveillance by S and, although his work efforts were essentially identical with those of B, they were more often perceived by S as a function of S's own power over him (p. 213).

This study suggests that allowing workers some initial independence and freedom from continued monitoring will not only aid the supervisor in evaluating their work, but will facilitate the development of mutual trust and respect.

Effects of Ingratiation on Those Who Engage in It

How are companies affected by decisions to employ ingratiation tactics to attract and keep their employees? In order to attract employees in the first place, company recruiters often present the firm in a positive and somewhat unrealistic light. Many writers have described the reality shock suffered by new recruits who find that the job does not even come close to meeting their expectations (see, e.g., Dunnette, Avery, and Banas, 1973; Hall and Schneider, 1973). After a short period of work, the recruit's attitudes toward the organization often decrease markedly (Vroom and Deci, 1971). In such cases, high turnover is often a serious problem. Since initial job training costs represent one of the major financial burdens that organizations incur (Campbell, Dunnette, Lawler, and Weick, 1970), it is obviously important to employ hiring practices that will minimize problems with turnover. One approach to this problem is for companies to eschew positive self-presentational styles for a more realistic job preview in which the positive and negative features of the job are revealed. In a recent review of this literature, Wanous (1975) has concluded that realistic job previews reduce initial expectations and minimize problems with turnover, usually without reducing the number of people who will accept the job.

What consequences are likely to accrue to the individual who employs ingratiation strategies to attract and keep a job? Each person who seeks a job is likely to have to make the same decision. Should he present himself honestly? Or should he try to discern the type of individual the firm is looking for, and then alter his self-presentation accordingly? This is assuming that it is possible to tell what the company is looking for, although that may not always be the case. Suppose a potential recruit has a naturally aggressive and flamboyant personality, but has read books in college suggesting that a more conservative, subdued type is preferred. In his effort to present himself in a favorable light, he may play down the very qualities that the firm is looking for.

Even if it is clear what the company wants, the decision to try and alter one's self-presentation to fit their bill is a complicated one. Obviously, it is better to be hired for (or in spite of) one's true characteristics. But many people may assume that their chances of landing a job are better if they present themselves differently and/or more favorably than they really are. Indeed, there is good evidence that information given in job interviews is often strikingly inaccurate (Weiss and Dawis, 1960). However, the façade is not likely to end there. The qualities that are important in getting the job will probably be important in keeping it, and the person will be forced to continue his dissimulation in order to survive. Although we know of no research on this problem, we believe the psychic costs of keeping up such a façade indefinitely are likely to be great.

This discussion highlights some more general problems that the potential ingratiator might encounter. One is that the more we distort our self-presentation to attain a particular positive response or goal, the less signifying value that positive feedback has. Thus, people who engage in such strategies never really learn about themselves.

It is somewhat sad that those who present themselves falsely never attain accurate self-information. What is even more unfortunate is that they do not know it. There is a great deal of research to suggest (see Jones and Wortman, 1973, for a review) that if an ingratiator receives positive reinforcement from others after employing a particular self-presentation, he is likely to take this feedback from others quite seriously and come to believe the things he has said about himself. Thus, any differences between the real person and the façade are likely to diminish over time. The ingratiator will unwittingly become what he is pretending to be.

Although some research has focused on the effects of ingratiation on those who deliver and receive it, we need to know more about the vicissitudes of the phenomenon in organizational settings. Only then can we begin to relate the phenomena discussed in this chapter to major issues within the organizational field. It is hoped the present essay will help to stimulate such work and to convince the reader of its importance.

References

Aronson, E., and Linder, D. Gain and loss of esteem as determinants of interpersonal attractiveness. *Journal of Experimental Social Psychology.* 1965, *1*, 156-71.

Bachman, J. G. Faculty satisfaction and the dean's influence: An organizational study of twelve liberal arts colleges. *Journal of Applied Psychology,* 1968, *52*, 55-61.

Backman, C. W., and Secord, P. F. The effect of perceived liking on interpersonal attraction. *Human Relations,* 1959 *12*, 379-84.

Baskett, G. D. Interview decisions as determined by competency and attitude similarity. *Journal of Applied Psychology,* 1973, *57*, 343-45.

Bavelas, A. Personal communication, December 6, 1965. Cited and discussed in Rosenthal, R., and Jacobson, L., *Pygmalion in the Classroom.* New York: Holt, Rinehart and Winston, 1968.

Berlew, D. E., and Hall, D. T., The socialization of managers: Effects of expectations on performance. *Administrative Science Quarterly,* 1966, *11*, 207-23.

Blakeney, R. N., and MacNaughton, J. F. Effects of temporal placement of unfavorable information on decision making during the selection interview. *Journal of Applied Psychology,* 1971, *55*, 138-42.

Blau, P. M. A theory of social integration. *American Journal of Sociology,* 1960, *65*, 545-56.

Bray, D. W., Campbell, R. J., and Grant, D. L. *Formative Years in Business: A Long Term AT&T Study of Managerial Lives.* New York: Wiley, 1974.

Brehm, J. W., and Cole, A. H. Effect of a favor which reduces freedom, *Journal of Personality and Social Psychology,* 1966, *3,* 420-26.

Broll, L., Gross, A. E., and Piliavin, I. Effects of offered and requested help on help seeking and reactions to being helped. *Journal of Applied Social Psychology,* 1974, *4,* 244-58.

Byrne, D. Interpersonal attraction and attitude similarity. *Journal of Abnormal and Social Psychology,* 1961, *62,* 713-15.

———. Attitudes and attraction. In L. Berkowitz (ed.), *Advances in Experimental Social Psychology* (vol. 4). New York: Academic Press, 1969.

Byrne, D., and Griffit, W. A developmental investigation of the law of attraction. *Journal of Personality and Social Psychology,* 1966, *4,* 699-702.

Byrne, D., Griffit, W., and Stefaniak, D. Attraction and similarity of personality characteristics, *Journal of Personality and Social Psychology,* 1967, *5,* 82-90.

Byrne, D., Nelson, D., and Reeves, K. Effects of consensual validation and invalidation on attraction as a function of verifiability. *Journal of Experimental Social Psychology,* 1966, *2,* 98-107.

Byrne, D., and Rhamey, R. Magnitude of positive and negative reinforcements as a determinant of attraction. *Journal of Personality and Social Psychology,* 1965, *2,* 884-89.

Campbell, J. P., Dunnette, M. D., Lawler, E. E., and Weick, K. E. *Managerial Behavior, Performance, and Effectiveness.* New York: McGraw-Hill, 1970.

Carlson, R. E. Effect of interview information in altering valid impressions. *Journal of Applied Psychology,* 1971, *55,* 66-72.

Carnegie, D. *How to Win Friends and Influence People.* New York: Simon & Schuster, Pocket Book ed., 1940. Orig. publ. 1936.

Chaiken, A., and Derlega, V. *Self-disclosure.* Morristown, N. J.: General Learning Press, 1975.

Cozby, P. C. Self-disclosure, reciprocity, and liking. *Sociometry,* 1972, *35,* 151-60.

Deutsch, M., and Solomon, L. Reactions to evaluations by others as influenced by self-evaluations. *Sociometry,* 1959, *22,* 93-112.

Dickoff, H. Reactions to evaluations by another person as a function of self-evaluations and the interaction context. Ph.D. dissertation, Duke University, Durham, N. C., 1961.

DiMarco, N. Life style, work group structure, compatibility, and job satisfaction. *Academy of Management Journal,* 1975, *18,* 313-22.

Dion, K., Berscheid, E., Walster, E. What is beautiful is good. *Journal of Personality and Social Psychology,* 1972, *24,* 285-90.

Dittes, J. E. Attractiveness of group as function of self-esteem and acceptance by group. *Journal of Abnormal and Social Psychology,* 1959, *59,* 77-82.

Downs, A. *Inside Bureaucracy.* Boston: The Rand Corporation, 1967.

Dunnette, M. D., Arvey, R. D., and Banas, P. A. Why do They Leave? *Personnel,* May/June (1973):25-39.

Farris, G. F., and Lim, F. G., Jr. Effects of performance on leadership, cohesiveness, influence, satisfaction, and subsequent performance. *Journal of Applied Psychology,* 1969, *53,* 490-97.

Fleishman, E. A., and Hunt, J. G. (eds.) *Current Developments in the Study of Leadership.* Carbondale, Ill.: Southern Illinois University Press, 1973.

Fleishman, E. A., and Peters, D. R. Interpersonal values, leadership attitudes, and managerial "success". *Personnel Psychology,* 1962, *15,* 127-43.

Fromkin, H. L., Klimoski, R. J., and Flanagan, M. F. Race and competence as determinants of acceptance of newcomers in success and failure work groups. *Organizational Behavior and Human Performance,* 1972, *7,* 25-42.

Geller, D. M., Goodstein, L., Silver, M., and Sternberg, W. C. On being ignored: The effects of the violation of implicit rules of social interaction. *Sociometry*, 1974, *37*, 541-56.

Gerard, H. B., and Greenbaum, C. W. Attitudes toward an agent of uncertainty reduction. *Journal of Personality*, 1962, *30*, 485-95.

Given, W. B. *How to Manage People.* Englewood Cliffs, N. J.: Prentice-Hall, 1964.

Gomersall, E. R., and Myers, M. S. Breakthrough in on-the-job training. *Harvard Business Review*, 1966, *44*, 62-72.

Greenberg, M. S., and Frisch, D. M. Effect of intentionality on willingness to reciprocate a favor. *Journal of Experimental Social Psychology*, 1972, *8*, 99-111.

Griffit, W. B. Anticipated reinforcement and attraction. *Psychonomic Science,* 1968, *11*, 355.

Griffit, W. B., and Veitch, R. Preacquaintance attitude similarity and attraction revisited: Ten days in a fall-out shelter. *Sociometry*, 1974, *37*, 163-73.

Gruder, C.L., and Cook, T. D. Sex, dependency, and helping. *Journal of Personality and Social Psychology*, 1971, *19*, 290-94.

Hakel, M. D., Ohnesorge, J. P., and Dunnette, M. D. Interviewer evaluations of job applicants' resumes as a function of the qualifications of the immediately preceding applicants: An examination of contrast effects. *Journal of Applied Psychology*, 1970, *54*, 27-30.

Hall, D. T., and Schneider, B. *Organizational Climates and Careers.* New York: Seminar Press, 1973.

Hansson, R. O., and Fiedler, F. E. Perceived similarity, personality, and attraction to large organizations. *Journal of Applied Social Psychology*, 1973, *3*, 258-66.

Harvey, O. J., and Clapp, W. F. Hope, expectancy, and reactions to the unexpected. *Journal of Personality and Social Psychology*, 1965, *2*, 45-52.

Heider, F. *The Psychology of Interpersonal Relations.* New York: Wiley, 1958.

Hewitt, J. Liking and the proportion of favorable evaluations. *Journal of Personality and Social Psychology*, 1972, *22*, 231-35.

Holstein, C. M., Goldstein, J. N., and Bem, D. J. The importance of expressive behavior, involvement, sex and need-approval in inducing liking. *Journal of Experimental Social Psychology*, 1971, 534-44.

House R. J. A path goal theory of leader effectiveness. *Administrative Science Quarterly*, 1971, *16*, 321-38.

Hunt, J. G., and Larson, L. L. (eds.). *Contingency Approaches to Leadership.* Carbondale, Ill.: Southern Illinois University Press, 1974.

Hurlock, E. B. An evaluation of certain incentives used in school work. *Journal of Educational Psychology*, 1925, *16*, 145-59.

Insko, C. A., Thompson, V. D., Stroebe, W., Shaud, K. F., Pinner, B. E., and Layton, B. D. Implied evaluation and the similarity-attraction effect. *Journal of Personality and Social Psychology*, 1973, *25*, 297-308.

Jacobs, L., Berscheid, E., and Walster, E. Self-esteem and attraction. *Journal of Personality and Social Psychology*, 1971, *17*, 84-91.

Johnson, D. W., and Johnson, S. The effects of attitude similarity, expectation of goal facilitation, and actual goal facilitation on interpersonal attraction. *Journal of Experimental Social Psychology*, 1972, *8*, 197-206.

Johnson, P. Women and power: Toward a theory of effectiveness. *Journal of Social Issues*, 1976, *32*, 99-110.

Johnson, P. B., and Goodchilds, J. D. How women get their way. *Psychology Today*, October 1976, *10*, 69-70.

Jones, E. E., Gergen, K. J., and Davis, K. E. Some determinants of reactions to being approved or disapproved as a person. *Psychological Monographs*, 1962, *76* (whole no. 521).

Jones, E. E., Gergen, K. J., and Jones, R. G. Tactics of ingratiation among leaders and subordinates in a status hierarchy. *Psychological Monographs*, 1963, *77* (whole no. 566).

Jones, E. E., and Gordon, E. M. Timing of self-disclosure and its effect on personal attraction. *Journal of Personality and Social Psychology*, 1972, *24*, 358-65.

Jones, E. E., Jones, R. G., and Gergen, K. J. Some conditions affecting the evaluation of a conformist. *Journal of Personality*, 1963, *31*, 270-88.

Jones, E. E., Stires, L. K., Shaver, K. G., and Harris, V. A. Evaluation of an ingratiator by target persons and bystanders. *Journal of Personality* 1968, *36*, 385.

Jones, E. E., and Wortman, C. *Ingratiation: An Attributional Approach*. Morristown, New Jersey: General Learning Press, 1973.

Jones, R. A. *The Self-Fulfilling Prophecy: Social, Psychological, and Physiological Concomitants of Expectancies*. Hinsdale, New Jersey: Lawrence Erlbaum Associaties, in press.

Jones, S. C. Self-and interpersonal evaluations: Esteem theories versus consistency theories. *Psychological Bulletin*, 1973, *79*, 185-99.

Jones, S. C., and Schneider, D. J. Certainty of self-appraisal and reactions to evaluations from others. *Sociometry*, 1968, *31*, 395-403.

Kaufman, H. G. Relationship of early work challenge to job performance, professional contributions, and competence of engineers. *Journal of Applied Psychology*, 1974, *59*, 377-79.

Kennedy, W. A., and Willcutt, H. C. Praise and blame as incentives. *Psychological Bulletin*, 1964, *62*, 323-32.

Kerr, S., and Schriesheim, C. Consideration, initiating structure, and organizational criteria: An update of Korman's 1966 review. *Personnel Psychology*, 1974, *27*, 555-68.

Kipnis, D., and Vanderveer, R. Ingratiation and the use of power. *Journal of Personality and Social Psychology*, 1971, *17*, 280-86.

Korman, A. K. "Consideration," "initiating structure," and organizational criteria—A review. *Personnel Psychology*, 1966, *19*, 349-61.

Landy, D., and Sigall, H. Beauty is talent: Task evaluation as a function of the performer's physical attractiveness. *Journal of Personality and Social Psychology*, 1974, *29*, 299-304.

Layton, B. D., and Insko, C. A., Anticipated interaction and the similarity-attraction effect. *Sociometry*, 1974, *37*, 149-62.

Lombardo, J. P., Weiss, R. F., and Buchanan, W. Reinforcing and attracting functions of yielding. *Journal of Personality and Social Psychology*, 1972, *21*, 359-68.

Lowe, C. A., and Goldstein, J. W. Reciprocal liking and attributions of ability: Mediating effects of perceived intent and personal involvement. *Journal of Personality and Social Psychology*, 1970, *16*, 291-298.

Lowin, A., and Craig, J. R. The influence of level of performance on managerial style: An experimental object-lesson in the ambiguity of correlational data. *Organizational Behavior and Human Performance*, 1968, *3*, 440-58.

Martin, N. H., and Sims, J. H. Thinking ahead. *Harvard Business Review*, 1956.

Mayfield, E. C. The selection interview—A re-evaluation of published research. *Personnel Psychology*, 1964, *17*, 239-60.

McClelland, D. C. *Power: The Inner Experience*. New York: Irvington Publishers, Inc., 1975.

McClelland, D. C., and Burnham, D. H. Power-driven managers: Good guys make bum bosses. *Psychology Today*, December, 1975, *9*, 69-70.

Mettee, D. R. Changes in liking as a function of the magnitude and affect of sequential evaluations. *Journal of Experimental Social Psychology*, 1971, *7*, 157-72.

Mettee, D., and Riskind, J. Size of defeat and liking for superior and similar ability competitors. *Journal of Experimental Social Psychology*, 1974, *10*, 333-51.

Mills, C. W. *White collar: The American middle classes*. New York: Oxford University Press, 1962.

Morse, S. J., "Help, Likeability, and Social Influence," *Journal of Applied Social Psychology*, 1972, *2*, 34-46.

Nemeth, C. Effects of free versus constrained behavior on attraction between people. *Journal of Personality and Social Psychology*, 1970, *15*, 302-11.

Organ, D. W. Social exchange and psychological reactance in a simulated superior-subordinate relationship. *Organizational Behavior and Human Performance*, 1974, *12*, 132-42.

Pelz, D. C. Influence: A key to effective leadership in the first-line supervisor. *Personnel*, 1952, *3*, 209-17.

Porter, L. W., and Lawler, E. E., III. *Managerial Attitudes and Performance*. Homewood, Illinois: Richard D. Irwin, Inc., 1968.

Potter, D. A. Personalism and interpersonal attraction. *Journal of Personality and Social Psychology*, 1973, *28*, 192-98.

Regan, D. T., Straus, E., and Fazio, R. Liking and the attribution process. *Journal of Experimental Social Psychology*, 1974, *10*, 385-97.

Roadman, H. E. An industrial use of peer ratings. *Journal of Applied Psychology*, 1964, *48*, 211-14.

Rosenfeld, H. M. Approval-seeking and approval-inducing functions of verbal and nonverbal responses in the dyad. *Journal of Personality and Social Psychology*, 1966, *4*, 597-605.

Rosenthal, R., and Jacobson, L., *Pygmalion in the Classroom*. New York: Holt, Rinehart, and Winston, 1968.

Schein, E. H. How to break in the college graduate. *Harvard Business Review*, 1964, *42*, 68-76.

———. Organizational socialization and the profession of management. *Industrial Management Review*, 1968, *9*, 1-16.

———. *Organizational Psychology* (2nd ed.). Englewood Cliffs, New Jersey: Prentice-Hall, 1970.

Scherwitz, L., and Helmreich, R. Interactive effects of eye contact and verbal content on interpersonal attraction in dyads. *Journal of Personality and Social Psychology*, 1973, *25*, 6-14.

Scrontrino, M. P. The effects of fulfilling and violating group members' expectations about leadership style. *Organizational Behavior and Human Performance*, 1972, *8*, 118-38.

Secord, P. F., and Backman, C. W. Interpersonal congruency, perceived similarity, and friendship. *Sociometry*, 1964, *27*, 115-27.

Senn, D. J. Attraction as a function of similarity-dissimilarity in task performance. *Journal of Personality and Social Psychology*, 1971, *18*, 120-23.

Sigall, H. Effects of competence and consensual validation on a communicator's liking for the audience. *Journal of Personality and Social Psychology*, 1970, *16*, 251-58.

Sofer, C. *Men in Mid-career: A Study of British Managers and Technical Specialties*, Cambridge, England: Cambridge University Press, 1970.

Stapert, J. C., and Clore, G. L. Attraction and disagreement-produced arousal. *Journal of Personality and Social Psychology*, 1969, *13*, 64-69.

Staw, B. M. Attribution of the "causes" of performance: A general alternative interpretation of cross-sectional research on organizations. *Organizational Behavior and Human Performance*, 1975, *13*, 414-32.

Strickland, L. H. Surveillance and trust. *Journal of Personality*, 1958, *26*, 200-15.

Taylor, D. A., Altman, I., and Sorrentino, R. Interpersonal exchange as a function of rewards and costs and situational factors: Expectancy confirmation-disconfirmation. *Journal of Experimental Social Psychology*, 1969, *5*, 324-39.

Tognoli, J., and Keisner, R. Gain and loss of esteem as determinants of interpersonal attraction: A replication and extension. *Journal of Personality and Social Psychology*, 1972, *23*, 201-4.

Tracey, W. R., "The empty inbasket trick." *Personnel Journal,* January, 1973.

Vroom, V. H., and Deci, E. L., "The stability of post-decisional dissonance: A follow-up study of the job attitudes of business school graduates." *Organizational Behavior and Human Performance,* 6 (1971): 36-49.

Vroom, V. H., and Mann, F. C. Leader authoritarianism and employee attitudes. *Personal Psychology,* 1960, *13,* 125-40.

Vroom, V. H., and Yetton, P. W. Leadership and Decision-making. Pittsburgh: University of Pittsburgh Press, 1973.

Wall, J. A., and Adams, J. S. Some variables affecting a constituent's evaluations of and behavior toward a boundary role occupant. *Organizational Behavior and Human Performance,* 1974, *11,* 290-408.

Walster, E. The effect of self-esteem on romantic liking. *Journal of Experimental Social Psychology.* 1965, *1,* 184-97.

Walster, E., Aronson, V., Abrahams, D., and Rottmann, L. Importance of physical attractiveness in dating behavior. *Journal of Personality and Social Psychology,* 1966, *4,* 508-16.

Wanous, J. P., Realistic job previews for organizational recruitment. *Personnel,* April, 1975.

Webster, E. C. *Decision Making in the Employment Interview.* Montreal: The Eagle Publishing Co., Ltd., 1964.

Weiss, D. J., and Dawis, R. V., An objective validation of factual interview data. *Journal of Applied Psychology,* 1960, *44,* 381-85.

Wexley, K. N., Yukl, G. A., Kovaks, S. Z., and Sanders, R. E. Importance of contrast effects in employment interviews. *Journal of Applied Psychology,* 1972, *56,* 45-48.

Whyte, W. F. *Money and Motivation.* New York: Harper, 1955.

———. *The Organization Man.* New York: Simon and Shuster, 1956.

Wortman, C. B., Adesman, P., Herman, E., and Greenburg, R. Self-disclosure: An attributional perspective. *Journal of Personality and Social Psychology,* 1976, *33,* 184-91.

Chapter Five

An Attribution Theory of Leadership

Bobby J. Calder

The study of leadership is one of the few areas of social science which has had a truly cumulative history of research and thought. This work has not always been at the forefront of advances in methodology and theory, but neither has it been subject to the ebb and flow of attention characteristic of many other areas. The pattern of leadership research has been one of discarding, extending, and introducing ideas as the limitations of existing ideas are realized. A progression of different orientations has guided modern psychological studies of leadership. From the turn of the century to the 1940s, researchers attempted to identify the personal attributes and personality traits which leaders possess. Hundreds of studies compared leaders and nonleaders on variables such as height, intelligence, and dominance, but failed to establish any strong relationship between these variables and leadership. The many inadequacies of this work were revealed by the reviews of Stogdill (1948), Hemphill (1949), Gibb (1954), and Mann (1959). Most important, the trait approach failed to distinguish between leadership as a process and the leader as a person. Research was not able to detect traits associated with leadership across situations or even to obtain high correlations within a given situation.

The next orientation shifted from the characteristics of leaders to the actual behavior of leaders and their style of leadership. Bales (1950) developed a methodology for observing group discussions and recording member actions. He found two kinds of leadership styles which he termed "task" and "maintenance" (interpersonal) behaviors. Similar categories of leader behavior, initiation of structure and consideration, were obtained by Shartle and his co-workers (1952). These categories were obtained from factor analyses of a questionnaire (the Leader

Behavior Description Questionnaire) containing items referring to more specific behaviors. Scores on this test, still a subject of research activity, have been found to correlate with measures of leadership effectiveness and to support the importance of structure and consideration. A related line of research by Kahn and Katz (1960) sought to determine those patterns of supervision (e.g., closeness of supervision and employee orientation) most related to productivity and morale. Although the behavioral approach did point out some important aspects of leadership, its descriptive orientation did not really provide an explanation of leadership processes.

The trait and behavioral approaches to leadership were followed by an explicit recognition of the importance of the situational context in which leadership occurs. Fiedler (1964, 1967, 1971a, 1971b) proposed a "contingency model" which hypothesizes that leadership effectiveness depends on the relationship between the leader's task versus interpersonal orientation and the favorableness of the situation. Although empirical support for this model has been mixed (see e.g., Hunt, 1967; Graen, Alvares, Orris, and Martella, 1970; Fiedler, 1971b, 1971c; Chemers and Skrzypek, 1972), it has clearly been valuable in stimulating research concerned with more than just the distinguishing characteristics of leaders. Katz and Kahn's (1966) discussion of leadership has also been influential in emphasizing the interaction of style and task demands in determining leadership effectiveness.

Recently an even broader view of leadership has begun to emerge, one fully recognizing the multiple contingencies of the leadership process. Hollander and Julian (1968, 1969, 1970) have developed a "transactional" approach to leadership which emphasizes the exchange relations between leaders and followers. The leader provides resources in achieving group goals and in return receives status, esteem, influence, and legitimacy. Gibb (1969a, 1969b), along the same lines, has discussed an "interactional" approach. Leadership is viewed as "a concept applied to the *inter*action of two or more persons, when the evaluation of one, or of some of the parties to the interaction is such that he, or they, come to control and direct the actions of the others in the pursuit of common ends" (Gibb, 1969a, p. 221). This general orientation has perhaps had the most impact in the narrower form of "path-goal" theory (Evans, 1970, 1974; House, 1971; House and Mitchell, 1974). Utilizing an expectancy theory framework, House argues that the leader attempts to influence the valences and expectancies of subordinates regarding their organizational performance. The leader may increase the value of work-goal attainment or clarify path-goal instrumental relationships. It is suggested that, for an unstructured task situation, enhancing the value of work goals is more likely to increase effectiveness than path-goal clarification, while the reverse is true for a structured task. Although such theories are not fully interactional, they do attempt to specify just what it is that leaders provide followers. As such, they are a step beyond descriptions of what leaders do.

Given this evolutionary pattern, one would expect that judgments of the contribution of leadership research would have been less harsh than they have been. Stogdill (1974), in a recent compendium of research findings, concludes that:

> It is difficult to know what, if anything, has been convincingly demonstrated by replicated research. The endless accumulation of empirical data has not produced an integrated understanding of leadership (p. vii).

This view is probably shared by a majority of social scientists, with research on leadership being held in vague disrepute. Nor does there appear to be any great optimism that the accumulation of research is really heading anywhere.

What is to be made of this paradox? On the one hand, even a superficial examination of the history of leadership research conveys the sense of steady progress in theoretical sophistication and data collection. Yet there is little sense of really having achieved anything in the way of a new or profound understanding of leadership beyond that available from everyday knowledge. It is suggested here that a new, alternative orientation to leadership is needed. While attention is directed at a particular theoretical perspective, namely attribution theory, this perspective is not suggested in the context of simply extending current leadership research. While it might be possible simply to graft attribution theory onto one or more present approaches to leadership, the objective here is to propose a reorientation of the entire leadership area in which attribution would become the central construct. Indeed, in this reorientation, leadership itself would cease to be a scientific construct.

First- and Second-degree Constructs

Ideas about leadership may be used at two levels of analysis. One is the level of social science theory which we have been examining. Explanatory terms derived at this level are sometimes called second-degree constructs. They are supposed to be of a high degree of abstraction and to be supported by scientific evidence. In contrast, first-degree constructs belong to the world of everyday explanation. They are the terms and language we use to give meaning to the events of everyday life. A powerful criticism of social science in general has been advanced by ethnomethodologists such as Circourel (1964) and by phenomenologists such as Schutz (1967, originally 1932). All too often social science theory confuses first-degree constructs with those of the second-degree. Explanations of everyday life are implicitly assumed to have some scientific status. The validity of these first-degree constructs, however, lies only in the social construction of reality by a group of actors.

In our view, the paradoxical state of leadership research stems from just such a confusion of first- and second-degree constructs. The major problem is with the construct of leadership itself. Certainly leadership is a meaningful part of our language for describing and explaining everyday events. As will be discussed shortly, this language is very rich indeed. It is institutionalized and taught to very young children, complete with colorful examples of presumed historical significance. The thinking of social scientists has of late even contributed to this language. But none of this necessarily implies the validity of leadership as a second-degree construct.

Faced with a social construction of reality stressing the importance of leadership, researchers have directly adopted the language and ideas of everyday explanation in their zeal to study the phenomenon of leadership. Unfortunately, this "phenomenon" still exists principally as a first-degree construct. There has been almost no attempt to define what a leader is in truly psychological, sociological, or anthropological terms. Instead, the reference of the construct is to our everyday conception of leadership. In turn, leadership research may be seen as an attempt to make even further use of our implicit notions that leaders possess certain traits, that the behavior of leaders is different from followers, that different tasks require different leadership styles, and the like. We should point out that this criticism does not deny that intuition may be a source of scientific theory. It does deny that the constructs and logic of everyday language can be accepted as scientific without additional support. Leadership research has not provided this support. *The paradox of leadership research is resolved by the realization that what has been attempted is not the development of scientific theory but the systematic and consistent use of everyday thought.*

The problem with leadership research does not lie specifically with leadership theories. It lies with the metatheory of leadership. At the heart of the problem is *conceptualization*. Science consists of the interrelationships of concepts (Bunge, 1967). The real world is too complex to be understood in and of itself. Conceptualization seeks to represent the real world in a simple enough way to allow understanding. Scientific concepts are abstracted forms and represent only limited aspects of real world objects and behaviors. As shown in figure 1a, two types of reference relationships are crucial to conceptualiza-

FIGURE 1   Metatheoretical Reference Relationships

(a) The Nature of Scientific Theory

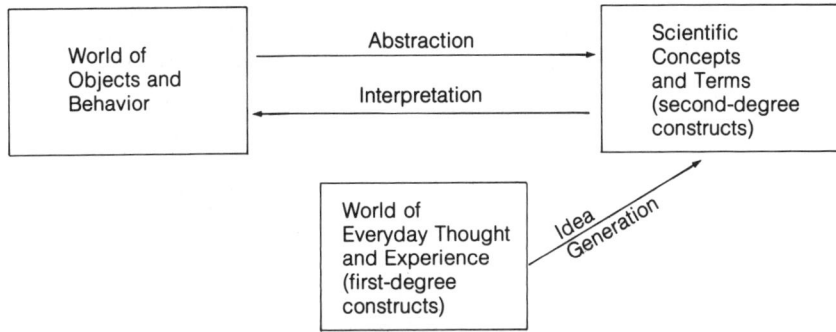

(b) The Nature of Leadership Theories

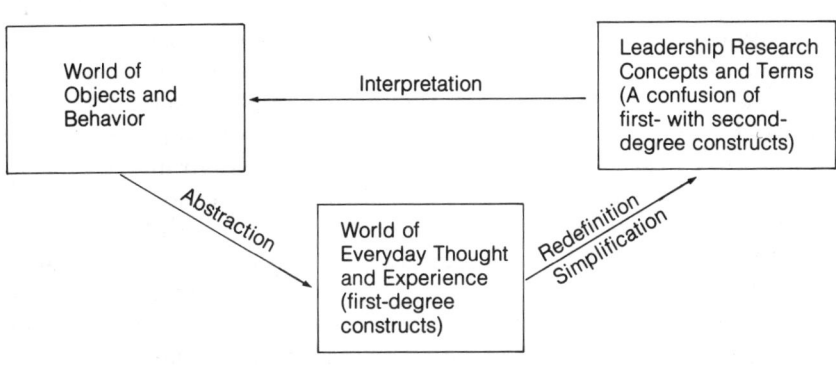

tion. Scientific concepts and the terms referring to them are abstractions of the real world in the sense that they are classes of objects depending on some common property or relation between the objects (Reichenbach, 1947). Concepts, in other words, are simplifications and idealizations of reality. The scientific process must work in reverse, too. We must be able to use scientific concepts to *interpret* the real world, to say whether real objects possess the properties or relations embodied in a conceptualization. Ostensive interpretation is the ability to name or point to real objects on the basis of conceptualization. Operational interpretation is more sophisticated. It is the ability to use a concept to measure real objects (Bunge, 1967).

The critical issue here is the nature of scientific concepts. In all of science the origin of concepts is somewhat problematic (Kaplan, 1964). How do we develop concepts? Where do they come from? Part of the answer seems to be that good theory spawns its own concepts (the best example being particle physics). There is also the process of reformulating old concepts in the face of empirical evidence. Still, there must be an external origin at some point in theory development, and this origin is the world of everyday thought and experience. In normal scientific discourse, this everyday world bears some unknown and largely irrelevant relationship to the real world. And its relationships to scientific conceptualization, when acknowledged at all, is meant to be limited to generating ideas, or "bootstrapping" (see figure 1a). Scientific concepts originating in this way are expected to be immediately subject to the most rigorous tests of interpretation and further abstraction.

When one looks at leadership research from the standpoint of metatheory, one is struck by its divergence from the philosophy-of-science view of conceptualization. Figure 1b attempts to characterize the problem in terms of the relationships of abstraction and interpretation. What has happened is that researchers have begun with an *unusually* strong bias toward the ideas of everyday thought and experience, or what we have called first-degree constructs. These constructs are in fact abstractions, albeit nonscientific ones, of the real world. As discussed more fully later, everyday conceptualizations of leadership represent people's nonscientific efforts to understand and give meaning to their world. The problem is that these everyday concepts have assumed such significance in our society that they seem to possess a higher-order legitimacy and credibility. The aura surrounding these concepts has led leadership researchers to adapt them with only minor redefinitions in terminology, but with even further simplification. Whereas everyday conceptualizations are highly situational in meaning, leadership researchers have tried to simplify them so that they are generalizable across situations. These overly-simplified everyday abstractions are the ostensible "second-degree" concepts of leadership research. Our point is that these "second-degree" concepts represent a confusion of first- with second-degree concepts and fundamental distortion of the scientific method. This confusion and distortion accounts for the failures of leadership research. The ostensible second-degree constructs of leadership research are difficult to use scientifically even for ostensive interpretation.

This basic problem has been compounded many times over by an unwillingness to change or discard leadership research concepts in the normal scientific way for fear of moving too far away from the original everyday ideas. This fear is natural since the presumed significance of leadership research stems directly from the clear importance of these everyday ideas. There are indications that leadership researchers are not entirely oblivious to this problem. Some researchers have implicitly begun to look for new ideas. Oldham (1976), for instance, addresses leadership in terms of the motivationl strategies of supervisors: "Personally Rewarding," "Personally Punishing," "Setting Goals," "Designing Feedback Systems," "Placing Personnel," "Designing Job Systems," "Materially Rewarding," "Materially Punishing," and "Designing Reward Systems." Approaches such as this may be seen, from our perspective, as efforts to move away from first-degree constructs while preserving the illusion that one is studying what it is that is important about those first-degree constructs. This need not be an illusion. It could be a viable research strategy, but to be so would require explicit attention to the relationship between first- and second-degree constructs. In any event, the strategy of trying to maintain some connection with the imagery of leadership while developing truly second-degree concepts is in fact a roundabout route back to the normal scientific relationships of figure 1a. While this strategy might have some pedagogical merit, it is far from optimal in moving toward scientific understanding. The more direct strategy of being unencumbered, beyond the idea-generation state, by second-degree constructs seems preferable.

What happens if we attempt to disentangle the second-degree constructs in leadership research from the first-degree? Although this is no doubt a matter for extended analysis, it seems clear that whatever second-degree constructs and hypotheses remain are not likely to be unique to the leadership area. They would in fact be those associated with other, more general models of behavior and interaction. The question, for instance, of what traits leaders possess becomes the question of whether trait models explain certain behaviors. The imagery of leadership may fit these behaviors, but this is irrelevant to the second-degree explanation. Leadership is a label applied in everyday life to the behaviors. Likewise, the transactional nature of leader-follower interaction reduces to models of interpersonal influence. In short, a scientific understanding of "leadership" does not depend on the construct of leadership. Now it may well be that general models, such as trait theory itself, also confuse first- and second-degree constructs. We would contend, though, that the hypotheses and constructs specific to the leadership area are the more blatant offenders.

It is not proposed that leadership research be abandoned as a unique line of inquiry. Acceptance of our view, however, does necessitate a basic reorientation. One possibility, as illustrated by Oldham's work, is the gradual drift away from second-degree leadership constructs toward new constructs which still implicitly bear on the everyday meaning of leadership. Unfortunately, researchers moving away from traditional concepts have fallen into the same trap. They tend to tie their new concepts to the world of everyday experience, producing the same confusion of first- and second-degree constructs. Perhaps the best example of this tendency is the work of Vroom and Yetton (1973). This work may be interpreted as an attempt actually to systematize everyday thinking in an overtly prescriptive fashion. Their model takes the form of a set of rules for managers to use in deciding how participative to be with their subordinates. The focus is "normative," but this may best be understood as "socially normative," rather than "scientifically normative" or "objectively optimal." This approach in fact dodges the confusion of first- and second-degree constructs by limiting itself to the former, the prescriptions of experience. The danger is that the scientific trappings associated with such models (e.g., basing rules at least partially on leadership research) do not make them any more scientific than any other statement of "principles of management."

A more viable reorientation for scientific inquiry is to make the everyday constructs and hypotheses of leadership an *object* of study. How people make inferences about and react to leadership is itself an important behavior to explain. To use a common analogy, we may investigate the behavior of people as "naïve scientists" of leadership. The term "naïve scientists" is apt, if a little too condescending, in view of our own use of "naïve" theory. Although there are several schools of thought (e.g., enthnomethodology and sociological phenomenology) relevant to this perspective, the "naïve psychology" of Fritz Heider (1958) seems best suited as a basis for our discussion.

Heider was concerned chiefly with interpersonal perception, the process through which people infer dispositions in others. An individual's actions may be attributed to a variety of causes, both environmental and personal, but according to Heider the common-sense rules of everyday explanation bias us strongly toward seeing people as the cause of their own behavior. The fact that a behavior has occurred at all tends to "engulf the field" of potential causes. Even so, people do make distinctions in the extent to which they assign responsibility for an action to the actor. Dispositions are inferred more strongly if external (situational) forces are weak and if the actor seems to have both the ability and the motivation to perform an action. Attributions to the actor serve to make the perceiver's world more predictable and managable. Heider's framework has subsequently been extended to make up the theoretical perspective called "attribution theory." Before turning to this theory, it may be useful to point up some of the subjective features of our everyday "naïve psychology" of leadership.

The Naïve Psychology of Leadership

Leadership is a prime manifestation of our bias toward perceiving personal causes for behavior. It is first of all something we say about other people, possibly including ourselves. It is not necessary to embrace the Whorf-Sapir hypothesis that thought depends on language to see that our language serves as a ready conduit for such statements. Leadership is a label which can be applied to behavior. It locates the reason for that behavior squarely in the personal dispositional nature of the actor. Certain inherent qualities of the actor are taken as causing both the behavior and its intended effects. These qualities concern both the ability and motivation of the actor. These qualities, however, are not invariant. This is an important point. Consider the following descriptions of two people.

Person 1	*Person 2*
Problem-solver	Physically imposing
Likeable	Shrewd
Warm speaker	Manipulative speaker
Selfless	Egotistical
Modest	Power-loving

Although the qualities of each person are very different, both in ability and motivation, the semantic constraints associated with our naïve concept of "leader" easily encompass each description. Both people could, given some behavior, be called a leader. That we might further specify the first person to be a "benevolent leader" and the second an "autocratic leader" is irrelevant. The point is that our naïve construct of leadership is very fuzzy. In general usage it refers only to some degree of personal potency. More specific qualitative meanings are largely situationally defined. It is not surprising that leadership has proven elusive as a scientific construct.

Judgments about leadership are made on the basis of observed behavior. An individual who labels another as a leader has no direct knowledge of the other's internal qualities. The other person's behavior must serve as evidence for the existence of these qualities.

Knowledge of this behavior comes either from direct observation or through indirect sources. The behavioral evidence itself may be only symptomatic, in that it is taken as reflecting the likelihood of more significant behaviors. That is, cues such as style of speech and physical attractiveness may be used as surrogate behaviors for judging leadership. In any case, leadership is an inference. An individual may be more or less confident about this inference. The central problem for the individual in inferring leadership is the adequacy of the behavioral evidence available.

The behaviors accepted as evidence of leadership depend on the particular set of actors involved. At the very least, the predominant social class composition of a group of actors and the purpose of the group's interaction renders some behaviors more appropriate than others for leadership inferences. Members of a street corner gang obviously focus on behaviors which are very different from those which are salient in the corporate board room. It may well be, as contended in leadership research, that there are dimensions of these behaviors which are the same, such as the structuring of group activities, but this should not be allowed to obscure what are very real qualitative differences. The meaning of leadership depends on the qualitative nature of the behavior taken as evidence of leadership. The meaning of leadership for members of the street corner gang is not nearly so fuzzy as indicated by the general usage of "leadership." This meaning is lost entirely in second-degree classifications of types of leader behavior.

Not only do evidential behaviors differ across groups of actors, but they are also distinct from other behaviors occurring within the group. If all the behaviors performed in a group were similar, there would be no basis for inferring leadership. The important point is that evidential behaviors must be *typical* of a class of behaviors which are *different* from those of most group members. Leaders, like deviates, cannot conform in their behaviors, otherwise there would be no basis for judging them different. Yet leaders are not deviates. Their behavior is perceived to belong to a special class of functionally positive behaviors. Hollander (1958) has advanced the well-known premise that leaders obtain "idiosyncrasy credits," that is, implicit permission to differ in their behavior in order to benefit the group. Granting of these credits is related to the supposed earlier conformity of leaders. This notion is clearly compatible with the present orientation. In our view, however, leaders are not in fact leaders until there is some basis for distinguishing their behavior.

Perhaps one of the most frequent distinguishing characteristics of evidential behavior is simply the extremity of that behavior. People who do more of something are likely to be perceived as leaders (or else as deviates). There is no better example of this than sheer verbal participation. Research indicates that people who talk more are more likely to be judged leaders. Consider a well-known experimental investigation by Bavelas, Hastorf, Gross, and Kite (1965). Industrial engineering and industrial psychology students were placed in four-person groups to discuss three human relations problems. The primary concern of the experiments was to modify one member's verbal output with operant conditioning techniques and to observe the effects of this behavioral difference on the perceptions of other group members. Each subject had in front of him a red and a green light which only he could see. The red light served as a negative reinforcer, flashing whenever the subject's comments supposedly hindered the discussion. The green light served as a positive reinforcer, flashing whenever the subject's comments supposedly contributed to the discussion. On the basis of the first discussion, the subject who ranked next to last in participation was selected as a target person (TP). Reinforcements were delivered during the second discussion to increase the TP's participation. During the third discussion, as in the first discussion, no reinforcements were delivered.

In the first experiment reported by Bavelas et al., the TP was positively reinforced and the other group members were negatively reinforced. The TP's participation increased significantly in the second discussion and remained higher during the third discussion. These increases were accompanied by increases on a questionnaire measure of the perception of the TP as a leader by the group members. A second experiment obtained the same effects when the reinforcements were delivered after some of the TP's remarks. Subsequent experiments failed to alter the TP's participation when only positive or only negative reinforcement was used. Zdep and Oakes (1967) replicated the Bavelas et al. findings and demonstrated that the presence or absence of the initial leadership questionnaire exerts no effect on the TP's leadership status.

According to a naïve psychology of leadership (which was not the perspective of this research), subjects employed talking as an evidential behavior—as an appropriate basis for inferring leadership. This is not at all surprising, considering what is known about verbal participation. Studies have shown that verbal behavior is strikingly systematic; it is plausible to speculate that people may well be aware of this regularity. The highest participator in a group usually accounts for about 40 percent of the total communication over a range of group sizes. Moreover, if the remaining group members are ranked in terms of participation, the percentages of participation for adjacent ranks approximate a constant ratio, and mathematical functions can be written to describe the data (Bales, Strodtbeck, Mills, and Roseborough, 1951; Stephan and Mishler, 1952; Coleman, 1960; Kadane and Lewis, 1969). Such regularities suggest that people may come to expect variations in verbal behavior and may use these variations along with other behavior to infer leadership.

Evidential behaviors must be typical as well as different. Not all behavioral variation in a group implies leadership. Certain classes of variation are even associated with deviance. Inferences about leadership are made only from differences in behavior which fit expectations of how leaders typically behave. As already noted, such expectations are different for different groups of actors. Just what these leadership expectations are is an empirical question. To imply leadership, an observed behavior must be typical in the sense that the differentiated behavior falls within a set of behaviors associated with leadership expectations.

According to Heider, the perception of personal causes of behavior may be tempered by the perception of situational forces. Certainly the meaning of leadership is particular to a given group of actors *and* their situational context over time. Heider's thought suggests, moreover, that the situation constitutes a potential alternative explanation of behavior. A given evidential behavior can be attributed not to leadership as a personal, internal cause but to external, situational forces. For example, if subjects knew that a target person's verbal participation was artificially raised by external reinforcement, this behavior would not result in the perception of leadership. Internal qualities would be discounted as a cause of the behavior.

The importance of situational factors as alternative explanations in the perception of leadership can be seen by contrasting "leadership" and "headship." Researchers have generally reserved "leadership" for social influence which is not based on formal authority (cf. Kochan, Schmidt, and De Cotiss, 1975). With headship, individuals acquire the right to exercise certain legitimate forms of influence in an organization as a consequence of occupying a certain position in the organization. It is widely supposed that such legitimate influence should not be confused with leadership, which is based on personal initiative and the voluntary compliance of others. The same assumption applies, though more loosely, in the naïve psychology of leadership. Behaviors which might otherwise constitute evidence of leadership are discounted in favor of the situational explanation that they are enacted because it is the individual's duty to perform them. In general, the perception of leadership is less likely whenever the role demands of other people are salient as causes of behavior. But the distinction between leadership and headship is not so rigid as researchers have tried to make it. (It is not a scientific distinction). Unless role demands are highly salient, people follow their bias toward personal causation. The fire chief who goes with a group of firemen into a burning building probably will be perceived as a leader even if going into the building is his duty.

Extreme behaviors sometimes "engulf the field" of perception to the extent that even highly plausible situational explanations are ignored. The executive who contributes heavily to a company task force may be perceived as a leader by members even though they know that this behavior is likely to earn the executive a large bonus.

In sum, the naïve psychology of leadership provides participants in a group with an understanding of their behavior. As a scientific construct, leadership is hopelessly ambiguous, as documented by Pfeffer's (in press) discussion of treatments in the literature. At the level of situational meaning for a given set of actors, leadership provides a rich, internal, personal explanation of behavior.

Attribution Theory Perspectives

Naïve psychology is presently being investigated under the rubric of attribution theory. While there has been little attempt to operationally define the term "attribution," the construct refers to the cognitive processes through which individuals infer causation from observed behavior. Attribution is a second-degree construct. It is less vague than the notion of "interpersonal perception," though both refer to the psychological processes underlying naïve psychology. Attribution studies rely heavily on two theoretical perspectives, one due to Kelley (1967, 1971, 1972), and the other to Jones and Davis (1965).

We have preceded our discussion of attribution theory with an informal overview of the naïve psychology of leadership, because in our view the two main attribution theory perspectives are not capable of providing a complete analysis. These perspectives do not address all of the complexities entailed in the attribution of leadership. Attribution theories are by no means a ready-made vehicle for the reorientation of leadership research which we have advocated.

Both major theoretical perspectives dwell on conditions which determine whether a behavior is attributed to internal, personal causes or to situational forces. Kelley posits an intuitive "analysis of variance" model. In inferring an internal state such as leadership from another person's observed behaviors, an individual analyzes the covariation between the behaviors and a possible internal state. There are four dimensions of possible covariation. Are the behaviors (1) "distinctive" in that an observer does not tend to attribute the internal state to most people? (If he does, the observer must make an internal attribution that he reacts to most people in a similar way rather than an external attribution that there is something different about the person observed.) Is there consistency over (2) time and (3) place (modality) in the observation of the behaviors? Is there consistency over (4) people by way of a consensus that the behaviors reflect the internal state? To the extent that behavior exhibits distinctiveness and consistency over time, place, and the reactions of others, it is accepted as evidence of a personal disposition such as leadership. Otherwise the behavior is

FIGURE 2   An Extension (shaded areas) of Jones and Davis' Treatment of Behaviors and Effects

		Effects	
		Observed	Unobserved
Behaviors	Observed	Jones and Davis' Correspondence Possible	Unnatural Description
	Unobserved	Correspondence Possible	No Correspondence Possible

discounted and attributed to situational factors. The former is termed an "internal" attribution, the latter, an "external" attribution. Although the consistency-across-other-people dimension appears to be more complex than the theory indicates, data from laboratory experiments generally support the theory (e.g., McArthur, 1972).

Jones and Davis cast their approach in terms of how an observer can be sure that the language he uses to describe a behavior is also descriptive of the personal dispositions of the performer. Their term for the match between observed behaviors and inferred dispositions is "correspondence." The problem for the observer is whether any disposition corresponds to the observer's description of another person's behavior. Correspondence depends on certain variables. These variables concern the "effects" produced by a behavior rather than the behavior itself. Jones and Davis rule out effects for which behaviors are unobserved as evidence of dispositions—that is, as candidates for possible correspondence. This restriction seems unnecessary. The theory may readily be extended, as shown in the shaded areas in figure

2. Correspondence is certainly possible where both behaviors and effects are observed. Jones and Davis do not allow, however, for the possibility that behavior can be assumed in the face of observed effects. If this logic is pursued, it becomes apparent that one of the main contributions of the theory lies in suggesting that attributions may be made on the basis of knowledge about the effects of a person's actions *even though these actions were not themselves observed.* To see the importance of this for the attribution of leadership, consider the situation in which a person is placed in a supervisory position and the performance results of his subordinates suddenly improve. Although no one may ever observe behaviors on the part of the supervisor which could have produced the improved results, these effects are still typically used as a basis for attributions.

Instances in which behavior is observed but effects are not are more problematic. The physical, or otherwise objective, description of behavior is rarely in itself meaningful. Behavior only acquires meaning when suppositions about effects and purposes are part of the description. Otherwise the description is unnatural, for the very reason that correspondence is precluded. One of the main values of Jones and Davis' work is to point up the sterility of any attribution theory that does not recognize the nonobjective nature of the description of behavioral observations. These descriptions are so weighted toward effects that the actual observation of behavior is hardly a necessary condition for correspondence.

Jones and Davis also limit their analysis to intended effects. Again we must recognize the weight given to effects in descriptions. Even unintended or accidental effects color descriptions. An observer might know that a successful new supervisor could not logically have produced all the improvement in his subordinates' performance, but these performance effects are part of the description of that supervisor's behavior anyway. Existing attribution theories are quite weak in capturing the meaningfulness of such descriptions. It is an oversimplification to focus separately on either behavior or effects.

Two key variables, according to Jones and Davis, affect correspondence: the number of noncommon effects produced by a choice, and the social desirability of a choice. The choice may be between implicit or explicit alternatives. In either case, the chosen alternative is associated with a set of observed effects, *and* each of the unchosen alternatives is associated with a set of effects which would have been the consequences had they been chosen. To the extent that the effects associated with the chosen alternative do not overlap with those of the unchosen alternatives, a stronger attribution can be made. For example, if a woman chooses to marry one of three boyfriends, where all three are handsome but the chosen one is richer while the other two are more intelligent and personable, the chosen alternative possesses fewer noncommon effects (being rich is the sole noncommon effect), and the attribution should be strong that the woman is materialistic, and so forth. The strength of an attribution is also increased if the assumed social desirability of the effects associated with the chosen alternative is low. People may choose what is socially desirable rather than personally desirable. If most people would have preferred the effects of the choice, it is less revealing of an internal, nonsituational cause than a choice involving less socially desirable effects.

FIGURE 3 An Analysis of Leadership Attributions Based on Jones and Davis' Theory of Correspondent Inferences

		Assumed Social Desirability of Effects	
		High	Low
Number of Noncommon Effects	High	Ambiguous and Doubtful Leadership	Interesting but Ambiguous Leadership
	Low	Doubtful Leadership	Correspondent Leadership

Jones and Davis' theory is not well developed. It does not recognize, for instance, the fact that selection of a set of alternatives involves as much choice as the final selection among alternatives. That is, the fact that all of a woman's boyfriends are handsome must surely affect attributions, even though the theory eliminates this effect because it is common within the choice set at a particular point. The theory has stimulated interesting research, however. In an experimental paradigm originated by Jones, Davis, and Gergen (1961), a subject observes a job interview and then makes attributions about the interviewee. The interviewee is either consistent with the role demands of this job (in-role) or is inconsistent (out-of-role). Out-of-role behavior presumably encompasses fewer noncommon effects and has lower social desirability. As predicted, attributions about the interviewee's personality traits are stronger for out-of-role behavior. Figure 3 displays a summary of the impact of the number of noncommon effects and the social desirability of effects on the attribution of leadership. Correspondent inferences are possible only when both variables are low. In this case, observers can be more confident that behavior which can be described in the language of leadership also reflects personal leadership qualities.

Attribution theories are not as mechanistic as our discussion indicates. The active nature of the perceiver's role is usually handled in terms of observer biases. Jones and Davis emphasize the possible consequences of an action for the observer. The effects on which an inference about correspondence is based may be interpreted differently, depending on the involvement of the observer. The effects may be "hedonically relevant" in that they constitute positive or negative outcomes for the observer; or they may involve "personalism" in that they are perceived to be directed at the observer personally. Both hedonic relevance and personalism may strengthen what would otherwise be a weak attribution. In general, if behavior is observed during the course of an ongoing interaction, the goals of that interaction will in part shape the nature of the attributions made (cf. Jones and Thibaut, 1958). Such biases are likely to be particularly important for the attribution of leadership in groups where goal compatibility among members is absent. If the goals embodied in an observed behavior conflict with an observer's own goals, the observer is less likely to make a leadership attribution regardless of the nature of the observed behavior.

An Attribution Theory of Leadership

We may now draw together our discussion in the form of a tentative attribution theory of leadership. As noted, it is felt that the theoretical perspectives of Kelley and Jones and Davis do not in themselves provide a complete approach. The present perspective seeks to point up the full complexities of the naïve psychology of leadership. Figure 4 provides an overview of the model.

Leadership is defined as a first-degree construct. It refers to a set of personal qualities which are described in ordinary language. These qualities and the words used to describe them differ for different groups of actors and situations. The investigation of the naïve psychology of leadership presumes some knowledge of the qualities and language which constitute the meaning of leadership. The scientific problem at issue is the explanation of how a set of actors, for whom leadership is situationally defined, infer leadership from observing each other's behavior. The internal qualities associated with leadership are not directly knowable. The individual who uses the first-degree construct of leadership must work backward from behavior and can never know with certainty whether or not leadership qualities actually exist as a personal cause of behavior.

FIGURE 4 Flow Diagram of the Attribution Model

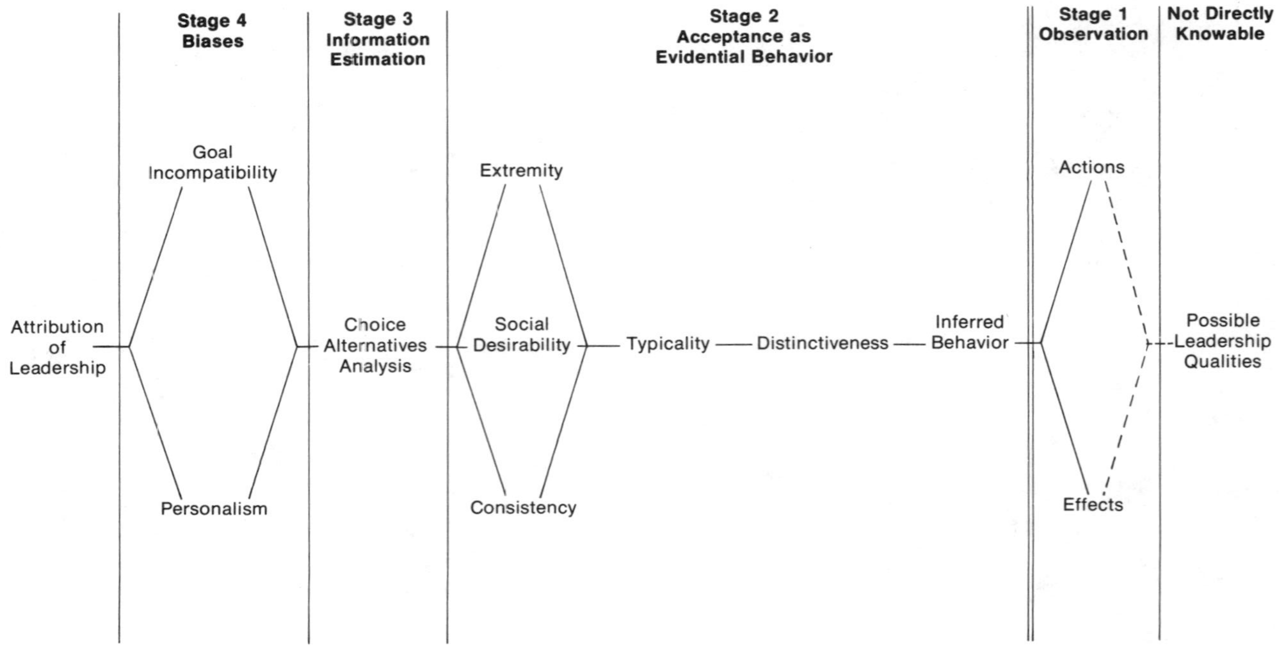

Leadership is a disposition and cannot itself be observed. The first stage in the attribution of leadership is therefore the observation of behavior by another and the effects of this behavior. (Note that the stages in fig. 4 are given from right to left to connote that the individual is working backward.) In the simplest instance, the individual observes both actual physical behavior and its consequences. The observation of physical behavior, however, is not a necessary condition for the attribution of leadership. Many behaviors are private or otherwise unobservable. Often description is available only second-hand from others. As discussed in connection with Jones and Davis' work, individuals may also rely heavily on knowledge about effects which are associated with a person, even though the requisite behavior for these effects has not been observed. If an effect is not in actuality due to a person, this is a source of attributional error.

Observed actions and effects may also imply entirely different behaviors which have no basis at all in actual observation. Individuals may infer the existence of important behaviors from observations which are trivial in themselves. Earlier we saw that simply observing the amount of time talking increased the likelihood of attributing leadership. Such relationships probably depend on the fact that such simple observations imply the existence of otherwise unobserved behaviors. Someone who talks a lot in a group probably makes relatively more money, knows important people, and so forth. These "inferred observations" supply indirect evidence to the attribution process. It is explicitly recognized in the next stage of our model that individuals may base their attributions on more information than they have in fact observed.

In the second state of the attribution process, actual and inferred observations are either accepted or rejected as evidence of leadership. Observations are first examined for distinctiveness. The actions and effects associated with a focal person are compared with other actors in the group. To be acceptable as evidence, the focal person's behavior must be distinguishable. By definition, leadership cannot describe everyone in the group; its very meaning calls for distinctive behavior. The process we have in mind is similar to Kelley's notion of distinctiveness. There the emphasis was on how a person sorts out his own reactions to people. Does he always react in a particular way to most people or is his reaction to a certain person distinctive? Only if the reaction is distinctive should it be attributed to some property of the focal person. Our contention is that a somewhat simpler notion will do.

An individual examines the variability in behavior across the group. If little variability exists, then there is no information on which to base inferences about leadership. With greater variability, more potential evidence is available to the attribution process.

Once potential evidence is detected, it is matched against expectations about how leaders should act. Figure 5 characterizes the nature of these "typicality" inferences. The meaning of leadership for a group is represented as a set of beliefs linking leadership qualities to specific behaviors. The individual has what amounts to an implicit theory of leadership. That is, he believes that personal leadership qualities

FIGURE 5   Processes Underlying Typicality Inferences

produce certain behaviors and effects. These beliefs are at the core of the first-degree qualitative meaning of leadership. The individual uses his implicit leadership theory to interpret potential evidential behaviors and effects. He does this by reversing the causal direction of his beliefs. As depicted in figure 5, expectations are formed by assuming that the behaviors and effects believed to be caused by leadership qualities themselves provide causal evidence for the existence of these qualities. That is, the belief that a certain leadership quality produces a certain behavior is transformed into the expectation that an instance of the behavior implies the existence of the quality. Logically this is to assert that if A implies B, then B implies A. While logically incorrect, these expectations provide a psychological basis for interpreting observed behavior. A potential evidential behavior or effect is compared with expected behaviors and effects. If the former is similar to the latter, a typicality inference is made. The inference is that the potential evidence, standing alone, implies leadership qualities.

It may be helpful to illustrate the psychologic of the putative typicality inference process. Remember that, by our account, leadership has meaning only as defined by a particular group of actors. Let us look at, what is for leadership research, a somewhat unusual group—apartment house janitors in Chicago. Intensive interviews by Gold (1964) suggest the tenor of the janitor's everyday life. "Cut-throating", for instance, is common. This is the practice of trying to force another janitor out of a building by reporting violations of union rules (e.g., the other janitor's wife helps him do the work), sabotaging the other janitor's building or equipment, and even going directly to the other janitor's boss to ask for that janitor's building. Now we might imagine that these janitors, in their interaction, have certain ideas about leadership, or personal potency. Suppose that this group thinks of leadership in terms of qualities such as manliness, aggressiveness, shrewdness, and egotisticalness. Whatever their own language for these traits, this constellation underlies the meaning of leadership for them.

The meaning of leadership must further depend on a set of beliefs which explain certain behaviors on the basis of these qualities. Corresponding to the first step in figure 5, suppose that the janitors' implicit theory of leadership looked something like that shown in figure 6 (arrows indicate that a quality leads to a behavior).

FIGURE 6   Janitors' Implicit Theories of Leadership

Qualities	Behavior
Manliness	Tries to cut-throat other janitors
Aggressiveness	Engages in intimidating rough-housing
	Makes fun of some janitors
Shrewdness	Takes up for his janitor friends
	Talks a lot about his exploits
Egotisticalness	Stands up to tenants

When janitors observe each others' behavior, their implicit theory of leadership is used in reverse. That is, they assume, corresponding to the second step in figure 5, that trying to cut-throat other janitors implies the qualities of aggressiveness and shrewdness. (That such underhandedness might indicate the opposite of leadership in some groups is irrelevant.) Engaging in intimidating rough-housing indicates manliness and aggressiveness, and so on for the other behaviors. Such reversals create leadership expectations. If a given observed behavior is judged distinctive (see fig. 4), it is compared with these expectations (the third step in fig. 5). If the two are similar—the observed behavior is *typical* of the expected—then the observed behavior is taken, other things being equal, to indicate leadership.

Typicality inferences are not sufficient for the attribution of leadership, however. Look back at figure 4. The next step is the determination of whether or not there are alternative explanations of the observed behavior which would discount the typicality inference. This is the major concern of most attribution theorists, and Kelley's ideas are important here. Although all possible alternative explanations can never be ruled out, not even psychologically, it is possible for the individual to examine the evidence for spuriousness, the possibility that the ostensible behavior-leadership link is actually due to some extraneous factor. The work of Kelley, discussed earlier, suggests three major dimensions for such an intuitive analysis. If the evidence does not hold up over time or across relevant situations, or if it is not supported by the opinions of other relevant actors, it may plausibly be attributed to nonpersonal situational sources. "Standing up to a tenant" on one occasion is not attributed to a janitor's leadership qualities unless this behavior is validated so as to minimize the possibility of spuriousness. Along with Kelley's validation dimensions, we would explicitly add Jones and Davis' criteria of social desirability. Group pressure is a powerful alternative explanation which must be ruled out in the attribution of leadership.

Coupled with the consistency evaluation of potential evidence in figure 4 is the evaluation of extremity. This is thought to be important in two ways. First, it is possible that evidence may not be judged extreme or important enough to imply leadership qualities. The nature of leadership is such that individuals may have quantitative standards for leadership. Even behaviors and effects which are distinctive and typical may not automatically be assumed to indicate leadership. Potential evidence is discounted unless certain cutoffs are exceeded. Standing up to a tenant might have to entail telling the tenant what he can and cannot request rather than merely a less extreme, passive refusal to comply with a request.

The extremity evaluation is also important as a possible bypass for consistency alternative explanations. This is why in figure 4 it is depicted as operating in parallel with consistency and social desirability. Any behavior or effect which is sufficiently extreme can override alternative explanations. This is the phenomenon Heider called "engulfing the field" of perception. It probably occurs frequently in the attribution of leadership. The rumor of a janitor's having once punched a tenant in the nose might be extreme enough to override any consideration of validity.

The third stage postulated in the attribution process involves what is termed "information estimation." The prior acceptance stage determines whether potential evidence should be interpreted as indicating leadership or should be discounted. Evidence, however, may be acceptable and still not be specifically informative about leadership qualities. Following Jones and Davis, the informativeness of the evidence is thought to depend on an analysis of the alternative behaviors presumably open to a focal person. For any behavior that a focal person performs, it is possible to construe various alternative behaviors and the effects associated with them. At a minimum there is the alternative of not performing the behavior. By comparing the evidential behavior and effects with hypothesized alternatives, the information value of the evidence can be estimated. Jones and Davis' notion of noncommon effects is illustrative in many ways of the process we have in mind.

Although a full analysis of the information estimation stage is beyond the scope of this discussion, what is plausible is that an observer evaluates the evidential worth of observed behavior and effects by comparing them to what he construes to be the *personal* alternatives of the actor. He compares the behavior performed with other things the actor might have done. The likelihood that an observed behavior is caused by leadership qualities as opposed to other qualities can be evaluated from these alternatives. A different sort of validity is at stake here, one more akin to what we might think of in scientific parlance as "construct" validity. The question is whether there is any evidence for "leadership" qualities causing the observed behavior versus other, perhaps unsuspected, qualities. The acceptance stage dealt with spuriousness, not the legitimacy of the inferred qualities themselves. It is informative in the latter regard to believe that the person observed could have performed other behaviors with different effects, which would have implicated nonleadership qualities. This is particularly true to the extent that the observed behavior could be explained by these same nonleadership qualities as well as possible leadership qualities. If a janitor were known to have other options for making extra money (for example, working part-time for his brother-in-law), but the janitor seemed to choose cut-throating instead, an observer would feel far more confident that the underlying qualities involved in cut-throating were aggressiveness and shrewdness, which are leadership qualities, rather than greediness, which is common to both behaviors. While the previous stage ruled out nonpersonal alternative explanations, in this stage more or less confidence in the evidential behavior results from attemps to rule out competing personal explanations which do not involve leadership qualities.

The final state shown in figure 4 recognizes the potential of individual biases to affect attributions. The major sources of bias have already been discussed. There is the broad class of goal incompatibility, which subsumes hedonic relevance, and the more specific effect of personalism. It is our hypothesis that the latter effect generally produces only minor distortions in comparison with goal incompatibility. It would seem very difficult to attribute leadership to someone whose goals run against one's own. On the other hand, the attribution of leadership would seem much easier if it facilitates attainment of one's goals.

Conclusions

Parts of the theoretical discussion here have of necessity been speculative. There are, to our mind, wide gaps in attribution theorizing. Moreover, attribution theorists in social psychology have never confronted the need for rich, qualitative understanding which their work implies. It is hoped that the present theory, and our comments on the naïve psychology of leadership, suggest a way in which it is possible, finally, to subject that aspect of everyday experience we call leadership to scientific scrutiny.

An attribution theory of leadership is likely to strike many as mere sophistry. They may feel that somehow there is nothing really new in it. There have long been studies of the perception of leadership. While true, this should not obscure the central point of the proposed theory: Leadership *exists* only as a perception. Leadership is not a viable scientific construct. It is, however, extremely important as naïve psychology. Attribution theory seeks to provide a scientific analysis of this naïve psychology. The problem for future research is not merely what variables affect the perception of leadership. Research must be directed at the underlying nature of the leadership attribution process. The theoretical proposals set forth in this chapter are intended to stimulate such research.

Attribution theory also has important implications for leadership training. Leadership cannot be taught as a skill. Skills may certainly help a person to perform more effectively, but leadership depends on how this performance and its effects are perceived by others. To teach leadership is to sensitize people to the perceptions of others—that is, to sensitize them to the everyday common-sense thinking of a group of people. The transfer of leadership from one group of actors to another thus becomes highly problematic. The would-be-leader must respond to attributions based on the meaning of leadership for each group with which he interacts.

If it does nothing more than call attention to the need for understanding the everyday, nonscientific, meaning of leadership for specific groups of actors, attribution theory represents an advance for both leadership research and training.

References

Bales, R. F. *Interaction Process Analysis: A Method for the Study of Small Groups.* Reading: Addison-Wesley, 1950.

Bales, R., Strodtbeck, F., Mills, T., and Roseborough, M. Channels of communication in small groups. *American Sociological Review,* 1951, *16,* 461-68.

Bavelas, A., Hastorf, A. H., Gross, A. E., and Kite, W. R. Experiments on the alternation of group structure. *Journal of Experimental Social Psychology,* 1965, *1,* 55-70.

Bunge, M. *Scientific Research I: The Search for System.* Berlin: Springer, 1967.

Chemers, M. M. and Skrzypek, G. J. Experimental test of the contingency model of leadership effectiveness. *Journal of Personality and Social Psychology,* 1972, *24,* 172-77.

Cicourel, A. *Method and Measurement in Sociology.* New York: Free Press, 1964.

Coleman, J. The mathematical study of small groups. In H. Solomon (ed.), *Mathematical thinking in the measurement of behavior,* Glencoe, Illinois: The Free Press of Glencoe, 1960.

Evans, M. The effects of supervisory behavior on the path-goal relationship. *Organization Behavior and Human Performance,* 1970, *55,* 277-98.

———. Extensions of a path-goal theory of motivation. *Journal of Applied Psychology,* 1974, *59,* 172-78.

Fiedler, F. E. A contingency model of leadership effectiveness. In L. Berkowitz (ed.), *Advances in experimental social psychology,* vol. I, Academic Press, 1964.

———. *A Theory of Leadership Effectiveness.* New York: McGraw-Hill, 1967.

———. Validation and extension of the contingency model of leadership effectiveness: A review of empirical findings. *Psychological Bulletin,* 1971a, *76,* 128-48.

———. *Leadership.* New York: General Learning Press, 1971b.

Gibb, C. A. Leadership. In G. Lindzey (ed.), *Handbook of Social Psychology,* vol. 2, Reading: Addison-Wesley, 1954, p. 877-920.

———. An interactional view of the emergence of leadership. In C. A. Gibb (ed.), *Leadership,* Baltimore: Penguin Books, 1969a, p. 214-22.

———. Leadership. In G. Lindzey and E. Aronson (eds.), *The Handbook of Social Psychology* (2nd ed.), vol 4, Reading: Addison-Wesley, 1969b, p. 205-82.

Gold, R. In the basement—The apartment building janitor. In P. Berger (ed.), *The Human Shape of Work: Studies in the Sociology of Occupations,* New York: Macmillan, 1964, pp. 1-49.

Graen, G., Alvares, K., Orris, J. B., Martella, J. A. Contingency model of leadership effectiveness: Antecedent and evidential results. *Psychological Bulletin,* 1969, *74,* 285-96.

Heider, F. *The Psychology of Interpersonal Relations,* New York: Wiley, 1958.

Hemphill, J. K. The leader and his group. *Educational Research Bulletin,* 1949, *28,* 225-29.

Hollander, E. Conformity, status, and idiosyncracy credit. *Psychological Review,* 1958, *65,* 117-27.

Hollander, E. P. and Jullian, J. W. Leadership. In E. F. Borgatta and W. W. Lambert (eds.), *Handbook of Personality Theory and Research,* Chicago: Rand McNally, 1968, p. 890-99.

———. Contemporary trends in the analysis of leadership processes. *Psychological Bulletin,* 1969, *71,* 387-97.

———. Studies in leader legitimacy, influence, and innovation. In L. Berkowitz (ed.), *Advances in Experimental Social Psychology,* vol. 5, New York: Academic Press, 1970, p. 34-69.

House, R. A path-goal theory of leader effectiveness. *Administrative Science Quarterly,* 1971, *16,* 321-38.

House, R., and Mitchell, T. Path-goal theory of leadership. *Journal of Contemporary Business,* 1974, *3,* 81-97.

Hunt, J. G. Fiedler's leadership contingency model: An empirical test in three organizations. *Organizational Behavior and Human Performance,* 1967, *2,* 290-308.

Jones, E. E. and Davis, K. E. From acts to dispositions. In L. Berkowitz (ed.), *Advances in Experimental Social Psychology,* vol. 2, New York: Academic Press, 1965.

Jones, E., Davis, K., and Gergen, K. Role playing variations and their informational value for person perception. *Journal of Abnormal and Social Psychology,* 1961, *63,* 302-10.

Jones, E. and Thibout, J. Interaction goals as bases of inference in person perception. In R. Taguiri and L. Petrullo (eds.), *Person Perception and Interpersonal Behavior,* Stanford: Stanford University Press, 1958.

Kadane, J. B., and Lewis, G. H. The distribution of participation in group discussions: An empirical and theoretical reappraisal. *American Sociological Review,* 1969, *34,* 710-23.

Kahn, R., and Katz, D. Leadership practices in relation to productivity and morale. In D. Cartwright and A. Zander (eds.), *Group dynamics,* Evanston, Ill.: Row, Peterson, and Co., 1960.

Kaplan, A. *The Conduct of Inquiry: Methodology for Behavioral Science,* New York: Intext Educational Publishers, 1964.

Katz, D., and Kahn, R. L. *The Social Psychology of Organizations.* New York: Wiley, 1966.

Kelley, H. Attribution theory in social psychology. *Nebraska Symposium on Motivation,* 1967, *15,* 192-238.

——. *Attribution in Social Interaction.* Morriston, N. J.: General Learning Press, 1971.

——. *Causal Schemata and the Attribution Process.* Morristown, N. J.: General Learning Press, 1972.

Kochan, T., Schmidt, S., and De Cotiis, T. Superior-subordinate relations: Leadership and headship. *Human Relations,* 1975, *28,* 279-94.

Mann, R. D. A review of the relationships between personality and performance in small groups. *Psychological Bulletin,* 1959, *56,* 241-70.

MacArthur, L. The how and what of why: Some determinants and consequences of causal attribution. *Journal of Personality and Social Psychology,* 1972, *22,* 171-93.

Oldham, G. The motivational strategies used by supervisors: Relationships to effectiveness indicators. *Organizational Behavior and Human Performance,* 1976, *15,* 66-86.

Pfeffer, J. The ambiguity of leadership. *Academy of Management Review,* in press.

Reichenbach, H. *Elements of Symbolic Logic.* New York: The Free Press, 1947.

Schutz, A. *The Phenomenology of the Social World.* Evanston, Ill.: Northwestern University Press, 1967.

Shartle, C. *Executive Performance and Leadership.* Columbus: Ohio State University Research Foundation, 1952.

Stephan, F., and Mishler, E. The distribution of participation in small groups: An exponential approximation. *American Sociological Review,* 1952, *17,* 598-608.

Stogdill, R. Personal factors associated with leadership. *Journal of Psychology,* 1948, *25,* 35-71.

Vroom, V., and Yetton, P. *Leadership and Decision-Making.* Pittsburgh: University of Pittsburgh Press, 1973.

Zdep, S. M., and Oakes, W. F. Reinforcement of leadership behavior in group discussion *Journal of Experimental Social Psychology,* 1967, *3,* 310-20.

Chapter Six

Information Processing and Decision Making in Organizations

Terry Connolly

This chapter attempts to synthesize two approaches to organizational research: the approach which views organizations as complex decision-making devices, and the approach which treats them as complex information-flow or communication networks. The synthesis is a view of the organization in terms of complex, decision-related communication networks. This notion is taken up in the first section of the paper, under the rubric of "The Diffuse-Decision Process." The discussion of these processes leads directly to consideration of the relationship between an individual's decision-making activities and the informational inputs he receives; these issues are taken up in section 2. Section 3 extends the approaches to the individual information-processing/decision-making phenomena to settings in which two or more individuals interact with the same streams of information—for example, in situations of conflict, consensus judgment, or training of diagnostic skills. Finally, section 4 returns to the network level, and addresses a number of issues of network structure in relation to the decisional activities with which the net is concerned. The broad intent is to draw together a number of normally separate issues in organizational communication and decision making, and to identify several promising research leads which flow from this synthesis.

Section 1: Individual Decision Events versus Diffuse-Decision Processes

At risk of only slight overgeneralization, it may be argued that most of the research on decisions has focused on single-individual choice events. That is, the predominant analytic framework addresses situations in which an individual—the decision maker—is confronted with some set of alternatives from which he is to choose. Further, this basic framework is founded on choice under conditions of certainty—a known set of alternatives, each with known costs and benefits, evaluated in terms of a known and stable set of preferences, goals, objectives, or criteria.

Given the substantial investment in this one-person, decision-event model, the tendency is to treat more complex decisional phenomena by attempting to reduce them to this basic model. Thus, the problem of unknown costs and benefits of alternatives may be handled within the basic model by means of the expected-value (or subjective expected-value) approach. Similarly, the problem of several dependent decision makers may be treated via the game-theoretical approach, in which formalized rules of interaction allow treatment of each individual separately in terms of the basic model. From this perspective, such developments as the theory of teams (e.g., Marschak and Radner, 1954) and models of negotiation and bargaining behavior (e.g., Nash, 1950; Cross, 1965) may be seen as efforts to treat complex decisional phenomena by reduction to the single-individual, choice-event model.

It appears that the success of these various extensions declines rather quickly as the departure from the basic decision-making model increases. Thus game-theoretic formulations are powerful for the two-person, zero-sum case, but quickly become unmanageable for more complex situations. Similarly, the treatment of unknown futures via expectations is powerful for the tightly-constrained situation known as "risk" (where the decision maker knows, or believes he knows, the probability of each outcome) but much less so in the case normally identified as "uncertainty" (where these probabilities are not known). As Conrath (1966) points out, the view of "uncertainty" as an unknown probability distribution across future states of the world is, in fact, highly restricted, and one can readily visualize situations of vastly greater uncertainty. For example, the decision maker may not know what his alternatives are or the possible outcomes of each. This highly uncertain situation is, Conrath argues, common in real-world decision problems and is not successfully treated by any of the extensions of the basic decision model.

The major thrust here is the proposal of an alternative to this "reductionist" approach to complex decisional phenomena. The essence of the alternative proposed here is that we may usefully approach such phenomena, not as a set of distinct decisions or events, but as an inter-active decision process. As will be argued below, the process orientation directs attention to the interrelationships between decisional and communicative activities in organizations, activities which have traditionally been treated somewhat separately. Such integration, it is hoped, will help to overcome certain existing limitations in the research literatures relating to the two activities, and open the way for further integrating research.

One limitation of research based on the individual decision-event model is that the decision maker is considered largely in isolation from the organizational environment which provides his input information, and to which he communicates his outputs. Decision-focused models of organizations typically introduce informational mechanisms, if at all, only on an ad hoc basis. For example, both Simon (1955) and Downs (1967) suggest models of information-search based on decisional variables; Cyert and March (1963) make a number of critical assumptions relating informational inputs to decisional behavior. However, none of these authors would claim to offer a broad and general treatment of organizational communication processes as they relate to decision making. Indeed, attempts at empirical validation of the informational assumptions (for example, Porat and Haas's [1969] examination of the Cyert and March assumptions) are typically partial, and not entirely supportive.

A similar isolation may be found in the literature on organizational communication. A highly competent review of this topic (Porter and Roberts, 1972) lists only one source (out of more than 150 references) in whose title the word "decision" appears. Interestingly, the one exception, Ference (1970) is an attempt somewhat parallel to the present one to link communications systems and decision processes in organizations.

The treatment of organizational communication as separate and distinct from such other organizational events as decision making has been somewhat limiting. For example, a study by Allen and Cohen (1969) of communications in research and development laboratories includes a number of interesting findings concerning the general patterns of technical information flow in such settings. However, the decisional relevance of the communications was not explicitly considered, and, as a result, questions of the purpose and impact of the observed communication patterns are unresolved. Similarly, the issue of how effective are the decisions made as a result of the information flows cannot be satisfactorily addressed.

It appears, then, that research leverage may be gained by attempting to treat decision making and communication in organizations within a single integrated framework, explicitly treating the impact of informational inputs on individual decision makers, the role of decision variables on communication events, and the communicative connections between multiple decision makers in large decision processes. One such approach, developing from the notion of the "diffuse-decision process," is advanced below.

The Diffuse-Decision Process

Consider the following situations in which important decisions are made:

1. The location of a major public utility, such as a new highway.
2. The planning and budgeting of expenditures in a large research laboratory.
3. The selection of a Presidential candidate by a major political party.
4. The setting of a price for a commodity in a competitive market.

For several reasons—the lack of an identifiable decision maker, the extended time period, the importance of structuring and linkage mechanisms—none of these decisions is conveniently treated in terms of the traditional decision-event model. It appears that such phenomena are more appropriately examined as decision processes than as decision events.

The adjective "diffuse" is here used to emphasize the characteristics of such processes which distinguish them strongly from decision events. First, the processes are temporally diffuse, covering extended periods of time, with indistinct end-points. Second, they are multiperson processes, with influence (and decision-making responsibilities) diffused across a number of individuals. Third, the participants are typically separated by nontrivial physical distances, so that these processes are geographically diffuse. Finally, when found in organizational settings, the processes often cover several organizational levels, and are thus organizationally diffuse.

There is no intention here of classifying decisional phenomena as either of the focused-event type or of the diffuse-process type. Rather, the suggestion is of a continuum from highly focused to highly diffuse along which a given decision may be located for analytical purposes. Without attempting to define the metric for "amount of diffuseness," it seems fair to suggest that at least some important decisions are diffuse in all four senses described above. The examples given earlier in this section all seem to be highly diffuse decisions. The extreme case of a diffuse decision is a process in which many participants, over an extended period of time, generate a decision in response to some decision problem, working with alternatives which may initially be unclear or unknown, with costs and benefits not reliably estimable, with unclear and/or conflicting preferences, and with modifiable resources and constraints. Activities concerned with the clarification of objectives, predictions of future states, generation of alternatives, resolution of preference conflicts, and so on, are thus treated as an integral part of the decision process, rather than as external to the decision itself, the traditional approach.

It is at once clear that the net of communicative activities in which the participants are embedded constitutes a critical part of the decision process. It is this net which connects the activities of the individual participant into the decision process, providing him with his decisional inputs, and connecting his outputs into the decisional activities of others. The notion of a decision-specific communication net thus serves as a bridge between the microscopic, individual-focused level of analysis and the more macroscopic, process-focused level. The individual is treated as an active node in a communication net, receiving, storing, searching for, transforming, and emitting information. We shall assume further that he has preferences of some kind (both personal, and those associated with his organizational membership); that he has stored information, both factual and procedural (for example, skills at information processing, expectations as to where specific information may be found); that his time is a scarce resource; and that his behavior is intendedly (though boundedly) rational, subject to certain limits of human information processing.

At the macroscopic level, we shall be concerned with the aggregate of these individual information-processing activities, that is, the decision-specific communication net. At this level, we shall consider such issues as the relationship between the "official" or imposed net connecting the participants and the "unofficial" or emergent net they actually use; the impact of decision-problem characteristics on net configurations; measures of net characteristics such as centrality, stability, and connectedness; and possible relationships between net characteristics and the effectiveness of the decision-making process.

In summary, then, the present chapter is an attempt to understand organizational decision making by focusing on the flows and transformations of information associated with the decision process. The first section examines these issues at the level of the individual, but—it is important to emphasize—viewing him not as an isolated decision maker but as a participant in a decision process. We therefore stress the mechanisms which connect him to the other decision participants. We will consider such issues as what activates his decision-related behavior, how he synthesizes his various informational inputs, how he searches for new information, and so on. A subsequent section will consider situations in which two individuals interact with identical informational inputs. Such situations arise in certain cases of bargaining and bilateral negotiation, in the formation of consensual judgments by two experts, and in the training of judgmental skills. The final section of this chapter returns to the aggregate or network level, drawing on a number of available research literatures to suggest approaches to research into, and design of, effective diffuse decision processes.

Section 2: The Individual

We consider the individual decision participant as a rather complex information-processing machine—receiving, storing, searching for, transforming, and emitting information of various categories. In this section, we will examine the various types of information processing in which individuals become involved, and outline a number of established research traditions which, in their approaches or in their findings, provide some insight into these activities.

The first issue to be examined is how an individual becomes a participant in a decision process. That is, what types of events initiate decision-relevant information-processing activities? Surprisingly little attention has been paid to this issue in either normative or descriptive treatments of decision making. One of the few systematic treatments is that of Pounds (1965) in his discussion of what he calls "problem finding." The basic activation mechanism proposed by Pounds is the individual's perception of some discrepancy (presumably larger than some threshold level) between an actual state of the world and some aspired-to or desired state (cf. Siegel, 1957; March and Simon, 1958, p. 49). Pounds' contribution is an attempt to specify the sources of the aspired-to states, which he attributes to certain "models" held (perhaps implicitly) by the manager to generate desirable levels of certain variables or goal states. He outlines four classes of such models —those based on historical data, those based on plans, those based on other people's expectations, and those generated outside the organization—which together accounted for virtually all the problem-finding events he observed in one case study.

Several comments are in order here. First (as Pounds himself notes), the analysis is quite preliminary. Even at the taxonomic level, the four classes of models he suggests appear neither mutually exclusive nor collectively exhaustive. For example, how would one classify a product quality complaint from a customer who, having built a planning model on the basis of prior learning-curve data, finds current product quality unacceptable? The case appears to have elements of all four classes of models. On the other hand, it is important for our purposes to note that activity is initiated by the discrepancy perceived between two informational events, those reflecting actual and those reflecting desired states of the world. Since information in these two classes will generally not be received by the individual simultaneously, his storage and forgetting mechanisms and the factors directing his attention, are clearly of importance. Finally, the discrepancy-activation model does appear to be quite general, covering processes from a routine request for specific information to major problem-solving and decision-making activities.

Apart from its intrinsic interest, the process of "problem finding" or, more generally, of the initiation of information-processing activities may be expected to have a critical impact on later parts of the process. For example, the individual's formulation of the problem he faces, the priority he assigns to it relative to his other work, the solution criteria he applies, the extent and direction of his information search, and the nature and direction of the information he finally puts out, are all plausibly related to the events which initiated his information-processing activity. It is clear, then, that the initiation phase is both little understood and important for an adequate understanding of later phases of the process.

Categories of Information

In addition to a more refined taxonomy of initiating events, we will need a vocabularly to describe the subsequent decision-related information-processing activities of the individual. It will expedite the later discussion if we make the following distinctions:

Information Source. Some decision-related information comes to the individual without any specific effort on his part—for example, as a normal part of his organizational role, from normal social contacts, from his regular reading or monitoring of professional and nonprofessional publications, specific communications from other individuals, and so on. For such information, the individual is a passive receiver. A second class of information is that actively sought out by the individual in response to a specific decisional activity—for example, a focused library search, a request to a colleague for specific information or advice, or a formal investigation aimed at discovering some specific fact. Finally, some part of the decision-relevant information used by the individual may have been acquired previously and stored (in his memory, personal library, notes, or whatever) so as to be accessible with little or no overt information search. Clearly, these three categories shade into one another in some cases, but the distinctions retain some value. For example, we would hypothesize that information acquired by active search will be more decision-specific than that acquired as a passive receiver; that the ease of acquiring information, or of converting it to usable form, will affect the extent to which it is used; and that important individual differences in ability and style exist between the three modes, with some individuals preferring to rely on, and performing more effectively in, one mode rather than another. We shall, then, make use of a distinction between three modes of information acquisition: passive receipt, active search, and retrieval from storage.

Information Function. A second potentially useful set of categories of information may be derived from consideration of the function the information serves in the individual's decision-making activity. The traditional model of the individual decision maker considers him as choosing from some set of alternatives in light of his evaluation of the expected consequences of each in terms of some set of goals, preferences, or criteria. With some extension, this suggests the following categories of decision-related information:

1. State-related: information concerned with the identification or clarification of either (a) the present, or (b) the aspired state of the system.

2. Alternative-related: information concerned with the identification or clarification of an action alternative.

3. Outcome-related: information concerned with the prediction or estimation of the consequences of choosing each alternative, its costs and benefits.

4. Criterion-related: information concerned with the specification or clarification (including relative weighting) of the criteria to be applied in making the choice.

5. Computation-related: information concerned with the processing of information in the first four categories into output information.

6. Process-related: information concerned with the specification or clarification of the individual's role in the decision process, or of the roles of others.

An application of this category scheme is given in Connolly (1975). One focus of that study was the perception of uncertainty by participants in a research-planning decision process. Perceived uncertainty was treated as the individual's feeling of being less than certain of the adequacy, accuracy, or relevance of his information in each of the six categories. It was hypothesized that these uncertainties would be experienced independently—that is, an individual may experience high uncertainty in one area, low uncertainty in another. This hypothesis was substantially supported. This finding raises a number of questions, discussed later in this essay, about the usual unitary treatment of uncertainty. It also suggests several interesting research issues, such as the determinants of perceived uncertainty (for example, the type of decision problem, the individual's role in the process), and the consequences of perceived uncertainty (for example, patterns of information search, satisfaction with decision outcomes). Without developing these issues in detail here, it does appear useful to consider the information used by the decision participant in terms of its relevance to his decisional activities.

Information Processing and Expert Judgment

Our view of the individual as an active node in a complex net of information channels suggests that useful linkages can be established to the large and well-developed literature treating human judgment as an information-processing phenomenon. Excellent reviews of this literature are available (e.g., Slovic and Lichtenstein, 1971; Pitz, 1975; Kleinmuntz, 1968). The present discussion will thus be limited to a brief overview of the basic paradigms of that work, its relationships to our current interests, and the identification of a few areas where suggestive findings are available, or could be generated with modest extensions of current directions of work.

The basic concern of the descriptive work on human judgment is with how an individual uses the information available to him in reaching a decision or forming a judgment in the face of uncertainty. Two distinct (and thus far little-connected) paradigms have guided most of this research. The first emphasizes the use of regression models to describe the relationships between (a) the information inputs to the judge ("cues") and his judgmental output; and (b) the cues and the true state of the world, the latter being considered as the source of the information contained in the cues. Following Brunswik's "lens model" conceptualization (Brunswik, 1952), the first of these relationships provides a model of the judgmental process of the individual, while the second models the environment in terms of the relationship between the accessible cue or stimulus dimensions and the inaccessible true state which they reflect. The relationships between the several statistical measures relating cues, response, and environment have been examined in some detail (e.g., Tucker, 1964).

The second major paradigm in judgment research is based on Bayes' Theorem, a simple result in elementary probability theory which provides a normative rule for revising probabilities in light of new information. A typical experiment in this paradigm asks the subject to revise his beliefs (probability estimates) as to which of several populations is being sampled in light of sample information. His revisions are then compared to those generated by Bayes' Theorem. Thus, in both the regression and Bayesian paradigms, insight into the subject's judgmental process is obtained by comparing his responses to those generated by a theoretical model which uses the same input information. The limitations of the "paramorphic representation" of the subject's judgmental processes thus achieved are thoughtfully discussed by Hoffman (1960).

In terms of the categories of informational events suggested earlier, most of the work on human judgment examines individuals operating in a passive-receiver mode on state-related information. That is, the subject is presented with some information and is asked either to estimate the value of some continuous variable, or to estimate the probability that some hypothesis is a true description of the present state of the world. Studies of subjects deciding how much information to use have been confined to the Bayesian paradigm (e.g., Pitz. 1968; Fried and Peterson, 1969), though rather simple extensions of the lens model formulation (Connolly, 1974) allow examination of the same phenomenon within the regression paradigm. Similarly, there appears to be no obvious problem in extending the content of the information processed to the other categories of information proposed earlier.

In several respects, then, the models guiding the research on human judgment phenomena are quite close to our present interest in the individual as an active node in a complex, decision-related communication net. As an example of the possibly fruitful interactions between the judgment literature and the diffuse-decision notions, consider one approach used in judgment studies to represent the individual. A large number of studies in the judgment literature have attempted to represent the individual's use of his input information in forming his judgments. One of the simplest approaches is to fit first-order linear-regression models to a series of judgments (see Slovic and Lichtenstein, 1971, pp. 677-80 for examples of such studies). This approach is often surprisingly successful in capturing a large percentage of the judgmental variance, even when the judge's self-insight suggests more complex nonlinear, configural, or sequential processes. (This is not necessarily to suggest that the actual process is as simple as the linear model implies; Dawes and Corrigan [1974] developing an earlier lead from Yntema and Torgerson [1961], have shown that linear models will frequently provide close fit to highly nonlinear processes, within quite broad ranges of process and task characteristics.) Other representations have been utilized by Einhorn (1971, 1972) for certain decision settings in which the linear tradeoff properties of the linear model are unattractive, and by researchers such as Wiggins and Hoffman (1968) for settings in which verbal protocols imply configural use of information. In general, it may be noted that these modifications of the first-order linear model have contributed little to the predictive accuracy of the representation; the linear model is highly robust in accounting for nearly all of the explainable variance.

This ability to represent the relationship between informational input and output at the individual level in a simple equation suggests a wide range of research opportunities in the diffuse-decision context. For example, the relative weights given to the informational cues might be compared across individuals performing similar decision functions, at different organizational levels, with different levels of experience, or differences in personality or cognitive style. The well-established discrepancies between the individual's insight into his weighting scheme and that revealed by analysis of a series of his judgments (e.g., Heopfl and Huber, 1970; Slovic, 1969) has a number of implications in areas such as design of management information systems (Ackoff, 1967). The ability to represent objectively the relative weights given to various information sources opens the door to studies of the relationship between amount of interaction with some particular information source (whether an individual, or a nonhuman source such as a library or data bank) and the impact the information gathered has on the output decision. Given the failures of self-insight noted above, it may be expected that this relationship is far from an optimal one in terms of balancing cost of information against quality of decision.

One particularly intriguing research possibility bridging the judgment studies with organizational decision-making phenomena may be derived from the finding familiar in Bayesian studies of conservatism—that is, subjects revise their probabilities in the appropriate direction, but less than is (normatively) justified by the diagnosticity of the information. (See, e.g., Edwards, 1968.) Stated otherwise, the conservatism phenomenon would require an individual to gather more information than is strictly necessary in order to reach some given level of confidence in the rightness of his decision. In a quite different context, Oskamp (1965) found that decisional accuracy was relatively unaffected by increments of information past a fairly low level, but that confidence continued to increase as more information was given. Add to these findings the errors of self-insight into weighting, particularly in the subjective overestimation of weights actually given to minor cues, and one can construct a plausible case that decision participants will, in general, gather and attempt to use more information than they need to. (This phenomenon is noted by Ackoff [1967, p. 149] as a serious problem in the design of management information systems [MIS]: ". . . the manager . . . with respect to information, wants 'everything.' The MIS designer . . . tries to provide even more than everything. He thereby increases what is already an overload of irrelevant information.") A further implication of this line of reasoning is that organizationally dysfunctional consequences may ensue, not just in terms of resources consumed in gathering excess information, but in lower ultimate decision quality, given the rather limited capacity of the human mind to process large quantities of input information (Miller 1956; Dorris, 1974). (The fundamental importance of the limitations on human cognitive capacity have been extensively discussed by a variety of authors [e.g., Simon, 1955, 1976; Bruner, Goodnow and Austin, 1956; Dawes, 1975; Taylor, 1975; Argyris, 1972; Mackenzie, 1974] and will not be further reviewed here.)

While the above represents some directions in which the judgment research could enrich studies of organizational decision making, enrichment in the reverse direction is also highly promising. For example, laboratory studies of judgment phenomena are only recently giving serious attention to the fact that decisions in the real world are rarely made on the basis of numbers alone. Far more frequently, the numbers are embedded in a meaningful verbal context which provides the decision maker with guiding concepts for his information use, and with ways of organizing and integrating his informational inputs. Several empirical studies have demonstrated the behavioral importance of including such frameworks on laboratory studies (Miller, 1971; Muchinsky and Dudycha, 1974).

These findings on the importance of the verbal context need to be considered in light of the work on perceptual processes in problem solving, particularly the "chunking" process suggested by Simon and Barenfeld (1969) as a critical part of expertise in chess. This line of research has established that expert chess players are vastly superior to weak players in reconstructing board positions after a brief exposure, but only if the position is a result of real play, not random arrangement of the pieces. Simon and Barenfeld interpret this as reflecting the experts' use of a vocabulary, allowing the board position to be stored in a few "chunks" of information instead of the much larger number of bits of information required by the weak player. Such chunks also serve to direct the strategic analysis of the position and thus suggest plausible moves, again providing large gains in cognitive efficiency over the novice attempting to examine all possible moves. The emphasis of the laboratory judgment studies on the numerical properties of the tasks may thus have ignored a critical aspect of the real-world judgment process: the judge's ability to understand the process generating the stimuli he sees, and to organize his information processing around a conceptual structure. Examination of the nature, sources, and consequences of these concepts appears to be a promising area for both laboratory and field research in the context of the relationship of information to decision making.

Further "mundane realism" (Aronson and Cartsmith, 1968) could be added to the laboratory settings by incorporating stress of various kinds (for example, significant money stakes, time pressures, or distractions); by opening up active search for, or selection from, available information, with real cost associated with acquiring information. Similarly, it would appear that in most real-world settings, the individual learns of the accuracy of his decisions or judgments, if at all, in ambiguous terms, a significant time after his judgment was made, and perhaps only in evaluative rather than factual terms. The impact of such feedback degradations on judgmental learning appears an important issue, and one which has only recently started to attract experimental attention (Miklausich, 1973; Rose, 1974).

Implicit in much of this discussion is the assumption that organizational decisions are frequently made in the face of considerable uncertainty. It thus becomes important to ask: "How do people assess probabilities and predict uncertain outcomes?" Much of the work addressing this question has been recently reviewed by Tversky and Kahneman (1974), who identify three heuristic strategies—representativeness, availability, and anchoring/adjustment—which are commonly used by individuals facing decisions under uncertainty. The heuristics are generally useful, but each is prone to systematic biases and errors, possibly quite large ones.

Using the representativeness heuristic, for example, a subject assigns probabilities by the extent to which the data he observes are representative of one or another population from which they might have come. Subjects using this strategy are prone to several errors: They do not take account of prior probabilities; they are insensitive to sample size; representativeness is judged in terms of an erroneous view of chance mechanisms; regression is commonly misunderstood intuitively, and so on. Similarly, serious biases distort probability assessments under the other two heuristics as well.

It should be noted that neither extensive training in statistics nor lengthy experience guarantees freedom from these biases and fallacies in making intuitive judgments of probability. However, it does appear that several of these distortions could be minimized or eliminated by suitable modifications of the decision maker's informational environment. For example, the familiar conservatism effect can be obviated by partitioning the decision task between an individual and a machine, with the individual generating the conditional probabilities of each datum, given each hypothesis, and the machine applying Bayes'

Theorem to integrate these assessments into posterior probabilities for each hypothesis (Edwards, 1962). The distortion of the availability heuristic caused by faulty search strategies—for example, the ease with which familiar or salient cases can be retrieved, or the differential ease of different search techniques—could be mitigated by appropriate computer-based retrieval systems. Even without use of computers, it may well be possible to arrange the individual's informational environment in terms of sequence of arrival of information, provision of accessible historical information, multiple information channels, and so on, so as to minimize the known judgmental errors. Such extensions of the laboratory findings on judgmental biases to real-world settings offers considerable potential, both in validating the findings and in developing decisional aids.

It should be noted in passing that several research literatures address the issues of individual differences in information processing, problem solving, and decision making. In addition to such obvious variables as age, sex, intelligence, and experience, a complete treatment of information processing at the individual level would have to take account of such variables as authoritarianism (Adorno et al., 1950; Harvey, 1963); dogmatism (Rokeach, 1960); cautiousness and tolerance for ambiguity (Messick and Hills, 1960); cognitive complexity/simplicity, and rigidity/flexibility (Bieri, 1955; Scott, 1960; Vannoy, 1965); category width (Pettigrew, 1958); and various aspects of conceptual structure (Sieber and Lanzetta, 1964; Streufert and Driver, 1966; Schroder, Driver and Streufert, 1967). Some recent studies (e.g., Taylor and Dunnette, 1974), have moved beyond identifying the effects of individual differences on information processing to assessing the relative magnitude of several effects in specific decisional settings. On the applications side, exciting work is going forward (e.g., Dyer, 1973; Geoffrion, Dyer, and Feinberg, 1972; Wallenius, 1975) in the area of man-machine interactive decision making, with the broad aim of combining the strengths of human and computer information processing into an efficient total system. No attempt to review these extensive bodies of work will be made within the space limitations of this chapter. The intent here is merely to alert the reader to the existence of these active research directions, and to suggest the considerable range of interesting studies possible addressing simultaneously personality and task or situational dimensions in information-processing/decision-making behaviors.

In summary, this section has presented a view of the individual participant in a diffuse decision process as an active node in a complex communication net. Several possible approaches to integrating his information-processing with his decision-making activities have been suggested, focusing on such questions as:

1. What informational events initiate decision-making or problem-solving activity, and how do different initiating events affect the subsequent activities?
2. How does the individual integrate his multiple informational inputs into his decisional outputs? What are the limitations and distortions on this process, and how may they be ameliorated in real-world settings?
3. To what extent have available laboratory judgment studies captured the essence of the real-world judgment process? What are the effects of such variables as verbal context, feedback degradations, real resources, decisional stress, large cue sets, and information search in modifying judgmental processes?
4. By what processes does an individual arrive at probability estimates for certain future events? What biases can be expected in such processes, and how may they be minimized in real-world settings?

The emphasis has been on formulations which treat information processing and decision making within a single framework, rather than as separable phenomena. Within such a framework, the aim has been to suggest areas in which laboratory and field research may enrich one another. In the next section, we shall attempt to extend this general approach from the single individual to pairs of individuals interacting with one another.

Section 3: Two-Person Interactions

The focus of this section is on the situation in which two individuals interact with the same informational inputs in forming their judgments, decisions, or other informational outputs. As before, the informational inputs may be considered either as a convergence of several information channels, or as a multidimensional stimulus of some sort. In particular we shall be concerned with two such situations:

1. Situations in which the two individuals attempt to make shared inferences as to the state of affairs reflected by their (shared) informational inputs. An example is two doctors forming a consensus diagnosis from a folder of information gathered from a patient.
2. Situations in which two individuals express preferences for some entity whose properties are reflected in their (shared) informational inputs. An example is two opposing negotiators each assessing the same labor contract containing a number of elements.

The two situations share a number of interesting formal features, being distinguished primarily by the inference/preference processes.

In the former, some "true state of the world" is thought to exist—for example, the patient's actual disease—and the aim of the interaction is to agree, not just with one another, but with this reality. In the latter, no such "true state" is thought of as underlying the stimulus; the reference point for preference is within the evaluator.

Much of the work on these two-person processes has been conducted by Hammond and his colleagues at the University of Colorado (e.g., Hammond, 1965; Hammond and Summers, 1972; Flack and Summers, 1971; Hammond and Brehmer, 1973; a number of relevant papers are collected in Rapoport and Summers, 1973). A good example of the work on negotiating processes is provided by Balke, Hammond and Meyer's (1973) modified reenactment of an actual labor-management negotiation. These authors point out that our normal assumption about such negotiations is that they reflect "motivational conflict"—that is, the two sides pursue divergent goals under constraints of scarce resources, rationally seeking partisan ends. Balke et al. suggest that, in addition to such motivational conflict, the known imperfections of the human judgment process may lead to what they call "cognitive conflict"—that is, conflict resulting from participants' inconsistencies in judgment, and their lack of insight into their own and their opponents' evaluative processes. Cognitive conflict thus reflects the inadequacy of human information-processing, suggesting that appropriate information-processing aids could reduce the conflict, and lead to improved decision making.

The Balke et al. study investigated the effectiveness of providing such information-processing aids. Their basic information-processing aid was the use of computer graphics to show each participant the judgmental strategy he was actually using in evaluating possible contracts. From preliminary discussions with the participants, the researchers identified four critical contract issues, and the ranges of each under dispute. They then prepared 25 "sample contracts" containing different levels of these four issues, and each participant evaluated them on a seven-point scale from "recommend acceptance" to "recommend rejection." Participants also predicted opponents' evaluations on the same scale. For each participant, the researchers computed a regression equation predicting overall evaluation from the values and squared values of each issue level. This equation formed the basis for feedback to the subject of (a) the relative weights he was assigning to each issue area; (b) the function-form relating issue levels to his overall evaluations; and (c) the degree of inconsistency with which he applied his weighting function. The computer graphics device allows presentation of these data in a variety of graphical and pictorial forms.

The first part of the study collected the above evaluation data, plus subjective weightings for each participant and his opponent. Three weeks later each participant reevaluated the 25 contracts after receiving graphic feedback on his objective weighting scheme, and again estimating his own weights. At this point, he was shown his opponent's actual (regression-based) weighting scheme, and asked to make new predictions of his opponent's evaluations. Finally, pairs of negotiators attempted to reach agreement on evaluations of all 25 contracts, with limited "bargaining" being allowed when agreement was not reached.

The main findings of the study were:

1. In spite of the negotiators' familiarity with the issues, and with their opponents, understanding of their own and their opponents' weighting schemes was found to be seriously inaccurate.

2. Consistency was low overall.

3. Predictions of opponents' evaluations were generally inaccurate, even after feedback on the opponent's weighting scheme.

4. Negotiators receiving the computer graphics feedback were able to reach significantly better agreement during negotiation than were negotiators receiving only conventional verbal explanations. Thus, despite a number of imperfections in this study (small numbers of negotiators; reenactment rather than "real-time" negotiation, etc.), the results are encouraging. In essence, they identify a number of psychological mechanisms which may lead to difficulties in a bargaining situation, and suggest an information-processing technology which may ameliorate the difficulties. Further extension and replication is urgently needed.

A situation formally similar to the bilateral negotiation problem arises when two experts are required to reach a consensus judgment, or when one is trying to teach his judgmental expertise to the other. An expert pathologist working either with another expert (a second opinion) or with an intern would be a typical example of such settings. Hammond (1971) has noted that considerable difficulty and frustration may arise in the training situation because, given the expert's poor self-insight, he will teach his student inappropriate strategies which, even when conscientiously applied, lead the student to judgments at variance with his instructor's. Einhorn (1974), noting the generally low degree of agreement between two experts, has pointed out the rather stringent requirements for agreement in complex judgment tasks. He notes that for agreement on global judgments, not only must the two judges weight and combine cues identically, but they must also agree on what are the relevant cues, and on "how much" of each cue appears in any particular stimulus. It seems unlikely that these stringent conditions will be met in most practical judgment situations.

As with the bilateral negotiation problem, the use of information-processing aids opens up the possibility of helpful intervention into such situations. Hammond (1971), in another example of the use of computer graphics techniques, has shown the facilitating effects on the learning of complex judgmental tasks of computer graphic feedback to the subject of his cue utilization strategies, and those required for successful task performance. As Hammond notes, the development and refinement of this approach in areas such as medical diagnosis suggests such exciting possibilities as the rapid, large-scale training of clinical competence in developing countries where access to both established experts and practical medical experience may be very limited. The simplicity of the representations of the judgmental processes should not disguise the significance of the issues involved. As Hammond suggests, ". . . of prime significance is the fact that, although crude, these representations of a person's cognitive processes mean something to the person. It may well be that such representations will make it possible for a man to enhance his understanding not only of his own judgmental processes, but those of others as well. Computer graphics may well mark a new era of research in the study of man" (Hammond, 1971, p. 907). Whether or not such dramatic impact is achieved, there does appear to be considerable potential for procedures and technologies which, by aiding human information processing in areas where the unaided individual is known to be weak, can facilitate decision making. This potential, which we have seen in both the one-person and the two-person case, turns on an understanding of the relationship between the individual, his informational inputs, and his decisional outputs. In the next section, we will return to our initial focus on these processes from the perspective of the network of communication activities which constitute the multi-person decision activities we have labeled "diffuse-decision processes."

Section 4: Some Aspects of Multiperson Processes

In this section we attempt to provide some approaches at the macro level. That is, we will focus on the decision process and its associated communication net as a whole, examining such issues as the imposed and emergent communication net, the characteristics of these nets, and their relationships to the decision problem faced and the effectiveness of the net in solving it. With such a broad target, the aim here is a highlighting of specific issues—namely, relevant research traditions, and directions for development.

One obviously relevant research tradition is that on problem-solving in restricted-communication small groups. The established paradigm for this work has survived almost unchanged from the original studies of Leavitt (1951) and Bavelas (1950). It consists of isolating the group members from one another by screens, and allowing interaction only by passing written messages through slots in the screens. Different arrangements of the slots allow the experimenter to impose different net configurations on the group, such as the circle (communication with each neighbor), wheel (communication only with one focal individual), and all-channel (communication with any other group member) patterns. With some minor modifications, this paradigm has generated a number of studies potentially relevant to diffuse decision processes. For example:

1. The original Leavitt (1951) study suggested that centralized communication nets led to more effective task performance, though with lower satisfaction for all subjects except the most central individual. However, an elegant, altered replication by Guetzkow and Simon (1955) suggests that the impact of the different nets was not on the groups' ability to perform these simple tasks, but on their ability to devise a procedure or organization for doing so. This conclusion is further supported by Guetzkow and Dill (1957).

2. Heise and Miller (1951), using a microphone and earphone arrangement to allow restricted verbal communication, showed that channel noise (in the form of reduced signal-to-noise ratios) accentuates the impact of communication-net restrictions, though the effect is moderated by the structure implicit in the task.

3. Macy, Christie, and Luce (1953) examined the effect of coding noise (that is, ambiguous symbol names) on task performance, and found that the high error-rate associated with increased coding noise was corrected only by nets which provided sufficient interconnection to allow detection of errors, and the evolution of shared vocabularies.

4. Shaw (1954) and Gilchrist and Shaw and Walker (1954) studied the effects of unequal initial distribution of information on task performance, and found that increasing initial information for a peripheral group member has much the same effects (e.g., on leadership, satisfaction) as increasing his position centrality.

5. Shaw (1954b), examining the effects of problem complexity, provides data suggesting that the original Leavitt finding of the superiority of centralized nets may be limited to very simple problems, and that more interconnected, less centralized nets may be more effective for more complex problems. His conclusions are challenged by Mulder (1960) who found that, given adequate learning, centralized nets performed well on more complex tasks.

A number of reviews and extensions of this work are available (e.g., Shaw, 1964; Guetzkow, 1965; Faucheux and Mackenzie, 1966; Mackenzie, 1967), and no attempt will be made here at a detailed review and synthesis. In general, there is little question that net structure does make a difference to task performance, and that which net is more efficient depends on the type of task being performed. Where the tasks are very simple (e.g., Leavitt, 1951), the group's problem is essentially that of collecting the information in one place. For such tasks, simple nets in which most individuals act merely as information relays are most efficient (though not very satisfying to the members). On more complex tasks (e.g. Shaw, 1954b; Macy et al., 1953), mere relaying of information to a central point becomes less efficient (or less feasible), and nets which connect one individual with several others perform better. Broadly speaking the findings in this area are consistent with the hypothesis that high-uncertainty tasks are better performed in richly interconnected, low-centrality nets, while low-uncertainty tasks are better performed in minimally interconnected, highly-centralized nets.

It may well be that a similar hypothesis holds for the decision-related communication nets which emerge at the organizational level. However, adequate testing of this hypothesis requires significant conceptual and methodological developments in regard to both net characteristics and decisional uncertainty. In the former area, the seminal work of Bavelas (1948) on the topology of connectedness provided both concept and metrics for much of the laboratory small-group work. Bavelas' approach, however, is limited to complete nets in which a communication link either exists or does not. In organizational studies, we will typically be unable to examine complete communication nets, and will also want to examine questions of amount of communication along a particular link—that is, our interest will extend beyond the question of whether or not two participants can, in principle, communicate with one another; we will want to ask how much they actually do communicate in some specific context. These two restrictions appear to limit the value of Bavelas' elegant approach for studies of actual organizational nets.

A sophisticated attack on the conceptual and methodological problems of measuring organizational communication nets has recently been undertaken by a group at the Stanford Institute for Communications Research (e.g., Richards, 1975; 1974a, 1974b; Richards and Lindsey, 1974; a nontechnical introduction is provided by Monge and Lindsey, 1974). This work, drawing on both systems theory and information theory, centers on topological analysis of actual communication nets, supplemented by conventional statistical analysis. It offers a rich conceptual framework developed to the point of providing data-collection instruments and standardized computer software. The approach appears highly promising for future studies of organizational communication nets.

This is not to suggest that useful work on this question is possible only for the mathematically sophisticated. It is quite easy to devise common-sense concepts and measures of interesting network proporties which can be applied to partial nets, or regions of larger nets, in which communication between any two participants is treated as a continuous variable. For example, a useful measure of the overall activity on the net could be provided by averaging the total communication along each link; a rough measure of how interconnected the net is can be generated by computing the ratio of the number of links carrying more than some minimum amount of traffic to the number of total possible links; the centrality of some participant can be indexed by considering the total communication activity in which he is involved as a ratio of the average activity of all participants; and (defining a decentralized net as one in which all participants have equal centrality) a measure of degree of centralization of the net (or of some region of the net) is provided by the variance in centrality measures over all participants. Such measures are, clearly, rough and ready, and may be misleading in unusual cases. However, in most simple cases they can be readily shown to correspond to intuitive notions of activity, connectedness, individual centrality, and net centralization.

This discussion of network characteristics has been offered in the context of the broad hypothesis that such characteristics are systematically related to the uncertainty of the decision problem activating the net. Concepts and measures of decisional uncertainty abound, though—as will be suggested below—it is not clear that any of them is adequate for our present purposes. Information theory treats uncertainty as ". . . the logarithm of the number of possible outcomes an event can have" (Garner, 1962, p. 9). As Rapoport and Horvath (1959) point out, this definition is limited to the syntactic characteristics of language, and is not obviously applicable to the semantic and pragmatic aspects of communication. The limitations of the decision-theoretic formulation of uncertainty were discussed earlier. Basically, it was noted that this formulation treats uncertainty only within a highly constrained framework, and that situations violating this framework can be readily imagined in organizational settings.

A growing body of work in organization behavior (e.g., Woodward, 1958; Burns and Stalker, 1961; Crozier, 1964; Thompson, 1967; Conrath, 1967; Lawrence and Lorsch, 1969; Duncan, 1971, 1972) has examined the relationships between the organization and its environment, generally including the uncertainty of that environment as a critical variable. While each of these authors would probably agree to a large extent with Thompson's view of uncertainty as ". . . the fundamental problem for complex organizations" (1967, p. 159), there is considerable variation between them in how uncertainty is to be conceptualized and measured. There is, for example, no clear agreement on whether uncertainty should be treated at the level of perceptions by organizational participants or as an "objective" property of the environment; if the former, whether or not individual perceptions can be satisfactorily aggregated into a single measure for a group of individuals; and whether uncertainty is uni- or multi-dimensional, either in the sense of multiple aspects of the decision function (as discussed earlier) or as relating to different sectors of the environment (as in Lawrence and Lorsch, 1969). Measurement procedures have reflected these conceptual differences.

Without attempting to resolve the complex issues here, we will suggest some tentative guidelines for development. First, it seems useful to maintain a clear distinction between the perceptions which are held by organizational members about the environment (the "enacted environment," in Weick's [1969] phrase) and measures which may be thought of as characterizing the "actual" environment (for example, Duncan's [1972] complexity and changeability dimensions): the rules for mapping one onto the other then become an empirical question of some interest. Second, there appears no compelling reason to expect, a priori, that these individual perceptions will be identical across individuals, or that such variance reflects error-prone perceptions of the same underlying reality; the degree of homogeneity across individuals and situations is an open empirical question. Third, it appears entirely likely that an individual will perceive different levels of uncertainty associated with different aspects of his decision problem (Connolly, 1975). Whether or not to aggregate these different dimensions into one overall measure of uncertainty will depend on the research issue. For example, such a single measure might be of value in studying the relationship between perceived uncertainty and stress-related illness. However, the disaggregated measures appear more promising for studying, say, the locations in which the individual will first search for uncertainty-reducing information, since such search will, presumably, be related to the type of uncertainty experienced. Overall, there appears to be considerable scope for development of concepts and measures of organizational uncertainty.

The somewhat primitive level of our present treatment of uncertainty in decision processes should stimulate, rather than inhibit, work in this area. Even with an unsophisticated, global notion of uncertainty, one can find support in the studies cited above for the hypothesis that, for collectivities ranging from small laboratory groups to entire organizations, effective decisional performance under high uncertainty requires noncentralized, richly interconnected, and flexibly organized communication nets. As more refined concepts and measures of uncertainty and net structure are developed, we may expect to be able to propose and test a range of more subtle hypotheses relating uncertainties to communication processes. In particular, it seems valuable to treat both process and outcome in such studies—for example, the individual-level mechanism suggested earlier whereby perceived uncertainty affects net structure via its impact on the individual's information-search activities. Such an approach seems close to Weick's (1969) emphasis on the process of organizing, rather than merely on the structure of the organization. Structure may emerge as partially the institutionalization of emergent communication nets invented by decision participants as they wrestle with their decision problems. Much as footpaths may be laid out by paving over worn paths on the grass, so may organization structures be partially created by the routinization and facilitation of communication channels forged by organizational participants in their daily work. Thus issues not only of organizational analysis, but of organizational design, are implicit in the developments proposed here. (See Galbraith, 1974, for further discussion of the design implications of an information-processing approach to organizations.)

There remain a large number of approaches to organizational decision-making phenomena which are, to greater or lesser extent, relevant to our present perspective. Studies such as those of Salancik and Pfeffer (1974) and Pfeffer and Salancik (1974), focusing on power in budget allocation decisions, share a methodological link to our present approach by their attempt to use the "policy capturing" technology to examine allocation decisions. A theory of managerial decision making has been proposed (Bowman, 1963) and evaluated empirically (Kunreuther, 1969) which is closely allied to the notion of "bootstrapping" developed independently in the human judgment literature (Dawes, 1971). Attempts to develop mathematical models of decentralized decisional processes (e.g., Arrow, 1959, 1964; Dantzig and Wolfe, 1963; Ruefli, 1971a, 1971b; Freeland and Baker, 1973) offer important insights, particularly as the structure and dynamics of the models approximate real-world flows of information, decision events, bargaining behaviors, and so on. At several crucial points Cyert and March's (1963) behavioral theory of the firm turns on specific assumptions about the mechanisms relating decision making to information available to the decision maker. Empirical testing of these assumptions (e.g., Porat and Haas, 1969; Rados, 1972; Carter, 1971) has stimulated refinement and revision of the model at several key points. Studies of ideas flow and communication in research organizations (e.g., Rubenstein and Hannenberg, 1965) frequently deal, if only implicitly, with the decisional impact of the information. Finally, field studies are starting to appear (e.g., Shumway et al., 1975) which trace aspects of diffuse decisions over time. (Interestingly, nearly all of these studies are of budgeting or resource-allocation decision processes; such critical decisions appear to demonstrate most clearly several fundamental phenomena of organizational functioning.)

Concluding Remarks

At the outset of this chapter, it was suggested that it is possible, and useful, to attempt a closer integration of research on information-processing and decision-making phenomena in organizations. It was further proposed that this integration may be achieved at a rather macroscopic level, using the notion of the diffuse-decision process in which decisions emerge from the interlocked activities of multiple-decision participants embedded in a complex net of information flows. The macroscopic properties of this process are treated as emerging, to a significant extent, from the activities of the individual participants coping with very local decision domains—for example, searching for information to reduce decisional uncertainty. The remainder of the chapter provided a sampling of research themes and findings which, at the individual, dyadic, group, and organizational level, offer leverage points for research on these processes.

It may be useful to place the notions presented here against the backdrop of some recent shifts in thinking about organizations. A strong case can be made (e.g., Georgiou, 1973) that virtually all organizational research has accepted, explicitly or implicitly, the "organizational goal" paradigm—that is, the assumption that organizations are, in some sense, purposive, whether or not the goals actually pursued are those publicly announced, or whether they are thought to be those of a dominant individual (the entrepreneur), a dominant coalition within the organization, the equity holders, or whomever. Recent challenges to this goal paradigm have included attempts (e.g., Clark and Wilson, 1961; Georgiou, 1973) to refurbish Barnard's (1938) primary focus on incentive systems, where the central strategic issue is not the attainment of organizational goals but the provision of sufficient incentive to each individual to continue his participation. Related heresies include notions of organizations as "organized anarchies" or "decisional garbage cans" (Cohen, March and Olsen, 1972; March and Olsen, in press), or as "loosely coupled systems" in which the central feature is the process of organizing, rather than the form of organization attained at some point in time, and in which goals are discovered in retrospect rather than pursued in prospect (Weick, 1969).

The present approach is compatible at several points with these perspectives. The primary focus is on the individual embedded in a decision process by means of his communicative links to other individuals. The extent to which the criteria he applies in his decisional activities are derived from personal or organizational purposes is not assumed a priori but presented as an empirical issue. Similarly, the structure of the total decision process is not assumed to be fixed, but as emerging in large part from the activities of the participants. Initially, all we require of structure is a "primitive orderliness" (Weick, 1969: p. 37) which initiates decisional activity for at least some participants, and spreads to other participants as the process unfolds. Much of the structure existing at some instant may be seen as the routinization of communication channels invented previously in the course of decisional work; much of the goal formulation may be seen as rationalization of previously applied criteria. The approach presented in this chapter, then, is largely compatible with the nongoal paradigms emerging in organizational research.

As a final comment, it should be reemphasized that the aim of this chapter has been, in a phrase of Lou Pondy's, less to celebrate the past than to invent the future. More modestly, its purpose will have been well served if it stimulates new empirical research. Opportunities for such research have been noted. What has not been emphasized is the exciting possibility of applied research addressing the broad issue of the management of organizational decision processes. Vroom (1973) has suggested that a critical part of the manager's role is the determination of ". . . which social process should be engaged in the solution of the problem or the making of the decision" (p. 64). As our understanding grows, we may aspire to develop a technology of the effective design and management of decision systems. The prospect is an exciting one.

References

Ackoff, R. L. Management misinformation systems. *Management Science,* 1967, *14,* 145-56.

Adorno, T. W., Frenkel-Brunswik, E., Levinson, D. J. and Sanford, R. N. *The Authoritarian Personality.* New York: Harper, Row, 1958.

Allen, T. J., and Cohen, S. I. Information flow in research and development laboratories. *Administrative Science Quarterly,* 1969, *14,* 12-20.

Argyris, C. *The Applicability of Organizational Sociology.* Cambridge, England: The University Press, 1972.

Aronson, E., and Carlsmith, J. M. Experimentation in social psychology. *Handbook of Social Psychology,* 2nd ed., vol. 2, Reading, Mass.: Addison-Wesley, 1968, 1-79.

Arrow, K. J. Optimization, decentralization, and internal pricing in business firms. In *Contributions to Scientific Research in Management,* UCLA, Western Data Processing Center, 1959.

———. Control in large organizations. *Management Science,* 1964, *10,* 397-408.

Balke, W. M., Hammond, K. R. and Meyer, G. D. An alternative approach to labor-management negotiations. *Administrative Science Quarterly,* 1973, *18,* 311-27.

Barnard, C. I. *The Functions of the Executive.* Cambridge: Harvard University Press, 1938.

Bavelas, A. A mathematical model for group structures. *Applied Anthropology,* Summer, 1948, 16-30.

———. Communication patterns in task-oriented small groups. *Journal of Acoustical Society of America,* 1950, *22,* 725-30.

Bieri, J. Cognitive complexity-simplicity and predictive behavior. *Journal of Abnormal and Social Psychology,* 1955, *51,* 263-68.

Bowman, E. H. Consistency and optimality in managerial decision making. *Management Science,* 1963, *9,* 310-21.

Brehmer, B., Azuma, H., Hammond, K. R., Kostron, L., and Varonos, D. A cross national comparison of cognitive conflict. *Journal of Cross Cultural Psychology,* 1970, *1,* 5-20.

Bruner, J. S., Goodnow, J. J. and Austin, G. A. *A Study of Thinking.* New York: Wiley, 1956.

Brunswik, E. *The Conceptual Framework of Psychology.* Chicago: University of Chicago Press, 1952.

Burns, T., and Stalker, G. M. *The Management of Innovation.* London: Tavistock Publications, 1961.

Carter, E. E. The behavioral theory of the firm and top-level corporate decision. *Administrative Science Quarterly,* 1971, *16,* 413-29.

Clark, P. B., and Wilson, J. Q. Incentive systems: A theory of organizations. *Administrative Science Quarterly,* 1961, *6,* 129-66.

Cohen, M. D., March, J. G., and Olsen, J. P. A garbage can model of organizational choice. *Administrative Science Quarterly,* 1972, *17,* 1-25.

Connolly, T. Information search in judgment tasks: A model and some research alternatives. *Proceedings of the American Institute of Decision Sciences,* Atlanta, Ga.: October, 1974.

———. Communication nets and uncertainty in R&D planning. *IEEE Transactions in Engineering Management,* 1975, vol. EM-22, 50-54.

Conrath, D. W. Organizational decision making under varying conditions of uncertainty. *Management Science,* 1967, *13,* B487-500.

Cyert, R. M., and March, J. G. *A Behavioral Theory of the Firm.* Englewood Cliffs, N. J.: Prentice-Hall, 1963.

Crozier, M. The Bureaucratic Phenomenon. Chicago: University of Chicago Press, 1964.

Dawes, R. M. A case study of graduate admissions: Application of three principles of human decision making. *American Psychologist,* 1971, *26,* 180-88.

———. Shallow psychology. *Oregon Research Institute Bulletin,* 1975, vol. 15.

Dawes, R. M., and Corrigan, B. Linear models in decision making. *Psychological Bulletin,* 1974, *81,* 95-106.

Doktor, R., Senn, J. A., and McNaul, J. P. *Organization and Information* (mimeo) School of Management, State University of New York, Binghampton, February, 1974.

Dorris, A. L. Decision making with large cue sets. Ph.D. dissertation, Georgia Institute of Technology, December, 1974.

Downs, A. *Inside Bureaucracy.* Boston: Little, Brown, 1967.

Duncan, R. B. Multiple decision making structures in adapting to environmental uncertainty: the impact on organizational effectiveness. Working paper no. 54-71, Northwestern University, Graduate School of Management, 1971.

―――. Characteristics of organizational environments and perceived environmental uncertainty. *Administrative Science Quarterly,* 1972, *17,* 313-27.

Dyer, J. S. An empirical investigation of man-machine interactive approach to the solution of the multiple criterion problem. In Cochrane, J. and Zeleny, M. (eds), *Multiple Criteria Decision Making.* Columbia, South Carolina: University of South Carolina Press, 1973.

Edwards, W. Dynamic decision theory and probabilistic information processing. *Human Factors,* 1962, *4,* 59-73.

―――. Conservatism in human information processing. In Kleinmuntz, B. (ed): *Formal Representation of Human Judgment.* New York: Wiley, 1968.

Einhorn, H. J. The use of non-linear, non-compensatory models in decision making. *Psychological Bulletin,* 1970, *73,* 221-230.

―――. Use of non-linear, non-compensatory models as a function of task and amount of information. *Organization Behavior and Human Performance,* 1971, *6,* 1-27.

―――. Expert measurement and mechanical combination. *Organization Behavior and Human Performance,* 1972, *7,* 86-106.

―――. Expert judgment: Some necessary conditions and an example (mimeo). Graduate School of Business, University of Chicago, February, 1974.

Faucheux, C., and Mackenzie, K. D. Task dependency of organizational centrality: its behavioral consequences. *Journal of Experimental Social Psychology,* 1966, *2,* 361-75.

Feather, N. D. Subjective probability and decision under uncertainty. *Psychological Review,* 1959, *66,* 150-63.

Ference, T. P. Organizational communication systems and the decision process. *Management Science,* 1970, *17,* 83-96.

Flack, J. E., and Summers, D. A. Computer aided conflict resolution in water resources planning. *Water Resources Research,* 1971, *7,* 1410-14.

Freeland, J. R., and Baker, N. R. A goal partitioning procedure for modelling coordination activities in a hierarchical decentralized organization. Research paper no. 184, Stanford Graduate School of Business, October, 1973.

Fried, L. S., and Peterson, C. R. Information seeking: optional vs. fixed stopping. *Journal of Experimental Psychology,* 1969, *80,* 525-29.

Galbraith, J. R. Organizational design: an information processing view. In Kolb, D. A., Rubin, I. M., and McIntyre, J. R. (eds), *Organizational Psychology: A Book of Readings.* Englewood Cliffs, N. J.: Prentice-Hall, 1974.

Garner, W. *Uncertainty and Structure as Psychological Concepts.* New York: New York: Wiley, 1962.

Geoffrion, A. M., Dyer, J. S., and Feinberg, A. An interactive approach for multicriterion optimization. *Management Science,* 1972, *19,* 357-68.

Georgiou, P. The goal paradigm and notes towards a counter paradigm. *Administrative Science Quarterly,* 1973, *18,* 291-310.

Gilchrist, J. C., Shaw, M. E., and Walker, L. C. Some effects of unequal distribution of information in a wheel group structure. *Journal of Abnormal and Social Psychology,* 1954, *49,* 554-56.

Guetzkow, H. Communications in organizations. In March, J. G. (ed), *Handbook of Organizations.* Chicago: Rand McNally, 1965, 534-73.

Guetzkow, H., and Dill, W. R. Factors in the organizational development of task-oriented groups. *Sociometry,* 1957, *20,* 175-204.

Guetzkow, H., and Simon, H. A. The impact of certain communication nets upon organization and performance in task-oriented groups. *Management Science,* 1955, *1,* 233-250.

Hammond, K. R. New directions in research on conflict resolution. *Journal of Social Issues,* 1965, *21,* 44-66.

―――. Computer graphics as an aid to learning. *Science,* 1971, *172,* 903-8.

Hammond, K. R., and Brehmer, B. Quasi-rationality and distrust: implications for international conflict. In Rappaport, L., and Summers, D. A. (eds), *Human Judgment and Social Interaction*. New York: Holt, Rinehart, 1973.

Hammond, K. R., and Summers, D. A. Cognitive control. *Psychological Review*, 1972, *79*, 58-67.

Harvey, O. J. Authoritarianism and conceptual functioning in varied conditions. *Journal of Personality*, 1963, *31*, 462-70.

Heise, G. A. and Miller, G. A. Problem solving by small groups using various communications nets. *Journal of Abnormal and Social Psychology*, 1951, *46*, 327-35.

Hoepfl, R. T., and Huber, G. P. A study of self-explicated utility models. *Behavioral Science*, 1970, *15*, 408-14.

Hoffman, P. J. The paramorphic representation of clinical judgment. *Psychological Bulletin*, 1960, *57*, 116-31.

Kleinmuntz, B. (ed). *Formal Representation of Human Judgment*. New York: Wiley, 1968.

Kunreuther, H. Extensions of Bowman's theory of managerial decision making. *Management Science*, 1969, *15*, B412-39.

Lawrence, P. R., and Lorsch, J. W. *Organization and Environment*. Homewood, Illinois: Irwin, 1969.

Leavitt, H. J. Some effects of certain communication patterns on group performance. *Journal of Abnormal and Social Psychology*, 1951, *46*, 38-50.

Mackenzie, K. D. Structural centrality in communications networks. *Psychometrika*, 1966, *31*, 17-25.

———. Measuring a person's capacity for interaction in a problem solving group. *Organizational Behavior and Human Performance*, 1974, *12*, 149-69.

Macy, J., Christie, L. S. and Luce, R. D. Coding noise in a task-oriented group. *Journal of Abnormal and Social Psychology*, 1953, *48*, 401-9.

March, J. G., and Olsen, J. P. *Ambiguity and Choice in Organizations*. In press, 1976.

March, J. G., and Simon, H. A. *Organizations*. New York: Wiley, 1958.

Marschak, J., and Radner, R. The firm as a team. *Econometrica*, 1954, *22*.

Messick, R., and Hills, J. R. Objective measurement of personality: cautiousness and intolerance of ambiguity. *Educational and Psychological Measurement*, 1960, *20*, 685-98.

Miklausich, V. M. The effects of error-prone feedback on performance in a multiple-cue inference task. Unpublished Master's thesis, Georgia Institute of Technology, 1973.

Miller, G. A. The magical number seven, plus or minus two: Some limits on our capacity for processing information. *Psychology Review*, 1956, *63*, 81-97.

Miller, P. McC. Do labels mislead? *Organizational Behavior and Human Performance*, 1971, *6*, 480-500.

Monge, P. R., and Lindsey, G. N. The study of communication networks and communication structure in large organizations (mimeo). Stanford Institute for Communications Research, April, 1974.

Muchinsky, P. M., and Dudycha, A. A. The influence of a suppressor variable and labelled stimuli on multiple cue probability learning. *Organizational Behavior and Human Performance*, 1974, *12*, 429-44.

Mulder, M. Communication structure, decision structure, and group performance. *Sociometry*, 1960, *23*, 1-14.

Nash, J. F. Non-cooperative games. *Annals of Mathematics*, 1951, *54*, 287.

Oskamp, S. Overconfidence in case study judgments. *Journal of Consulting Psychology*, 1965, *29*, 261-65.

Pettigrew, T. F. The measurement and correlates of category width as a cognitive variable. *Journal of Personality*, 1958, *26*, 532-44.

Pfeffer, J., and Salancik, G. R. Organizational decision making as a political process: The case of a university budget. *Administrative Science Quarterly*, 1974, *19*, 135-51.

Pitz, G. F. Information seeking when available information is limited. *Journal of Experimental Psychology,* 1968, *76*, 25-34.

———. Decision making and cognition. (mimeo): Paper given at Fifth Research Conference on Subjective Probability, Utility and Decision Making, 1975.

Porat, A. M., and Haas, J. A. Information effects on decision making. *Behavioral Science,* 1969, *14*, 98-104.

Porter, L. W. and Roberts, K. H. Communication in organizations. Tech. report no. 12, University of California, Irvine: July, 1972.

Pounds, W. F. The process of problem finding. Massachusetts Institute of Technology, Sloan School working paper no. 145-65, November, 1965.

Rados, D. L. Selection and evaluation of alternatives in repetitive decision making. *Administrative Science Quarterly,* 1972, *17*, 196-206.

Rapoport, A. and Horvath, W. J. Thoughts on organization theory. *General Systems,* 1959, *4*, 87-93.

Rappoport, L., and Summers, D. A. *Human Judgment and Social Interaction.* New York: Holt, Rinehart, 1973.

Richards, W. D. Network analysis in large complex systems: Metrics (mimeo). Stanford Institute for Communication Research, April, 1974.

———. Network analysis in large complex systems: The nature of structure (mimeo). Stanford Institute for Communication Research, April, 1974.

———. A systems methodology for the study of information and information processing systems (mimeo). Stanford Institute for Communication Research, March, 1975.

Richards, W. D., and Lindsey, G. Social network analysis: an overview of recent developments (mimeo). Stanford Institute for Communication Research, October, 1974.

Rokeach, M. *The Open and Closed Mind.* New York: Basic Books, 1960.

Rose, D. E. The impact of evaluative feedback on learning and performance in a multiple-cue decision problem. Unpublished Master's thesis, Georgia Institute of Technology, March, 1974.

Rubenstein, A. H., and Hannenberg, R. C. Idea flow and project selection in several industrial research and development laboratories. In Tybout, R. A. (ed.), *Economics of Research and Development.* Columbus, Ohio: Ohio State University Press, 1965.

Ruefli, T. W. A generalized goal decomposition model. *Management Science,* 1971, *17*, B505-18.

———. Behavioral externalities in decentralized organizations. *Management Science,* 1971, *9*, B649-57.

Salancik, G. R., and Pfeffer, J. The bases and use of power in organizational decision making: the case of a university. *Administrative Science Quarterly,* 1974, *19*, 453-73.

Scott, W. A. Cognitive complexity and cognitive flexibility. *Sociometry,* 1962, *25*, 405-14.

Schroder, H. M., Driver, M. J., and Streufert, S. *Human Information Processing.* New York: Holt, Rinehart, 1967.

Shaw, M. E. Some effects of unequal distribution of information upon group performance in various communication nets. *Journal of Abnormal and Social Psychology,* 1954, *49*, 547-53.

———. Some effects of problem complexity upon problem-solving efficiency in different communication nets. *Journal of Experimental Psychology,* 1954, *48*, 211-17.

———. Communication networks. In Berkowitz, L. (ed.), *Advances in Experimental Social Psychology,* *1*, 111-47, New York: Academic Press, 1964.

Shumway, C. R., Maher, P. M., Baker, N. R., Souder, W. E. Rubenstein, A. H., and Gallant, A. R. Diffuse decision making in hierarchical organizations: An empirical examination. *Management Science,* 1975, *21*, 697-707.

Sieber, J. E., and Lanzetta, J. T. Conflict and conceptual structure as determinants of decision making behavior. *Journal of Personality,* 1964, *32*, 622-41.

Siegel, S. Level of aspiration and decision making. *Psychology Review,* 1957, *64,* 253-62.

Simon, H. A. A behavioral model of rational choice. *Quarterly Journal of Economics,* 1955, *69,* 99-118.

────. *Administrative Behavior* (3rd ed). New York: Free Press, 1976.

Simon, H. A., and Barenfeld, M. Information-processing analysis of perceptual processes in problem solving. *Psychology Review,* 1969, *76,* 473-83.

Slovic, P. Analyzing the expert judge: A descriptive study of a stockbroker's decision process. *Journal of Applied Psychology,* 1969, *53,* 255-63.

Slovic, P., and Lichtenstein, S. Comparison of Bayesian and regression approaches to the study of information processing in judgment. *Organizational Behavior and Human Performance,* 1971, *6,* 548-745.

Streufert, S., and Driver, M. J. Conceptual structure, information load, and perceptual complexity. *Psychonomic Science,* 1966, *3,* 249-50.

Taylor, R. N. Psychological determinants of bounded rationality: implications for decision-making strategies. *Decision Sciences,* 1975, *6,* 409-29.

Taylor, R. N., and Dunnette, M. D. Relative contribution of decision-maker attributes to decision processes. *Organizational Behavior and Human Performance,* 1974, *12,* 286-98.

Thompson, J. D. *Organizations in Action.* New York: McGraw-Hill, 1967.

Tucker, L. R. A suggested alternative formulation in the developments by Hursch, Hammond and Hursch, and by Hammond, Hursch and Todd. *Psychological Review,* 1964, *71,* 528-30.

Tversky, A., and Kahneman, D. Judgment under uncertainty: Heuristics and biases. *Science,* 1974, *185,* 1124-31.

Vannoy, J. S. Generality of cognitive complexity-simplicity as a personality construct. *Journal of Personality and Social Psychology,* 1965, *2,* 385-96.

Vroom, V. H. A new look at managerial decision making. *Organizational Dynamics,* Spring, 1973.

Wallenius, J. Comparative evaluation of some interactive approaches to multi-criterion optimization. *Management Science,* 1975, *21,* 1387-96.

Weick, K. E. *The Social Psychology of Organizing.* Reading, Massachusetts: Addison-Wesley, 1969.

Wiggins, N. and Hoffman, P. J. Three models of clinical judgment. *Journal of Abnormal Psychology,* 1968, *73,* 70-77.

Woodward, J. *Management and Technology.* London: H.M.S.O. 1958.

Yntema, D. B., and Torgerson, W. S. Man-computer cooperation in decisions requiring common sense. *IRE Transactions in Human Factors in Electronics,* 1961, *HFE-2,* 20-26.

Chapter Seven

Power and Resource Allocation in Organizations

Jeffrey Pfeffer

We live in an organizational society (Boulding, 1953). Organizations control most of the productive resources and capital, and provide most of the goods and services that we use in our daily lives. Most of us work for organizations. For the large majority of U.S. citizens, our wealth consists primarily of our position in an organization and the income that we derive from that position. Stratification is mediated by organizations. We are filtered by organizations such as schools (Heyns, 1974), hired by other organizations, and filtered further, so that very few persons reach the top of organizations and draw large incomes. Positions and jobs, as well as money and capital equipment, are resources allocated largely within organizations by administrative mechanisms. Pondy (1970) explicitly recognized the importance of organizations in the allocation of resources in society, and indeed, because of the relationship between position in the social structure and organizational position, organizations allocate social status as well.

That the criteria, the processes, the bases by which such allocation decisions are made are important is self-evident. Anyone who has ever, in his own capacity or as a subunit leader, applied for a job, a promotion, or a share of some budget or access to some resource has been exposed to and affected by organizational resource allocation decisions. The decisions and choices made within and by organizations affect every aspect of social life. Moreover, it might be fair to say that the decisions and choices of organizations are what is meant when we write of "organizational behavior." It is the purpose of this chapter to examine this topic—the allocation of resources in organizations—in detail, paying particular attention to the role of social influence, the processes by which this influence is exercised, the bases of this influence, and the consequence of this perspective on organizations for our understanding of some critical organizational decisions.

Rational Criteria

One reaction to the subject matter of this chapter might be that everyone knows how decisions are made—by using rational criteria such as maximizing profit, or effectiveness or efficiency, or, in more elaborate fashion, by maximizing subjective expected utility. This model of choice behavior, while developed on an individual level, has found wide acceptance in the social science literature to describe both individual and group behavior. For instance, expectancy models such as Fishbein's (1963) attitude-belief relationship, or Vroom's (1964, pp. 17-18) model of force to perform some act all have an underlying structure closely resembling the utility maximization models of decision theory (Mitchell, 1974). All of these formulations operate from the premise that individuals have desired goals, preferences, or objectives. Intermediate outcomes (such as promotion, pay, a compliment) can be evaluated according to how they contribute to achieving this ultimate outcome and, in turn, possible actions are evaluated in terms of the expectation that they will lead to obtaining the intermediate level reward or outcome. Thus, working hard is evaluated according to the person's expectations of the consequences of working hard, where these consequences are related to some ordering of preferences or goal states. The utility maximization model is found throughout the economics literature and, indeed, is a necessary element for the definition of rational behavior as proposed by social choice theorists.

Regardless of its usefulness in predicting behavior, this is a model of man that is both socially desirable and psychologically comforting. Rational choice is a valued social ideal (Parsons and Smelser, 1956). Mental institutions are one possible home for persons who behave "irrationally." In every school of administration, there are courses on decision making which emphasize how to rationalize the choice process. Even at the governmental level, planning-programming-budgeting systems were attempts to make the allocation process in government more rational.

Rationality is a part of the theory of bureaucracy. For instance, Udy (1962) noted that bureaucratic rationality was achieved when ascriptive characteristics of individuals, such as the social characteristics of family background, race, and sex, no longer were important in selection and promotion in organizations. Weber's (1947) description of bureaucracy was an attempt to outline a system of organization that would insure that organizational members would make decisions and take actions considering the organization's goal—or, in other words, would make organizationally rational decisions. This was to be accomplished through the imposition of various control mechanisms such as rules and the promotion and reward of persons according to their performance in their organizational roles. The control of behavior to insure conformity to organizationally relevant standards of action has formed the focus of much subsequent research on organizational structures (e.g., Child, 1972, 1973; Meyer, 1972).

Because rationality is so desirable according to social values, the possibility of nonrational decision making is resisted. And the notion that decision making, particularly in organizations, is likely to be almost inevitably nonrational is even more abhorrent to social values. If decision making is nonrational, it must be because we haven't trained people, introduced enough computers, optimized, simulated, or something else. The driving notion behind much current management thought is that with enough training and study, any decision-making situation can be rationalized, and, implicitly, improved in the process.

Limits to Rationality

Various authors, however, have recognized limitations to the ability of persons or groups to make rational decisions. The first constraint on rational decision making is the limited cognitive and information-processing capabilities of individuals. Consider again the expectancy models of Vroom (1964) or Fishbein (1963). For each possible action, there may be a variety of possible outcomes, each with its own probability of occurrence and with its own value to the individual. The computational task involved in assessing a large number of actions with a large number of outcomes is tremendous, and would probably leave any person who tried to do it immobilized. Simon's (1955) concept of satisficing recognized the limits to the individual's ability to search for alternatives and process information. Simon argued that rather than examining the full range of consequences over every conceivable alternative, individuals searched until they found a satisfactory alternative, and then stopped the decision-making process. The idea of bounded rationality (March and Simon, 1958) is, however, not a threat to the fundamental premises of rational decision making. It leads to prescriptions designed to enhance information-processing capabilities, including computerization. The basic premise remains that man desires to be rational, and is rational within the limits of his cognitive capabilities.

A more serious attack on the concept of rational choice is to be found in Weick (1969). Arguing from Schutz (1967) and other phenomonological sociologists, Weick maintained that the meaning of behavior was inferred ex post. Rather than having behavior directed by or toward some goal or preference, the goal was constructed after the action occurred in order to rationalize the behavior. While, in this framework, behavior is always goal-directed and, hence, rational, it is clear that this view of human behavior is in conflict with the notion that persons have well-defined goals and preference orderings that they use to evaluate ex ante possible actions. The inference of motivation or meaning to action, either by external observers or by the person himself, forms the subject of attribution theory (Kelley, 1971) in social psychology. Schachter (1959), in an early experiment, used chemical arousal and a role model on naïve subjects to induce feelings of anger or excitement or happiness. The premise of this research was that the meaning of action is derived from a social process, which would tend to question the notion of well-defined goals and preferences guiding behavior. The concept that we act first and infer meaning to that behavior after it has occurred is disquieting, but empirical evidence is accumulating that this provides a valid alternative perspective on human behavior (Bem, 1972).

Thus far, we have dealt with limits to individual rationality. At the group or organizational level, an additional constraint becomes salient. Rational decision making presupposes a goal or set of objectives, or at least well-defined and transitive preferences. If, however, we view the organization as a coalition of interests (March, 1962; Cyert and March, 1963), it is impossible to define a consistent set of preferences or criteria. Goals not only become constraints (Simon, 1964) imposed by various coalition participants, but the evaluation of action becomes dependent on who in the coalition is doing the assessing. There is evidence that organizations are coalitions comprised of interests with different and conflicting standards of assessment and preferences. Friedlander and Pickle (1968), studying the effectiveness of 97 small businesses in Texas, found that there were negative or small correlations among the measures asking how well the organizations satisfied each of 7 different interests. Baldridge (1971), examining decision making in a university, concluded that the coalition model was the most appropriate description of reality. Yuchtman and Seashore (1967), in their discussion of organizational effectiveness, rejected the goal approach, noting that organizations served many interests with conflicting criteria.

When there are different preferences among organizational participants, Arrow (1951) demonstrated that it is impossible to develop a social choice mechanism that takes into account the various preferences and does not violate at least some of the postulates of rational decision making. Rational action is defined with respect to some goal or preference ordering (Friedland, 1974). In the absence of an agreed-upon goal or preference ordering, the rationality of organizational action is dependent on the particular group that is doing the assessment. What is rational given the standards and criteria of one group, such as employees, may be quite irrational given the standards and criteria of another organizational group, such as the owners.

The problem is not that organizations do not seek to use rational, bureaucratic criteria, but that it is impossible to do so because of dissensus concerning preferences, criteria, and definitions on what the organization should be doing. Unless goals and criteria are shared among all participants in the organization, the use of power and influence is inevitable in organizational decision making. For, in some way, the relative weighting of the various demands and criteria must be determined. Since there is no way of rationalizing away the dissensus, political strength within the coalition comes to determine which criteria, whose preferences are to prevail. Wildavsky (1961) has explicitly recognized the almost inevitable political nature of the resource allocation process:

> The crucial aspect of budgeting is whose preferences are to prevail in disputes about which activities are to be carried on and to what degree, in the light of limited resources. The problem is not only "How shall budgetary benefits be maximized?" as if it made no difference who received them, but also "Who shall receive budgetary benefits and how much?" (p. 184).

Two examples from the university setting will illustrate the inevitability of the use of power in resource-allocation decisions. Consider the allocation of faculty positions to departments in the organization. Further, assume that it has been agreed that only the workload, or students taught will be used in making this decision. Here, certainly, is a situation that can be rationalized. We can count precisely both students and faculty, and it is a simple computational process to allocate the additional positions to the most needy subunit. But, students come in different varieties—there are doctoral students, master's students, advanced and beginning undergraduate students, students who are majoring in the subject offered by your department, and students who are merely taking the courses as electives from other departments. Certainly, all of these students should not be equally weighted in assessing work load or student demand. Similarly, there are differences in professors—some are instructors, others are assistant, associate, or full professors. Again, differential weighting would seem to be logical. But while we can precisely compute the distribution of students and faculty, the weights accorded to each subgrouping must be determined, and in an arbitrary fashion. It is here that power comes into use. So, even in a situation where there is apparently one simple criterion, we see that the complexity of the actual decision-making context means that influence will be used in the process.

Alternatively, consider the hiring process. We certainly want to hire into our organization the most outstanding applicant, but, how can merit be measured? If there is a shared paradigm among the faculty, if there is consensus concerning the important dimensions, how they are weighted, and how the dimensions can be measured, then objective indicators can be used. But, in the absence of such consensus, merit or worth becomes a concept which is difficult to assess. As Perrow (1972) has noted, "Competence is hard to judge so we rely on familiarity" (p. 11). This example illustrates one condition for the use of influence—that there be some dissensus concerning preferences or in the definition of the situation.

TABLE 1 Amount of Control Possessed by Organizational Authorities

	Low	High
Consensus about Goals/Technology (certainty)	Professional Model	Bureaucratic Model
Dissensus about Goals/Technology (uncertainty)	Political/Coalition Model	Centralized Model

There may be disagreement, however, without the decision-making situation resembling the coalitional or political model of organizational functioning. If there is some authority in the organization that has a great deal of control, then decisions will be made in a centralized fashion by this authority. There are, then, two dimensions that appear to be relevant in determining the form decision making takes within the organization: (1) whether there is consensus or dissensus about goals and preferences and technology, and (2) the amount of control possessed by the authorities in the organization. Table 1 illustrates the relationships.

When there is consensus about goals and technology, or there is certainty, but authorities have little control, the professional model describes organizational decision making. There is self-control by the professionals, and because of the common norms, standards, and beliefs, collegial decision making works. When there is certainty and the authorities have more power and control in the organization, it is possible to implement rules, standardized forms, and procedures to govern behavior. Child (1973) has referred to this as the "bureaucratic model" of organizational control. When there is dissensus and uncertainty, and when there is no strong central authority, a situation resembling the political or coalitional view of organizations is likely to emerge. There is still a dispersed distribution of influence, but in the absence of shared norms and values, political struggles ensue to resolve the differences. When there is strong central authority, centralized decision making can be imposed, leading to what Child (1973) has called the "centralized model" of organizational control. The importance of dissensus or uncertainty for determining the form of decision making is evident, and has also been emphasized by Thompson (e.g., Thompson and Tuden, 1959). It is uncertainty, we would argue, that is important in determining whether the bureaucratic or centralized model of control is employed. The imposition of the bureaucratic model, with its associated characteristics of specialization and the development of formal rules and procedures, presupposes the ability to subdivide and allocate the task and to develop rules that will be applicable over a period of time. Furthermore, rules, as the organization's quasilegal system, also presuppose a reasonable degree of consensus concerning the definition of the situation. In circumstances of uncertainty, it is likely that personal mechanisms of control are more likely to be employed.

Allocation Process

The social value attached to rationality and objectivity means that, in the allocation process itself, the use of power must be relatively unobtrusive. Every attempt is made to legitimate the decision process and the decision outcome through recourse to objective, universalistic standards of assessment. Any discussion of the process of the use of power must consider the mechanisms through which power is exercised unobtrusively.

The Selective Use of Objective Criteria
"One use of organizational power may be to influence the criteria

used in organizational decision making" (Salancik and Pfeffer, 1974, p. 462). Organizational participants will, typically, fare differentially well in a decision, depending on what criteria are used. Promotion decisions based on intelligence, technical skill, having a pleasing personality, or loyalty will likely lead to different results, depending on the criterion chosen. Similarly, resource allocation decisions will have different outcomes depending on the bases of the allocation.

This fact would suggest that organizational members would be likely to, first, assess the relative position of their subunit depending on the choice of criteria; and, second, to use their influence to implement the use of those criteria that most favor their own position. There is some evidence that this is the case. In a study of resource allocation decisions made at a university, Salancik and Pfeffer (1974) found that there were high correlations between the department heads' assessment of their relative position on a given dimension within the university and their actual position for those dimensions that were important factors in allocating resources. These authors further reported that when asked what the basis of allocating the budget within the university should be, the department heads tended to favor those dimensions on which their departments scored relatively well (pp. 462-63).

In the allocation process, there are typically available a number of legitimate, objective criteria. Organizational members use power and influence to have those legitimate criteria selectively used that tend to favor their own relative positions. It is, therefore, difficult to observe the use of power directly. Decisions are discussed in terms of acceptable, legitimate criteria. The legitimation of the use of power has obvious advantages both in terms of legitimating the decision outcome and in not provoking as much opposition.

The Use of Legitimate Decision Procedures

To maintain the unobtrusiveness of power, it is also important to use legitimate, accepted procedures for allocating resources in organizations. It is generally believed that participation by a variety of organizational interests in decision making insures that influence in the decision will also be shared. Consequently, committees are frequently used to legitimate allocation decisions in organizations.

While the term "cooptation" originally referred to a strategy employed with respect to groups and organizations in the focal organization's environment (e.g., Selznick, 1949), the cooptation of interests is a more general phenomenon occurring within as well as between organizations (Gamson, 1968). If there is a dominant coalition in control of an organization, with enough power and influence to obtain the resources or policies desired, it is nevertheless the case that it may be useful to coopt other interests within the organization to avoid provoking opposition and to insure a broader base of support for the decision. Committees in organizations frequently are used for the purpose of such cooptation of other interests.

The use of committees to make resource allocation decisions offers several advantages. First, responsibility for the decision is diffused. With a committee, the responsibility for the decision can be attributed to all of the committee members, rather than to a single individual.

Second, if the committee is composed of persons representing various interests within the organization, it is likely that these interests will be effectively coopted. Participation in decision making has typically been found to increase the likelihood that the decision made will be accepted (e.g., Coch and French, 1948; Vroom and Yetton, 1973, p. 10). The representation of interests on a committee will tend to insure that the various groups will feel they have had an effect on the decision, and will increase the likelihood of acceptance and decrease the probability of the decision being contested.

Third, the committee form of decision making may be perceived as more legitimate. After all, democratic norms and values are also strongly held. Decisions made by a single person are likely to be perceived as being arbitrary or autocratic. The use of a committee to make the decision may provide a legitimate mechanism for action. The legitimacy of an outcome is determined by the process as well as by the actual result (e.g., Dowling and Pfeffer, 1975).

While the use of committees may provide legitimation or cooptation in the resource allocation process, it is unlikely that it alters the final result. In most decision contexts, committees operate with the information provided to them, under the rules provided, and under time constraints. With limited time, specified rules, and with the options for choice already developed, the relative amount of variance possibly accounted for by the committee is limited. Further, power and influence will operate in the committee decision-making context as well as in the larger organization. Influential subunits may again be able to get their way (Stagner, 1969).

While the committee is a pervasive form of decision-making structure in organizations, there have been few studies exploring the conditions of its use. The above discussion suggests, however, that the use of committees is more likely when: (1) there is conflict among organizational participants concerning the criteria for decision making, and, therefore, the cooptation of competing interests is possible; (2) no single group or perspective has such dominance or authority that it can impose its way without regard to the rest of the organization, so that cooptation is necessary. Further, committees are more likely to be employed when the situation can be so structured that the decision outcome can be manipulated by the dominant coalition. We would argue that the first two conditions operate in a multiplicative fashion so that committees are used only when there is both dissensus and the necessity for coopting the other interests. When there is consensus about criteria and preferences, every person would decide like every other person, and, consequently, all are indifferent about who makes the decision. In this case, the committee is not necessary because there are no competing or alternative interests to be represented. And, only when influence is more dispersed is cooptation necessary to insure the acceptance of the decision without serious opposition. When the authorities possess strong centralized control, competing interests can more readily be disregarded. The use of committees is probably also related to the legitimacy of this mode of decision making and the need for legitimating the decision.

Centralization Through Majority Rule

The extension of this legitimation strategy is to use a committee composed of all organizational participants. The effects of such a decision system are likely to also be observed in relatively large committees.

The participation of all subunits or organizational participants in a decision is something that is generally thought to be desirable. The literature dealing with participative decision making and power equalization in organizations is normatively and value-oriented, and the operating assumption is that the greater the participation, the better for both the organizational participants and the organization (subject, of course, to constraints involving technical knowledge and the availability of information). Yet, it is possible that while more complete sharing of decision-making responsibility does lead to more legitimacy for both the decision and the decision-making system, in actual effect, the greater the participation, the more the reality conforms to a very centralized decision-making structure. This result leads to the apparent paradox of centralizing decision making by moving to greater participation by more people in the decision-making process—centralization through majority rule. Mulder and Wilke (1970) demonstrated this effect in an experimental study.

Decision making takes time. Just as it would take time for a citizen to study the issues carefully in choosing among candidates or in deciding whether or not to communicate with a representative, so time is required for organizational members to familiarize themselves with the information relevant to resource-allocation decisions. Second, it is necessarily true that the decisions will be a function of both the preferences or goals of the individuals and the information they have about available options and the likely consequences of various courses of action. While the decision-making process itself may involve a wide sharing of responsibility, it is seldom the case that the information-collection and alternative-generation process operates in a decentralized fashion. Access to information is limited, and responsibility for information gathering is given to a few people. Further, a large number of people can vote on alternatives, but drafting alternatives is only possible in a relatively small group.

The consequence of these two facts is that participation in decision making may be avoided because of the time commitment required and the feeling that any individual's impact will be small. Furthermore, participation will be with respect to previously developed alternatives, and the choices will be heavily constrained by the information developed in a centralized structure. Schattschneider (1960, p. 68) perceptively noted that "the definition of the alternatives is the supreme instrument of power."

For example, consider the case of hiring in a university department. Several different possible decision structures could be imagined, including having the choice made solely by the department head, by a committee composed of persons representing various interests (subfields, research or teaching orientation, etc.) within the department, or the decision could be made by the department as a whole, voting in a meeting. If the decision is made solely by the department head, it is virtually certain that everyone in the organization will know this. Consequently, the locus and responsibility for the decision is well-defined, and those in the organization who are interested know where and how to make their concerns and preferences known. Since the behavior of any organizational member, even one in a leadership position, is constrained by the demands and expectations of those in his role set (Pfeffer and Salancik, 1975), the department head will make the decision only after being exposed to and considering the various positions of the interests in his department. If the decision structure is composed of representatives of the various interests, then it is obvious that there will be shared decision making among the various groups. But, in the case of the department as a whole making the decision, the representation of various interests becomes much more difficult. First, responsibility for the decision is diffused, which means that a person or group has a difficult time knowing where and how to exert influence. Second, the department as a whole cannot, obviously, interview people or develop information on candidates. This task will devolve to a small group, or even a single individual, who may be identifiable or not, but in any event who can always claim to be acting under the mandate of majority governance. Opposition or support is harder to focus and organize and, as a consequence, it is my prediction that the decision situation is, in operation, the most centralized of all.

The Control of Information

Anyone who has ever been associated with an organization as a customer, client, or employee knows that all information is not available to all persons who are in or in contact with the organization. Information is sometimes kept secret. Surprisingly, the role of secrecy in organizational operations has received virtually no empirical attention, in spite of the fact that it seems obvious that the distribution of information and access to information in an organization are important factors affecting the decisions made. The control of information—always, of course, claimed on the basis of some legitimate purpose—is another important aspect of the allocation process in organizations.

Information is essential in order to affect any organizational decision. Consequently, secrecy, or the limitation of access to information is used strategically by power holders to enhance and maintain their capability for action in the organization. Various aspects of an allocation decision may be kept secret. First, the information used to make the decision may be kept secret. Thus, for example, in deciding who to promote, the general types of information may be known, but the specific information, such as the content of letters of reference or actual performance evaluations, may be withheld. Second, the decision-making process itself may be secret. This may involve not divulging the names of the decision makers, or, more usually, the content or process of the deliberation. And third, occasionally even the results of the decision making may be kept secret. Though this is customarily difficult to do, it is the case that, in many organizations pay is secret. Each of these aspects of secrecy can vary independently of the others, so that any combination of secret and nonsecret information is possible.

The function of secrecy for maintaining the influence of the decision makers is evident. In the case of the first variety of secrecy, where the information used for the decision is withheld, second-guessing or criticism of the decision is prevented. The decision makers can always say that those who did not like the decision outcome were not privy to all the facts (an explanation occasionally used by high government executives to justify their actions). As long as information is controlled, it is virtually impossible for anyone to challenge the decision. Not knowing who the decision makers are, a component of the second variety of secrecy, obviously makes it impossible to attempt to influence the decision. Keeping the decision process itself secret also acts to protect those making the decision from influence attempts. They may present their actions in public as being something different from what went on in private. Keeping the results of the decision secret, the third form of secrecy, will also tend to forestall opposition to decisions. People assess their relative well-being in a process of social comparison (e.g., Adams, 1965). Comparisons are made between various indicators of objective need or worth and outcomes of the allocation process. To the extent that either or both of these pieces of information are withheld, it becomes impossible to engage in this process of social comparison and, consequently, easier to convince people that the decision has been fair. Thus, secrecy may be used to forestall social comparison processes, hide responsibility for the decision, or to permit information justifying the decision to be produced and disseminated.

In order to withhold information, a legitimate reason for this action must be provided. Hiding the responsibility of decision makers or preventing social comparisons are not legitimate reasons. Thus, in any organization that practices secrecy, it is almost inevitable that a rationalization or mythology develops justifying the practice of secrecy. The most common theme is that secrecy is somehow necessary for universalistic, legitimate criteria to be applied to the allocation decision. Thus, exposure to pressure is presumably something that will interfere with the workings of an otherwise rational process, and exposure of information, will, perhaps, constrain the providers of that information. Because of constraints of length, a detailed discussion of all the various rationalizations for processes of secrecy is not possible in this paper. Suffice it to say that we have already argued that resource allocation is almost inevitably a political process. Thus, the idea that secrecy will facilitate the use of more rational, universalistic criteria is suspect. Care should be taken to separate the rationalizations for an organizational practice from the real causal variables.

Secrecy almost invariably leads to decisions and a decision process that are different from what would have otherwise occurred. If this were not the case, there would be no point in the secrecy and no necessity to develop and reinforce the mythologies that support it. Moreover, the decisions are likely to be more different to the extent that there is greater dissensus associated with the decision process. If everyone agrees on objectives and on the definition of the situation, then whether the decision is made in public or in private, by one person or many, will not affect the outcome. The result of adding a column of numbers, to take an extreme example, is invariant over these conditions. Therefore, we can hypothesize that secrecy will make the most difference, and, consequently, be the most necessary and desirable, under conditions of greater dissensus in the decision-making situation. Furthermore, secrecy is likely to be more needed and useful when power is more equally distributed among conflicting interests. Just as in our discussion of cooptation and the role of committees, if there is very centralized, powerful authority, secrecy is not as necessary. It is when there is dissensus and power is more dispersed that secrecy is required for the influentials to be able to make decisions they desire without arousing powerful opposition.

The Effects of Power on Allocation Outcomes

While we have discussed the political nature of decision making in organizations, and how processes and ideologies are constructed to hide the use of power and influence, it is also true that not all allocation decisions are equally political or are equally likely to be affected by the power of the organizational participants involved. In this section we will discuss some of the conditions that affect the use of power in organizational decision making and resource allocation.

Characteristics of the Resource

The first dimension that affects the use of power in decision making is the nature of the resource being allocated or the policy being determined. Two characteristics of the resource would appear to be important. First, is the resource scarce? Unless the resource being allocated is scarce within the organization, there is, in a sense, no problem of allocation, and certainly no need for subunits or individuals to use power and influence to acquire the resource. In the absence of scarcity, organizational subunits will be able to obtain all of the resource that they want or need without resorting to influence attempts. As Gamson (1968) has noted, influence requires the expenditure of resources, and there is no reason to incur the cost of influence attempts when the subunit will receive the resources it wants in any event.

While the condition of scarcity appears obvious as a prerequisite to observing the effects of power on resource allocation, it is, nevertheless, an important variable distinguishing among organizations both over time and at a point in time. If power is more likely to be used in conditions of greater resource scarcity, then, for example, it follows that: (1) power has become a more important basis for allocating resources in universities as funding has become tighter over time; (2) power has become a more important basis for allocating research grants as more and more persons have applied for a smaller or constant pool of money; (3) power is more important in hiring and promotion decisions when jobs and promotions are scarce. The point is that the scarcity hypothesis on the use of power has wide implications and is applicable in a large number of contexts.

The second characteristic of the resource that is important in determining whether or not power is used in its allocation is whether or not the resource is critical to the subunit. Resources vary in their importance or criticality. Just as a subunit is not likely to have to contest for a resource which is not in scarce supply, so it is the case that it will not want to contest for a resource that is not critical to its operations. The effects of power on resource allocation, then, should be observed more for resources which are critical to most subunits within the organization.

In order for power to be used in allocating resources, the resource must be both critical to most subunits within the organization and scarce as well. If the resource is critical, but not scarce, or if the resource is scarce, but not critical, power will not be used in its allocation. Further, it is possible to think of the two dimensions of resource criticality and scarcity as being independent of each other. However, if a resource is generally critical for the operation of subunits, it is more likely to be scarce than if it is less critical, since more subunits will require it.

In a study of the allocation of four resources at the University of Illinois, Salancik and Pfeffer (1974) provided support for the position taken here. They reported that the correlation of subunit power with the allocation of resources was highest for the most critical and most scarce resource, graduate university fellowships, and was insignificant for the least critical and scarce resource, summer faculty fellowships. These results held when objective measures of allocation were introduced into the analysis. In this study, resource criticality and scarcity were almost perfectly correlated, so separate tests of the effects of the two dimensions were not provided.

Decision-maker Discretion

The use of power to influence resource allocations presumes that the allocation decisions involve some discretion on the part of decision makers, and are subject to adjustment in response to influence attempts. But, occasionally, resource allocations within organizations are subject to factors outside of the organization in question. In such instances, it is possible that the subunits' power, relevant within the organization, is of no consequence in affecting these external influences on organizational decisions.

As an example, consider the study of Pfeffer and Salancik (1974) in which the allocation of budget to 29 departments at the University of Illinois was examined. In that study it was found that subunit power had an equal effect with instructional units taught on resource allocations, and that for many of the more powerful departments, there was actually a zero or negative correlation between changes in instructional units and changes in resources over time. Assume, however, that a state law were passed setting a formula for budget allocation in state universities based solely on students taught. Now, an analysis accounting for variations in budget allocation would show no effect of power.

There are many situations in which legal constraints or other external pressures limit or even eliminate discretion in the allocation of resources within organizations. In these instances, subunit power within the organization will not have an affect on allocation outcomes. Rather, allocation outcomes depend on the ability to affect the external regulations and influences which dictate organizational decisions.

Public or Private Decision Making

Another dimension of the decision situation that may affect the use of power is whether the decision-making process is public or private. There are two plausible arguments that can be advanced. One is that power is more likely to affect decision outcomes when decisions are made in private. The premise is that the social context will constrain the actions of decision makers more when that social context is immediate, as in a public situation, and when decisions and the decision process are visible to this context. This rationale probably lies behind the many open-meeting laws and the continuing attempts to make decision-making meetings and information public.

The second argument holds that the only effect of public decision making would be to force the use of more acceptable and legitimate criteria to justify the decision that would have been made anyway. The argument is that the decisions would be made, if desired, still out of public scrutiny in informal meetings, but that because of the public nature of the formal process, greater attention would be paid to the forms of legitimating the decision-making process. While process and appearances might change, the results would remain the same. This is because, given the same degree of dissensus and the same actors in the decision situation, power becomes the only way of arriving at a choice.

The example of hiring and promotion decisions may provide support for this argument. Under pressure from the federal government, employers, including universities and business firms, were told not to use the friendship network (or "old boy") method of recruiting and hiring personnel. This led to extensive advertising and a wide search process, and the preparation of elaborate descriptions of job requirements and documentation of nondiscriminatory or affirmative action behavior. But, in the final analysis, it is not clear that the same social networks did not operate in tandem to produce the final result. After all, job descriptions and criteria can be developed to favor a certain candidate, just as criteria for allocating budgets can be developed to favor any one of a number of subunits in the organization. Indeed, it is possible that the supposed opening up of the decision-making situation may only make it more difficult to cope. If hiring is accomplished through an old boy social network, and this is openly known, then at least persons know the rules of the game and can potentially gain access to the network. But, if the network operates and fewer people know about it, assuming the process actually being used is the openly advocated one, then it is less likely they will attempt or be able to gain access.

Given the faith placed in opening up decisions as an antidote to the use of power in decision making, this seems to be an area that is in need of investigation. It is possible that the use of power is unaffected by the public or private nature of the allocation process, or that the use of power is inhibited. While it has not been argued, it is even possible that public decision contexts can increase the use of power in allocating resources by providing increased legitimacy for what would have been otherwise a problematic, political issue.

Uncertainty

The effect of uncertainty on the use of power has already been mentioned in our earlier discussion of the limitations of rational decision making. Thompson and Tuden (1959) developed a typology of decision types based on whether or not there was consensus about goals, and whether or not there was consensus on the connections between actions and outcomes, or causes and consequences. They argued that when there was consensus both about goals and about the relationship between actions and results, a computational (or bureaucratic) form of decision making was employed. When there was consensus on goals but not on the means of achieving the goals, judgment was the decision type employed, while consensus on the connections between actions and consequences but dissensus on goals led to a compromise strategy of decision making. When there was consensus on neither aspect of the decision situation, then Thompson and Tuden characterized the situation as requiring a decision strategy of inspiration. In their framework, only the bureaucratic or computational form of decision making does not involve the use of power. Compromise and inspiration involve the use of power and so does judgment, in which power is used to implement one's definition of the situation.

The social psychological literature also provides support for the position that power will be used in decision making under conditions of uncertainty. Festinger (1950, 1954) has argued that in uncertain social situations people attempt to stabilize their perceptions and beliefs through a process of social comparison. Social influence occurs as a consequence of the social comparison process, operating under conditions of uncertainty which cannot be reduced by recourse to objective standards or physical reality (Smith, 1973, chap. 2). Under conditions of uncertainty, social referents for beliefs and perceptions are sought, and the social consensus that emerges defines the situation and the reality for the people involved. Reality becomes socially constructed and defined, and social influence operates to affect decisions and judgments.

The concept of paradigm (Kuhn, 1962) provides a way of quickly summarizing the concept of uncertainty as it is being discussed here. As Lodahl and Gordon (1972) measured the concept of paradigm in science, it represents consensus on the important issues to be researched, on the subject matter of the field, and on the methodologies to be employed. While paradigm development as consensus has been discussed in the literature of the sociology of science, it is a concept equally applicable to organizations. We can speak of organizational paradigms, and ask whether they are well or poorly developed. In an organization with a certain technology, in which the connections between actions and consequences are well known and consensually agreed upon, and where there is agreement concerning the situation of the organization, the organization has a well-developed paradigm of operation, and should, therefore, be less subject to the effects of social influence in decision making than an organization which has a poorly developed paradigm. The consequences of high- or low-paradigm development for organizational structures and decision making, examined by Lodahl and Gordon (1973b), should be directly translatable to other organizational contexts.

In a study examining the effect of uncertainty on the use of social influence in organizational decision making, Pfeffer, Salancik, and Leblebici (1976) found support for the preceding argument. Examining National Science Foundation (NSF) grant allocations to universities in four social sciences that varied in terms of their degree of paradigm development, these authors found that social influence had the greatest effect on allocations decisions in those fields that were the least paradigmatically developed. Social influence effect was assessed by the consequence of institutional representation on the various advisory panels for each field. Proceeding from a similar theoretical perspective, Pfeffer (in press) found that institutional representation on editorial boards of journals had more effect on publication outcomes in sociology and political science than in chemistry, a field with a more highly developed paradigm. Both studies are consistent with the theoretical position that power will be used and have more effect when there is greater uncertainty in the decision-making context.

In the absence of consensus or certainty, greater emphasis will be placed on the structural characteristics of the decision-making process, such as who has access, whether it is public or private, and the formal methods and procedures used. When there is consensus, when there is a widely held normative belief, the form of the decision-making process does not matter and will be considered less important. While it is interesting and important that social influence operates to affect decisions more under conditions of uncertainty, an even more intriguing question is what determines which particularistic criteria come to be employed. While in the NSF and journal studies mentioned above, there is some indication that institutional similarity is the important dimension, it remains to be investigated under what circumstances other components of similarity, such as similarity in backgrounds, orientations, sex, age, or so on, become the important characteristics used in making decisions.

The specific particularistic criteria used in decision making can lead to different consequences. Consider the practice by scholarly journals of using anonymous reviewing for deciding upon publication or rejection of articles. In a discipline with a great deal of dissensus concerning theory and methodology, decisions will probably be made on the basis of perceived similarity in theoretical orientation between the reviewers and the author. If reviewing were not anonymous, decisions might be made more on the basis of similarity in current affiliations and academic backgrounds. It is not clear that this latter basis of particularism would not result in more diversity in theoretical orientation and points of view than the former, though it would restrict access to the journal along another dimension.

The Effect of Allocations on Power

While we have, thus far, been concerned with the effect of power on resource-allocation decisions, and the conditions and processes by which power is used, it is also the case that the allocation decisions themselves have consequences for the relative influence in the organization of various groups and subunits.

First, allocation decisions have symbolic value, serving to reinforce the prestige and the position of those who fared well in the allocation process. Social power, after all, is not a physical reality. Uncertainty may exist in the organization as to the exact influence position of various subunits and participants. Allocation decisions provide a reality by which power can be assessed. Decisions provide ratification for the perceptions of relative influence that before were, perhaps, only loosely held.

Since some components of power, such as prestige, are reputational in any case, the symbolic value of having a subunit's position of influence reaffirmed should not be underestimated. As long as one social actor believes the other has power and acts accordingly, then, in fact, the other does have power. In the allocation of resources, a process of attribution may occur (e.g., Schopler and Layton, 1972). The observation is made that certain participants receive favorable allocation outcomes; then the attribution may be made that these participants had the power to affect the allocation decisions. The attribution of influence as a consequence of the observation of allocation outcomes becomes an independent source of influence for the participants.

The second effect of allocation outcomes is directly to affect the relative power and influence of organizational participants. Gamson (1968) has noted that power depends on the possession of resources. Clearly, obtaining resources in an allocation process will facilitate the enhancing and maintaining of the subunit's power position within the organization. Power is used to obtain critical and scarce resources, which then can be used to maintain the subunit's position of power.

This effect can be observed in almost any social system in which power and influence operate. For example, in the University of Illinois, power within the organization enabled subunits to obtain more of the budget (Pfeffer and Salancik, 1974). These extra resources, then, could be expended hiring better faculty, supporting more and better graduate students, and doing more research. In turn, as a consequence of these activities, the department could develop more national prominence in its field and could use this increased national prominence to obtain outside funding in the form of grants and contracts. Since, in this organization, prestige, graduate education, and outside funding were related to subunit power (Salancik and Pfeffer, 1974), the cycle could continue. Power is used to acquire resources, which are then used in such a way as to enable the subunits to acquire more power.

Similar consequences can be observed from the allocation of positions in organizations. Power can be used to hire candidates that are favored by a particular group within the organization. Once hired, these persons become sources of additional strength for the group. And, in the case of promotions, again power can become institutionalized in the organization. Once a subunit or group acquires positions of power, these positions can be used to further selectively promote allies and punish opponents. And rules, information systems, and definitions of organizational reality which all favor the positions of the current power holders can be developed and implemented because of their power.

Because power can be used to affect allocation decisions, which then provide symbolic reaffirmation of relative influence as well as the resources to maintain power, it is the case that the distribution of power within organizations is most often quite stable. Only external contingencies that can no longer be adequately handled, or mistakes in managing the internal coalition can produce meaningful shifts in the distribution of influence within organizations.

Acquiring and Maintaining Power

An examination of how power is acquired and maintained requires exploration both of the determinants of power in organizations and how, strategically, actions are taken to employ these determinants to attain influence. While there has been some small amount of empirical research concerned with the determinants of power, there has been virtually no research on the processes; that is, the dynamics by which power and influence are acquired in organizations.

The Role of Uncertainty

The most completely articulated perspective on the determinants of power in organizations is probably the strategic contingencies theory (Hickson et al., 1971). This model evolved from earlier theorizing on the determinants of power in organizations. Crozier (1964) had studied bureaucracies in France, and in one French factory in particular, had noticed that the maintenance engineers, though not particularly high in the organizational hierarchy, exerted a great deal of influence in the organization. Crozier found that the breakdown of the machinery was the only remaining uncertainty confronted by the organization. Consequently, the maintenance engineers, who controlled this important uncertainty, had power in the organization. Cyert and March (1963) had also argued that organizations sought to avoid uncertainty. Those in positions to absorb the organization's uncertainty, they argued, would have influence in the organization.

Thompson (1967, chaps. 9 and 10) further elaborated the idea that power accrues to subunits because of their ability to cope with critical organizational uncertainties. He noted that persons would form coalitions within organizations when their resources were not adequate to deal with the uncertainties they confronted. The basis for the coalition was the mutual reduction of uncertainty among participants. Further, organizations would bring into the dominant coalition those persons who could deal with important organizational uncertainties. The more sources of contingency for the organization, the larger the dominant coalition. And Thompson noted that organizations, to solve current uncertainties, would give power to subunits or persons who could cope with the current conditions. Then, when contingencies changed, the organization would find it had bargained away its future capability for dealing with new uncertainties, because those in power would be those brought in to deal with past problems.

Hickson et al. (1971) further elaborated the idea of the importance of uncertainty as a source of power. They noted that uncertainty itself didn't create power but rather the ability to cope with uncertainty. Further, uncertainty coping itself was not sufficient to provide power to an organizational subunit. The ability of the organization to find a substitute for the coping capability affected subunit power, as did the importance of the uncertainty for the organization, assessed partially by how connected the subunit doing the coping was to the rest of the organization. The importance of substitutability for determining power is found in the earlier formulations by Emerson (1962) and Blau (1964), both of whom noted that power and dependence were reduced to the extent that resources or outcomes could be obtained from alternative actors.

An empirical test supporting the strategic contingencies theory was reported by Hinings et al. (1974). Perrow (1970) examined departmental power in a sample of industrial firms, and found that the marketing department was consistently the most powerful. He interpreted these results by saying that in this consumer-oriented economy, the most critical problem faced by firms was the ability to sell their products. The idea that uncertainty is a critical problem confronted by organizations and, consequently, coping with that uncertainty may provide power within the organization is consistent with Weick's (1969) model of an organization as a system for registering and removing equivocality from the informational environment, as well as being consistent with the theses of those authors who have stressed the importance of environmental uncertainty for determining organizational structure (e.g., Lawrence and Lorsch, 1967; Duncan, 1972).

Some of the processes by which uncertainty can be used to

acquire power are derivable from this research. If uncertainty coping brings power only to the extent that such coping cannot be easily replaced, then to acquire power subunits will want to attempt to insure that their expertise cannot readily be acquired outside of their boundaries. This may be done by destroying sources of information relevant to how the job is done (e.g., the destruction of maintenance manuals as described by Crozier, 1964), developing specialized language and terminology which inhibits the understanding of the job by outsiders, and by restricting the distribution of knowledge concerning how the task is accomplished. All of these techniques are visible in organizations. Jargon is pervasive and while justified as making communication more efficient among those who know the terminology, it also serves to keep knowledge private and to make the task appear more complex and important than, perhaps, it really is. One effect of secrecy not already discussed is the maintenance of the power of those operating in secret because their jobs can be pictured as more difficult and complex than they really are. If no one knows exactly how the job is done, it can be made to look more difficult and more uncertain than it is.

If uncertainty and the capability to cope with it provides power in an organization, then this suggests that it may occasionally be functional for a subunit to cause problems by failing in its tasks. In the case of Crozier's factory, if the machines never broke down, it would not make any difference whether the expertise to repair them was widely distributed or not. Thus, one strategy to increase power in the organization is occasionally to cause problems which the subunit can then handle. Related to this strategy is to define ex sting or occurring organizational problems as being within the subunit's particular expertise. Since organizational uncertainties are ambiguous, it is not difficult to maintain that one's own subunit has the particular expertise required to cope with the organizational problem.

Since uncertainty frequently derives from the organization's interactions with external organizations, the strategic contingencies theory suggests how the environment affects organizations. Much of the research on the effects of organizational environments on organizations has not specified a process by which such effects operate. The strategic contingincies theory suggests that external uncertainties create power within the organization for those subunits that can cope with the uncertainties. In turn, this power enables these subunits to affect organizational decisions.

This argument suggests that in attempting to acquire or maintain power, coalitions with those responsible for the external contingencies is a useful strategy to pursue. In the relationship between union and management in corporations, the union leaders and the industrial relations department in the organization may easily find themselves in a symbiotic relationship. In order for the union officials to maintain their power, they have to show that they are handling strategic contingencies for the members, and that they have some unique capabilities in these areas. This perception is enhanced by portraying the employing organization as hostile to the workers' interests and by indicating that the bargaining process is arduous and requires skill. The industrial relations department will enhance its power in the organization to the extent it can convince other subunits that union relations are problematic, and that the bargaining and negotiating process requires expertise that is not obtainable elsewhere. Note that in this instance, it is in the interests of both parties to maintain the outward appearance of conflict and to portray the negotiating process as difficult.

Resources

Related to, but at the same time different from the strategic contingencies theory is the idea that power accrues to those subunits that are most instrumental in providing important resources for the organization. The acquisition of resources as a source of subunit power within the organization was the focus of Salancik and Pfeffer's (1974) analysis of the determinants of subunit power in a university. In that study, subunit power was most highly related to the subunit's outside grant and contract funds.

To the extent that resources are a critical contingency for organizations, it could be argued that the focus on a subunit's ability to bring in critical resources is equivalent to the subunit's capability of coping with a critical organizational contingency. The principal difference, if there is one, concerns the ease of measurement of the concepts. The flow of resources into an organization and responsibility for resource flows appear to be more precisely specified than the concept of uncertainty or contingency.

In a loosely coupled coalition, such as a university, a United Fund, or a conglomerate firm, the importance of being able to acquire outside resources for power within the organization may be derived directly from Emerson's (1962) and Blau's (1964) notions of power and dependence. To the extent that the subunit brings in outside resources, it lessens its dependence on the rest of the organization for internally allocated resources. Conversely, the subunit increases the rest of the organization's dependence on it. That this power can be used to increase the share of internally allocated resources has been seen in Pfeffer and Salancik's (1974) study of university budgeting and Lodahl and Gordon's (1973a) examination of external and internal funding for university physical and social science departments. In both instances, power derived from the acquisition of outside funds was employed to increase the subunits' share of internally allocated funds.

The importance of resources for determining subunit power argues for the importance of the subunit's external relationships. The ability to acquire funds or other resources critical to the organization insures the subunit of a powerful position. This also suggests that a position involved in measuring, negotiating for, or allocating resources increases subunit power within the organization.

Allies

Subunits in organizations can achieve power through alliances with internal and external groups, as well as through direct control of resources or the capability of coping with critical uncertainties. If we assume, following Riker (1962), that the size of coalitions formed is only just large enough to win, to avoid splitting the benefits with more participants than necessary, then it must be true that in order to form an alliance, the subunit must have something to offer in the first place. Thompson (1967) has argued that when cause/effect resources are inadequate to cope with the uncertainty, subunits will find it in their interests to pool resources. What this means is that when individual groups cannot cope with critical contingincies, but jointly they can achieve the capability of dealing effectively with contingencies, then alliances among the groups are likely to be formed.

While there is a history of research on coalition formation (e.g., Caplow, 1956; Gamson, 1961; Stryker and Psathas, 1960), virtually all of the studies of coalitions have focused either on experimental situations or on legislative bodies. But coalitions and alliances form within bureaucratic structures as well. It is possible that when no single subunit possesses enough control over resources, or enough uncertainty-coping capability to unilaterally enforce its will, in alliance with other subunits it can achieve control over organizational decision-making processes and outcomes.

Alliances with groups outside of the organization are particularly likely. The external group may want some specific organizational action or performance, and the subunit may want increased authority and control over the organization. A mutuality of interest may exist so that the external group can create contingencies and demands, which the subunit can then proceed to handle, paying off the external group with the action or performance desired, and leaving the subunit in control of the organization. Or the subunit may seek external allies to buttress its claims for a greater share of the organization's resources.

The development of external constituencies is a practice of most public bureaucracies. Interest groups and client organizations are carefully cultivated so that external pressure can be brought to bear on the organization to favor the particular subunit. One good external ally is a respected consultant organization. The use of outside expertise to either eliminate some opponent or else bolster the subunit's own position is probably more frequent than supposed. The external ally in this case provides legitimacy and the appearance of objectivity, which is frequently desirable, given the social norms favoring rationality.

Like any group structure, alliances must be continually reaffirmed through the exchange of important commitments or contingencies among the partners. Alliances are particularly stable when the resources that are especially critical to one subunit are not critical to another, so that each can help the other acquire a critical resource but not be in direct competition for the resource themselves.

In organizations, as in other political systems, some unifying theme or rationale is helpful to build cohesiveness in the coalition and to provide a legitimate and coherent rationalization for its decisions. In universities, coalitions form around the rationale of research excellence, or public service, or teaching. When departments act in concert to influence allocation decisions, it is important that there be a legitimate explanation for their behavior. Much like goal statements, the rationales articulated by coalitions of interests within organizations serve more to justify their concerted action than to predict the basis for their behavior.

A coalition can be identified by a common set of actions with respect to various types of decision situations. Subunits within organizations form implicit or explicit structures that are both enduring and socially meaningful. Regularities in the patterns of support and opposition to various policies and allocation actions can frequently be observed in organizations. Coalition theory would predict, of course, that those consistently on the losing side would make efforts to negotiate their way into the winning coalition. However, if the winning coalition is of minimum size, this may not be possible.

The examination of coalitions within formal organizations is only one of the aspects of the resource allocation process that requires additional investigation. As the bulk of the existing research on coalitions assumes single trials with no ongoing relationship, much of the theory for this inquiry will have to be developed. Focus must include the coalitions formed with external pressure groups, because this form of coalition behavior is probably frequent.

Conclusions

The separation of the normative and descriptive aspects of the study of organizations is always problematic, but in the examination of decision making in organizations, the tendency to confuse preferences with reality is especially pronounced. The literature of organizational decision making has been dominated by a prescriptive orientation.

It is, therefore, appropriate to conclude this chapter with some prescriptions pertaining to power and resource allocation in organizations. These prescriptions, however, do not call for the application of more statistical decision theory, more optimization, more computerized analysis. It should be evident from the first sections of this chapter that we believe such efforts to be futile in those situations in which there is dissensus and the absence of centralized power. Optimization requires a specified goal and statistical decision theory requires estimates of costs and payoffs. Such elements are not available when there are contesting interests with incompatible preferences and inconsistent definitions of organizational reality. Indeed, the presence of those conditions that we have specified as making bureaucratic decision making impossible might be hypothesized to be related to the failure of rationalist decision-making procedures.

The model of organizational resource allocation we have described is one in which power and influence operate to affect decision outcomes, but through a variety of tactics the operation of power and influence are made as unobtrusive as possible. These tactics include (1) the use of legitimate criteria in a selective fashion; (2) the use of legitimate decision procedures; and (3) the control of information and the use of secrecy. All three procedures for making power less visible rely, to some extent, on organizational myths, with the myth of the rational decision-making system being the most common. Since rationality and universalism are valued social ideals, the identification of allocation procedures and outcomes with these values shields the procedures from both criticism and inspection. Further, our model posits that the allocation outcomes, themselves affected by power, serve to reinforce the position of the influentials. This occurs both through the operation of an attribution process in which power and influence are attributed to those acquiring resources, thereby giving them more power, and because the resources obtained can be invested and used to maintain and acquire power. Power is based on resources, one of which is the ability to cope with critical organizational contingencies.

Legitimacy of the allocation outcomes and procedures is critical. As a consequence, the meaning attached to decisions and outcomes becomes, itself, a focus for the use of power. Those in power will seek to have meaning defined so as to construct a universalistic, rational definition of social reality. Those in opposition will seek to have reality socially constructed to portray particularism and the arbitrary use of power. The construction of meaning given to organizational actions becomes an arena for the use of influence. The definition of social reality is critical in maintaining the stability of the organization and the positions of those individuals and subunits with power.

The point, therefore, is that all of the elements of the organization tend to be consistent with each other, and to act to reinforce the stability of the current influence structure. Allocation outcomes are determined by subunit power, and the allocations then are used to maintain and enhance the power of the subunits. Further, organizational ideologies and mythologies are developed to legitimize the status quo. Of course, this becomes easier to do because the influential groups have differential access to information, communication channels, and resources. It is not unusual, consequently, to observe that fundamental changes in influence within organizations occur only when the organization is faced with a severe crisis. For instance, in a series of case studies of proxy fights (Wattel, 1966), the analogy was made between the proxy fight and revolution, and the anecdotal evidence supports the position that such revolutions are likely to occur only in instances of the most blatant mismanagement of organizational problems.

Our prescriptions are to recognize the inevitability of the political nature of resource-allocation decisions, the role of organizational mythology and techniques of legitimation in making the operation of power less obtrusive, and the fact that power accrues to those who control critical resources or who, either alone or through alliances with other internal or external groups, are capable of coping with critical organizational uncertainties. It is invariably the case that the use of power has observable consequences. More attention to the actual consequences of organizational decisions, and less concern with the mythology and rhetoric associated with the decision-making process, will produce better insights into organizational functioning. And such understanding of organizational operation is, after all, the necessary prerequisite to effecting organizational change. As Pettigrew (1973) aptly noted, "An accurate perception of the power distribution in the social arena in which he lives is . . . a necessary prerequisite for the man seeking powerful support for his demands" (p. 240).

References

Adams, J. S. Inequity in social exchange. In L. Berkowitz (ed.), *Advances in Experimental Social Psychology* (vol. 2), New York: Academic Press, 1965.

Arrow, K. *Social Choice and Individual Values*. New York: John Wiley, 1951.

Baldridge, J. V. *Power and Conflict in the University*. New York: John Wiley, 1971.

Bem, D. J. Self-perception theory. In L. Berkowitz (ed.), *Advances in Experimental Social Psychology* (vol. 6), New York: Academic Press, 1972.

Blau, P. M. *Exchange and Power in Social Life*, New York: John Wiley, 1964.

Boulding, K. E. *The Organizational Revolution*, New York: Harper, 1953.

Caplow, T. A theory of coalitions in the triad. *American Sociological Review* 1956, *21*, 483-93.

Child, J. Organizational structure and strategies of control: A replication of the Aston study. *Administrative Science Quarterly* 163-77. 1972, *17*, 163-77.

———. Strategies of control and organizational behavior. *Administrative Science Quarterly*, 1973, *18*, 1-17.

Coch, L., and French, J. R. P. Jr. Overcoming resistance to change. *Human Relations*, 1948, *1*, 512-32.

Crozier, M. *The Bureaucratic Phenomenon*. Chicago: University of Chicago Press, 1964.

Cyert, R. M., and March, J. G. *A Behavioral Theory of the Firm*. Englewood Cliffs, N. J.: Prentice-Hall, 1963.

Dowling, J., and Pfeffer, J. Organizational legitimacy: Social values and organizational behavior, *Pacific Sociological Review*, 1975, *18*, 122-36.

Duncan, R. B. Characteristics of organizational environments and perceived environmental uncertainty. *Administrative Science Quarterly*, 1972, *17*, 313-27.

Emerson, R. E. Power-dependence relations. *American Sociological Review*, 1962, *27*, 31-41.

Festinger, L. Informal social communication. *Psychological Review*, 1950, *57*, 271-82.

———. A theory of social comparison processes. *Human Relations*, 1954, *7*, 117-40.

Fishbein, M. An investigation of the relationships between beliefs about an object and the attitude toward that object. *Human Relations*, 1963, *16*, 233-49.

Friedland, E. I. *Introduction to the Concept of Rationality in Political Science*. Morristown, N. J.: General Learning Press, 1974.

Friedlander, F., and Pickle, H. Components of effectiveness in small organizations. *Administrative Science Quarterly*, 1968, *13*, 289-304.

Gamson, W. A. An experimental test of a theory of coalition formation. *American Sociological Review*, 1961, *26*, 565-73.

———. *Power and Discontent*, Homewood, Ill.: Dorsey Press, 1968.

Heyns, B. Social selection and stratification within schools. *American Journal of Sociology*, 1974, *79*, 1434-51.

Hickson, D. J., Hinings, C. R., Lee, C. A., Schneck, R. E., and Pennings, J. M. A strategic contingencies' theory of intraorganizational power. *Administrative Science Quarterly*, 1971, *16*, 216-29.

Hinings, C. R., Hickson, D. J., Pennings, J. M., and Schneck, R. E. Structural conditions of intraorganizational power. *Administrative Science Quarterly*, 1974, *19*, 22-44.

Kelley, H. H. *Attribution in Social Interaction*. Morristown, N. J.: General Learning Press, 1971.

Kuhn, T. S. *The Structure of Scientific Revolutions*. Chicago: University of Chicago Press, 1962.

Lawrence, P. and Lorsch, J. *Organization and Environment*. Boston: Division of Research, Harvard Business School, 1967.

Lodahl, J., and Gordon, G. The structure of scientific fields and the functioning of university graduate departments. *American Sociological Review,* 1972, *37,* 57-72.

———. Funding the sciences in university departments. *Educational Record,* 1973a, *54,* 74-82.

———. Differences between physical and social sciences in university graduate departments. *Research in Higher Education,* 1973b, *1,* 191-213.

March, J. G. The business firm as a political coalition. *Journal of Politics,* 1962, *24,* 662-78.

March, J. G., and Simon, H. A. *Organizations.* New York: John Wiley, 1958.

Meyer, M. W. *Bureaucratic Structure and Authority.* New York: Harper and Row, 1972.

Mitchell, T. R. Expectancy models of job satisfaction, occupational preference and effort: A theoretical, methodological, and empirical appraisal. *Psychological Bulletin,* 1974, *81,* 1053-77.

Mulder, M., and Wilke, H. Participation and power equalization. *Organizational Behavior and Human Performance,* 1970, *5,* 430-48.

Parsons, T., and Smelser, N. J. *Economy and Society.* Glencoe, Ill: Free Press, 1956.

Perrow, C. Departmental power and perspective in industrial firms. In M. N. Zald (ed.) *Power in Organizations,* Nashville: Vanderbilt University Press, 1970.

———. *Complex Organizations.* Glenview, Ill.: Scott, Foresman, 1972.

Pettigrew, A. M. *The Politics of Organizational Decision-Making.* London: Tavistock, 1973.

Pfeffer, J. Paradigm development and particularism: journal publication in three scientific disciplines. *Social Forces,* (in press).

Pfeffer, J., and Salancik, G. R. Organizational decision making as a political process: The case of a university budget. *Administrative Science Quarterly,* 1974, *19,* 135-51.

———. Determinants of supervisory behavior: A role set analysis. *Human Relations,* 1975, *28,* 139-54.

Pfeffer, J., Salancik, G. R., and Leblebici, H. The effect of uncertainty on the use of social influence in organizational decision making. *Administrative Science Quarterly,* 1976 *21,* 227-45.

Pondy, L. R. Toward a theory of internal resource-allocation. In M. N. Zald (ed.), *Power in Organizations,* Nashville: Vanderbilt University Press, 1970.

Riker, W. H. *The Theory of Political Coalitions.* New Haven, Conn.: Yale University Press, 1962.

Salancik, G. R., and Pfeffer, J. The bases and use of power in organizational decision making: The case of a university. *Administrative Science Quarterly,* 1974, *19,* 453-73.

Schacter, S. *The Psychology of Affiliation: Experimental Studies of the Sources of Gregariousness.* Stanford, Calif.: Stanford University Press, 1959.

Schattschneider, E. E. *The Semi-Sovereign People.* New York: Holt, Rinehart, and Winston, 1960.

Schopler, J., and Layton, B. D. *Attributions of Interpersonal Power and Influence.* Morristown, N. J.: General Learning Press, 1972.

Schutz, A. *The Phenomenology of the Social World.* Evanston, Ill.: Northwestern University Press, 1967.

Selznick, P. *TVA and the Grass Roots.* Berkeley: University of California Press, 1949.

Simon, H. A. A behavioral model of rational choice. *Quarterly Journal of Economics,* 1955, *69,* 90-118.

———. On the concept of organizational goal. *Administrative Science Quarterly,* 1964, *9,* 1-22.

Smith, P. B. *Groups Within Organizations.* New York: Harper and Row, 1973.

Stagner, R. Corporate decision making: An empirical study. *Journal of Applied Psychology,* 1969, *53,* 1-13.

Stryker, S. and Psathas, G. Research on coalitions in the triad: Findings, problems, and strategy, *Sociometry,* 1960, *23,* 217-30.

Thompson, J. D. *Organizations in Action,* New York: McGraw-Hill, 1967.

Thompson, J. D., and Tuden, A. Strategies, structures, and processes of organizational decision. In J. D. Thompson, P. B. Hammond, R. W. Hawkes, B. H. Junker, and A. Tuden (eds.), *Comparative Studies in Administration,* Pittsburgh: Pittsburgh University Press, 1959.

Udy, S. H. Administrative rationality, social setting, and organizational development. *American Journal of Sociology,* 1962, *68,* 299-308.

Vroom, V. H. *Work and Motivation.* New York: John Wiley, 1964.

Vroom, V. H. and Yetton, P. W. *Leadership and Decision-Making.* Pittsburgh: University of Pittsburgh Press, 1973.

Wattel, H. L. (ed.) *Proxy Fights as Managerial Revolutions.* Hempstead, N. Y.: Hofstra University, Yearbook of Business, ser. 3, vol. 1, 1966.

Weber, M. *Theory of Social and Economic Organization.* New York: Oxford, 1947.

Weick, K. E. *The Social Psychology of Organizing.* Reading, Mass.: Addison-Wesley, 1969.

Wildavsky, A. Political implications of budgetary reform. *Public Administration Review,* 1961, *21,* 183-90.

Yuchtman, E., and Seashore, S. E. A system resource approach to organizational effectiveness. *American Sociological Review,* 1967, *32,* 891-903.

Chapter Eight

Enactment Processes in Organizations
Karl E. Weick

With the introduction of open systems analyses into organization theory, it has become fashionable to talk about the interaction between organizations and their environments. One byproduct of this has been a potential overestimation of the ease with which distinct organizations can be differentiated from their distinct environments. The presence of explicit boundaries separating distinct, internally-constrained entities has been assumed so that investigators could move on to other issues. These assumptions of distinct units, however, have influenced the form that other arguments about organizations take. For example, having assumed that boundaries are not problematic, investigators have examined issues such as how things "cross" boundaries, how organizations react to their environments and occasionally try to influence them, and how organizations go about learning what is really out there that they have to deal with.

The perspective to be developed in this essay argues that organizations[1] are more active in constructing the environments that impinge on them than is commonly recognized. That is, organizations often impose that which subsequently imposes on them. From this perspective, organizational scholars should pay particular attention to the conditions under which organizations implant that which they later rediscover and call "knowledge" or "understanding" of their "environment." The nature of the processes whereby organizations create the

---

I have learned much about enactment from discussions with Michel Bougon, discussions which I acknowledge with gratitude. The National Science Foundation provided support for this work through Grant SOC 75-09864.

environments that subsequently constrain their actions can be illustrated using banks, physicians, and actors as examples.

Enacted Investment

Large banks are institutional investors in the stock market. They collect money from individual clients and use it to purchase stock, bonds, and other securities for their clients' benefit. These large institutional investors account for a sizeable portion of the trading that occurs on the exchanges (currently, almost 60 percent of the shares traded). Presumably, the interaction between these investors and the market could be examined as one of investors reacting to market fluctuations in such a way as to raise the probabilities that their investments will be profitable.

The sheer size of these investors, however, also means that their activities can be understood as the creation of the environments that then impose on them. The fate of Polaroid Corporation stock during 1972 is a good example. During 1972 Polaroid sold for as much as $149 per share,

> . . . a price that reflected near-unanimous agreement among institutional investors that Polaroid was a growth company with hot consumer prospects: After all, it had just developed a new color camera that would ultimately be in every household. Yet, sometime that year, the fund managers who thought so highly of Polaroid began wondering how they could ever unload the huge Polaroid blocks they had accumulated, since at that point anyone who was likely to buy Polaroid stock had probably already done so. Suddenly, institutions began to bail out of Polaroid, causing the price to fall. This drop led other institutions to sell ever-larger blocks of Polaroid shares, causing the price to drop even more sharply. At one point in 1972, Polaroid dipped as low as $86; last year it bottomed out at $15 (Rottenberg, 1976, pp. 21-22).

Doubts concerning the attractiveness of Polaroid investments created the environment which then was imposed on investors and made Polaroid stocks less attractive to hold, thereby validating the initial definition that they might be less attractive than originally thought—a self-fulfilling prophecy.

This example of an enacted environment in banking illustrates the more general case that there may be a closed-loop quality to much organizational "sensemaking." There are conditions under which organizations do not act like open systems, conditions under which they create the environment that they make sense of. Campbell (1975) has made a similar observation:

Adaptive evolution is a negative feedback steering device, and therefore works best when the evolving social organization is a small part of the total environment, so that variations in the social organization do not substantially change the selective system, that is, the overall environment. It is on these grounds that one might well doubt that any adaptive social evolution is going on at the level of nations today. Major nations are so few in number, and so much the dominant part of each other's environment, that each variation initiated by one nation may fundamentally change the overall system, thus altering the selective system and creating something closer to a runaway positive feedback rather than a stabilizing negative feedback (p. 1106).

Unless an evolving organization is only a small part of the environment, then, its actions will change the selection system. As an organization increases in size it becomes more and more its own selection system and finally quite literally does impose the environment that imposes on it. As should also be apparent, the distinction between organization and environment becomes hopelessly blurred under these ultimate conditions, a blurring that was apparent in the Polaroid sell-off.

Enacted Medicine
Physicians also create some of the environments that impose on them. A particularly clear example of this enactment is "physician-induced disease" (iatrogenics). The concept of iatrogenics has been invoked by Scheff (1965) in his studies of errors in medical diagnosis. He notes that the predominant decision rule in medicine is, "When in doubt continue to suspect illness." If we use the language of "type 1" errors and "type 2" errors, a type 1 error would occur when the physician dismisses a patient who is actually ill and a type 2 error would occur when a physician retains a patient who is not ill.

Scheff presents considerable data demonstrating that physicians overwhelmingly make type 2 errors. The chief medical errors, in other words, consist of the physician diagnosing someone as sick who in fact is really well. This preference for type 2 errors seems to rest on two assumptions: (1) "Disease is usually a determinant, inevitably unfolding process, which if undetected and untreated, will grow to a point where it endangers the life or limb of the individual, and, in the case of contagious diseases, the lives of others" (p. 71); (2) "medical diagnosis of illness, unlike legal judgment, is not an irreversible act which does untold damage to the status and reputation of the patient" (p. 71). These two assumptions which buttress a preference for type 2 errors imply that type 2 errors are relatively harmless. It is this conclusion to which Scheff takes strong objection.

He argues that it is possible for a physician to create illness where none exists by inadvertently giving labels to his patients at a time of high suggestibility. In response to this labeling, patients then proceed to act out a career of chronic illness. Had the labels not been available, had the person's symptoms remained unorganized (see Miller, Hampe, Barrett, and Noble, 1970), and had the person not been as suggestible, then a career of illness would not necessarily have occurred. The effects of a diagnosis of false positive may be much more serious than is now realized in the medical profession.

To carry the analysis one step further, among physicians it is probably the case that they can be sorted into those who favor active intervention to alleviate sickness and those who prefer to "let nature take its course." The proposition suggested by this categorization is that those who favor active intervention will make more type 2 errors than those who view intervention as a means to assist natural processes. The "interventionists" more frequently impose a world that subsequently presents them with medical environments requiring their skills.

Enacted Theater

Actors, especially those who engage in improvisational theater, frequently impose environments which then organize their subsequent activities. A good example of theatrical enacted environments is Keith Johnstone's "Theatre Machine" company in London (Jencks and Silver, 1973, pp. 144-45). In one routine, two performers are given a deck of cards with one sentence of dialogue written on each card. The deck is shuffled, after which the actors take turns reading lines from the cards and trying to make dramatic sense of them. In another sketch two players improvise dialogue while two additional players move the speakers' body parts through "suitable" actions. Obviously the body movements always lag slightly behind the words that are being said, thereby creating some striking incongruities. Members of the company also create a situation where two actors mime something in slow motion while a third person comments on it. "A scene like this involves triple discoveries, with each performer supplying information to the others that he then uses in some generally unexpected way; successive transformations take place" (p. 145).

In each of these instances, the players build up an environment that informs their subsequent actions. Frequently, the actors do not know what they have done until the action is completed. A person, for example, who tries to make random dialogue meaningful, may not know what he has just said until he hears the tone of voice used by his partner in the next remark. The actors steadily build up a plausible world, but it is a world of their own design put in place by their own actions and then rediscovered as something to which they accommodate their subsequent actions. The actors are literally talking to themselves, but in doing so, they are not becoming more confused. Quite the contrary. Their world is developing a sense of sorts.

Conclusion

In all three cases—investment policies, iatrogenics, and improvisational theater—people had a major role in creating the world toward which they subsequently "responded." The separations between the organization and the environment were decidedly blurred in each case (e.g., the physician sees himself when his diagnosis implants a "disease" which is then presented to him for treatment). Sensemaking in each of these cases often involves individuals examining reflectively their own actions in order to discover what they've done and what the meaning of those actions is. Finally, the process of sensemaking in each case is better understood by examining what is in people's heads and imposed by them on a stream of events than by trying to describe what is "out there."

Conceptualizations of Enactment

We will now try to locate the phenomenon we are interested in by means of organizational concepts. Relevant assertions made by Filley, House, and Kerr (1976), Katz and Kahn (1966), and Piaget (1962) will be examined.

Control Imagery

In the examples of banks, physicians, and actors, there was an activist imagery. Organizations were proactive toward their environments rather than reactive to them. The theme that organizations try to control their environments whenever possible has appeared often in the organizational literature:

> Organizations seek to control environments by increasing their power over environmental units, and seek to adapt to environments by monitoring environmental demands and by designing structures and practices to permit effective response to such demands (Filley, House, and Kerr, 1976, p. 299).

Generally, organizations that face complex, unpredictable environments tend to have complex structures, including high differentiation among units and high decentralization of decision making.

The enactment perspective used in this essay highlights different features in organization-environment interactions than are emphasized by Filley, House, and Kerr. For example, distinctions between *the* organization and *the* environment are treated as more problematic (see the following discussion of Katz and Kahn), and the activity of controlling is also viewed differently. The importance of control from an enactment perspective lies in the fact that to control something is to take actions with respect to it. These actions become the raw materials from which a sense of the situation is *eventually* built. The controlling actions are what the organization examines retrospectively to see what it is up to. Filley, House, and Kerr also say little about how the organization knows what it faces. The environment portrayed in this proposition is already thick with meaning, and the problem we are interested in is how organizations invest their settings with meaning and modify these understandings over time. In a sense, Filley, House, and Kerr intercept the problem of adaptation later than we do. They assume that the organization "knows" its environment and can then decide which portions can be controlled and which require accommodation. The question we focus on is how does the organization even come to use labels such as "controllable" or "coercive" to punctuate its stream of experience? Why not other labels? Why assume organizations strive to control environments rather than their own perceptions (Powers, 1973)?

Organizations have to build their environments before they can even have the luxury of controlling them. The ways in which they construct them cognitively will have strong effects on their actual actions of control. Furthermore, in the act of controlling their constructed environments, organizations learn quite vividly what those environments consist of. It is the understanding and sensemaking which accompany the Filley, House, and Kerr controlling and adapting activities that are given most attention in the enactment perspective.

Systems Imagery

Some of the issues broached in the preceding section concerning boundaries can be illustrated in terms of open systems theory. As mentioned earlier, in their enthusiasm for the imagery of organizations as open systems, some investigators have taken as a given the distinction between an "organization" and its "environment." They have been vague, however, about what that environment is toward which those organizations are open and where it "begins." Thus, much of the talk about environments faced by organizations suffers from misplaced concreteness. As a result, boundaries are drawn between the supposed "environment" and the supposedly corresponding "organization" with more certainty than seems warranted.

To illustrate the issue of misplaced concreteness, consider the following statement:

> The first problem in understanding an organization or a social system, is its location and identification. How do we know that we are dealing with an organization? What are its boundaries? What behavior belongs to the organization, and what behavior lies outside it (Katz and Kahn, 1966, p. 14)?

In their first sentence, Katz and Kahn declare that the identification and location of systems are problematic. In their second sentence the problem is said to be epistemological (i.e., a problem in the acquisition of knowledge). But in their third and fourth sentences Katz and Kahn ignore the caveat imposed by the first two sentences; they assume the *existence* of boundaries, insides, and outsides—an existence which they had just declared problematic. Predictably, in their following section Katz and Kahn also ignore their caveats and talk about inputs and outputs that take place between *an* open system and "*the* external environment" (p. 19, emphasis added). Inclusion of the article "the" before "external environment" implies a unique, objective environment that exists independent of actors and actions and that appears similar to all observers. Furthermore, the qualifier "external" placed before the word "environment" implies that there is another environment, presumably labeled "internal," that is not to be confused with the external one.

While the categories external/internal or outside/inside exist logically, they do not exist empirically. The "outside" or "external" world cannot be known. There is no methodological process by which one can confirm the existence of an object independent of the confirmatory process involving oneself. The outside is a void, there is only the inside. A person's world, the inside or internal view is all that can be known. The rest can only be the object of speculation. Therefore, when we object to internal/external or inside/outside as arbitrary partitions that tend to confuse issues, what we mean is simply that logical distinctions in this case do not necessarily correspond to empirical distinctions. Actors immersed in experiential streams organize and punctuate those streams by positing organizations and environments (and gods and traits), however, and the last thing we want to do is define away their solutions to sensemaking by imposing for them the logical but empirically empty distinction between internal and external worlds. *If* organizational members discover that inside/outside is a useful punctuation, and impose it, and retain it because it allows them to take reasonable actions, fine. We simply don't want to put words in their mouths or images in their eyes.

The misplaced concreteness of talk about *the* organization and *the* environment diverts the attention of organizational theorists from crucial problems. If one asserts the existence of a mythical entity, then observers are tempted to search for its properties rather than treat its "existence" as problematic. If it were viewed as problematic, the more crucial questions would consist of queries such as under what conditions its "existence" is posited, what that positing accomplishes for the positer, and how people operate when they punctuate their streams of experience with other nouns than "the external environment."

Environments are problematic, but not their substances and properties and parts. It is their existence as an entity that is problematic. How does it come to pass that an organization finds it useful to say of its flow of experience, "we face an environment" or "we face the environment"? To what questions asked by organizational members is the positing of an environment or the environment an answer? Yet organizational theorists don't worry about problems such as this. They act as if it is obvious what the environment is and where it is. Given these a priori certainties, what investigators tend to dismiss is the assertion that the environment is located in the mind of the actor and is imposed by him on experience in order to make that experience more meaningful. It seldom dawns on organizational theorists to look for environments inside of heads rather than outside of them. Neither Filley, House, and Kerr, nor Katz and Kahn, sensitize organization watchers to this issue. One person, however, who has taken seriously the possibility that environments are in the head, waiting to be imposed, is Jean Piaget.

Cognitive Imagery

An unusually thorough summary of the sensemaking mechanism we are proposing is found in the following phrase translated from Piaget (1962, pp. 191-93):

> . . . the initial universe [of a person] is not a network of causal sequences, but a simple collection of events surging in extension of *his* own activities" (pp. 191-92, emphasis added).[2]

Virtually all of the elements that we associate with enacted sensemaking are found in that sentence. The closest approximation to the enactment process per se is contained in the phrase, "surging in extension of his own activities." The imagery of surging suggests that things are not well delineated, they change as a consequence of the intensity and nature of an individual's activities, and that what a person does is what he eventually will know.

The process of transforming these enacted raw data into information is suggested by Piaget to be a two-stage affair. First, there is a crude punctuation phase in which the undifferentiated flow is turned into "a simple collection," a phrase that implies that portions are bracketed and separated (the flow of the stream of experience has been frozen and divided into units), that only the crudest relations, if any, have been established among the units, and that a modest transformation from raw data into information has occurred. One might even argue that this crude breaking up of a stream into a simple collection of events lies somewhere between bracketing a portion of the stream of experience for further work and labeling and connecting that which has been bracketed.

The second stage of the transformation from raw data to information, however, is the more influential one for conduct. The person continues to do cognitive work on the collection of events until they become transformed into a "network of causal sequences." The final product of enactment, therefore, will be a causal map (Weick, 1975) depicting how the events in the simple collection are causally related.

It is interesting that Piaget describes the events as surging rather than emerging, implying that these events occur suddenly rather than gradually. The course of sensemaking implied here is jagged and discontinuous rather than smooth and continuous. Surprises should be plentiful and puzzles more dogged than any actor would wish. Again it should be emphasized that the person is active, both cognitively and physically, when the environment is organized. The person is not a data collector, is not accumulating replicas of the environment, and is not copying outside events. Instead, the person is punctuating and enacting the flow of experience, the results of these activities being retained in a network of causal sequences or causal map.

The key ideas in Piaget's description can be illustrated by considering the following stream of experience:[3]

adhadhadhadhadhadJameswhileJohnhadhadhadhadhadha
dhadhadhadhadhadmoreinterestfortheteacherhadhadh.

Enactment is partially the process of stumbling onto that string. Enactment also means bracketing some portion of that stream as in the following:

JameswhileJohnhadhadhadhadhadhadhadh
adhadhadhadmoreinterestfortheteacher

These dual enactment activities of generating and bracketing occur at the initial stage of sensemaking, can be constrained by past experience, produce raw data rather than information, and partially constrain sensemaking because they exclude portions of the stream of experience. So far, we have an exhibit of what exists as "extensions of a person's own activities."

Once a person has generated/bracketed part of the stream, then the activities of punctuation and connection (parsing) can occur in an effort to transform the raw data into information. One way to punctuate that stream is to separate it by equal spaces into 19 "words," an arbitrary, reasonable, initial way to organize that stream. The result looks like this:

James while John had had had had had had had
had had had had more interest for the teacher

Now, we have a "simple collection of events," namely words, but we have no idea how they might be connected or organized in terms of meaningful "causal sequences."

Even though the initial punctuation was reasonable, it did not prove to be sensible. We still don't know what is being asserted. Therefore, we try another form of punctuation, this time using unequal spaces between the words.

James   while John had had   had had   had had   h
ad   had had   had had more interest for the teacher

The use of unequal spacing as a punctuation scheme looks promising, because connections among sets of words are suggested. If we insert punctuation marks in place of the unequal spaces to concretize the connections, we arrive at the following display:

James, while John had had "had had," had had "had."
"Had had" had had more interest for the teacher.

Punctuated in that manner, the work produced by John was found more interesting by the teacher than was James' work. John has "caused" an increase in the teacher's interest. A meaningful causal sequence has appeared. Exactly the opposite conclusion can be reached if we punctuate those same raw data like this:

James, while John had had "had," had had "had had."
"Had had" had had more interest for the teacher.

Now James, rather than John, becomes the favored person and James, rather than John, is responsible for heightening the teacher's interest.

Notice some salient properties of this episode of sensemaking. There is a certain arbitrariness to the activity. One set of punctuations and connections is frequently as plausible as another. Those punctuations that are made are also consequential; the identity of the favored person in this example changes depending on which punctuation scheme is used. Furthermore, the enactment of the reader-actor was intimately woven into that final information both by means of the activity of punctuation and by means of the initial bracketing.

Enactment processes generated and bracketed the raw data; punctuation and connection processes (parsing) transformed the raw data into information—and the *result* was an enacted environment. Notice that the enacted environment is something more than a simple collection of events. Depending on how the initial sequence is parsed, either James or John "caused" a change in the teacher's interest. It is not just that each of the two men possesses some "had hads" and the teacher possesses more interest; rather it is the fact that these assorted possessions have become causally linked. They were not intrinsically or inherently causally linked. Instead, the sequences became causally related only as an extension of the actor's own activities of bracketing and parsing.

It is important to note that even though enactment looks like a relatively insignificant portion of the process of doing interpretations, in fact it is of major importance. The only possible raw materials that are available for subsequent parsing and retention, are those materials initially generated and/or bracketed by enactment processes. Enactment drives everything else in an organization. *How enactment is done is what an organization will know.* Even though parsing and enactment are constrained by past experience (e.g., I will often do what I can label), what I am trying to specify are those processes that affect the invention of environments, in order to see more clearly how organizations generate self-validating knowledge of those environments.

Characteristics of Enacted Sensemaking

This essay represents working notes about a class of phenomena, the observation of which will allow observers to render these observations obsolete. That is, a definitive characterization of enacted sensemaking remains to be written. It is possible, however, to state some preliminary considerations that may be relevant to defining the concept.

Reality Is Treated Metaphorically

Elsewhere, I have noted that "reality is a metaphor" (Weick, 1969a). By that, I meant that talk about "a reality" is simply one way that people try to make sense out of the stream of experience that flows by them. To say that there is a reality, an environment, and then to search for and discover underlying patterns in those superimposed structures is one way to make sense of that stream. But the tenuousness of this process, as well as the actor's central role in its execution, are captured only if we remain attentive to reality *as* metaphor. Failure to view reality in these terms is usually associated with underestimation of the ways in which individuals contribute to the worlds they think they see.

Literally, to enact an environment can mean to "create the appearance of an environment" or to "simulate an environment for the sake of representation." Those two meanings are compatible with the position taken in this essay. Members act as if they have environments, create the appearance of environments, or simulate environments for the sake of getting on with their business. These organizing acts are acts of invention rather than acts of discovery, they involve a superimposed order rather than underlying order, and they are based on the assumption that cognition follows the trail of action.

One of the more dramatic examples of the metaphorical quality of reality is found in attempts by technicians, engineers and astronauts at NASA to make sense out of unaccountable electrical phenomena

> ... like the light on an instrument panel suddenly turning on when the machine it serviced was most definitely off. That was sometimes not merely hard to explain, but impossible to explain. So they called it a glitch. God's own luminescence was in the switch! Give a better explanation! "I just threw a glitch into the light when I was turning my warning lights off and on," said Gordon Cooper during the flight of Murcury-Atlas 9 when a gravity signal showed on his switchboard during an orbital freefall. Cooper was renowned for his phlegm, but one butterfly of the night must have beat its wings in his throat when he looked at a dial which showed the force of gravity was present at a time when he knew he must be without weight. Yet note: Whether it is with vanity, woe, or awe, he still takes credit for throwing the glitch.

Who indeed has not felt the force of his own personality before a sensitive machine? (Mailer, 1970, pp. 167-68).

NASA brackets (generates?) a puzzling portion of its stream of experience and invents the label "glitch" as an explanation for the origins of and causal connections among mysterious phenomena. "God's own luminescence was in the switch." The enacted environment of "glitch" is then retained as one more causal map available to be superimposed as an "explanation" for puzzles such as those which confronted Cooper. When the normal presumption of an "earthy" reality proved inadequate as a means for NASA to organize what it thought it saw, the extraordinary presumption of an additional, more ethereal reality was introduced, after which it was again sensemaking, as usual. NASA may not have treated reality as a metaphor prior to "glitch," but it's a safe bet that they now hedge their epistemological and metaphysical bets, given a glitch's "existence."

Soliloquies Define Cognition

"An explorer can never know what he is exploring until it has been explored" (Bateson, 1972, p. xvi). The organizational equivalent of that assertion is "an organization can never know what it thinks or wants until it sees what it does." In the case of organizations, what they say and what they do provide the displays which can be examined reflectively after their occurrence in order to understand what is occurring. The sequence in that prototypical soliloquy is crucial. Talk or some kind of action occurs first and provides the occasion for an eventual articulation of cognitions and desires.

Consider the following question, one commonly uttered by organization members in the interest of sensemaking: "How can I know what I think until I see what I say?"

If we apportion the several activities in that sentence among the organizing processes of retention, selection, and enactment (Weick, 1969b), the apportionment will be as follows. "Know what I think..." is the outcome and conclusion of an effort at sensemaking. Knowledge of what one thinks, therefore, is stored in the retention process in the form of an enacted environment. Thus, an enacted environment is the residue of a sensemaking episode that is stored in the retention process as past wisdom. An enacted environment is the output from an episode of sensemaking, not the input to it.

Environments enacted on previous occasions can constrain contemporary enactment. When it is said that an organization is influenced by what it already knows, we mean that contemporary activities of generating and bracketing are affected as well by the present stream of experience as by environments that have been enacted on previous occasions.

The phrase, "until I see" is the process of selection and involves the activities of punctuation and connection. Punctuation means chopping the stream of experience into sensible, namable, and named units, and the activity of connection involves imposing relationships, typically causal relationships, among the punctuated elements. Another way to describe the selection activity is to say that it involves parsing. To parse something means to analyze and describe it grammatically, which also means to point out parts and their interrelations. Pointing out the parts is the activity of punctuation; interrelating these parts is the activity of connection; and the joint activities of punctuation and connection are the activity of parsing.

Other investigators (e.g., Watzlawick, Beavin, and Jackson, 1967, pp. 54-59) have also talked about the activity of punctuation, but their analyses imply that punctuation involves imposing different relationships among given variables. Never specified in these discussions is how the variables become singled out and named in the first place. Instead, it is argued that people can see different sequences in a long stream of pre-punctuated activities. What I wish to emphasize is the fact that punctuation involves chopping a stream of experience into event-variables that are labeled but that these labels are rather arbitrary. Once the variables have been named, the individual has not yet completed the sensemaking activities because the events must be grouped in some meaningful way. This grouping activity was referred to as "connection" by David Hume (1748; reprinted, 1955) and there is no reason to depart from his term. The activity of *seeing* what one has said implies for us organizing, in meaningful ways, raw data of letters and words.

This means that the phrase, "what I say" contains the enactment process. Raw talk is the data on which subsequent sensemaking operates. The talk—the saying, the soliloquizing—is what is meant by the activity of enactment.

Thus, taken in reverse order, there is the enactment process of saying, which is followed by the selection process of transforming the saying into information, a process that involves parsing (punctuation and connection). Once the enacted stream of talk has been parsed, an enacted environment exists. This enacted environment is something that the organization's members momentarily "know" and "feel they understand." The retained enacted wisdom may, on future occasions, serve as a constraint on actions that generate and bracket the stream of experience and/or as a constraint on the labels, punctuation marks, and relationships that are imposed on new chunks of raw data.

When it is asserted that organizations talk to themselves and engage in soliloquies, that shorthand expression maps across the process of enactment, selection, and retention in the manner specified above. That mapping suggests that the enacted environment is primarily an output rather than an input, that enactment generates raw data rather than information, and that the so-called "serious" work of sensemaking involves parsing which occurs as a selection activity.

Organizing soliloquies can affect such diverse phenomena as motivation, decision making, and communication. Robert Faris, for example, suggests the motivational importance of retrospecting soliloquies:

> The reward for the mountain climber, as well as for the pursuer of many a distant goal, must then be spread over a process of imagination extending over a long period of time in which images of past and future intermingle. In the months before the activity begins, for example, the climber not only imagines the experience of climbing, but relishes the more distant future when he can look back on the adventure. . . . Sometimes, at the moment of consummation of a long-term project, the event goes by so quickly that the person hardly experiences it, and has afterward only a confused memory. Such is often reported for weddings and graduation exercises which presumably culminate long periods of effort and planning. . . . It may be that even when a brief sense of ecstasy is felt, its power and influence yet lie in the longer term of anticipation and retrospection in imagination. It is the suggestion of this argument, in any case, that motivation for long-range goals is mainly, perhaps entirely, in the time-extending anticipatory and retrospective imagination, along with anticipation of retrospection and retrospection of anticipation, applied not only to the moment of goal consummation, but to various significant stages of the process of activity before and after (1968, p. 66).

Thus, what may sustain interest in activities with brief moments of consummation, are the anticipation of retrospection and retrospecting the anticipation. Not only do soliloquies stretch the duration of the activity but they also make a larger portion of it sensible.

The potential importance of soliloquies in decision making has been described by Garfinkel:

> In place of the view that decisions are made as the occasions require, an alternative formulation needs to be entertained. It consists of the possibility that the person defines retrospectively

the decisions that have been made. *The outcome comes before the decision*. . . . The rules of decision making in daily life . . . may be much more preoccupied with the problem of assigning outcomes their legitimate history than with the question of deciding before the actual occasion of choice the conditions under which one, among a set of alternative possible courses of action, will be elected (1967, p. 114).

The game of charades is a superb metaphor for enacted sensemaking as it affects communication. In charades, an actor enacts an environment which puzzled observers try to parse. Imagine that you are the person in charades who must act out the title of a movie and imagine that you are given, as your title, the movie *Charade*. As the presenter, you probably would try somehow to get "outside" of the game and point to it so that the observers would see that the answer is the very activity they are now engaged in. Alas, the observers are likely to miss this subtlety and instead to shout words like, "pointing," "finger," "excited," "all of this," and so forth.

There are several interesting features of enactment in charades. The person doing the gesturing knows what he is perceived as enacting only after he hears the observers' guesses. That is, the actor produces a soliloquy, the punctuation of which is done by others. The actor produces an enacted environment as an output but the observers are faced with a display which they can punctuate and connect in numerous ways. The actor imposes meanings on his environment that come back and organize his activities, except that the observers see these implanted meanings as puzzles rather than certainties. If the actor has enacted a puzzling or complicated or subtle environment, that enactment comes back and organizes him in the sense that he has to do enormous work to salvage, patch up, and redirect the observers' efforts to invent plausible constructions for his subtleties.

Notice that in mountain climbing, historicizing an outcome, and charades the actual actions available for sensemaking are loosely organized. They remain susceptible to numerous interpretations, interpretations that will be imposed after the fact. Organizations talk to themselves in order to clarify their surroundings and learn more about them. These soliloquies frequently are closed systems. Organizations examine retrospectively the very displays that initially they created as pretexts for sensemaking. Organizations talk in order to discover what they are saying, act in order to discover what they are doing.

Enactment Brackets Raw Data
In another work (1969b) I described enactment in a rather confus-

ing manner: "The enactment process creates the information that the system adapts to, and in doing so removes a small amount of equivocality" (p. 91). If that sentence had contained the words "raw data" instead of "information," the meaning would have been clearer. While I am retaining the ideas that enactment is an active process and that it creates some of what the organization has to deal with, it is also clear that the creation of information occurs later in the process of organizational sensemaking than I realized. In the earlier analysis, enactment simultaneously put an environment before the organization and partially labeled that environment. For the sake of clarity, I think the activities of enacting the raw data and of labeling it need to be separated so that it is possible to get a clearer idea of what affects each activity. In the earlier example involving James, John, the teacher, and a host of "hads," information appeared quite late in the example when, finally, "words" were identified and separated. Left unexplained was the genesis of the raw data on which meanings were superimposed. That same questionable origin of raw materials available for sensemaking is present in my description of enactment quoted at the beginning of this paragraph.

The temptation is strong to conclude that the analysis is complete once an environment has been described in terms of information. What is left out by this description is an explanation of how the raw data were generated and bracketed in the stream of experience as potential candidates for sensemaking. The concept of enactment, as a sensemaking activity, is now being assigned exclusively to the initial steps when experience is both generated and bracketed under the partial constraint of retained wisdom.

The distinctions among information, raw data, meaning, and communication have been illustrated by Thayer (1967):

> A [manufacturing] plant does not operate on the basis of the existence of certain raw materials, but on the basis of certain *information* about the condition, place, price, utility, and so on, of those raw materials: ". . . any characteristic of an operation that can be observed and recorded, constitutes potential information for the communication network" (Miller and Starr, 1960). Materials and parts are thus legitimate units of information (p. 92).

It could be argued, as I did in 1969, that enactment is the process by which an organization generates its own information. However, that usage obscures the crucial distinction between data and information. As Thayer (1967) said:

It is not the "things" of the world—material or nonmaterial—with which we deal. We deal with "information" about these things . . . the things themselves are physical data that are sensed and transduced by the individual sensorium to provide him with raw sensory data. The function of the psychological system, at this point, is to select out and convert that raw data into information— i.e., into "mental" material for thought or "decision." It is this event or occurrence—that of consciously or unconsciously ascribing meaning or significance to raw sensory data and thus of converting it to information—that I prefer to call "communication." Thus communication *occurs* when some raw data input has been meaningfully related to some portion of the total psychological system for immediate or later use in thought or action. It follows from this, and other notions of intrapersonal functioning, that the *meaning* of *any* experience is constituted by the very process of its accommodation into the dynamic psychological system (p. 89).

Given the distinction between raw data and information, I want to argue that enactment involves generating the raw data which is eventually transformed by other processes into information and action. Enactment processes shape an organization's experience at the raw data stage, not at the information stage. Influences from enactment are there from the beginning and it is this sense in which enactment involves the creation of an organization's environment.

When people talk about organizations operating on information as an environment, they often fail to specify what the raw data are or how they were created. This failure makes it difficult to understand how organizations do interpretation, how they know, or what they know. The concept of an enactment process tries to fill that gap by highlighting the difference between raw data and information and by asserting that actions generate the raw data that eventually may be parsed into sensible experiences.

Thus, when it is asserted that enactment processes generate raw data, this means that actions serve to bracket and single out some portions of the stream of experience for further examination. The bracketing is exceedingly crude in the sense that it involves nothing more than the suggestion that observers should pay more attention to *this* ill-defined portion of the stream than to that one.

Enactment, viewed as the generation and bracketing of raw data, can also be described using imagery associated with an evolutionary epistemology. If we consider the common sequence of trial and error, then enactment is pure trial with no judgments of error being made.

Perception of error is a selection activity. Error is a particular way of parsing the ongoing stream of experience under the constraint of retained wisdom. Enactment generates raw data from which one may conclude that an error has been made, but those very same data might just as easily be punctuated as a truth has been spoken, a truism has been blurted, an absurdity has been confirmed, and so forth. If you cannot mentally disentangle truth from error in a sequence of trials, then you've got the image of what is meant by an enactment process and you can begin to sense the modest constraints that shape it.

Implications of the point that enactment is largely unconstrained can be seen if we examine the assertion that organizations engage in lots of random actions. Members of organizations often do things with little warrant and it is often these episodes of bumbling and galumphing that produce rich variations which can be serendipitously parsed into novel definitions of what has occurred (Weick, 1976). Enactment is the organizational equivalent of unjustified variation (Campbell, 1974), and is often only weakly constrained by retention and causal maps. It is that sense in which "galumphing" is an accurate description of what happens in enactment. Miller (1973, p. 92) has described galumphing as the "patterned voluntary [i.e., controlled by retention and causal maps] elaboration or complication of process, where the pattern is not under the dominant control of goals."

Activities that are not under the predominant control of retention and causal maps are activities that can wrap themselves in novel ways around novel "objects" in the environment, thereby providing occasions for novel parsing and adaptation. The veneer of rationality that overlies much talk about organizations tends to minimize the role of random activities. If enactment is described as pure trial, as random activity, as indiscriminate bracketing, as generating raw data, and as loosely coupled actions, as well as activity that may be constrained by previous enactment, then the subtle mixture of chaos and order that seems to characterize this initial process has been captured.

Reasonableness Supersedes Accuracy

If one assumes that sensemaking involves invention rather than discovery, then validation takes on a different appearance. One cannot say that a superimposed order is right or wrong. Such a judgment would presume an underlying order that is waiting to be discovered. Validation of superimposed patterns involves judgments of reasonableness, and if one superimposed order is reasonable and is no less plausible than some other imposed order, then the imposition is valid.

The notion that reasonableness is the appropriate criterion of validity in superimposed orders is found in our research on model cultures (Weick and Gilfillan, 1971). We composed three-person groups, implanted a specific strategy that the founders were to use in solving the Common Target Game, and then steadily for 11 generations replaced these founders one at a time with naïve subjects. The question was, what would happen to the initial strategies or punctuations that were implanted? Previous research suggested that the implanted strategies would disappear by about the sixth generation due to spontaneous innovations introduced by newcomers. What we found was that this occurred in one condition but not in another. It all depended on the kind of tradition present. One form of punctuation was perpetuated indefinitely. Thus, spontaneous innovation does not inevitably erode a tradition or displace an enacted environment.

When a culture started with a strategy that was just as good as another one they could have used, this strategy persisted. Even when occasional subjects tried to revolt against this "reasonable" strategy and replace it, these efforts were never successful. We labeled this type of strategy, "warranted arbitrary." By this we mean that arbitrarily choosing this particular strategy is warranted or reasonable because no real world criteria exist that suggest it is any worse than other ones. Other similar strategies are equally functional and it's a toss-up as to which one should be used. Thus, the choice among these equivalent strategies can legitimately be made on grounds such as personal preference, esthetic qualities, whatever.

But if a less functional strategy is adopted (its dysfunctions outweigh its functions), it will rapidly disappear due to counterpressures from reality. We have labeled this kind of item "unwarrantedly arbitrary." A group is in trouble if it ignores rational criteria and adopts a strategy that is *not* obviously as good as other ones it can imagine. The group is in trouble because this strategy is vulnerable to spontaneous innovations and will soon disappear. This is fortunate in the sense that there seems to be a self-correcting mechanism that operates in groups even when its personnel is changing. It is less fortunate because these changes expose the groups to uncertainty and low productivity during the intervals when the unwarranted strategy is gradually being replaced.

We were struck by the fact that this apparent cultural wisdom in the choice and perpetuation of strategies clearly is not tied to specific people. By the fourth generation in all cultures, no one knows precisely what strategy that culture started with and all participants know that their task is to hit the target numbers in any way they please. Nevertheless, naïve subjects continue to use the exact strategy their culture started with *if* that strategy is just as good as any other one, and refuse to use the initial strategy the culture started with if there are alternative strategies that are more reasonable. Once the poorer strategies have been replaced by more reasonable ones, the replacements also become resistant to spontaneous innovation.

Thus, to state that an organization makes reasonable punctuations of its experience is not a bland assertion. To make reasonable punctuations is the best that an organization can do when it constructs an enacted environment.

It will be recalled that parsing is an act of invention, not an act of discovery. It is an invention in the sense that decisions about punctuation and connection single out an economical network from the few networks posited which, in turn, are but a handful of all possible causal networks that could have been invented. A crucial property of an invented network or causal map is that its validity cannot be proven in a logical sense. Instead, the only assertion that can be made about conclusions contained in the map are that they are as likely, as possible, and as reasonable as some other conclusion.

Thus, when it is stated that an imposed structure is reasonable, that description carries a great deal of meaning. It means that we are talking about inductions rather than deductions, about likelihoods rather than certainties, about contingencies rather than necessities, about plausible explanations rather than proofs, about exceptions rather than uniformities, about invention rather than discovery, and about the pragmatically sensible rather than the strictly logical. Reasonableness, not accuracy, is the topic of interest in enacted sensemaking.

Ideas Are Real-ized

One of the best ways to capture the nuances in the view that environments are enacted is to say that people act out and real-ize their ideas. In the processes of acting out and of real-izing their ideas, they create their own realities. The crucial phrase is "real-izing their ideas." By this I mean literally that people make real, or turn into a reality, those ideas that they have in their heads. It is that sense in which the phrase, "believing is seeing" is more than a play on words; it captures part of the mechanism by which organizing processes unfold and create their own environments.

Similar imagery suggesting that ideas control what is seen is found in the following quotation from Popper (1962):

> Without waiting, passively, for repetitions to impress or impose regularities on us, we actively try to impose regularities upon the world. We try to discover similarities in it, and interpret it in terms of laws invented by us. Without waiting for premises, we

jump to conclusions. These may have to be discarded later, should observation show that they are wrong (p. 73).

Thus, people invent organizations and their environments and these inventions reside in ideas that participants have superimposed on any stream of experience. This contrasts with the view that organizations and environments consist of underlying structures that are revealed to inquisitive discoverers. The one quibble I have with Popper involves the last sentence. The phrase "should observation show that they are wrong" implies a reality underlying the appearances, an implication that I find dispensible. I don't think observation would suggest that something should be discarded because it is wrong. Instead, I think observation would simply suggest that there are alternative, arbitrary ways to make sense out of a stream of experience, and that these alternative-imposed regularities might be more useful or more esthetic or more pleasant or more novel than the regularities currently being imposed.

Another way to phrase the issue of ideas being real-ized is to say that sensemaking is an efferent activity. The modifier "efferent" means "centrifugal" or "conducted outward." The person's idea is extended outward, implanted, and then rediscovered as knowledge. The discovery, however, originated in a prior invention by the discoverer. In a crude, but literal sense, one could talk about efferent sensemaking as thinking in circles. Action, perception, and sensemaking exist in a circular, tightly-coupled relationship.

This tight coupling between enactment and selection processes, has been talked about in the guise of several concepts. Perhaps the most common one is the notion of the self-fulfilling prophecy (e.g., Archibald, 1974; Bateson, 1951; James, 1956; Kelley and Stahelski, 1970; Merton, 1948; Henshel and Kennedy, 1973):

A self-fulfilling prophecy may be regarded as the communicational equivalent of "begging the question." It is behavior that brings about in others, the reaction to which the behavior would be appropriate reaction. For instance, a person who acts on the premise that "nobody likes me" will behave in a distrustful, defensive, or aggressive manner to which others are likely to react unsympathetically, thus bearing out his original premise. . . . Pragmatically, we can observe that this individual's interpersonal behavior shows this kind of redundancy, and that it has a complementary effect on others, forcing them into certain specific attitudes. What is typical about the sequence, and makes it a problem of punctuation, is that the individual concerned conceives of himself only as reacting to, but not as provoking, those attitudes (Watzlawick, Beavin, and Jackson, 1967, pp. 98-99).

The essence of efferent sensemaking is summarized in the last sentence of that quotation.

People frequently isolate particular items, presume that they are indicators of some underlying pattern, and use this tentative pattern identification both to search for and to label subsequent particulars which, in turn, flesh out the underlying pattern which, in turn, fleshes out the sensibleness of current particulars, etc. This kind of tight circularity is what has been called, the "documentary method of meaning."

> The [documentary] method consists of treating an actual appearance as "the document of," as "pointing to," as "standing on behalf of" a presupposed underlying pattern. Not only is the underlying pattern derived from its individual documentary evidences, but the individual documentary evidences in their turn, are interpreted on the basis of "what is known" about the underlying pattern. Each is used to elaborate the other (Garfinkel, 1967, p. 78).

Eloquent exhibits of the documentary method in operation are found in McHugh's (1968) experimental counseling protocols. He had subjects, under the guise of testing a new format for counseling, pose questions to a concealed counselor about their current problems that the counselor could answer with a yes or no. The counselor decided whether to answer yes or no by flipping a coin. The phenomenon of interest is how the troubled subjects make do with the fragments of contradictory and disjointed advice that they get from the counselor such that they transform the "interaction" into a sensible occasion. Clients literally real-ize their own ideas when they overlay them on the counselor's equivocal display.

There's an eerie sense in which McHugh's "random counseling" resembles client-centered counseling (Rogers, 1951). The client-centered counselor basically reflects back to the patient whatever the patient says and little more. Thus, the client is forced to impose new meaning on very little new data. In fact, the client may find the reflected comments to be almost as puzzling as are the bits and pieces of advice purveyed by the coin-flipping counselor. It is conceivable that client-centered counseling is nothing more or less than intensified usage of the documentary method.

That possibility aside, however, the point I wish to make is that how people make sense of randomized counseling may be prototypic of organizational sensemaking. In random counseling, the subject generates a display that is susceptible to multiple punctuations, gets an answer from the counselor which is even more puzzling than his initial enactment, and then visibly has to repunctuate, readjust, and reemphasize all that has accumulated up to that point. In the McHugh studies (and those done by Garfinkel) the subject thinks out loud while trying to make sense of the counselor's cryptic advice and these protocols are unusually rich displays in which one can examine punctuation, repunctuation, and alternative attempts at connection. Garfinkel presents detailed analysis of what people are doing when they try to make sense of the counselor's remarks (1967, see pp. 89-94), and similar detailed analyses are found in McHugh, the latter study being of interest because McHugh varied the proportion of yes's and no's that occurred during the exchanges.

Concepts such as real-ized ideas, self-fulfilling prophecies, and the documentary method share an imagery of efferent sensemaking. The documentary method perhaps most clearly contains the elements of a tight coupling between retention and punctuation that, working in the manner of a closed loop, generates a self-validating and compelling interpretation of the world. Efferent sensemaking assumes that an idea is projected or imposed and then discovered and punctuated by the imposer.

I think prevailing images of organizations incorporate too much passivity. The organizations are thought of as sitting back and examining a presumably separate, prestructured environment in order to figure out how to adapt to that environment. If we shift to a more self-conscious efferent imagery and if we blur the boundaries between organizations and environments, and if we selectively use open systems imagery, then we put ourselves in a better position to say that a substantial number of the enacted environments associated with organizations consist of personal ideas that are extended outward, implanted, and rediscovered.

Enacted Sensemaking in Orchestral Organizations

The purpose of the present section is to give an extended example of how one talks about enactment in an organization; that is, to demonstrate what observers notice when they take seriously the possibility that organizations enact many of their environments and how observers label, punctuate, and connect what they notice. Although the illustration describes orchestras, the ideas apply more broadly to other kinds of organizations.

In a field experiment (Weick, Gilfillan, and Keith, 1973), 38 musicians in two functioning jazz orchestras rehearsed three compositions written by composers whose attributed credibility was given as either high or low. Composer credibility is of potential importance in musicmaking because it is thought to influence the amount and kind of effort a musician will put forth to comprehend a new piece of music. Meyer has argued that efforts to comprehend new music are mediated by the "presumption of logic." "Without faith in the purposefulness of, and rationality of art, listeners would abandon their attempts to understand, to reconcile deviants to what has gone before or to look for their *raison d'etre* in what is still to come" (1956, p. 75). We predicted that musicians would find it difficult to presume logic when a composer was portrayed as nonserious. Consequently, the musicians would make more errors when they played that composer's music due to initial indifference or doubts, would downgrade the worth of the music, and would forget it sooner. However, when the *very same* piece of new music was given to a comparable orchestra and was attributed to a serious composer, we expected that the musicians would presume the music was purposeful and would expend more effort to comprehend it. This greater effort would be evident in such things as fewer errors and higher evaluation and better memory for the tune relative to its fate when attributed to a nonserious composer.

The predicted difference in errors occurred on the first play-through of the new music but disappeared on the second play-through, due to a combination of additional nonserious rehearsing plus direct observation that the composition itself was purposeful (the three selections were written by two established jazz composers, Alf Clausen and Don Piestrup). The predicted difference in evaluation did not occur, but when assessed by a recognition test the compositions given as written by serious composers were remembered significantly better 24 hours after the rehearsal. These data suggest that the attribution of credibility can be self-confirming. Closer attention to the work of the credible composer resulted in fewer errors and a better-sounding performance relative to the work of the noncredible composer, thereby confirming the credibility prophecy. When the musicians believed that the music was of higher quality, they generated, by their own heightened attentiveness, a better-sounding tune, which then constrained their subsequent playing.

Viewed more broadly, any orchestra rehearsal where musicians process new music is an ideal setting in which to observe the ways in which a strange piece of music is made more sensible. There are numerous sources of equivocality when new music is rehearsed. The music itself is equivocal because it is unknown, it contains some amount of musical complexity, it contains certain amounts of *calculated* or intentional disorder, many of its performance characteristics (such as the tempo where it plays well) have to be established, it is equivocal relative to the style in which the band prefers to play, and the tune shows a greater or lesser departure from convention in music. These and other questions are what an orchestra tries to resolve when it rehearses.

The environment that the orchestra members face is not simply the composition placed in front of them, but rather what they do with that composition when they play it through for the first time. The musicians don't react to an environment, they *enact* the environment. In the credibility study the enacted environment available to the musicians after their first play was an undifferentiated "soup." As observers, we might label this soup with nouns such as "sounds," "tempos," "themes," "shadings," and "errors." The first play-through of the composition could be made sensible by participants in a variety of ways. The crucial point is that the play-through, not the sheets of music, was the environment the musicians tried to make sensible.

Once musicians enact an environment, they then punctuate or break that environment into discrete events that are available for relating (e.g., "those 12 notes are thrilling," "those 6 bars are impossible," "that portion is ugly," "the notes are hard to read," "the tempo at which we start seems to be crucial"). Essentially, the musicians punctuate the stream of enacted music into reasonable nouns and then try to relate or connect the nouns in a reasonable manner. It is important to emphasize that (1) punctuation is arbitrary, (2) punctuation is a precondition for sensemaking, and (3) punctuation imposes a figure-ground relationship on the enacted environment, thereby making it more manageable.

Once a musician parses the stream of experience into a set of variables, he is able to make the inference that some of these punctuated variables co-vary. When one of the punctuated variables changes its value, one or more other variables are seen to move also, and these movements may be in the same or opposite directions. Based on these movements, the observer then infers a connection among the variables and may also infer, in the case of temporally separated but co-moving variables, a relationship of "causality." It is crucial to note that this act of connection is based on the experience of recurrent co-movement among the variables of interest and takes place in the mind of an individual participant. In a like manner, the organization is in the mind.

It is at this point in the argument where the thinking of David Hume (1748) is especially pertinent.

All events seem entirely loose and separate. One event follows another, but we can never observe any tie between them. They seem *conjoined,* but never *connected.* . . . But when one particular species of events has always, in all instances, been conjoined with another, we make no longer any scruple of foretelling one upon the appearance of the other, and . . . we then call the one object "cause," and the other "effect." We *suppose* [emphasis added] that there is some connection between them, some power in the one by which it infallibly produces the other and operates with the greatest certainty and strongest necessity. . . . The mind is carried by habit, upon the appearance of one event, to expect its usual attendant and to believe that it will exist. This connection, therefore, *which we feel in the mind* [emphasis added], this customary transition of the imagination from one object to its usual attendant, is the sentiment or impression from which we form the idea of power or necessary connection . . . . This is the sole difference between one instance, from which we can never receive the idea of connection, and a number of similar instances by which it is suggested (Hume, 1955, pp. 85-86).

Returning to the musicians who perform music by high- or low-credibility composers, they might punctuate this experience into seven variables: (1) attributed credibility; (2) playing effort exerted; (3) tolerance for errors; (4) attention to notes; (5) willingness to reconcile deviant notes; (6) willingness to suspend judgment; and (7) quality of tune when judged retrospectively. These seven variables are specified solely to illustrate the argument. It should be apparent that we can maintain consistency in our argument only if these variables are specified by the participant, *not* by an observer.

Given these seven variables, it is possible for the musician to connect them causally. For example, on the basis of repeated experience he might note that as credibility decreases, playing effort and attention to notes decrease and tolerance for error increases; when effort decreases, this decreases both the judged quality of the tune and the attention that the musician pays to the notes; when the tolerance for errors increases, this serves to decrease the attention to the notes, the willingness to reconcile deviant notes, and the willingness to suspend judgment about the tune; and finally the musician may note that all of these relationships may decrease the perceived quality of the tune, which then leads to a further lowering of credibility. If these connections are summarized graphically, then we would obtain the set of causal connections shown in figure 1. This is a causal map. It summarizes those punctuations and connections that are inferred by a person after repeated exposures to a stream of experience.

We assume that musicians, as well as people in general, retain causal maps in their minds. These maps, in the case of musicians, are superimposed on flows of experience that involve music making. What the maps do in part is suggest which variables can be punctuated out of that flow of experience (e.g., "I should single out from the flow of experience the amount of effort I am exerting because this is a significant portion of this experience"). These maps also suggest which punctuated variables are connected with which other punctuated variables. Notice that the map in figure 1 is an overlay or a template that the individual imposes on a stream of enacted experience to separate portions of that display into a figure-ground relationship.

FIGURE 1 Causal Map

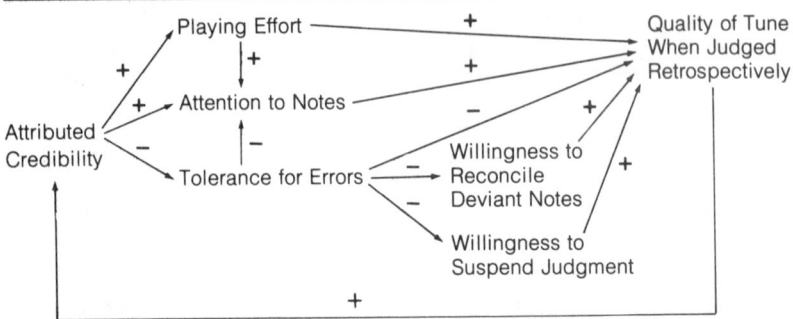

It is an interesting property of superimposed structures that they are often self-validating structures. To see this, reexamine the causal map of figure 1. It contains several loops by which one can start with the variable "attributed credibility" and trace a path that returns to the starting variable. The interesting property of each pathway is that it is a positive feedback loop. For example, if credibility decreases, this causes an increase in the tolerance for errors, which causes a decrease in the judged quality of the tune, which causes a further decrease in credibility, and so forth. A musician who imposes this particular structure on his music making will generate self-fulfilling prophecies that reinforce the map and confirm the initial attribution of credibility. If we treat "presumption of logic" as a variable, this means that a musician may find it easier or harder to presume that the composer is credible and that his composition will be serious or reasonable. If the musician increases the presumption of logic, then he raises the level of attributed credibility and through the imposition of the causal map produces the higher-quality tune—which confirms the initial presumption. If, however, he doubts the presumption of logic, then this lowers the level of credibility and *through the very same causal map* produces the lower quality tune which confirms the initial doubts about credibility.

The point is, the causal map in figure 1 may *be* the orchestra. If we then ask *where* that orchestra is, the answer is, in the minds of the musicians. It exists in the minds of the musicians in the form of the variables they routinely punctuate and the connections they routinely infer among these variables. These maps are then superimposed on any gathering where the announced agenda is music making.

So far, most of the points made deal with processes that take place in the minds of solitary actors. Within the orchestra it is true that the causal maps differ among 38 musicians and it is also true that any one musician has his own doubts about the stability of some of the punctuations and connections he makes. These differences and doubts suggest two things. First, there should be residual equivocality even after individuals impose their own idiosncratic versions of what has happened. Second, coordination will be problematic until some agreements can be reached among the participants as to what has happened and what should be done about it.

Elsewhere, we have argued (Weick, 1969b) that equivocality removal is essentially an interpersonal process and involves at least two members interlocking some behaviors to accomplish this removal. Using the ideas already presented, we can state more precisely how interlocked behaviors remove equivocality. The crucial collective act in organizations may consist of members trying to negotiate a consensus on which portions of an enacted display are *figure* and which are *ground*. More specifically, members collectively try to reach some workable agreement as to which portions of elapsed streams should be punctuated into variables and which connections among which variables are reasonable.

Thus, when we assert that equivocality is removed by interlocked behavioral cycles (i.e., by sequences of double interacts; Weick, 1969b, p. 33), we mean that members negotiate over specific issues of punctuation (e.g., "I don't think that the temperature of this room is important, but you seem to think it is") and issues of connection (e.g., "We seem to agree that temperature is crucial to our performance, but I think we play better when we are warmer and you think we play better when we are cooler"). Once members can reach some agreement as to what is consequential and what is trivial in their elapsed experience, and once they can get some kind of agreement as to the nature and direction of the connections among these consequential elements, then the elapsed experience becomes more sensible. That is, there is more overlap in the separate maps that are stored in the minds of the musicians when they leave the rehearsal and there is a greater likelihood that they will interlock their activities of music making more tightly when they confront new music at subsequent rehearsals.

The crucial point is that equivocality removal is both a social and a solitary process. What we are trying to specify is precisely what in that social process is crucial for what is basically a private, singular, and solitary activity. Sensemaking is largely solitary in the sense that structures contained within *individual* minds are imposed on streams of *individual* elapsed experience that are capable of an infinite number of *individual* reconstructions.

As we said in the *The Social Psychology of Organizing* (1969b), behaviors rather than people constitute groups. That being the case, a substantial portion of the variance associated with "group" activities can be explained if we concentrate on those behaviors that are interlocked and on those occasions when individual causal maps prove to be too idiosyncratic for coordinated activity to occur. While we want to be sure that we stay attentive to crucial determinants at both the group and individual level, we also do not want to have the proverbial "tie that binds" be a tie that blinds us to the ways in which individuals impose the organization that organizes the imposer.

To recapitulate, musicians *enact an environment* when they first play a piece of music and the outcome of this first play-through is an *equivocal display*. Based on previous experiences in processing new music, the musicians impose a *figure-ground structure* on this undifferentiated enacted display. This *imposed structure*, which is in the form of *causal map, punctuates* the display into a set of variables that are *connected* by means of *reasonable causal* linkages. The act of superimposing a causal map involves *retrospecting* elapsed experience. Although an imposed causal map makes the equivocal display more sensible for an individual musician, there remains the problem that the punctuations and connections are both uncertain within individuals and different between individuals. Causal maps are approximations and deal with likelihoods, not certainties. Since residual equivocality remains after individual causal maps are superimposed, it is necessary to gain some consensus among musicians as to what the orchestra is confronted with and how it is to be handled. Members activate *sets of interlocked behavior cycles* to deal with this residual equivocality. Initially, they try to *negotiate* a consensus on which portions of the display are figure and which are ground. When people collectively try to shrink the possible meanings attached to an equivocal input, they essentially are negotiating issues of punctuation and connection (e.g., "What did we or the composer do that caused that horrible chord?"). Having consensually made the enacted environment more sensible, the members then store their revised and presumably more homogeneous causal maps for imposition on future similar circumstances.

Conclusion

Oliver Wendell Holmes has written a charming fable that summarizes the intent of this essay. He writes:

> When we are as yet small children . . . there comes up to us a youthful angel, holding in his right hand cubes like dice, and in his left spheres like marbles. The cubes are of stainless ivory, and on each is written in letters of gold—*Truth.* The spheres are veined and streaked and spotted beneath, with a dark crimson flush above, where the light falls on them and in a certain aspect you can make out upon every one of them the three letters, *L, I, E.* The child to whom they are offered very probably clutches at both. The spheres are the most convenient things in the world; they roll with the least possible impulse just where the child would have them. The cubes will not roll at all; they have a great talent for standing still, and always keep right side up. But very soon the young philosopher finds that things that roll so easily are very apt to roll into the wrong corner, and to get out of his way when he most wants them, while he always knows where to find the others, which stay where they are left. Thus he learns—to drop the streaked and speckled globes of falsehood and to hold fast the white angular blocks of truth. But then comes Timidity, and after her Good-nature, and last of all Polite-behavior, all insisting that truth must *roll,* or nobody can do anything with it; and so the first with her coarse rasp and the second with her broad file, and the third with her silken sleeve, do so round off and smooth and polish the snow-white cubes of truth, that, when they get a little dingy by use, it becomes hard to tell them from the rolling spheres of falsehood (1901, pp. 98-99).

I like that fable because it warns against glibness. Investigators who study organization-environment relations sometimes lean toward separatist imagery. Environments are separated from organizations and things happen between these distinct entities. This way of carving up the problem of organizational analysis effectively rules out certain kinds of questions. Talk about bounded environments and organizations, for example, compels the investigator to ask questions such as how does an organization *discover* the *underlying* structure in *the* environment? Having separated the "two" entities and given them independent existence, investigators have to make elaborate speculations concerning the ways in which one entity becomes disclosed to and known by the other. But the firm partitioning of the world into the environment and the organization excludes the possibility that people *invent* rather than discover what they think they see. We have tried to provide an alternative to "discovery" formulations of organizational knowing.

What this essay supplies, then, is a way to talk about organizations. It contains a set of punctuations and connections that can be superimposed on streams of happenings viewed by organizational watchers. As is true of any enacted environment, the proposed punctuations and connections are arbitrary though possibly useful. As people begin to become comfortable with talking about enactment, they will undoubtedly find the ideas sketched in this chapter more fallible and less reasonable. That's fine, because when present concepts are improved, we should then be in a good position to understand a final example of enactment at its finest hour.

Truck drivers have a running feud with ICC inspectors who check for overweight loads. Truckers lose few opportunities to make their sentiments known to the people who man the scales. A driver nicknamed Ole Red was a past master at enacting environments for inspectors.

He'd pull into entry points when he was carrying nothing, just to drive those guys crazy. He'd pull up to the scales, get out of his truck, and start pounding all over his trailer with a little hammer. The operator would come out and ask him what the hell he was doing. Red would start at him real good and tell him that he was overloaded, but was carrying a load of canaries and he wanted to get them all into the air before he got weighed (Krueger, 1975, p. 118).

Notes

1. Since a tacit message of this essay is that nouns like "organization" and "environment" are dormitive, we encounter some genuine problems of exposition. The theory on which this work is based views organizations as flows of experience. As members enact and punctuate in parallel their individual flows of experience, they develop inferences about their experiences. These inferences are arranged cognitively in causal maps which in turn predispose future behavior. Individual member's causal maps are altered and developed through experience. This development produces some cognitive and behavioral correspondence which defines, for them, an organization.

When it is asserted that "an organization" acts, believes, soliloquizes, and so forth, reification is avoided because we mean that at least one member enacts on behalf of others some experience, punctuates that experience using in part a retained and superimposed causal map, some of whose variables have been jointly parsed, and produces an enacted environment which occasionally has vicarious relevance.

2. This passage translated into English by Michel Bougon from the following: "... l'univers initial n'est pas un reseau de séquences causales, mais une simple collection d'evénèments surgissant en prolongement de l'activité propre."

3. This example was inspired by James Fixx (1972, p. 29) and by Karen Weick's solution of the Fixx puzzle.

References

Archibald, W. P. Alternative explanations for self-fulfilling prophecy. *Psychological Bulletin*, 1974, *31*, 74-84.

Bateson, G. W. Conventions of communications: Where validity depends on belief. In J. Reusch and G. Bateson (eds.), *Communication, the Social Matrix of Society*. New York: Norton, 1951, pp. 212-27.

———. *Steps to an Ecology of Mind*. New York: Ballantine, 1972.

Campbell, D. T. Unjustified variation and selective retention in scientific discovery. In F. J. Ayala and T. Dobzhansky (eds.), *Studies in the Philosophy of Biology*. New York: Macmillan, 1974, pp. 139-61.

———. On the conflicts between biological and social evolution and between psychology and moral tradition. *American Psychologist*, 1975, *30*, 1103-26.

Faris, R. E. L. Graduate education in social psychology. In S. Lundstedt (ed.), *Higher Education in Social Psychology*. Cleveland: Case Western Reserve University, 1968, pp. 53-72.

Filley, A. C., House, R. J., and Kerr, S. *Managerial Process and Organizational Behavior* (2nd ed.), Glenview, Ill.: Scott, Foresman, 1976.

Fixx, J. *Games for the Superintelligent*. New York: Doubleday, 1972.

Garfinkel, H. *Studies in Enthnomethodology*. Englewood Cliffs, N. J.: Prentice-Hall, 1967.

Henshel, R. L. and Kennedy, L. W. Self-altering prophecies: Consequences for the feasibility of social prediction. *General Systems Yearbook*, 1973, *18*, 119-26.

Holmes, O. W. *The Autocrat of the Breakfast Table*. London: Walter Scott, 1901.

Hume, D. *An Inquiry Concerning Human Understanding*. New York: Bobbs-Merrill, 1955.

James, W. Is life worth living? In W. James, *The Will to Believe*, New York: Dover, 1956. pp. 32-62.

Jencks, C. and Silver, N. *Adhocism*. Garden City, New York: Anchor, 1973.

Katz, D. and Kahn, D. L. *The Social Psychology of Organizations*. New York: Wiley, 1966.

Kelley, H. H. and Stahelski, A. J. Social interaction basis of cooperators and competitors' beliefs about others. *Journal of Personality and Social Psychology*, 1970, *16*, 66-91.

Krueger, R. *Gypsy on 18 Wheels*. New York: Praeger, 1975.

Mailer, N. *Of a Fire on the Moon*. Boston: Little, Brown, 1970.

McHugh, P. *Defining the Situation*. New York: Bobbs-Merrill, 1968.

Merton, R. K. The self-fulfilling prophecy. *Antioch Review*, 1948, *8*, 193-210.

Meyer, L. B. *Emotion and Meaning in music*. Chicago: University of Chicago, 1956.

Miller, D. W., and Starr, M. K. *Executive Decisions and Operations Research*. Englewood Cliffs, N. J.: Prentice-Hall, 1960.

Miller, S. Ends, means, galumphing: Some leitmotifs of play. *American Anthropologist*, 1973, *75*, 87-98.

Piaget, J. *La construction du reel ches l'enfant*.2 ème éd. Neuchâtel: Delachaux and Niestlé, 1962.

Popper, K. R. *Conjecture and Refutation*. New York: Basic, 1962.

Rogers, C. R. *Client-centered Therapy*. Boston: Houghton Mifflin, 1951.

Rottenberg, D. The moneyweight champion. *New York Times Magazine*, Feb. 22, 1976. pp. 16-26.

Russell, B. *Introduction to Mathematical Philosophy* (2nd ed.). London: Allen and Unwin, 1948.

Scheff, T. J. Decision rules, types of error, and their consequences in medical diagnosis. In F. Massarik and P. Ratoosh (eds.), *Mathematical Explorations in Behavioral Science*. Homewood, Ill.: Dorsey, 1965, pp. 66-83.

Thayer, L. Communication and organization theory. In F. E. X. Dance (ed.), *Human Communication Theory*. New York: Holt, Rinehart, and Winston, 1967.

Watzlawick, P., Beavin, J. H., and Jackson, D. D. *Pragmatics of Human Communication*. New York: Norton, 1967.

Weick, K. E. Social psychology in an era of social change. *American Psychologist*, 1969a, *24*, 990-98.

———. *The Social Psychology of Organizing*. Reading, Mass.: Addison-Wesley, 1969b.

———. Organizations as enacted settings. Paper presented at Massachusetts Institute of Technology, Cambridge, May 1975.

———. Careers as eccentric predicates. *Executive*, 1976, *2*, 6-10.

Weick, K. E., and Gilfillan, D. P. Fate of arbitrary traditions in a laboratory microculture. *Journal of Personality and Social Psychology*, 1971, *17*, 179-91.

Weick, K. E., Gilfillan, D. P., and Keith, T. The effect of composer credibility on orchestra performance. *Sociometry*, 1973, *36*, 435-62.